Sisters in Crisis

Ann Carey

Sisters in Crisis

The *Tragic Unraveling* of Women's Religious Communities

Our Sunday Visitor Publishing Division
Our Sunday Visitor, Inc.
Huntington, Indiana 46750

Contents

Preface 7

1: Introduction: Sisters in Crisis 11

2: Ready for Renewal — or Revolution 18

3: Rome Calls for Renewal 36

4: Alarm in the Vatican 55

5: The LCWR's "Radical Rethink" 76

6: The Coup 88

7: The Many Faces of Indoctrination 108

8: The Re-Education of Sister Lucy 133

9: How Did Feminists Gain Control? 149

10: The Deconstruction of Ministry, Community, and Prayer 162

11: Communities vs. the Hierarchy:
    The IHMs and the School Sisters of St. Francis 184

12: The Quinn Commission Examines Religious Life 211

13: The Ideological Transformation of Sisters' Organizations 234

14: The Leadership Conference Splits 266

15: Turn out the Lights:
    Finances, Vocations, the Elderly, and Denial 293

16: Where Do the Sisters Go from Here? 311

Notes 331

Selected Bibliography 356

Index 360

Preface

Catholic sisters have been the backbone of the Catholic Church in the United States for more than one hundred fifty years. Sisters literally built the parochial school system as well as the Catholic health care and social service systems. Sisters helped Catholic dioceses and parishes spread the Catholic faith to the unchurched while at the same time ministering to the spiritual needs of the Catholic people. Perhaps most importantly, sisters have dedicated their lives to giving visible witness to the transcendence of God and to the spiritual aspect of our humanity.

Between 1965 and 1995, the number of Catholic sisters decreased by almost one-half. By the year 2000, there will be more retired sisters than working sisters. Sisters have nearly disappeared from many Catholic institutions, and some of the sisters who are still visible seem to be very angry with the Catholic Church in general and with the male hierarchy in particular. In many orders, the sisters themselves seem to be divided about how religious life should be lived, as some wear religious garb and continue to work in Catholic institutions, while other sisters in the same order live alone in apartments and work in secular occupations.

Journalists are trained to ask questions referred to as the five "Ws" and the "H." During the fifteen years that I have worked as a journalist in the Catholic press, I have often pondered these questions: *Who* led the changes in religious life for sisters, and who was most affected? *What* events and ideas influenced these changes? *When* did the philosophy of religious life change? *Where* have all the sisters gone? *Why* was the renewal of religious life interpreted so differently by so many sisters? And *how* did religious life for sisters evolve to its current crisis? This book is an effort to answer those questions.

In order to simplify a complex topic, consistent terms have been used throughout the book. Strictly speaking, there are some canonical differences between the terms "institute," "community," "congregation," and "order." However, in general usage, these terms are used interchangeably, as they are in this book. Similarly, the term "nun" refers canonically to a woman who belongs to a cloistered or contemplative order who remains behind convent or monastery walls, while "sister" is the canonical term for women Religious who belong to congregations that are engaged in apostolic work among the people of God. Most lay people are not aware of this distinction, so these terms also will be used interchangeably in this book. However, the topics covered in this book refer only to sisters who are members of apostolic communities, and do not refer to the approximately four thousand nuns who belong to contemplative institutes.

An additional matter of clarity involves the approximately five hundred different religious institutes of women in this country. Some of these institutes are provinces of international orders which have headquarters in other countries. For example, the general motherhouse of the Sisters of the Little Company of Mary is in London, England, but their United States provincial house is in Evergreen Park, Illinois. On the other hand, some United States religious institutes are international, and have their headquarters, or generalate, in this country, with provinces in other countries. The larger institutes of women Religious, whether they are international or domestic, usually are divided into several provinces in this country.

However, the province of a particular order should not be confused with an autonomous order. Many of these diverse institutes of women Religious were founded on the same tradition or rule, and the names of their institutes are very similar. Hence, many lay people think that institutes founded under the same rule are somehow connected. This is not the case except for provinces of the same institute. Also, the charism — the spirituality that guides the institute's way of life and approach to the apostolate — in each institute is distinct.

For example, the Dominican Sisters of St. Cecilia in Nashville, Tennessee, founded in 1860, are a very traditional order whose primary ministry is education in Catholic schools. The Dominican Sisters of the Congregation of the Most Holy Rosary in Sinsinawa, Wisconsin, founded in 1847, are a very diverse order with multiple ministries. These two Dominican orders are not connected. Likewise, the Franciscan Sisters of Our Lady of Perpetual Help of St. Louis, Missouri, founded in 1901, cite Christian formation as their primary ministry. But the Franciscan Missionaries of Our Lady of Baton Rouge, Louisiana, founded in 1913, have health care as their primary ministry — again, two distinct Franciscan orders with different charisms as well as different ministries.[1]

The title "mother" was always used in pre-Vatican II days to designate a sister who was superior general of an order, or superior of a province. In some institutes, the title "mother" was retained after a sister went out of office, but this was not always the case. After Vatican II, the title "mother" was dropped by many institutes of women Religious. For consistency, the title "sister" is used throughout this book for all sisters, even though they may have been superiors with the title "mother" at the time they are referenced.

Another possible source of confusion is that prior to Vatican II most orders required their sisters to take a religious name, quite often prefixed by "Mary" in honor of the Blessed Mother. However, following Vatican II, and with the Vatican's approval, many orders allowed their sisters to use their baptismal and family names if they so desired. So, some of the sisters mentioned here were known by their religious names at one time, then later resumed the use of their given names. An effort has been made to indicate in parenthesis the alternate name of the sister where there is the possibility of confusion.

Additionally, there is some confusion over the name of the Congregation for Institutes of Consecrated Life and Societies of Apostolic Life. This is the Vatican Curia administrative department that has authority to establish and give general direction to religious and secular institutes, to oversee renewal and adaptation of the institutes, to review and approve their constitutions, and to set up and communicate with conferences of major superiors. This congregation had three different names during the years covered in this book. Before 1967, it was the Congregation of Religious; from 1967 until 1988, it was the Congregation for Religious and Secular Institutes. Since 1988, the title has been Congregation for Institutes of Consecrated Life and Societies of Apostolic Life. This congregation will be referred to throughout the book as Congregation for Religious.

In another matter of terminology, I am uncomfortable with using the terms "liberal" and "conservative" because of their political connotations, and also because the terms carry negative images for many people. Therefore, I follow the example of sociologist Helen Rose Fuchs Ebaugh by using the term "change-oriented" to describe sisters or religious institutes inclined to seek a new definition of religious life by expanding the boundaries usually associated with the religious state. I use the term "traditional" to describe sisters or institutes which adhere to the traditional understanding of religious life as contained in Vatican II and documents and other Church teachings. Neither term should be construed as inherently negative.

I wish to acknowledge the valuable contribution of the many sisters who have contributed their experiences, prayers, and suggestions for this work. These sisters belong to a variety of religious institutes, including Benedictine, Carmelite, Daughters of Charity, Dominican, Franciscan, Holy Cross, Immaculate Heart of Mary, Little Sisters of the Poor, Loretto, Mercy, Notre Dame, St. Joseph, Sisters of Charity, Sisters of Christian Charity, and Sisters of the Holy Names of Jesus and Mary. Most of these sisters have asked not to be named, as they did not want to be perceived as criticizing their religious institutes, to which they are unfailingly loyal. Some of them wanted to remain anonymous because they feared retribution from congregational leaders who hold a divergent view of how religious life should be lived.

I also am indebted to the staff of the Archives of the University of Notre Dame, who graciously and patiently helped me access material in their holdings. Among the collections at the Notre Dame Archives which I studied were the records of the Leadership Conference of Women Religious, the National Assembly of Religious Women, and the Consortium Perfectae Caritatis. Much of the material gathered from primary sources in those collections, such as correspondence and meeting minutes, is original research published here for the first time.

1: Introduction: Sisters in Crisis

"[There is] a resistance on the part of many people to see what a crisis we're in and what a crisis we're facing."[1]

Sister Miriam Ukeritis, CSJ

Nearly every Catholic over the age of forty recalls the influence of sisters in parishes, schools, hospitals, and other Catholic institutions. Not only did sisters unselfishly serve the needs of the people and the Church, but they were walking reminders to the laity that there is a good deal more to life than the affairs of this world. By their presence and their example, sisters invited and challenged us to exercise the highest virtues for the glory of God, the good of our neighbors, and the salvation of our eternal souls.

Many Catholics treasured the sisters for who they were as well as for what they did, but too many Catholics, including priests and bishops, probably took sisters for granted. As we shall see in Chapter Two, sisters were too often treated simply as the workers of the Church and very seldom consulted about their own needs or ideas. Perhaps because sisters were so consumed by their seemingly endless work, they did not take the time to analyze carefully their own way of life and realize that customs they habitually practiced were not well suited to the modern apostolates they were pursuing. Nor was an overly authoritarian convent structure conducive to promoting an emotionally healthy lifestyle for adult women. In many cases, the result was overworked and over-stressed sisters who often were not professionally well-prepared for the jobs they were assigned and were too often treated like children by superiors and clerics.

Spiritually, many sisters were caught up in rote prayer exercises that became so routine that they had no opportunity to grow in prayerfulness or expand their spiritual insights. Long before Vatican II, the pope and the Congregation for Religious encouraged women Religious to re-evaluate and update some of their practices and attitudes that dated back to the middle ages. However, most orders of sisters were resistant to such changes.

Then the Second Vatican Council, which met over a three-year period from 1962 to 1965, mandated that all religious orders renew and adapt themselves to modern times. Chapter Three summarizes the major decrees and documents dealing with religious life that came out of Vatican II or were follow-ups to Vatican II. Also reported in Chapter Three are the reactions of different groups of sisters to the teachings coming from Rome. With a few exceptions, sisters were enthusiastic about the directives of Vatican II, and they set about renewal with more dedication than any other group in the Church. However, as Chapter Three discloses, sisters did not always get accurate information about Church teaching on religious life. And some sisters who were eager for change and determined to discard an authoritarian lifestyle gave an overly broad interpretation to the documents, resulting in deviations from the renewal set forth in Church directives.

The result was that a few orders simply didn't renew significantly at all and continue to remain in a pre-Vatican II mindset, even as they approach the third millennium. A few orders managed to steer a moderate course and adapt themselves to modern conditions, while still retaining the significant elements of religious life, as the Vatican II fathers had envisioned. But the majority of orders of women Religious in this country discarded most of their significant traditions and fashioned a new definition of religious life that is more descriptive of a secular institute than a religious institute.

A word about this important distinction. Both the religious institute and the secular institute are organizations of consecrated life officially recognized by the Church, but they are quite distinct. Members of a religious institute take public vows of poverty, chastity, and obedience, and exercise the apostolate of their institute in the name of the Church. Canon law directs that Religious are to observe a common life in their own religious house and wear the habit of the institute. Religious institutes are required by canon law to furnish all elements necessary for their members to achieve the purpose of their vocation. On the other hand, members of a secular institute live "in the world," and take private vows. Nonclerical members of a secular institute retain their married or single status and pursue their regular occupations.

As Chapter Four outlines, the Vatican tried repeatedly to get renewal of the sisters back on track, but too many sisters in positions of authority were determined to define renewal of religious life in their own terms, not according to the definitions coming from the Vatican or the hierarchy. The result has been disastrous in terms of new vocations, service to Church institutions, witness to the transcendent, and polarization of sisters within orders.

How did this misinformation and rebellion transpire?

Vatican II took place during the turbulent 1960s. Women religious were not immune to the cultural upheaval occurring all around them, and many sisters resonated with the feminist movement as an expression of their disenchantment over authoritarianism in religious life and in the Church. And, since women's religious institutes generally were functioning in a nineteenth-century pattern badly in need of updating and renewal, orders of women Religious were quite vulnerable to revolutionary new concepts being promoted by articulate, charismatic leaders.

Sisters also became sensitized during the 1960s to the needs of the poor and oppressed, so many of them gave up their traditional apostolates of education and health care to work directly with the poor. Furthermore, a movement begun in the 1950s to make higher education more accessible to sisters resulted in an emerging generation of sisters during the 1960s who were well-educated, self-confident, and politically astute. Thus, the leadership in many institutes of women Religious had a socio-political agenda unprecedented in previous years and the know-how to put that agenda into effect.

Chapters Five and Six examine the history of the Leadership Conference of Women Religious, the most influential group of sisters in the United States. This organization was set up in the 1950s and approved by the Vatican to aid communication between Rome and the sisters, as well as among institutes of women Religious. Originally, the conference was composed only of superiors general or provincial superiors. As the 1960s progressed, the superiors' conference became increasingly independent from Rome and actively engaged in securing for women a more powerful role in the Church. The conference changed its statutes in 1971, distancing itself from dependence on the Holy See, and opening its membership to include not only superiors, but also members of leadership teams.

Many of the leaders emerging in the conference in the late 1960s and early 1970s espoused an agenda of profound change for religious life, citing the documents of the Second Vatican Council as the basis for the renewal they envisioned. However, the documents of Vatican II often were interpreted so broadly that even the most sweeping innovations in religious life were falsely rationalized as mandates of the Council. In fact, no document of Vatican II ever remotely proposed the kind of "renewal" led by change-oriented sisters who convinced their institutes to abandon the very essentials of religious life, such as common prayer, religious garb, community life, and a corporate apostolate exercised in the name of the Church. This renewal led by change-oriented sisters rejected Church authority in the convent, in the diocese, and in Rome, and proposed a radical new lifestyle and purpose for sisters based on the liberation of women and the oppressed. Ironically, it was through the women superiors' conference that the change-oriented sisters were able to assert their influence on more traditional sisters who wished to preserve the essentials that had characterized religious life for hundreds of years, even as they updated their institutes according to the Second Vatican Council.

How was the influence of the change-oriented sisters promulgated?

Chapter Seven describes one method used by the Leadership Conference to deliver this revolutionary vision of religious life to grassroots sisters — a 25-year conference project called the Sisters' Survey. One phase of the Sisters' Survey was a massive questionnaire circulated to 157,000 sisters in 1967. Its advertised purpose was to see where sisters stood on a myriad of issues so that their readiness for renewal could be assessed. But critics of the survey saw it as an indoctrination tool designed to create dissatisfaction with the prevailing state of religious life and to promulgate a version of renewal supported more by some of the superiors' conference leaders than by Vatican II teachings.

Other influences in the 1960s and early 1970s also affected Religious and their attitude toward renewal. Among these influences discussed in Chapter Eight are programs and workshops for Religious that range from sensitivity training to encounters with the New Age movement. The result has been that some sisters became more versed in knowledge of yoga, astrology, Jungian psychology, and earth goddesses than in the doctrine of their own Catholic faith or the theology of religious life or the documents of the Second Vatican Council.

Even sisters trained at Catholic colleges and universities or in their own religious institutes often did not get a solid grounding in the faith, as Chapter Eight relates. The Sister Formation Movement, begun in the 1950s, promoted proper education of sisters before they began their apostolic works as teachers or nurses or social workers or catechists. As such, the Sister

Formation Movement was a very positive influence on sisters and the Church. But this movement also felt the effects of the popular culture of the 1960s and 1970s, and what had begun as a noble program to prepare sisters professionally for their working careers eventually changed its thrust and became an agent for promulgating the version of renewal being promoted by the most change-oriented sisters.

As a result of these various influences on sisters, the renewal of religious orders as mandated by the Second Vatican Council took on many forms. As Chapters Nine and Ten relate, when institutes of women Religious undertook the revisions of their constitutions to update their lives, many sisters were heavily influenced by the women's liberation movement and by some contemporary theologians who questioned the validity of Church teaching and the authority of the magisterium. The result has been chaos in many institutes of women Religious. Quite often it was not the majority who set the agenda for an order, but rather the sisters who were the most politically astute and the least committed to apostolic works.

As a result of these reforms, in many religious institutes, more sisters live away from their communities than with their communities. Many sisters have left their jobs in Church institutions and moved into the secular workplace, and the common apostolate that used to characterize religious communities has given way to individual works of individual sisters. As a result, many orders of women Religious have lost their corporate identity, their unifying mission, and their sense of community. Two case studies of renewal are presented in Chapter Eleven, which explain how sisters within the same order became polarized over what changes should be instituted in religious life.

This chaotic renewal in women's religious institutes has resulted in a record number of women leaving religious life and few new candidates joining religious orders of women. This situation, along with declining vocations among religious priests and brothers, so alarmed Pope John Paul II that in 1983 he ordered the United States bishops to study religious life in this country and to dialogue with Religious to try to figure out what was happening. The pope appointed Archbishop John Quinn to direct this study of religious life, and directed the Congregation for Religious to issue a document that summarized the Church teachings on religious life. As Chapter Twelve reveals, many of the Religious who had pushed for radical change in their institutes resented the pope's mandated study of religious life, and some sisters in particular viewed the study as a effort to get sisters "back in line." As a result, many change-oriented Religious used the Quinn Commission study as an opportunity to instruct Rome on how American Religious were creating their own democratic version of religious life.

Sisters in Crisis

However, women and men Religious who were concerned that religious life was becoming too laicized welcomed the study and the Vatican document on essential elements of religious life. But these same traditional Religious found that the study of religious life was conducted unevenly in the various dioceses, and some charged that the whole process was a whitewash designed to satisfy the Vatican and to present an overly optimistic picture of religious life in the United States. As Chapter Twelve reports, the papally-mandated study of religious life did little more than further polarize traditional Religious from change-oriented Religious.

The change-oriented sisters promoted their vision of religious life in their own communities, and also through national organizations of sisters and other high-profile groups. While these national organizations have never attracted large numbers of nuns to their memberships, they have done much to shape the public image of sisters, a distorted image in most cases, since the media are more likely to publicize sisters picketing the Vatican than sisters going about their work in a parish or nursing home or school or daycare center. Chapter Thirteen profiles some of these organizations, such as the National Coalition of American Nuns.

The evolution of the women superiors' conference from the 1970s to the 1990s also is reported in Chapter Thirteen, for the Leadership Conference of Women Religious continued to distance itself from the authority structures of the Church and went on to concentrate on causes that were more socio-political than religious. Many sisters were very unhappy with the independent direction taken by the Leadership Conference of Women Religious and by new definitions of religious life that were developed by experimenting sisters without the consent or approval of Rome. Sisters also were disturbed that their orders withdrew from many of the Catholic institutions that sisters traditionally staffed. This dissatisfaction resulted in groups of more traditional sisters coming together for mutual support and eventual recognition by the Vatican. Chapter Fourteen traces the evolution of some of these groups of traditional sisters who eventually broke with the Leadership Conference of Women Religious and then went on to receive the approval of the Vatican as an alternate superiors' conference.

The recognition of two superiors' conferences — one representing the traditional sisters and the other representing the change-oriented — demonstrates how polarized women Religious in the United States have become. The sisters suffering most from this polarization have been the elderly, who make up a majority of the population in change-oriented institutes. But a sizable number of the elderly in these institutes did not approve of the style of renewal that their institutes took, and they have struggled to live their vows in congregations that are not supportive of Church teachings about religious life — or about other areas of life as well.

Chapter Fifteen examines how many religious institutes of women struggle to support an aging population of sisters as the number of sisters drawing a salary declines and the number of retirees increases. Yet, the very institutes that are in the most serious decline — the change-oriented institutes — are the least concerned about their plight or their lack of vocations and seem to be in a state of pathological denial. Some sisters accept very stoically the fact that their institutes will not survive, and they continue to focus their energies on individual projects rather than on efforts to revitalize their own orders. The elderly sisters in such institutes often feel betrayed and forgotten as they watch the institutes in which they spent their entire lives edge closer to extinction as their leaders seem unable or unwilling to reverse the process.

Meanwhile, as the final chapter explains, the agenda of the most vocal women Religious deals not with revitalizing religious orders or increasing vocations to religious life or supporting Religious in staffing Church institutions. The highest profile women Religious seem more interested in liberating the poor and oppressed and in consolidating power for women in society and in the Church, as well as in an ecological agenda of saving the earth. Indeed, Benedictine Sister Joan Chittister, a former president of the Leadership Conference of Women Religious and an influential international speaker on religious life, was quoted in a 1994 conference publication professing these priorities: "In this culture, the rape of the earth and the oppression of women are the paramount issues with which we grapple. . . .

". . . Eco-feminism is the great question facing this period of ours. For religious to be blissfully absent from these questions is to abandon the very meaning and purpose of religious life."[2]

So some women Religious still are not ready to answer the invitation issued in 1996 by Pope John Paul II to return religious life to the norms outlined by the Church. Rather, they feel their "lived experience" is a better guide than a male hierarchy anchored in a European culture.

Yet, the end of the second millennium is a crucial time for many institutes of women Religious, for the decisions they make during these final years of the 1990s will determine, in many cases, whether their institutes will survive into the 2000s and once again flourish as vital signs of the vocation of every Christian to be united with Jesus Christ. The events, experiences, and personalities which brought the women Religious to this crucial point in their history are reported in the following chapters.

2: Ready for Renewal — or Revolution

"I have not come here to preach peace, but to call for a revolution, a revolution in the life of active nuns. . . ."[1]

Cardinal Leon Joseph Suenen

Cardinal Leon Joseph Suenens made headlines in 1963 when he made the above proclamation on a trip to the United States. But he was not the first high-ranking churchman to call for reform in convents, though he was the first to use the terms "revolution" and "war." During his papacy, from 1939 to 1958, Pope Pius XII had tried repeatedly to get women Religious to modernize, but in terms less flamboyant than Cardinal Suenens, who had a flair for the dramatic.

However, the leaders of women Religious generally had resisted these reforms, partly out of comfort with the status quo, and partly because the needs of the Catholic Church in the United States kept the sisters so occupied that they had little time to sit back and evaluate their own situation. Most priests and bishops also were reluctant to encourage change in the women's orders because sisters were key workers in parishes and dioceses that were burgeoning with Catholic families after the post-World War II baby boom. These Church leaders did not want to encourage any changes in convents that would restrict the number of sisters available to staff Catholic institutions. Thus, like most revolutions, the revolution in American convents took place because reform was desperately needed, but the leaders responsible for implementing reform had failed to do so.

The need for renewal

Customs and daily schedules for the sisters often were based on a European lifestyle that was hundreds of years old and rooted in an uneducated, rural society. Even in the 1950s, many American convents still followed schedules that had been devised before the widespread use of electricity. Thus, the sisters' day began at dawn to take advantage of the daylight, and their activities outside convent walls — and often inside, too — ceased at sunset.

While contemplative orders devote the majority of their time to prayer, active orders engage in outside works, or apostolates. Yet, before the Second Vatican Council, many of the active communities of women lived a monastic lifestyle and spent up to four hours a day in prayer. Often that prayer time was devoted to a recitation of routine devotions, with little consideration given to spiritual enrichment, Scripture study, liturgically-related prayer, or personal prayer. And a lengthy prayer schedule could be quite taxing for sisters holding down full-time jobs, particularly teachers, who needed evening hours to plan classes and grade papers. (Some retired sister-teachers readily admit that they regularly threw student papers in the trash because they simply did not have time to look at them.) Sisters also had little time for personal enrichment or even reading a newspaper or news magazine to keep up with current events. In many convents, reading of such outside materials was strictly controlled by the superior, and many sisters had no idea about what was going on in the outside world.

Custom and rule books that hadn't been revised in modern times usually controlled the day-to-day lives of sisters and were sometimes so detailed they even described how certain foods should be consumed. Horariums prescribed a sister's activities for each hour of the day, and even dictated bedtime. Mail usually was censored, and some orders restricted the number of letters a sister could write, even to her own family. Little courtesies, such as offering a cup of coffee to a visitor, had to be cleared through the superior in some communities, and most orders did not allow a sister to venture outside the walls without a sister companion.

Some of the changes proposed by the pope and the Congregation for Religious included putting more flexibility in the convent schedule, discarding outmoded acts of devotion or penance, updating religious garb, providing better professional training, improving religious formation, and teaching a stronger theology of the vows.[2] For example, in the apostolic constitution *Sponsa Christi*, released November 21, 1950, Pope Pius XII said: "And so, while fully maintaining all the basic and principal elements of the venerable institute of nuns, we have decreed, in relation to other elements, which are to be regarded as extrinsic and accessory, to introduce cautiously and prudently those adaptations to present-day conditions, which will be able to bring not only greater dignity but also greater efficacy to this institute."[3]

Again, on September 15, 1952, Pius XII brought up the matter of updating when he told the superiors general of women's institutes who were meeting in Rome: "In this crisis of vocations, be watchful lest the customs, the way of life or the asceticism of your religious families should prove a barrier or be cause of failures. We are speaking of certain usages which, if they had once a certain significance in a different cultural setting, do not possess it nowadays." The pope went on to give the example of the habit, saying it should be "suitable and meet the requirements of hygiene." He also warned the superiors to give their sisters the necessary education to put them on equal footing with their lay colleagues and to give the sisters the means to keep their professional knowledge up to date.[4]

Again, in a 1958 radio message, Pius XII observed: "Let monasteries and orders of nuns have esteem for their own special character . . . but they must not defend it in a narrow, inflexible spirit, and still less with a certain stubbornness which is opposed to any form of timely development and would not lend itself to any form of adaptation, even when the common good demands it."[5]

At the September 1952 meeting of mothers general in Rome, Claretian Father Arcadio Larraona, secretary of the Congregation for Religious, had advised that custom books and some convent practices should be updated: "Notwithstanding all their good qualities, it is undeniable that custom books, because of their detailed regulating of many aspects of daily life, can and do become oppressive, or at least embarrassing. There are superiors of all types and temperaments, and some of them are unduly attached to the letter of the prescription, without considering the spirit. . . ."[6]

Still, change was resisted by most women's orders, and it was not uncommon in many orders, even in the early 1960s, for sisters to be required to ask "permissions" from their superior every month to be allowed to perform routine tasks such as bathing, obtaining toothpaste and soap, doing assigned work, and even praying. It was also necessary for a sister to ask permission for normal adult activities such as using the telephone, even when using the telephone was an implicit part of the sister's job. The idea behind asking these permissions was an interpretation of the vow of obedience that everyday activities didn't have merit unless those activities were done as an act of obedience. Thus, all actions, even daily routines that every adult must perform, came under the vow of obedience.

The "Chapter of Faults" was also a common monthly spiritual practice convened under the direction of the mother superior, where members publicly confessed their faults to the rest of the community. "Faults" might include common human experiences such as breaking a dish, spilling food on one's clothing, or crossing one's feet. And, in some orders, if a sister neglected to accuse herself of a fault, the other sisters were obliged to accuse her.

Many orders also had rules that were unusually restrictive for normal human activity, such as the rule limiting exercise to a weekly walk, or the rule that prohibited sisters from eating in the homes of lay people. Such rules resulted not only in unhealthy nuns, but also in some bizarre situations, such as sisters being forced to eat their meals on the porches of their own parents' houses while on home visits, since eating in the house with lay people was prohibited.

Even worse, some orders routinely refused a sister permission to visit her family, even for the serious illness of a parent or the wedding of a sibling. Certainly, intentions may have been the best, for superiors did not want their sisters to be distracted from their lives of dedication, and a sister did embrace a new family — her community — when she made the decision to enter the convent. Still, Pius XII and other members of the hierarchy began to realize that families might be more supportive of their daughters' vocations if those daughters weren't expected to sever family connections and obligations entirely. The daughters would be happier sisters if they were permitted to have an ongoing relationship with their families and lead a lifestyle more appropriate for a rational adult.

Another area greatly in need of reform was the absolute tyranny of some mother superiors. Often these women were superiors for life, and many of them ruled their subjects with an iron hand and very little Christian charity, all in the name of the Church. At the same time that they acted in the name of the Church, some superiors also strongly resisted the directives of the pope and the Vatican Congregation for Religious to get rid of outdated customs. Often, a superior reveled in the custom of having the sisters kneel and kiss her hand or the hem of her habit when they addressed her or when they served her food. Others made life generally miserable for sisters who had incurred their wrath, and it was not unknown for superiors to give the least desirable assignments to the sisters who fell into disfavor. Indeed, some superiors abused power and treated their sisters like naughty little children constantly in need of supervision. Some superiors also were prone to assign infirm or obstinate sisters to parishes where the pastor and the superior did not see eye-to-eye, as a subtle way of keeping Father in line.

Sisters in Crisis

But even in congregations with moderate, loving superiors — and certainly there were many — life could be very difficult and stifling for sisters when rigid rules in their communities offered little possibility for personal growth or responsible decision making. So-called "recreation" time often consisted of sisters being required to show up in the recreation room for a forced chit-chat with the other members of the community, even if their own idea of recreation was to read a book or take a walk or simply to be alone. And all the duties of daily life, such as caring for one's habit, doing household chores, and participating in community prayer often left little time for any other activity or any possibility to expand one's horizons.

Undoubtedly, many of these practices were designed to make community life more orderly. As a Benedictine priest once noted, custom books contained detailed instructions such as how to crack open a soft-boiled egg so that the sister didn't squirt cooked egg onto the other diners. Such regulations probably could also be traced back to a time when young women entering religious life may not have had proper training in their own homes. The practice of silence during meals and specified times of the day also had its practical as well as spiritual appeal, for as one sister observed, silence made the company of obnoxious individuals much more tolerable. But the long periods of silence that often were mandated in many congregations permitted little opportunity for healthy adult discourse or community building. And while performing "busy work" tasks assigned by superiors may have been an exercise in obedience for sisters, many of the time-consuming tasks they were given had no other apparent benefits. In addition, some extreme interpretations of obedience seemed to suggest that a sister abdicate her own conscience.

Many sisters who lived this lifestyle accepted it with good humor as simply part of the cross they agreed to bear when they entered religious life. One sister recalled a former practice of her congregation that required the novices to kiss the floor if they were late for any of their activities. It was an old French custom, sister explained, and she simply took it in stride, pretending that she was kissing the feet of Jesus whenever she was required to kiss the floor.

Sister of Charity Julia Marie wrote in 1967: "The long day of domestic tasks, the restriction of athletic activity to a weekly walk . . . the hampering of freedom in visits and letters were all part of what we had more or less expected when we surrendered to God's call.

"It is true that my recollections do not emphasize genuine tyranny, or pettiness, or narrowness of vision. . . . We grew with varying degrees of success in prayerfulness, dignity of movement, friendship for each other . . .

life was good, and the girlish vitality and freedom that we had brought with us was 'changed but not taken away.' "[7]

Sister Marcella Marie Holloway, a Sister of St. Joseph of Carondelet, recalled a demanding mother superior she knew during the 1930s who required her sisters to observe such strict etiquette that they dare not make a sandwich at the dinner table "even though the hot dog seemed to cry for a bun." And after the superior lost a game of dominoes to Sister Marcella one night at recreation, the superior informed the young sister that her desire to win was a character flaw that should be moderated. But forty years later, Sister Marcella had nothing but praise for her superior, whom she credited with building character that eventually would give Sister Marcella strength to handle difficult situations that arose later in her lifetime.[8]

Of course, the lifestyles, customs, and rules of sisters varied from congregation to congregation, and even from convent to convent, depending on the local superior. And certainly some sisters found the lifestyle more difficult and dysfunctional than did others. What might have been comforting and spiritually uplifting to one sister may have been stifling and humiliating for other sisters. One former sister reported that her order accepted aspirants as young as twelve years of age. So, many of the sisters in her order had been in the convent since pre-adolescence and never really learned to function as independent adults, since they went from the authority of their parents to the authority of their superiors without ever making decisions on their own. Thus, sisters who had been independent adults before entering religious life often felt stifled by regulations that seemed perfectly acceptable to sisters who had been in the convent practically since childhood.

In addition to accepting girls at such a young age, prior to the Second Vatican Council many orders did not carefully screen candidates. Some young women entered the convent who were not well suited for religious life, and some women entered the convent for the wrong reasons — fear of marriage, a failed romance, escape from an abusive home, the opportunity for a free education, etc. Yet, with dioceses begging for more sisters to staff their institutions, congregations were not inclined to turn away candidates, and psychological testing was virtually unknown before Vatican II. Dr. J. T. Nix, a medical doctor who surveyed women Religious, reported in 1961 that:

1. Health education, health counseling, periodic health examination, and health records are nonexistent or inadequate.
2. Psychological screening as part of the preadmission examination is the exception rather than the rule.
3. Overwork is the rule rather than the exception, and in many communi-

ties retreats and attendance at conventions are synonymous with vacation.
4. Half of the community infirmarians have no nursing training.
5. Two-thirds of religious communities have no hospital insurance.
6. Admission requirements vary with every community and many communities apparently have none at all.
7. Catholic medical and hospital care is not always available to Negro sisters in certain sections of the country.[9]

Clearly, many elements surrounding the religious life of sisters were in need of reform — physical and psychological as well as spiritual. But most orders of nuns were like Tevye, the fictional main character in "Fiddler on the Roof," who clung to tradition simply because that was how things always were done. Even though many nuns had no idea why their communities practiced many of their traditions, they adhered to these traditions tenaciously and resisted suggestions by Rome to modernize. But while tradition is important to any institution or society, traditions that do not promote the goals of the community or the society should be re-evaluated, as Tevye found out when the modern world intruded into his village.

Addressing this issue, Jesuit Father Joseph Gallen wrote in 1961 that "any custom, practice or observance that is queer, odd, peculiar, or artificial is evidently wrong, simply because you will never find such a quality in the model of all sanctity, Jesus Christ." His examples of exaggerated practices included "Kneeling on meeting or leaving a superior, bowing from the waist when encountering him, kneeling when talking to him, and kissing the hand of a superior." But what concerned Father Gallen even more was the possibility that "unintelligent and excessive customs" might be identified with sanctity, thus leading to their "multiplication and obstinate retention." The unfortunate result of retaining mindless customs, he pointed out, is that a Religious might misinterpret these activities as holiness instead of placing holiness where it belongs, in the interior life.[10]

As one Dominican sister observed, many of these customs had no substantive meaning; they were simply done by rote, and no one was able to explain why. The problem was, she explained, since so much of the sisters' life was done by rote, many sisters didn't understand the meaning behind essential customs and traditions, either. So, when orders undertook renewal as mandated by Vatican II and discarded their excessive and empty customs, many of them moved too quickly and without adequate planning, also discarding customs that were meaningful and that had served to bond the community together, such as periods of silence and times for community prayer. As a Franciscan sister put it, "It was like removing tiles from a mosaic. At first, removing a few small tiles didn't hurt the big picture. But we kept going, and when we took away some of the essential pieces, the whole thing collapsed."

The habit of habits

The habit was another aspect of religious life that needed reform, and Pope Pius XII also approached this topic, telling the sisters to modernize their habits.

Most of the habits of women religious were modeled after clothing that was typical at the time their religious institutes were founded, as long ago as several hundred years. But what might have been suitable attire for six-teenth-century sisters who rarely stepped foot outside the walls of cool, damp European convents was simply not appropriate for twentieth-century women in active apostolates. The long, heavy wool habit and elaborate head-dress were impractical and uncomfortable in warm weather and so awk-ward in cold weather that many sisters wore only shawls in bitter cold be-cause coats would not fit over their habits. (In some orders, life was so regimented that the calendar — not weather conditions — governed when the sisters were allowed to start wearing their winter apparel.) Sisters had to sew the complicated habits themselves, and upkeep of the garments was quite time-consuming. While underclothing could be changed daily, it was impossible for sisters to change their entire habits as often as good hygiene would dictate.

Moreover, many habits were downright unsafe. Most sisters knew of nuns who had caught their long skirts or cinctures in a car or bus door and been dragged along behind the vehicle. In 1958, the Vatican Congregation of Religious warned sisters to do something about the veil to enable sisters driving cars to have unrestricted vision. Sisters even knew of some state driving examiners who purposely failed sisters on their driving tests, not because the sisters lacked driving skills, but because the officials felt the veil restricted the sisters' vision, which it did. In 1962, the California fire marshal even got into the act by alerting sisters that the cellulose nitrate material in some *guimpes* — the starched fabric covering the neck and shoulders — was extremely flammable.[11] And it does not take much imagi-nation to realize how dangerous the long, flowing sleeves and skirts were in kitchens near stoves and in other locations where machines were in use. Virtually every order had its own horror story about sisters who suffered burns after their habits became entangled in the mangle irons that were common in convent laundry facilities.

Sisters in Crisis

Yet, many communities pegged their identity on their distinctive habit, and some sisters were reluctant to modernize for fear their community might lose this identity. Sisters also were aware that as cumbersome as their habits might be, the habit was a specific element that attracted young women to religious life, for the habit made a clear statement that a sister was a woman who had devoted her life to God and service to the Church. And because of this symbolism, the habit immediately garnered the respect of lay people for the sisters. Many sisters also feared that modernizing the habit would make them too "worldly," both in appearance and in attitude. As one sister put it, "I knew that if the habit went, all the other stuff would come in, like beauty parlors and permanents."

Ill-prepared professionals

Perhaps even more important than lifestyle of the sisters was the issue of education. Even into the 1960s, it was common practice for sisters to be sent into the classroom or the hospital without completing their professional training. A 1952 study by Franciscan Sister M. Brideen Long looked at the educational background of 1,286 teaching sisters. Sister Brideen found that only eighteen percent of those sisters had finished three or more years of college education before they began teaching in the elementary schools. Nearly fifty percent of them had less than two years of college.[12]

Pope Pius XII addressed this problem repeatedly, saying that Religious working in Catholic institutions should have the same professional training as their lay counterparts. The pope's concern was not only for the welfare of young sisters who were placed into professional positions without adequate preparation, but also for the people served by those professionals. In his 1951 remarks to teaching sisters, Pope Pius called on religious orders to give their teachings sisters good professional preparation and support.[13] This same topic was covered in a 1951 circular from the Congregation of Religious which had instructed superiors to give their sisters the proper "pedagogical and technical training." The circular also warned the superiors that sending a young sister into the classroom to teach without the proper professional preparation was "rash."[14] On a similar note, in an April 24, 1957, discourse to nursing sisters, the pope admonished superiors not to let "certain horariums and usages" make the nursing sisters' work with the sick more difficult.[15]

Yet it was common practice for sisters to be on what was often referred to as "the twenty-year plan," with many sisters taking twenty to thirty years to complete their education because they could attend school only during the summers, when they weren't teaching. Sister of Loretto Carolyn Mary

Tighe remembers that her teaching order sent sisters into the classroom after a period of six months of postulancy and two years of novitiate. During this preparation time, the sisters took two years of course work at the motherhouse toward their bachelor's degrees. Then the nuns were assigned to teach full time during the school year and to attend school every summer. If they were stationed in a college town, sisters also went to school on Saturdays during the school year. But most sisters accepted the whole experience with remarkable good humor and few complaints.

It took Sister Carolyn Mary ten years to get her bachelor's degree, and then she started over again on the master's degree, which took eleven more years. "I'm sure it was hard, but we just took it as a matter of course," Sister Carolyn Mary recalled. As a teaching order, "We went to school, and we went to school, and we went to school. I used to say we studied so hard I didn't have time to wash my socks." But Sister Carolyn Mary pointed out that she enjoyed the summers of school, with special activities and the camaraderie of sisters from many different orders: "I loved my summers at Loyola [Loyola Marymount University in Los Angeles, California] so much I didn't care if we ever quit," she said.[16]

One Holy Cross sister recalls starting her teaching career before she was even old enough to vote. She was assigned an experienced teacher as her mentor in her school, and then she walked into a classroom of nearly fifty children, where, she said, "I managed to keep a few pages ahead of the children." She, too, eventually obtained her college degree by going to summer school over a several-year period. Another sister who was a college professor related that she finally obtained her degrees after nearly thirty years of going to summer school. The most difficult part for her, she said, was that the summer graduate courses were very demanding and intense, and it was difficult after nine months away to pick up where she had left off. The experiences of these sisters were typical of many tens of thousands of others.

Another burden the teaching sisters had was a large and often overcrowded classroom. Holy Cross Sister Rosaleen Dunleavy, a retired Saint Mary's College professor of biology, started out as a grade-school teacher. One year her elementary grade classroom was so crowded with the fifty-eight children in her class that she literally could not fit another desk into the room when a transfer student arrived. So, sister simply had the little boy sit at her desk for the rest of the school year. In spite of such difficult conditions, sisters rarely complained. As Sister Rosaleen explained, "I didn't need to sit down — I was young then!"

Sister Rosaleen probably was lucky to have only fifty-nine students, for many teaching sisters had considerably larger numbers to deal with. Author

Sisters in Crisis

Jim Trelease recalls having ninety-six classmates in his first grade class at St. Michael's School in Union, New Jersey, in 1947. He also recalls that the only time the children were all quiet was when Dominican Sister Elizabeth Francis read to them immediately after recess every day.[17]

The teaching orders were in a real quandary. The superiors wanted their young sisters to have a good education, but they were under great pressure from pastors and bishops to provide teachers for the record numbers of children enrolled in parish grade schools and parochial high schools.

In 1940, there were just over 2 million students in parochial and diocesan grade schools.[18] By 1955, that number had jumped to over 3 million, and by 1965, it had more than doubled to about 4.5 million. Diocesan and parochial high school enrollments also increased, from under 300,000 students in 1945 to over 500,000 in 1960, and nearly 700,000 in 1965. Some orders even cut short the spiritual formation for young sisters to prepare them more quickly for the classroom, a practice condemned by the Vatican. It also was a practice that was short-sighted, for Religious need a strong formation experience to sustain them in their vocation, and many young sisters simply didn't receive substantial formation to prepare them for the challenges of religious life, particularly during an era of profound change.

Why didn't the women's religious institutes heed Rome's warnings prior to Vatican II to reform their practices?

It was probably a "Catch-22" situation, in which the need for reform was acknowledged by at least some women Religious, but the methods for actually achieving that reform were elusive. It was almost impossible for superiors to send young sisters to college for four years in order to obtain a degree when pastors and bishops were pleading, even demanding, more sisters to staff parochial schools. With many orders strapped for money and without a college of their own, it was impossible to come up with the tuition fees to educate sisters who were drawing no income. It was easy for Rome to say that sisters should have the same professional training as their lay counterparts, but to make that actually happen was another matter indeed.

An overworked, under-appreciated work force

Probably the greatest abuse in need of reform was the way the local Church and lay people took sisters for granted. The Church expected so very much from the sisters and gave little in return. Catholics just assumed that the sisters would always be there to serve the parish and that they were happy to work for wages that barely covered their living expenses — or sometimes didn't cover their living expenses. Parents appreciated the music and art lessons the sisters gave in their spare time, but few lay people realized that sisters often worked those long hours to supplement their income, which in 1957 averaged $25 to $50 a month.[19] Author George Stewart observed in his comprehensive history of American sisters, *Marvels of Charity*, that in spite of such limited incomes, sisters lived so frugally that they still managed to save money to invest in their institutions, indeed even to construct buildings, and at times to loan money to pastors who got into dire financial straits.[20]

Still, Catholics expected after-school tutoring — and a myriad of other services — to come for free. Little thought was given to the sisters' retirement needs or the needs of the elderly sisters who were being supported by the working sisters. And it was simply assumed that the sisters should do menial tasks that could have been handled quite easily by lay parishioners. Many Catholics had little consideration for the sisters' need for recreation, vacation, cultural enrichment, family visits, or even just a little time to themselves. Perhaps even worse, meddling pastors often tried to tell sisters how to do their jobs in the parish schools, even though the priests knew far less about education than the sisters. And the priests and parishioners just smugly assumed the sisters would always be there to serve their needs.

These abuses prompted Jesuit Father John E. Coogan to write an article in *The Priest* magazine in 1957, suggesting ways that pastors could make life easier for sisters. Among his suggestions were to offer the school gym to the sisters on a regular basis, since the sisters had no place to exercise; to furnish the parish convent comfortably; to encourage parishioners to "shower" the sisters with food items occasionally; and to provide a car for the use of sisters, who usually had to depend on volunteer parishioners to drive them for their errands or medical appointments. Father Coogan also suggested that pastors should not expect sisters to act as janitors, secretaries, money counters, or sacristans.[21] Of course, many parishes and priests did treat the sisters with great esteem, but too many did not.

Vocations flourish

In spite of these difficulties in religious life, vocations flourished. In 1965, there were about 180,000 sisters, the largest number the American Church had ever seen. Experts say there are many reasons for this phenomenon. The most obvious explanation is that in the mid-1960s, the children born in the post-World War II "baby boom" would have been in their late teens, the age most women entered religious life in that era. But there were many other factors, too. The sisters were role models and walking vocations campaigns for millions of children they saw every day in the classroom, and they inspired many of their students to join them in dedicating their lives to God. The largest source of new vocations for many orders of sisters were the high schools operated by the order.

Furthermore, prior to 1960, there were few opportunities for women to engage in social service work outside of Church structures, and many young women saw the sisterhood as a way to serve humanity. Religious life also gave women an opportunity to serve the Church, a possibility not open to lay women before Vatican II. Some young women also perceived religious life as a means to obtain an education and professional stature that was not attained by many lay women before the 1960s. In fact, Catholic sisters were probably the only women managing large institutions prior to the women's movement of the 1960s. And certainly many young women entered the convent because they had a calling from God to sanctify themselves in a lifestyle that specifically attempted to imitate the life of Jesus, who Himself was poor, chaste, and obedient as He spread the Gospel message.[22] They were "people who are consumed by God, people who are on fire," as sociologist Sister of Charity Patricia Wittberg puts it.[23] They were women who wanted to serve the Church and live in community with other like-minded individuals who supported each other in pursing the vocation of every Christian to achieve union with Christ.

In 1965, when the Second Vatican Council ended, more than 104,000 nuns were teaching in Catholic schools in this country. Over 13,000 sisters staffed some 808 hospitals that were owned and operated by religious orders.[24] Sisters also worked in numerous social service settings, and they operated most of the 250-plus Catholic orphanages that sheltered nearly 25,000 children. But these numbers were to be short-lived, for the revolution in the convents was already underway, and as we shall see in the following chapters, the revolution had a dramatic impact on vocations and the Catholic institutions the sisters staffed.

The tumultuous sixties

The 1960s was a volatile decade in the United States, and women Religious were just as profoundly affected as the rest of American society by the cultural, political, and social turmoil of the 1960s. Author Jules Archer observed in *The Incredible Sixties* that the years 1963 to 1968 were the stormiest years ever in American history, with the exception of the Revolutionary and Civil War years.[25] The events of the 1960s had a significant impact on how the teachings of the Second Vatican Council were interpreted and received by Catholics in America, including Religious. During this decade, when many Americans were experimenting with radical new lifestyles and questioning authority and tradition, religious orders were being asked by the Church to update their lives and rewrite their own constitutions — hardly the most stable time to be undertaking a transformation process. As some scholars of Vatican II have pointed out, the impact of the Second Vatican Council would no doubt have been quite different if the Council had taken place in any other decade than the turbulent 1960s.

Passionist Father John Kobler, who has written extensively on the Second Vatican Council, believes the cultural revolution of the 1960s had a profound impact on how Religious and laity interpreted the work of the Council. He also believes that renewal by some Religious was more political than spiritual. He observed in 1994 that:

> It should come as no surprise, then, that an unreflective incarnation of the spirit of Vatican II in the secular, social concerns and values of the '60s often resulted in a "religious" product somewhat resembling "Rosemary's Baby": e.g., the urge to change The System, the push for People Power in the Church, more Participatory Democracy in governance, greater opportunities for women and racial minorities, and advocacy for the laity to assume positions of responsibility in the Church. However worthy these intentions may have been, this radically "prophetic" stance has often been hard to distinguish from empowerment as a political movement.
>
> The decidedly massive changes which have taken place in religious institutions over the past thirty years have eventuated in a certain confusion about roles both for congregations as a whole and for their individual members. As a result, there has been a great deal of experimentation: e.g., dropping distinctive habits, leaving the cloister, encouraging participation by the laity, joining in the activities of a local parish, and ceasing to sponsor many Catholic institutions such as schools and hospitals.[26]

During the 1960s, sisters were especially affected by a brand of feminism that went beyond the reasonable agenda of "equality feminists," who simply sought equal treatment for women. Many sisters during the 1960s instead bought into a more militant brand of feminism that is described by Professor Christina Hoff Sommers in her book *Who Stole Feminism?* as "gender feminism." Sommers' conclusion is that gender feminists are zealots who claim to speak for all women, but can produce no evidence or experience to back up that claim. These gender feminists push an agenda that seeks not merely equality, but confrontation that sets women against men in all areas of life.[27]

Certainly, sisters had legitimate cause to complain about an insulting, paternalistic attitude toward women by many men in the Church. Sisters were too often considered to be the work force of the Church and too seldom consulted about their opinions, ideas, needs or desires. And, often clergy and hierarchy enjoyed a plush lifestyle at the expense of sisters. Chaplains for religious orders often were provided a comfortable salary and room and board by the sisters, and still collected frequent stipends for Masses for the deceased or ill of the order. And it was common for sisters to be expected to present members of the hierarchy with monetary gifts on special occasions, such as anniversaries of ordination.

For example, in 1957, the new Conference of Major Religious Superiors of Women's Institutes (the predecessor to the Leadership Conference of Women Religious) coordinated a campaign to raise money for a jubilee gift to Cardinal Valerio Valeri, prefect of the Vatican's Congregation of Religious. The Conference suggested each member congregation donate $5.00 per one-hundred working sisters, with the hope that $5,000 could be raised for the gift to Cardinal Valeri.[28] Now, $5,000 was a great deal of money in 1957, especially considering that the average sister earned less than $50 per month. While most sisters felt that clergy and hierarchy deserved their respect and admiration, many began to resent the expectation of some — not all — men in the Church that they be treated like royalty by sisters who often worked longer hours than the men and had fewer financial resources.

These examples of paternalism and clericalism no doubt fueled the anger of some of the sisters who embraced the feminist movement in the 1960s in the hope of correcting these sexist practices.

The vanishing sister

The turmoil of the 1960s profoundly affected renewal in religious institutes. The orderly reform of religious life envisioned by the Second Vatican Council succeeded in some convents, but failed miserably in others because reform was not intelligently planned, and change was introduced at a pace too rapid to allow for adequate evaluation. Furthermore, some sisters used the process of renewing their orders to push their ideology that women Religious should assert their independence from the authority of the Church, which was symbolized by the all-male priesthood and hierarchy.

The result was that many sisters left religious life because the changes were so profound that the new model of religious life bore no resemblance to the life they had entered before renewal began. Others left because they felt reform wasn't happening fast enough and going far enough. And during the unstable time of renewal, fewer young women chose to commit themselves to a life that appeared to be transforming itself before their very eyes.

By 1970, the revolution in the convents was well underway, and the casualty figures were high. In just 5 years, the number of sisters declined by 19,000, to about 161,000. Those numbers continued to drop because of death, departures, and few new vocations, to a total of about 89,000 sisters in 1996 — half the number of sisters there were in 1965 — with a median age in the late 60s.

This dwindling number of sisters, as well as a trend to move away from traditional apostolates of teaching and health care, had a dramatic impact on Catholic schools and hospitals. While various demographic and economic factors also came into play in the closing of many of these institutions, certainly the declining number of sisters contributed to the demise of many Catholic institutions in which sisters were the primary work force. Another contributing factor was the new policy of "open placement," in which sisters in many congregations became free to select their own jobs and living arrangements. As the president of the Leadership Conference of Women Religious told the 1995 assembly of her organization, "We struggle with a desire to participate in a clear corporate mission, yet our members feel called to meet new needs often beyond our present institutional commitments."[29]

Thus, the Catholic schools that had enjoyed over 104,000 teaching sisters in 1965 lost almost half of those sisters in just 10 years; by 1975, there were approximately 56,000 sisters teaching in Catholic schools. By 1985, the number of teaching sisters had declined to just over 30,000; and by 1995, fewer than 13,000 sisters were teaching in Catholic schools — an 88 percent drop in just 30 years.

During those same 30 years, the number of parochial and diocesan elementary schools declined from about 10,500 schools serving about 4.5 million children in 1965 to about 6,900 schools serving just under 2 million children in 1995. Diocesan and parochial high schools didn't fare any better. There were more than 1,500 of these high schools in 1965, enrolling around 698,000 students. By 1995, there were about 379,000 students in 823 parochial high schools. Private Catholic high schools declined from about 900 with about 390,000 students in 1965 to 527 schools with approximately 273,000 students in 1995.

Sisters in Crisis

Catholic colleges also decreased in number during this period. In 1965, there were 295 Catholic colleges and universities.[30] In 1995, there were 235.[31] Some of these schools closed, while some, such as Webster College in St. Louis — founded and operated by the Sisters of Loretto — remained open but ceased to be identified as Catholic institutions.

Catholic hospitals likewise decreased in number, although the reasons for closing or selling hospitals also are complex and include finances, government regulations, insurance implications, and a number of other issues. Nevertheless, the declining number of sisters and the policy of open placement surely have contributed to the fact that more than 200 Catholic hospitals have closed or been sold to non-Catholic corporations between 1965 and 1995. In 1965, there were 808 Catholic general hospitals. The 1995 figure was 605, but that number continues to drop, with acquisitions and mergers rampant in the hospital industry. As of 1994, only about 20 percent of Catholic hospitals still had a sister as chief executive officer, compared to 50 percent in 1980.[32]

With fewer and fewer sisters working in Catholic hospitals or sitting on hospital boards, there is growing pressure for hospitals to forfeit their Catholic identity. Dr. Alan Sager, an associate professor at the Boston University School of Public Health, discovered that some congregations of sisters that operate Catholic hospitals feel pressured by lay boards and physicians to diminish the Catholic mission of their hospitals.[33] And certainly the Catholic tradition of caring for the poor is being tested by competition for contracts with health maintenance organizations and health networks.

Ironically, in those thirty years between 1965 and 1995 when Catholic institutions were closing their doors at an alarming rate, the Catholic population needing those institutions grew by nearly fifteen million people. Certainly a myriad of dedicated lay people heeded the call of Vatican II to become responsible for many of the works of the Church. Today, the remaining Catholic schools and hospitals are staffed predominantly by lay people, and most of those lay people do an outstanding job of teaching the Catholic faith and preserving the Catholic identity of their institutions. But, as Pope John Paul II pointed out in his 1996 apostolic exhortation *Vita Consecrata,* consecrated life is at the heart of the Church as a manifestation of every Christian's calling to be united with Jesus. "Jesus himself, by calling some men and women to abandon everything in order to follow him, established this type of life which, under the guidance of the Spirit, would gradually develop down the centuries into the various forms of the consecrated life. The idea of a church made up only of sacred ministers and lay people does not therefore conform to the intentions of her divine founder, as revealed to us by the Gospels and the other writings of the New Testament."[34]

The following chapters examine many of the circumstances which have contributed to the unraveling of women's religious communities in the United States.

3: Rome Calls for Renewal

"I think it would be safe to say that all communities have suffered greatly during this post-Conciliar period. Sufficient time was not taken to read and absorb the documents."[1]

Sister M. Claudia Honsberger, IHM

The documents issued by the Second Vatican Council and subsequent related documents called for updating religious life in many of the areas mentioned in the last chapter, such as modernizing habits, eliminating meaningless rules and regulations, enriching spiritual and liturgical experiences, and applying apostolates to contemporary needs. But none of the documents called for transforming the basics of religious life, which many sisters in the United States actually did. Rather, the Council documents reaffirmed the rich heritage of religious communities, praised the value of the teaching and health care apostolates, stressed life in community, designated religious habits as important signs of consecrated life, and emphasized the importance of prayer in common.

Why, then, do many well-intentioned sisters who are doing wonderful work sincerely believe that they are following the wishes of the Church regarding religious life when they live alone in apartments, wear secular clothing, interact only rarely with members of their community, and engage in occupations totally unrelated to the Catholic Church?

This chapter examines how the content of the Council documents was misinterpreted, transposed, and even ignored by Religious and their "expert" advisors. Thus, the renewal of religious institutes foreseen by the fathers of Vatican II did not resemble what really happened in many American convents, where some of the most zealous proponents of change embraced a radical concept of religious life quite different from the vision of Vatican II and sold that vision to other unsuspecting sisters.

The *Decree on the Appropriate Renewal of Religious Life*, 1965

Perfectae Caritatis, the *Decree on the Appropriate Renewal of Religious Life*, was issued toward the close of Vatican II, on October 28, 1965. *Perfectae Caritatis* expanded on Chapter Six of another Vatican II document, *Lumen Gentium*, the *Dogmatic Constitution on the Church.* As one commentator noted, *Lumen Gentium* had specified "that life consecrated by the evangelical counsels is a distinct, different, and identifiable manifestation of the holiness to which all Christians are called and, as such, is integral to the life and holiness of the church itself."[2]

A relatively short document, *Perfectae Caritatis* dealt with general principles for renewal and directed religious institutes to return to the original inspiration of their institute and to adapt those principles to the changed conditions of contemporary times. In doing this, the religious institutes were to retain their heritage while adapting the life, prayer, work, and government of their institutes to the needs of their members. The institutes also were urged to be more aware of cultural circumstances and to respond to contemporary apostolic needs. To achieve this end, *Perfectae Caritatis* directed religious institutes to employ community-wide consultation to revise their rules and constitutions to reflect the updated vision of religious life that was set forth by Vatican II.

While *Perfectae Caritatis* directed that the essentials of religious life be retained, it was hardly a status quo document, for the renewal vision set forth in *Perfectae Caritatis* called for changes significant enough to mandate rewriting and updating the constitutions and rules of religious institutes.

Regarding the vows, *Perfectae Caritatis* reaffirmed as a special symbol and effective means for fostering service. The document urged new forms of that would include material as well as spiritual . Obedience was emphasized as both the member's cooperation and "the superior's obligation to foster mature and responsible expressions of obedience in consecrated life." *Perfectae Caritatis* also affirmed the "importance of common life as expressed in prayer, in the sharing of the same spirit, in living together, and in bearing one another's burdens." The religious habit was described as a symbol of consecration that should be "simple, modest, poor, and becoming as well as in keeping with the requirements of health and adapted to various times and places and apostolic needs."*Perfectae Caritatis* was so important that entire portions were incorporated into the revised *Code of Canon Law* of 1983.[3]

Following *Perfectae Caritatis* less than a year later was Pope Paul VI's *Ecclesiae Sanctae*, which gave specific directives for implementing the broad mandates of *Perfectae Caritatis*. *Ecclesiae Sanctae* was a *motu proprio* — a document written by the pope on his own initiative and applying as legislation to the entire Church. However, both *Perfectae Caritatis* and *Ecclesiae Sanctae* were widely misinterpreted or simply ignored by a large number of American Religious. On top of this, some confusion was caused by the documents themselves.

Ecclesiae Sanctae directed that all religious institutes hold a special general chapter (meeting) on renewal by October 11, 1969, in order to approve changes in their constitutions that would allow for experiments in religious life which would respond to the mandates of Vatican II. A general chapter determines the important business of a religious institute and is convened anywhere from every three years to every ten years. Rather than mandating certain changes in religious institutes, the Vatican wanted to preserve the unique charisms of the various religious institutes by having each institute make changes appropriate for its own specific spirituality and way of life. The experiments were supposed to safeguard the purpose, nature, and character of the institute and were to be temporary. Then, the experiments were to be evaluated at the next regular chapter meeting of the institute. The beneficial experiments were then to be incorporated into the institutes' constitutions, and the experiments that were not helpful were to be discontinued. If further experimentation was deemed necessary at that first regular chapter meeting that followed the special renewal chapter, that experimentation could continue, but it was to be evaluated at the next chapter meeting and then either incorporated into the constitution or discontinued.

Experimentation gets out of hand

Since religious institutes had chapter meetings at various intervals, the period of experimentation would have worked out to a minimum of just a few years to a maximum of about twenty years, or until promulgation of the new *Code of Canon Law* — which occurred in 1983. Thus, since the period of experimentation was somewhat fluid, experiments tended to go on much longer than the Council fathers or the pope had intended. Some religious institutes purposely expanded the years between general chapters so that experiments could be stretched out. Others purposely incorporated items into their constitutions that they knew would never be approved by Rome so they could continue experimenting endlessly. And a few religious institutes are still doing just that today — continually rewriting their constitutions, which are then continually rejected by Rome because they contain items contrary to canon law or to the documents on religious life.

Certainly the Council and the Holy Father intended that the experiments would address some of the needed reforms mentioned in the previous chapter of this book. In January of 1965, about a year before the Second Vatican Council closed the following December, Holy Cross Father Bernard Ransing made this point at a meeting of the executive committee of the Conference of Major Religious Superiors of Women's Institutes. Father Ransing was an American member of the staff of the Congregation for Religious and religious advisor to the superiors' conference. He explained to the executive committee that: "There are changes that are necessary, and that, therefore, certainly should be made — adaptations in the religious life. As religious we are consecrated to the service of God and the service of the Church . . . therefore, if the Council, or, after the close of the Council, the Holy See, would call for changes or should open the way to changes, then we must be ready to adapt ourselves." But Father Ransing cautioned the superiors to make sure "the Church is responsible for the change and not just some one who writes an article for one or other of the many periodicals now in existence." He also stressed that "Whatever changes are made should be made, not in the end or in the essentials of religious life, but in the accidentals."[4]

Examples of appropriate experimentation were given by Holy Cross Father Edward Heston, a canon lawyer and soon-to-be-named secretary of the Vatican Congregation for Religious, in a 1967 presentation at the summer Institute for Local Superiors at the University of Notre Dame. Among the topics for experimentation that Father Heston cited were: modifying and modernizing the habit; eliminating the separation between novices and professed sisters; extending the period of temporary vows beyond the maximum of six years; modifying the length of the canonical year of the novitiate; doing away with the regular appointment of ordinary and extraordinary confessors; changing the term of office for a superior; changing the method for designating local, provincial, and general superiors; and altering other details of the administrative structure of the congregation.[5]

Father Heston further explained that during the experimentation period, the Holy See would not approve constitutions. The whole idea was for the religious institutes to try out the new ways of doing things, and then after ten years or so, the institutes would know what worked and what didn't. After this period of trying out the new, when an institute knew what worked well, its constitution could then be sent to Rome for approval.

However, almost prophetically, Father Heston also warned of the dangers of experimentation:

"It should be borne in mind in every community that this period of experimentation, when no texts of constitutions will be definitively approved by the Holy See, does not mean that a religious institute remains completely without constitutions or without concrete norms for its life and activities. Every special general chapter should make it clear to all members that the constitutions presently in force remain binding until the next definitive approval of the Holy See, except in those parts which may have been changed by this same special general chapter. Thus there will be no grounds for claiming that everything is lawful because the constitutions are to be regarded as being in a state of abeyance."[6]

Unfortunately, some religious institutes acted as if they indeed had no constitutions during the period of experimentation. Also unfortunately, some institutes ignored or did not realize the fact that *Ecclesiae Sanctae* required that any experimentation that was contrary to the *Code of Canon Law* in effect at the time had to be specifically approved by the Vatican. The code in effect had been approved in 1917, and there were several canons on religious life which eventually would be dropped or updated in the 1983 revised code. For example, the 1917 code required a period of postulancy for non-clerical members of religious institutes, whereas the 1983 code does not even mention postulancy. The 1917 code had about 200 canons pertaining to Religious, and the 1983 code has 173 canons covering consecrated life, including new forms of consecrated life such as secular institutes.

During the experimentation period, Religious knew that the *Code of Canon Law* was being updated, and some of them saw this as an opportunity to simply abrogate the old code without bothering to get the permission of the Vatican. The National Assembly of Women Religious — a small, independent organization of sisters from a variety of orders — declared that "Continued insistence on observance of the *Code of Canon Law* is anachronistic, the Sisters insist, since the Code itself is being totally revised."[7]

Immaculate Heart of Mary Sister Sandra Schneiders observed: "Much of what developed in the life experience of religious was either actually contrary to the [canon] law or so original as to have no real relationship, positive or negative, to it. . . . Superiors found themselves challenged to

40

lead their congregations into an uncharted future for which present law was inadequate; individual religious experienced the call to venture beyond the limits of what was permitted by common [canon] or particular [congregational] law and often into conflict with superiors."[8]

Indeed, some of the old canons were outdated, but *Ecclesiae Sanctae* did not give religious institutes the *carte blanche* many of them assumed in implementing experiments and rewriting their constitutions. It was made clear that any deviation from the 1917 *Code of Canon Law* was to receive special permission from the Vatican, but apparently this permission was not always sought.

For example, a 1972 letter to the superior general of an American order of sisters from Congregation for Religious secretary Archbishop Augustine Mayer, a Benedictine, pointed out some problems in the acts of the sisters' 1968-69 chapter. Archbishop Mayer told the superior to keep in mind that "it is necessary to have a Local Superior" and that a special chapter may modify the habit but "it may not authorize its suppression." He also questioned the chapter acts, which authorized three areas of experiments that the archbishop said were contrary to canon law. The chapter acts reported that permission was being sought from the Congregation for Religious to set aside those canons, but Archbishop Mayer informed the superior that there was no such request on record at the Vatican for acting contrary to those canons.[9]

Note that there was a gap of at least two years between the submission of the chapter decrees and any response from Rome. Understandably, American Religious grew impatient waiting for responses from the slow-moving Vatican bureaucracy, and, as with any bureaucracy, paperwork very likely did get lost occasionally. But in any event, religious institutes did not have authority to put into effect any decrees that deviated from canon law without that specific Vatican permission, even if it was slow in coming.

Complicating the picture was the fact that a good deal of erroneous information circulated about the canons governing religious life. Many sisters confused the rules or customs of their own congregations with actual canon law, thinking that practices of their own community, such as the chapter of faults, were mandated by canon law, when in fact the chapter of faults was not even mentioned in canon law.[10] Part of this confusion resulted because English translations of canon law were not widely available to sisters, and women were not admitted to study in canon law departments until after the Second Vatican Council. (Adding to the confusion later, the 1983 book *Religious Women in the United States*, which is widely used as a resource for information on women Religious, erroneously reported that the

Sisters in Crisis

1917 code had approximately two thousand canons pertaining to Religious,[11] when in reality there were only about two hundred.)

Many religious institutes went far beyond the boundaries for experimentation set by *Ecclesiae Sanctae.* These communities radically transformed the purpose, nature, and character of their institutes, all under the guise of obedient renewal. Some communities gave their members total freedom in deciding when and how they would pray, where they would live, what work they would do, what hours they would keep, and what they would wear — a freedom that led to excesses, such as mini-skirted nuns smoking, drinking, and dating. And some sisters simply took it upon themselves to change religious life. Sister Elizabeth Kolmer of the Adorers of the Blood of Christ wrote that: "Frequently enough individual sisters did not wait for those in authority to make the first move or, faced with reluctance on the part of the superior, made their own decision."[12] Many sisters left religious life because of this rapid transformation in their lifestyle, since their communities no longer resembled in any way the communities they had entered.

Archbishop Mayer observed in 1973: "Now it is bewildering to see some constitutions. . . .

"We cannot have all the forms of committed life in our institutes. A great source of confusion in many institutes is that now they want to live all the forms of consecrated life at the same time. . . . That is not possible. . . . If, in the end, some communities think they want the life of a secular institute, then they should say it. . . . Then Mother Church will find a category for them but they shouldn't try under the name of religious life to put in everything. That doesn't go; that only makes for confusion."[13]

In her book *Out of the Cloister,* Helen Rose Fuchs Ebaugh, a former Sister of Divine Providence and a sociologist, presented case studies of three orders. One of those orders, which she described as "change-oriented," already had made the following changes by 1970: Regarding government, "While president administers, all sisters cooperate in discovering and serving the needs of man. . . . Spirit speaks in all members, not just superiors." In job assignments, "Open placement puts responsibility for job on the individual. The order is to assist the person; the person herself is to discern where the Spirit is directing her." On prayer, "Frequency, place, and type of communal prayer to be determined by the local group." On dress, "Each individual may wear what she wishes in regard to dress, veil and any external symbol of her religious consecration."[14]

As early as September 1967, at the annual assembly of the Conference of Major Religious Superiors of Women's Institutes, Father had alluded to

42

defective experimentation that was already taking place. This was less than two years after the close of the Second Vatican Council and the issuance of the council document on religious life, *Perfectae Caritatis*. Furthermore, *Ecclesiae Sanctae*, the blueprint for implementing Vatican II reforms, had been issued just one year before.

Father told the superiors' 1967 assembly: "But it is unfortunately true, also, that a considerable amount of unauthorized experimentation has been initiated, due to misunderstandings or wrong interpretations of the 'mind of the Holy See.' Because these experiments have been premature, they have lacked that wise preparation desired by the Holy See and the prudent deliberation of the General Chapter itself. Worst of all they have caused confusion among the Communities, and have led to unrest and disquiet among certain individual religious who are eager for change."[15]

Christian Brother Bernard M. Ryan observed in 1969 that some experiments in religious communities were really not experiments, for they had no preparation, premise, method, or evaluation.[16] And one group of sisters wrote the Congregation for Religious in 1972 that "Five years of well-meant but illogical experimentation in unlimited adaptation have all but destroyed religious life in our country."[17]

A reformer recalls renewal

In a interview with the author, Sister S., who describes herself as one of the leaders of radical change in her own community, agreed that extreme experimentation had indeed destroyed religious life. She recalled that her mind-set after Vatican II was that there should be "no holding back." Sister S. said that she and other reformers felt that they had a mission, and they needed unlimited freedom to fulfill that mission. "We redefined the past to accommodate the present we wanted," she recalled.

When the reformers first began, she said, "We were thinking it's an experiment." But as time went on, "It became clear that there was no turning back; we had changed, and we couldn't become other." One of the older sisters who had been a mentor to Sister S. told her that she was saddened to see Sister S. "destroying religious life at its foundation." But Sister S. sincerely believed that she was doing the right thing for religious life. The reformers also felt that sisters opposed to all the changes they proposed simply "hadn't seen the light" and were thus dismissed as being conservative and reactionary.

Sister S. said she herself was elected as a chapter delegate on conservative credentials. The older sisters who opposed radical change had no voice, she said, since the reformers were so well organized. And the young sisters were easily persuaded. "All you had to do was convince the delegates [to chapter]; we were so convinced what had to happen had to happen." And in deciding what had to happen, the sisters were prompted by several outside speakers, including priests and religious brothers. Sister S. recalled one brother who told her chapter: "Sisters can't make sisters free; only God can. All you can do is restore the freedom you took from them." But Sister S. does not blame these men, for she said that her community chose guest speakers because they had "liberal credentials" and the reformers knew the speakers would say just what they wanted them to say.

Sister S. was the first one in her community to wear secular clothing, to live outside the convent, to live alone. By the early 1970s, Sister S. said she realized her sister/mentor friend had been right.

"I believe we did destroy the foundations of religious life," she said. "We over-emphasized the professional at risk of the spiritual. . . . As much as I love my community, I wouldn't enter my community now; there's nothing distinctive about it. We're no different from the lay life, and that's where we went wrong." A vocation to religious life is sustained by prayer and community support, Sister S. said, but "now we're in do-it-yourself religious life."

Redefining , , and obedience

The meaning of the vows underwent a radical redefinition in many communities. In a matter of just a few months, some sisters found themselves rocketed from a life of burdensome and meaningless restrictions and regulations to a lifestyle that was hardly recognizable as Religious. Obedience was often redefined as "response to the Spirit." was considered to consist of open dialogue and availability to people. was probably the least changed of the vows, but many Religious felt it was perfectly acceptable to date. Some Jesuits even coined a name for the notion that there was a third lifestyle situated between the married state and the priestly or religious state, which they called the "Third way."[18]

One Franciscan sister recalled that her congregation wanted the young sisters to learn to be more comfortable in the company of men, so social occasions were arranged for the sisters with priests and brothers. At first, the sister said she didn't notice that couples were pairing up, but the message became clear to her when some of these sisters left the order to marry the brothers or priests they had met at those community-sponsored events. Another sister and her traveling companion reported leaving a three-day regional meeting of priests and nuns in Chicago when the evening entertainment was a "mixer" at which the priests and nuns were invited to dance together.

Some examples from chapter decrees demonstrate how the Vatican directives were interpreted — or misinterpreted — by some of the renewal chapters. In June of 1969 the Franciscan Sisters of Perpetual Adoration of LaCrosse, Wisconsin, approved their interim statement of renewal, "Unity in Diversity." Regarding their apostolate of education, the statement reaffirmed "our commitment to Catholic education." But, the statement also asserted, "We shall broaden the term 'education' to include the involvement of Sisters in parish, ecumenical and civic organizations, and in public schools and universities." The document also permitted sisters to "be open to serve in whatever apostolate seems most beneficial to the Church and within the limits of available personnel," a departure from the original purpose of the institute.

Regarding prayer life, the statement urged sisters to "esteem" the Mass and "cherish" the privilege of participating in daily Mass. As for the habit, "Sisters shall be free to wear a black habit and veil or to continue in further experimentation in appropriate contemporary dress." The only specific requirement for dress was that the sister should retain her medal of the Blessed Sacrament and her ring.[19]

In the 1967 chapter of the Medical Missionary Sisters, "the habit of the society was retained, but liberty was given to each Sister to determine whether or not it would be more beneficial for her service to the Church to wear lay clothes."[20] Indeed, canon law did allow for lay clothing in exceptional circumstances, but those circumstances were to be unusual, and determined by the superior, not by the individual Religious themselves. Of course, the role of superior also was diluted by many congregations. For example, the Franciscan Sisters of the Poor in Brooklyn, New York, changed the title of superior general to community service coordinator, whose primary responsibility was leadership.[21] Many other communities followed suit.

The July 9, 1969, issue of *National Catholic Reporter* noted that the Sisters of Charity of the Blessed Virgin Mary "have gone all the way from a typically monarchial and authoritarian form of government to complete democracy" in which "There are no 'superiors' named from on high. Each local group of sisters is asked to designate a community representative to handle official correspondence and serve as contact person for the house. Apart from this, each house is free to set up whatever structures the sisters want." And, "Instead of being assigned to a teaching or other kind of job by a superior's fiat, each sister can now apply for whatever work position she thinks she is qualified for, and she can work out her own living arrangements as long as they are financially feasible." The orders' *Kinetics of Renewal* also provided that "each sister is now free to make her own decisions about the details of her life — whether she goes to mass today, the clothes she wears, the amount of time she spends with friends outside the community."[22]

The impact of this kind of radical change on the lives of individual sisters has been enormous, and many grassroots sisters have been very disturbed about what has transpired in their orders.

A survey of a Detroit province of sisters around 1972 indicated the concerns of some of these sisters regarding their "renewed" order. Respondents to the survey cited some of these problems: self-determination of person and community fostered selfishness, with groups selecting only their peers. Because sisters self-selected their work, some institutes of the order were over-staffed, while others were under-staffed. There was no authority figure. Convents built by parishioners were being abandoned by sisters who preferred living in apartments with a select group. Some sisters indulged themselves in leisure, travel, and recreation, while talking of the poor only in broad terms. The governing board was top-heavy, with too many coordinators who had too much power. One sister expressed her concern about a *laissez faire* lifestyle, noting, ". . . failure to observe the vows, lack of external expression of prayer and growing secularization appear to be condoned by the governing board as an individual's right of self-expression." Another sister wrote, "We need guidelines, just like Boy Scouts or a union."[23]

A renewal success story

Not all religious congregations of women exceeded the limits of reasonable experimentation and watered down the vows. Some orders very successfully updated their constitutions and lifestyles to the modern model of religious life envisioned by the Second Vatican Council, and it is those institutes which are most successful in attracting new vocations today.

The author asked Sister Judanne Stratman, a member of the Franciscan Sisters of Christian Charity, to describe the renewal effected by her order. The order has its motherhouse in Manitowoc, Wisconsin, and members of the order serve in sixteen dioceses. Sister Judanne explained that her community has consistently consulted the official Church documents, and in fact the order involves the entire community in ongoing studies of the various documents referring to religious life. *Perfectae Caritatis* was made available to all the sisters when it was issued, she said, as were subsequent documents relative to religious life. In 1996, the sisters began their study of *Vita Consecrata,* the apostolic exhortation on consecrated life by Pope John Paul II.

The Franciscan Sisters of Christian Charity spent time studying the spirit and aims of their foundress, as directed by the Council, and then tried to identify their charism more clearly in their revised constitution and mission statements. Sister Judanne identified the cornerstones of her order's charism as "simplicity built on faith in a loving God, joyful acceptance of, love for the Church, and selfless dedication to the service of others." These cornerstones, she said, are witnessed in the sisters' community life and in their apostolates.

In their renewal process, the Franciscan Sisters of Christian Charity retained their traditional apostolates of education and health care, but have expanded these apostolates to include pastoral ministry and catechesis, as well as contemporary health care settings. Their missioning process for these apostolates is done in the context of religious obedience. Each sister is expected to discuss with her superior her interests, needs, and personal abilities regarding her work in the apostolate. The sisters may make suggestions about apostolates, but they do not actively search on their own for a position. The community leadership identifies needs in Catholic institutions, and then discusses those needs with the sisters, being sensitive to the personal and psychological needs of the sisters. But the ultimate decision to mission a sister in an assignment rests with the major superior. Sisters are missioned only to assignments where they can live in community with other members of their institute. The sisters accept a salary that is only the amount needed for sustenance and their retirement fund.

In adjusting observances and customs, as directed by Vatican II, the sisters modified their habit to a street-length suit and short veil. Eliminated from the horarium were a common rising time, common meditation time, and common retiring time. The sisters continue to share daily Mass and Morning and Evening Prayer from the Liturgy of the Hours. Each sister also spends at least one hour a day in contemplative prayer and reading of Scripture. Sister Judanne reported that there is an ongoing effort in her order to promote better understanding of Sacred Scripture and Franciscanism.

While most of the sisters in the order have college degrees, the order also welcomes women who prefer domestic work benefiting the community. While this order does not have a large number of candidates entering every year, it does continue to attract some young women, as well as some sisters who have transferred from other orders. (In 1996, the order had 551 professed sisters, 15 temporary professed sisters, 1 novice, and 1 postulant.) Sister Judanne credited strong leadership for initiating and continuing to direct her order along the renewal path outlined by the Second Vatican Council, as well as the sisters' growth in prayer and generous service in their apostolates.

How good was the expert advice?

Adding to the confusion of unlimited experimentation was the fact that religious institutes, in trying to respond enthusiastically to the reforms of Vatican II, sought advice from many sources. It was not uncommon for "experts" to be consulted about renewal chapters and new constitutions. Many of these people no doubt gave their best advice, but even experts who were priests or Religious were not always familiar with the unique charism or spirituality of an institute, and sometimes not very familiar with Vatican II documents.

In her book *Climb Along the Cutting Edge*, Sister Joan Chittister (president of the Leadership Conference of Women Religious in 1976), described her 1968 Benedictine chapter. She wrote that normally chapters had one consultant present during a general chapter — a Benedictine priest who was a canon lawyer. However, for the 1968 renewal chapter, fourteen consultants were invited to be present — a mixture of lay, Religious and clergy. In 1969, there were sixteen consultants. These consultants included canonists, theologians, a scripture scholar, a philosopher, an anthropologist, a sociologist, a psychologist, an attorney, and a parliamentarian.[24]

Many religious institutes thought they could solve structural problems by modeling their organizations on successful business models. Hence, management consulting firms such as Booz, Allen and Hamilton, were frequently called in to help with constitutional changes and reorganizations. These secular firms no doubt were conscientious in advising sisters on efficient management techniques and organizations, but they did not always have a firm grasp of canon law, or a clear understanding of the meaning of religious life or the charism of a particular institute. Nor did management advice based on the manufacturing of products always work well in religious institutes, which are neither democratic organizations nor for-profit entities oriented toward placing products in the marketplace.

Canon law itself also could be variously interpreted for the sisters, and sisters had to rely on priest canon lawyers, for women weren't allowed to become canon lawyers until after Vatican II. For example, Passionist Father Paul Boyle, who was president of the Conference of Major Superiors of Men from 1969 to 1974, was a canon lawyer and president of the Canon Law Society of America from 1964 to 1965. Father Boyle consulted for several orders of women Religious on canonical questions, and frequently addressed sisters about experimentation and renewal chapters. However, some of Father Boyle's recommendations and writings were controversial because of his interpretations of various laws and documents.

In a lengthy article in the October 1972 issue of *Sisters Today*, Father Boyle argued that there are two schools of thought regarding interpretation of law. The first school is that "the wording of the law is the primary source of interpretation." The second school is that "the purpose of the law is the controlling element in interpretation." Father Boyle wrote that most American canonists were trained in the " 'verbal' theory school," but he claimed that Vatican officials had stressed the goal theory in the past twenty-five years. He then went on to interpret some of the Vatican documents or instructions based on the goal theory.

One of these documents alluded to by Father Boyle was a February 25, 1972, letter from Cardinal Ildebrando Antoniutti, prefect of the Congregation for Religious, which had stated, in part:

> . . . Religious institutes, in their general chapters, may, and in some cases ought to, modify the traditional habit in accord with practical requirements and the needs of hygiene, but they may not abolish it altogether or leave it to the judgment of individual sisters.
>
> The basic criterion to be observed is that the habit prescribed by religious institutes, even as modified and simplified, should be such that it distinguishes the religious person who wears it.
>
> On the other hand, purely secular clothes, without any recognizable exterior sign, can be permitted, for particular reasons, by the competent superiors to those sisters to whom the use of the religious habit would constitute an impediment or obstacle in the normal exercise of activities which should be undertaken in certain circumstances. Even in this latter case the dress of the religious women should not depart from the forms of , simplicity, and modesty proper to the religious state. It should always be "in some way different from the forms that are clearly secular." [25]

Yet, Father Boyle inverted the very clear message of Cardinal Antoniutti, and in a curious linguistic exercise, he tried to justify his own conclusion that the habit was *not* required: "All that the letter says is that General Chapters 'may not abolish it (the habit) altogether. . . .' If the habit is retained for certain liturgical or more formal occasions it is clear that the Chapter has not abolished it altogether. There is no effort to require that this distinctive sign be worn all or even most of the time." He also reasoned that, "Since purely secular clothes, without any apparent sign of commitment, are permitted for particular reasons, it is clear that no particular reason is required to justify purely secular clothes worn with some readily recognizable exterior sign. This combination constitutes a religious habit. The purpose of the various statements concerning a habit is public manifestation of consecration. Whatever serves to clearly identify one as a dedicated person is a habit."[26]

Further confusion was provided by other canonists, including Dominican Father Kevin O'Rourke, who likewise consulted frequently for women Religious during the renewal period. In a 1973 article in *Review for Religious*, Father O'Rourke also addressed the hot topic of the habit. He wrote, ". . . insofar as the law is concerned it is very clear that there is a right to experiment with the religious habit, not only in regard to its style but whether it is going to be worn or not."

Father O'Rourke went on to explain that "The renewal and the rewriting of the *Code of Canon Law* is very badly bogged down, and as a result we have a situation where many laws which are obsolete are not being observed. . . .

"It is my personal opinion — and I put it forward as opinion — that in the area of the religious habit, the law is being changed by custom. It is being modified in such a way that religious women and religious men will not be identified with habits in the future. . . . I believe the law is changing through custom, because the law-making body has not kept up to date with the signs of the times and with the needs of the people. . . ."

Father O'Rourke concluded that ". . . no matter how much we try to explain, some people are not going to be satisfied because they are unable to accept the theology which brings them away from the rigid, conforming, and authority-centered way of life, to a theology that brings them rather to an emphasis on personal responsibility, upon changing times, and upon the needs of the people being served."[27]

Father O'Rourke's article was cited in some chapter meetings by advocates promoting secular dress for Religious. One sister reported that a duplicated copy of Father O'Rourke's article was used as a source in her order's chapter meeting, rather than the Vatican II document on religious life, *Perfectae Caritatis*. (In spite of speculation that the new *Code of Canon Law* would not include the requirement for a habit, Canon 669 of the new code reads: "Religious are to wear the habit of the institute made according to the norm of proper law as a sign of their consecration and as a testimony of .")

Another source of misinformation was faulty or hasty unofficial translations of Vatican documents. Even before the documents were officially translated, private translations often were made and promulgated to Religious, who were understandably eager to see what the Council had to say about religious life. For example, there were occasions when a canon lawyer, who was versed in the official Church language of Latin, would do his own private translation of a Vatican document prior to release of the official translation, and then pass along to the sisters that private translation.[28]

A former president of the Sisters of Loretto, Sister Maureen McCormack, later wrote that "Our reading added momentum to our transformation. In the early years of renewal, we had access, through translations by our sisters, to writings not yet available in English. The thinking of forward-looking theologians was shared while their ideas were still germinating. Scripture scholars were invited to discuss their latest findings with us. Because we had our very own official auditor at the Vatican Council [Sister of Loretto Mary Luke Tobin, who was president of the Conference of Major Religious Superiors of Women's Institutes in the U.S.] who informed us about changes as they were happening, we set ourselves on the path to renewal in advance of decrees from Rome to do the same."[29]

Even with official translations, Religious often paid more attention to commentary on the Council documents than they did to the actual documents themselves. And many so-called Council experts warned against literal interpretation of Council documents, as if the contemporary Council documents needed the same kind of interpretation as Sacred Scripture, which must be interpreted in terms of historical background and literary genre. This idea that the documents should be interpreted rather than taken literally also encouraged a variety of subjective renditions that neatly fit the interpreters' agenda. Thus, if a sister got hold of a faulty translation or commentary — or perhaps even worse, heard a so-called "expert" speaker who substituted opinion or speculation for fact — misinformation was the unfortunate result.

The Congregation for Religious was so concerned about this problem that in January 1967, Cardinal Egidio Vagnozzi, apostolic delegate to the United States, brought the topic to the attention of Sister Mary Luke Tobin, president of the Conference of Major Religious Superiors of Women's Institutes. The Conference of Major Religious Superiors of Women's Institutes was the official organization recognized by the Vatican as representing women Religious, and part of its role was to act as a communications link between the Vatican and the various institutes of women Religious in the United States. Cardinal Vagnozzi told Sister Mary Luke that the Con-

51

gregation for Religious had directed him to ask the Conference of Major Superiors to inform its members that unqualified people should not be invited to lecture to sisters about Vatican II or the renewal of religious life. He stressed that communities of sisters should not be addressed by anyone not previously approved by the local bishop.[30]

At the September 1967 assembly of the Conference of Major Religious Superiors of Women's Institutes, a Congregation for Religious representative, Father Bernard Ransing, again addressed this issue:

> . . . There are so many forces working against the proper understanding and execution of the texts of the Decrees and the will of the Church.
>
> Frequently, "the mind of the Church" is quoted as authority for certain changes that are suggested. Superiors are told that if they do not adopt this or that innovation they are not acting according to this mind. But where is the mind of the Church to be found, if not in these documents that we have quoted?
>
> We have had reason to remark before, a number of times, on the self-constituted authorities who are giving their own personal interpretation of the religious life and how it is to be lived, and on how much harm they are doing in speaking or writing about something of which they have only superficial knowledge or no knowledge at all. . . . Quantities of books and articles are still being published, that propose personal views, and that, unfortunately, seem to be read and accepted by a certain class of religious much more readily than the official documents of the Church. And most unfortunate it is that some preachers, retreat masters, and spiritual directors plant erroneous ideas in the minds of religious, or encourage them in false concepts of their own. The main difficulty is always that they do not know or refer to the sources. They overlook and neglect the documents of the Church in elaborating their theories. And, of course, there is always that articulate minority within the religious family itself, which agitates for its own ideas and which not infrequently either undertakes on its own to start a trend, or forces the hand of the superiors to permit practices that have not been properly authorized.[31]

But how many sisters actually were able to obtain and read *Perfectae Caritatis* and other documents on religious life? Apparently, many sisters did not have access to the Council documents or to correct interpretations of the documents. On July 8, 1966, Monsignor Joseph T.V. Snee, assistant vicar for religious of the Archdiocese of New York, wrote Sister Mary Luke Tobin, president of the Conference of Major Religious Superiors of Women's Institutes, asking to be placed on the Conference mailing list, and observing: "I think that some of our communities are not being properly briefed on the various directives coming from the Holy See."[32]

Rome had assumed that superiors would conscientiously pass along pertinent information to the grass-roots sisters. According to Canon 592, it is the duty and responsibility of the religious superior to disseminate all relevant Vatican documents to the religious in her institute: "The moderators of every institute are to promote knowledge of the documents of the Holy See which affect members entrusted to them and be concerned about their observance of them." Certainly, many leaders of women's religious institutes adhered faithfully to this canon, but there is plenty of evidence that a good number of sisters in local convents never came into contact with the Vatican documents because their superiors did not feel the sisters needed to have the information or because the superiors disagreed with the contents of those documents.

And often, the basis for this disagreement with official Vatican pronouncements was resentment that women were not in decision-making positions in the Church, a feeling that had been emphasized by the feminist movement of the 1960s. Indeed, it seems that a good number of sisters took the advice that Jesuit Father John Haughey gave at the 1970 assembly of the Conference of Major Religious Superiors of Women's Institutes: ". . . We should make two things perfectly clear. That whatever ecclesiastical authority does not have the common courtesy to communicate directly to you, those directives and decisions that have been made about your lives; that such directives and decisions will be treated by you as if they do not exist; and secondly, if there is not clear proof that subsequent directives and decisions have had the benefit of consultation with representatives of those most immediately affected by these, that you have absolutely no intention of complying with them."[33]

Much of the misinformation about the Vatican II call for renewal of religious orders was promulgated by the very people who were responsible for directing that renewal — the leaders of some religious institutes, who perhaps were misinformed themselves, or who simply put their own interpretation on documents and teachings emanating from Rome. And certainly some responsibility for misdirecting the renewal belongs to pseudo-experts who created their own concept of what Vatican II intended for the renewal of religious life and then sold that concept to religious institutes. Thus, many women's religious institutes in the United States proceeded along a precipitous renewal journey that was directed more by the politics of women's liberation than by the documents of the Second Vatican Council.

The next chapter reports on efforts by the Church to get renewal of religious communities back on track.

4: Alarm in the Vatican

"Rome and America simply do not share the same value systems: they do not speak the same renewal language. American religious men and women no longer look to Rome for regulations and directives. They operate from a milieu that encourages the responsible freedom of the individual within the framework of her personal commitment to Christ and his church."[1]
National Assembly of Women Religious

As the process of renewal proceeded in religious communities, Church officials became alarmed about experimentation that exceeded canon law, a secularized lifestyle, rejection of authority, unprecedented numbers of Religious departing from religious life, declining numbers of new vocations, and the abandonment of community life and prayer as well as the traditional apostolates of health care and education. During the 1970s and 1980s, the Holy See consequently undertook several initiatives to refocus the renewal of religious life on the proposals laid out by the Second Vatican Council. Some of these initiatives were directed to Religious all over the world, and some were focused on Religious in the United States. But, as with the mixed reception of the Vatican II documents, these initiatives by the Holy See often were met with resistance by some Religious who were determined to pursue their own version of renewal. And this inclination to reject Rome's guidance and authority was supported by some bishops, priests, and laity who wanted more independence for the American Catholic Church.

Pope Paul's evaluation

The *motu proprio* giving implementation guidelines for renewal in religious institutes had been out for about five years when Pope Paul VI issued the apostolic exhortation *Evangelica Testificatio* on June 29, 1971, in which he set forth his observations about renewal efforts.

Paul VI praised Religious for their dedication and generosity. But he also alluded to "certain arbitrary transformations," an "exaggerated distrust of the past," "too hardy" experimentation, and "a mentality excessively preoccupied with hastily conforming to the profound changes which disturb our times." Paul VI also reminded Religious of the necessity and dignity of work, importance of the religious habit and communal sharing, importance of obedience, faithfulness to prayer, importance of silence, centrality of the liturgy, and primacy of an interior life.[2]

The pope's rather gentle criticism of renewal in religious institutes was not what some Religious desiring a more radical renewal wanted to hear, and some even claimed that Paul VI was trying to undo the renewal called for by the Second Vatican Council.

Christian Brother Gabriel Moran wrote that "I can hardly imagine anyone's life being influenced by these words [in *Evangelica Testificatio*]." Brother Gabriel claimed that "the document shows no awareness of the kind of problem tearing at the church today." He continued, "A document on 'religious life' and 'evangelical counsels' ought to be concerned with the lives of hundreds of millions of people. Instead, the papal letter, like the inadequate Vatican II document on which it is based [*Perfectae Caritatis*], presumes that religious life and religious order are interchangeable terms. This presumption is a cul-de-sac which produces a flow of rhetoric going nowhere except back on itself."[3]

The apostolic exhortation *Evangelica Testificatio* continued to be criticized in 1972 when the Theology Committee of the Leadership Conference of Women Religious launched a project to elicit responses to the exhortation, which in reality was an attempt to refute the papal document. Directing the project was Sister Sandra Schneiders, who later would write in her book, *New Wineskins,* that *Evangelica Testificatio* was, "in general, a theological step backward toward pre-conciliar understandings of religious life."[4]

The Leadership Conference's *Evangelica Testificatio* project soon thereafter published the book *Widening the Dialogue*, a collection of essays on the papal document. The book questioned the authorship of the apostolic exhortation (even though Pope Paul VI had signed it) and impugned the validity of the Latin translation. One essay by Franciscan Sister Francis Borgia Rothluebber (Leadership Conference vice-president in 1972, president in 1973) reveals the origin of the title of the sisters' book. In her essay, Sister Francis Borgia wrote that *Evangelica Testificatio* was ambivalent and rooted in the past rather than the future, and she invited "a searching dialogue!" on the exhortation.[5] The essays from this book were then used by the superiors' conference in workshops for sisters, so the interpretation of, and challenge to, *Evangelica Testificatio* by the Leadership Conference of Women Religious was thus promulgated to sisters all over the country.

A reminder from the Congregation for Religious

Less than a year after *Evangelica Testificatio*, the Congregation for Religious issued *Experimenta Circa* on February 5, 1972. This decree reminded Religious that purely democratic forms of government were unacceptable in religious institutes, for a superior must exercise personal authority. Then, on July 10, 1972, the Congregation for Religious sent a letter to all mothers superior stating that the Congregation had asked (in 1967) to see the acts of special general chapters in order to be aware of experiments and to be certain that chapters stayed within the limits of *Ecclesiae Sanctae*. The letter explained that the decrees from chapters that had been seen thus far had some common problems. Therefore, the Congregation for Religious was making observations and suggestions so that future chapter decrees could be modified or improved.

The letter reminded sisters that the purpose, nature, and character of their institute must be preserved, and that "every derogation from common law must have a dispensation explicitly granted." The letter also admitted that in some cases, the Congregation may have overlooked some change that was contrary to canon law, but "This would have been due to an oversight and may not be interpreted as an explicit concession."

Among the observations made by the Congregation for Religious about problematic chapter decrees:

1. Chapter decisions that dispense with any kind of dependence or accountability are not acceptable.
2. The obligation and right of the superior to exercise personal authority must be respected.
3. The formula for religious profession should be based on *Ordo Professionis* and approved by the Congregation for Religious. This formula is to be the same for each sister in the institute.
4. Sisters in temporary vows may not hold positions of authority.
5. Small communities are acceptable if the lifestyle is that of a religious community, with a person in authority. Small communities should not be composed of only peer groups nor according to personal choice.

6. Chapters should not hesitate to prescribe a minimum of time for daily prayer.
7. "The religious, not as a private individual but as a member of her Institute, engages in apostolic work which is according to the end of her Institute."
8. Chapter decisions on habit should follow *Perfectae Caritatis,* that the religious habit is an outward mark of consecration to God and should be simple, modest, and poor.
9. Some chapters leave to the individual all decisions about recreation, vacations, etc. In these matters, superiors cannot totally abdicate their authority.
10. The spirit of foundresses should permeate the constitutions.
11. Constitutions should include juridical matters, such as eligibility for active and passive voice, practice of poverty, manner of admittance to profession, etc.[6]

Later in 1972, French Cardinal Jean Danielou, in an interview on Vatican radio, observed that religious life in the Western world was in crisis. He blamed the crisis on false interpretation of Vatican II found in journals, conferences, and theology. Cardinal Danielou cited "a false concept of liberty which brings in its wake contempt for constitutions and rules, and exalts the whim of the moment and improvisation." He called for an end to experiments and decisions which were contrary to the directives of the Council, and suggested that in religious institutes where this was not possible, religious who wanted to be faithful to their constitutions should be allowed to set up their own distinct communities.[7] (Some traditional women Religious took Cardinal Danielou's suggestion, and a few new communities of sisters were established, such as the Sisters of St. Joseph the Worker in Walton, Kentucky. This new order was established in 1973 by eighteen former Sisters of Charity of Nazareth who felt their order was becoming too secularized.)

As the 1970s passed, the direction of renewal in many religious institutes continued to trouble Rome, and some sisters made it very clear that they felt the Vatican had nothing of value to tell American Religious and that American Religious were not obliged to listen to Rome. In June of 1976, Cardinal Jean Villot, Vatican secretary of state, asked the Leadership Conference of Women Religious to circulate to its members the May 24, 1976, address of Pope Paul VI at the consistory with the Church's cardinals in Rome. The address dealt with polarization in the Church on the part of those who would not accept the authority of Vatican II, namely Archbishop

Marcel Lefebvre and his followers, and at the other pole, those who were moving beyond the teachings of Vatican II. Cardinal Villot directed that the sisters pay particular attention to the section of the address in which the pope wrote about abuses of the teachings of Vatican II. Abuses cited by the pope included:

> Those who believe themselves authorized to create their own liturgy, sometimes limiting the sacrifice of the Mass or the sacraments to the celebration of their own lives or of their own struggle. . . .
>
> Those who minimize the doctrinal teaching in catechetics or distort it according to the preference of the interests, pressures or needs of the people. . . .
>
> Those who pretend to ignore the living tradition of the church, from the fathers to the teachings of the magisterium, and reinterpret the doctrine of the church, and the gospel itself. . . . This is all the more dangerous when it is done by those who have the very high and delicate mission of teaching Catholic theology.
>
> Those who interpret theological life as the organization of a society here below, reducing it indeed to a political action.[8]

The *Essential Elements* of Religious Life

By the time 1983 arrived, eleven years had passed since Pope Paul VI had written his assessment of renewal, *Evangelica Testificatio*, and many religious institutes as well as individual Religious still did not seem to grasp the directives of *Perfectae Caritatis* (1965) and the *motu proprio Ecclesiae Sanctae* (1966). Additionally, some communities were continuing to experiment widely with their lifestyle and governance, some seventeen years after *Ecclesiae Sanctae* authorized temporary, limited experimentation. So, at the direction of Pope John Paul II, on May 31, 1983, the Congregation for Religious issued a summary of canonical norms for religious life called *Essential Elements in the Church's Teaching on Religious Life as Applied to Institutes Dedicated to Works of the Apostolate*. This document followed a letter from the pope to the bishops of the United States, in which the pope appointed Archbishop John Quinn to head a commission to study religious life in the United States. The pope was requesting this study because of concern over the rapidly diminishing number of vocations to the religious life in this country and the unprecedented departure of Religious from Catholic institutions. The pope asked the Congregation for Religious to issue *Essential Elements* as a guideline for bishops in performing this study of religious life.

Essential Elements was just what its title indicated, and was simply a restatement and clarification of Church teaching and canon law regarding religious life. The document repeated Pope John Paul II's 1979 call for Religious "to evaluate objectively and humbly the years of experimentation so as to recognize their positive elements and their deviations."[9] *Essential Elements* also signaled an end to the period of experimentation mandated by *Ecclesiae Sanctae*, for the new *Code of Canon Law*, which was promulgated by the pope January 25, 1983, would become effective November 27, 1983.

Essential Elements stressed the importance of the vows, which included: putting all gifts and salaries in common as belonging to the community; obedience to superiors and the Holy Father; community living, which includes sharing prayer, work, meals, leisure, and a common spirit; directing the works of all members to a common apostolate; wearing "a religious garb that distinguishes them as consecrated persons"; and placing personal authority in a superior, not a group.[10]

While the more traditional Religious praised the *Essential Elements* document, it did not sit well with some very vocal change-oriented American Religious, who were beginning to relish a certain independence from Rome. Some Religious were further angered that the Holy Father had called for a study of religious life in the United States, regarding this action as an insulting inquisition that singled out American Religious. And some Religious continued to put their own spin on the "spirit of Vatican II," and insisted that Rome was trying to reverse the mandates of the Second Vatican Council, even though *Essential Elements* was obviously a rehashing of canon law and Vatican II documents, including the popes' exhortations on religious life. Unfortunately, too many Religious were unfamiliar with those documents, so they accepted and even joined the Rome-bashing undertaken by some very vocal and high-profile Religious and laity.

In her introduction to the 1985 book she edited, *Midwives of the Future*, Loretto Sister Ann Patrick Ware wrote that: "One of the reasons for publishing this book at this time is that ominous signs are in the air. In 1983, the Congregation of Religious and Secular Institutes (SCRIS) issued a document, *Essential Elements of Religious Life,* which in effect would undo the work of renewal that religious communities of women have carried out."[11]

Sister Dorothy Vidulich, a Sister of St. Joseph of Peace and a co-member of the Loretto Sisters who is a columnist for *National Catholic Re-*

porter, made it clear that some American Religious felt that their "lived experience" made them more qualified than the pope or Vatican II to define authentic religious life. She wrote in *Midwives of the Future*: "The 1983 SCRIS [Congregation for Religious] *Essential Elements of Religious Life* is a feeble recall to a lukewarm monastic style completely divorced from Vatican II theology. Its critique by so many United States women and men religious is a healthy and encouraging sign that our lived experience is basic to the emerging new theology of religious life."[12]

Sociologist Jesuit Father Joseph Fichter wrote that "Tension and resentment seem to be growing among American sisters over 'vacillating' instructions from Rome. Paul VI mandated renewal in all religious communities. John Paul II ordered a reversal. Religious were informed in the 1983 document from the Congregation for Religious, *Essential Elements in the Church's Teaching on Religious Life*, that 'the lessons learned from their two-decade experience of renewal are abrogated in favor of a return to a preconciliar closed system of religious life.' "[13]

A casual reader will no doubt assume from the structure of the preceding sentence that the quotation about returning to a "preconciliar closed system of religious life" was taken from *Essential Elements* itself. But, if the reader paused to look up footnote twelve, she would discover that the quote is actually from an essay in *Midwives of the Future*. The essay was written by the controversial School Sister of Notre Dame Jeannine Gramick, a founder of New Ways Ministry, a ministry among gays and lesbians. (A commission was appointed by the Congregation for Religious in 1994 to examine the teachings of Sister Jeannine and her colleague in New Ways Ministry, Salvatorian Father Robert Nugent. As of late 1996, the Vatican had not announced a decision about its findings.)

Anita Caspary, who had been superior of the Los Angeles Immaculate Heart of Mary sisters before she and the majority of her order became laicized in 1971 rather than follow Rome's directives on renewal, wrote in *National Catholic Reporter* on March 2, 1984, that some sisters were quite rightly ignoring *Essential Elements*, and she issued a veiled threat. She wrote that some nuns ". . . have set the whole matter aside to go on with the work at hand rather than using time to readdress questions they have settled for themselves. But among a sizable group of sisters of various communities, there is emergent anger, a growing frustration with the system. The more outspoken predict another exodus of sisters like that of the 1960's should the Vatican intervention be carried out to the letter." Caspary further lamented that Rome was directing bishops to "lead the sisters back into a pre-Vatican mode of life."[14]

Sisters in Crisis

Essential Elements did not sit well with some members of the Leadership Conference of Women Religious, either. Former executive directors of the conference, Sister Mary Daniel Turner, a Sister of Notre Dame de Namur, and Providence Sister Lora Ann Quinonez (who was executive director in 1983), reported that at their 1983 assembly, forty-three members publicly repudiated "the characterization of religious life in *Essential Elements* as alien to the experience of American sisters."[15] The sisters speaking were particularly disturbed that *Essential Elements* offended "American cultural sensibilities — the voice of the people is conspicuously absent from the document; its approach is ahistorical, nonexperimental; it is an attempt to quell what Rome sees as rebellion; it is an anonymous document, produced in secret; its fuzzy, ambiguous legal force leaves the door wide open for unchecked administrative abuse." Sisters Mary Daniel and Lora Ann called this incident at the superiors' meeting "A clear demonstration of the growing acknowledgment of the legitimate role of culture in shaping religious identity."[16]

Some canon lawyers even suggested that *Essential Elements* was not an authoritative document since the pope had not signed it. However, this point was refuted by Cardinal Eduardo Pironio, prefect of the Congregation for Religious, who said that the document did not require a signature because it was mandated and approved by the pope and related to his letter to American bishops. Cardinal Pironio further explained that on September 19, 1983, the Holy Father had told some American bishops on their *ad limina* visit to Rome that he had "approved a summary of the salient points of the Church's teaching on religious life prepared by the Congregation of Religious and Secular Institutes" to be used as guidelines by individual bishops as well as the commission appointed to study United States religious life.[17]

Some Religious reacted to the new *Code of Canon Law*, also released in 1983, in the same manner they reacted to *Essential Elements*. Sister of Notre Dame de Namur Marie Augusta Neal, a sociologist who was very influential in shaping renewal among women Religious, indicated that the new code was a step backward and had ignored the teachings of Vatican II. Writing in 1990, she elevated "lived experience" and experimentation as being superior to canon law in determining the structure of religious life: "Many Catholic sisters face a serious dilemma of obedience in the 1980s and will continue to do so in the 1990s. This dilemma takes the form of a conflict between honoring Vatican Council mandates to prophetic ministry and resuming the traditional form of the vow of obedience. . . . In the area of governance, the latest revision of canon law has re-affirmed the sacred character of the decision-making power of one person as administrator and ultimate authority figure. . . . Set aside and discounted are the nearly quarter century's experiments and lived experience of collegial governance and shared authority, adopted as a model of holiness by many congregations of women religious."[18]

Margaret Susan Thompson, a lay member of the National Coalition of American Nuns and a Syracuse University professor who has written extensively on American Catholic sisters, observed in 1994 that "retrogressive initiatives" of Pope John Paul II were "signified most pointedly by provisions in the 1983 revised *Code of Canon Law*, in *Essential Elements of Religious Life* [also 1983], and the Quinn Commission."[19]

But Sister Claudia Honsberger, a past superior of the Sisters, Servants of the Immaculate Heart of Mary, Immaculata, Pennsylvania, wrote a lengthy defense of *Essential Elements* in 1984. A former regional chairperson in the Leadership Conference of Women Religious, Sister Claudia had parted company with official Conference positions several times before. She wrote that religious communities did not take sufficient time to read and absorb the Vatican II documents, resulting in many misinterpretations and subsequent confusion for Religious. She suggested that some Religious disputed the content of *Essential Elements* because they were living a totally different lifestyle than the lifestyle for Religious described by the pope in the document.

Sister Claudia struck a poignant note when she alluded to the turmoil caused by unlimited and unevaluated experimentation in religious communities, writing that ". . . every religious knows what a time of anxiety and confusion it was, and still is, for many of the outgrowths of the period and the Chapters have been a source of pain, if not real agony."[20]

Collapsing community life

Most change-oriented communities of women Religious did not apply the Church guidelines in *Essential Elements* to their lifestyle and governance, but rather continued to define religious life in their own terms. One of the most apparent deviations from *Essential Elements* is demonstrated by the fact that many orders of women Religious have more sisters living away from their community than living with the community.

In a study of eight orders of women Religious, Sister Patricia Wittberg, a sociologist, found that in 1990 forty-two percent of the sisters in those eight communities lived alone, and another eighteen percent lived with just one other sister.[21] Thus, a full sixty percent really weren't living in what is normally defined as community. In many congregations, only the ill or retired live in community. In her presidential address to the 1995 Leadership Conference of Women Religious assembly, Conference president Andree Fries, a Sister of the Adoration of the Most Precious Blood, noted, ". . . we rarely have the luxury of a meal together, much less of quality time for prayer and community."[22]

This lifestyle apparently is quite typical for many communities of sisters. For example, a sizable number of Loretto Sisters reside in the Denver area, where the sisters formerly operated Loretto Heights College and staffed several parochial schools. Denver is the current site of the Loretto central staff office and development office. The 1993-94 Loretto Directory listed sixty-one Loretto Sisters living in Denver. Of those, twenty-four were listed as living alone; twenty-two living with one other sister; and there was one household each of three, four, and five sisters. The directory indicated that three sisters lived with one or more lay persons.

Even in cities where a motherhouse is located, it is not at all uncommon for sisters to live alone, with only one other sister, or with lay people, in apartments or houses. The sisters of the St. Louis province of the Sisters of St. Joseph of Carondelet live at over one hundred separate addresses in the St. Louis area, according to the 1995 Archdiocese of St. Louis yearbook. Many of these addresses are local convents or religious institutions. For example, seven "communities" have addresses at the provincial house, with a total of thirty-one sisters. Approximately one-hundred-fifty retired sisters are listed as residing at the retirement center. But there are thirty-eight addresses — most of which are apartments — at which only one St. Joseph sister is listed as residing. There are twenty-five addresses at which two St. Joseph sisters are listed as residing, some of which are apartments and some of which are houses.

It was no surprise, therefore, when the Vatican Congregation for Religious issued the document *Fraternal Life in Community* on February 19, 1994. In that document, the Congregation for Religious observed that the emphasis of mission over community "has had a profound impact on fraternal life in common to the point that this [community] has become at times almost an option rather than an integral part of religious life."

The Congregation for Religious made several observations about Religious, including: a culture of individualism has weakened commitment to community life and projects; a lay mentality stresses the material over the spiritual; some Religious have become consumers, not builders, of community; authority is misunderstood to the point that no one is in charge; and adequate time for prayer is not set aside. The document further noted that Religious should not live alone or away from community without serious reason, nor should religious live with laity. Institutes in which the majority of the members live apart "would no longer be able to be considered true religious institutes," according to the *Fraternal Life in Community* document.[23] Nor was this a new ruling from the Vatican; it was merely a reiteration of the definition of community already in existing Church documents and a re-emphasis on the fact that community is one of the key elements of religious life.

So, again, clear directions about religious life were given from the Vatican in this document, but apparently many Religious either rejected, ignored, or simply were not aware of the contents of the document. Some Religious protested that there can be many definitions of community, including "community without walls." However, the document on community set forth specific guidelines which call for Religious to actually live day-to-day with other members of their institute.

For religious institutes that have not heeded this or other Vatican documents, the result has been quite detrimental. Studies over several years by the Georgetown University Center for Applied Research in the Apostolate consistently show that religious institutes which actually live in community are much more successful in attracting new vocations than those which permit members to live on their own. The comprehensive 1992 "Future of Religious Orders in the United States" (FORUS) study, discussed later in this book, reached the same conclusion.

A synod on religious life

During the entire month of October 1994 the World Synod of Bishops took up the topic of consecrated life. But many American Religious were not happy that a body of bishops would be discussing the state of consecrated life and making recommendations to the pope. Furthermore, some religious superiors saw no reason to even make the members of their institutes aware of the synodal topic, even though Rome wanted all Religious to be involved.

In preparation for the synod, the synod secretariat issued a preliminary study document in November 1992, called the *lineamenta*. Archbishop Jan Schotte, general secretary of the synod secretariat, solicited "the widest possible involvement of clergy, religious and laity" in responding to the document. The *lineamenta* asked questions such as: "What are the greatest difficulties today facing women and men religious in offering an authentic Gospel witness to their special consecration in the midst of the people of God? How are problems treated resulting from the dwindling numbers in communities and the abandonment of works, especially those which have a valid social meaning in the field of education and health care assistance? What is the manner of dealing with the demise of an institute or its difficulty in surviving?" The responses to the *lineamenta* were then to be used by the synod secretariat in preparing the synod agenda.

In some dioceses of the United States, listening sessions were set up for this discussion to take place, but this was not a universal practice. Some religious institutes also created a framework for Religious to discuss the *lineamenta* and to offer further ideas for reflection at the synod. Unfortunately, a large number of Religious were never even made aware that the *lineamenta* existed and that their input had been solicited. Many Religious did not even receive this information from their superiors, who have a canonical obligation to inform their members about communications coming from the Vatican.

This fact became very clear in mid-1993 when the author received a telephone call from a sister-friend who was concerned that many Religious were not being given the opportunity to have any input on the synod. The sister had attended a meeting with about eighty sisters from many different congregations, and was amazed to find that only one other sister at the meeting even knew about the *lineamenta*. Further investigation by the author revealed that sisters in several different congregations had never even heard of the *lineamenta*, nor had their congregations asked them for any input on the upcoming synod on consecrated life.

Reaction to the *lineamenta* by Religious who did hear about it was quite mixed. The *lineamenta* enumerated several positive "fruits of renewal," which included: 1) "clearer awareness of the consecrated life's biblical and theological foundations, and its relationship to Christ, the Holy Spirit and the church"; 2) "better understanding and celebration of the liturgy"; 3) "greater openness to the meaning of community life"; 4) "greater awareness of the charismatic aspect of the life and work proper to each institute"; 5) "better ecclesial sense of the consecrated life"; and 6) signs of "genuine models of sanctity," "witness of charitable efforts," and "witness of martyrdom."[24]

But the *lineamenta* also identified some negative results of renewal, including: 1) "signs of a disorientation in persons and groups as a result of changes in constitutions and a divergence from past practices," including problems in the areas of liturgy, prayer, asceticism, obedience, poverty, communal life, and "generous dedication to the apostolate"; 2) "indications of individualism and secularism, contrary to the sense of consecration and to the striving toward perfection"; 3) "tension with the hierarchy and manifestations of dissent in both theory and practice in relation to authority and the magisterium of the Apostolic See and bishops, or in liturgical practice"; and 4) a "serious problem in vocations," placing some institutes in danger of extinction.[25]

Archbishop Schotte made it clear that the *lineamenta* was not an exhaustive treatment of the synod topic, and should not be interpreted as anticipating any possible conclusions of the synod. But, the more change-oriented Religious were wary about the synod discussing consecrated life, and some people predictably speculated that the pope was trying to return religious life to a pre-Vatican II model and that the *lineamenta* was a thinly disguised blueprint for conclusions that would eventually emanate from the synod.

In a response to the *lineamenta*, the executive committee of the Conference of Major Superiors of Men observed that there was an overemphasis upon consecration and communion in the document. The committee suggested additional themes "of great importance for understanding United States religious," including pluralism, globalization, democracy, and transformation of traditional institutions and structures.[26]

In its reflection paper on the *lineamenta*, the national board of the Leadership Conference of Women Religious remarked that "In many ways the synod, like other official church convocations, stands before the judgment of the church's women, and other women as well, in an age that finds the practice of exclusively male groups making decisions for women incomprehensible."[27]

In a later "Draft Responses by LCWR to Select Questions from the *lineamenta* for The 1994 Synod on Consecrated Life," the Conference executive committee revealed its philosophy on religious life in disagreeing with several points in the *lineamenta*:

On community: "The demands of ministry frequently make it impractical or impossible for groups of apostolic women religious to live under a single roof. Religious institutes are creatively experimenting with new ways of gathering, praying, and sharing. These new forms witness to the value of community and provide the necessary support for members. It is essential that such experimentation continue and that women religious have the opportunity to clarify, claim, and hold themselves accountable to a definition of community that is appropriate for the apostolic life."

On charismatic identity and mission: "New expressions of ministry, some of them not explicitly church-related, need to be tried and tested."

On the perspective of women Religious: "Women religious recognize that the exclusion and denigration of women that permeate society have their counterparts in the church. Lack of participation in decision-making, exclusionary language and ritual, and patriarchal structures run counter to movements of reform in society and to the Gospel itself. Exclusion and discrimination cause some sisters to be alienated from the liturgical and sacramental life of the church; they cause others to move from church-related ministries into the secular arena; they cause some to leave religious life altogether, and deter new membership."

On feminism: "Women religious have been conscientised [sic] to the systemic denial of women's gifts, insights, and persons in church and society. They have aligned themselves with and championed the desire of women everywhere for full equality."

On ambiguity of identity and role: "There are many tensions between canonical and traditional definitions of religious life and the new self-understanding of religious women. The consequences are felt in the relationships of religious with bishops, clergy, laity, and one another. For all are lacking for respectful dialogue and clarification of new understandings."

On difficulties in the particular church: "For example, women religious are often victims of unjust and unprofessional employment practices. They serve at the pleasure of a pastor and can be dismissed without cause or redress. Compensation is sometimes inadequate."

At the spring 1993 meeting of the United States bishops, Immaculate Heart of Mary Sister Margaret Brennan, a former president of the Leadership Conference of Women Religious, took issue with the *lineamenta*'s statement that "in some cases a mistaken idea of feminism has laid claim to the right to participate in the life of the church in ways which are not in keeping with the hierarchical structure willed by Christ." Sister Margaret told the bishops:

> It must be said that a statement of such dogmatic certitude appears to many women as one that denies our birthright as baptized Christians to be the church as women and denies women any role in decision-making bodies.
>
> It is important for you as bishops to understand that the commitment of many women religious to the feminist movement in the church is not to overthrow our rich tradition, but rather to challenge and to overcome the dualisms that have taken root in its structures and its symbol system as well. An emerging feminist consciousness has enabled us to invite others into an expanded experience of God and our world. This is particularly true in the way that women theologians have been able to revision our Chris-

tian tradition and to bring feminist theology to a new level of discussion. In this area we cherish the hope that continued theological reflection and dialogue can open wider vistas of inclusion that can lead to a discipleship of equals.[28]

The National Coalition of American Nuns called the *lineamenta* "a sad Paper with Pitiful Nuances," which was "symptomatic of a dysfunctional curia."[29]

In her column in the *National Catholic Reporter*, Sister Dorothy Vidulich contended that the synod was being convened because "Pope John Paul II thinks it is about time to let the good Catholic sisters know he is their Holy Father. This is because the Vatican suspects that women religious, in the United States especially, are getting out of control." But, she continued, "For women religious who have experienced the pain of change — spirituality, life-style, dress, ministry, mission, governance — plus the joy of creative response to the emerging postmodern world, many of the questions posed in Rome's preliminary study document, *lineamenta*, are couched in pre-Vatican II language. It's almost as if the past two tumultuous decades never happened. . . ."

"The synod will not hold back the tide of feminism, which reclaims women's birthright as baptized Christians to be the church as women."[30]

Referring to expectations that the synod might recommend that Religious be required to adhere more closely to Church guidelines for religious life, the president of a congregation of women Religious warned that: ". . . the toothpaste is already out of the tube. There's no putting it back."[31]

The synod convened during the month of October 1994 following an agenda set forth in a working paper that had been developed from responses to the *lineamenta*. Since a synod is advisory and not legislative, propositions for future action were sent to Pope John Paul II for his consideration in preparing his apostolic exhortation on the synodal topic. The propositions were not made public, but reportedly some of the propositions included the suggestions that Religious adhere to Church teaching as part of their witness and that bishops and Religious dialogue more on the topics of the magisterium and the relationship of Religious to the local church.[32]

The interventions of the bishops generally were not publicized either, but press sources reported on a few of these presentations, giving some flavor of the discussions. Bishops from various countries were full of praise for the contributions of consecrated persons to the Church, and they emphasized that consecrated life was vital to the Church. But many bishops also indicated that they shared some of the same concerns that had appeared in the synod's working paper.

Archbishop Augusto Vargas Alzamora of Lima, Peru, called for a return to distinctive garb for Religious, saying that one reason for a decline in vocations was that Religious cannot be distinguished from lay persons.[33] Archbishop Oscar Andres Rodriguez Maradiaga of Tegucigalpa, Honduras, a member of the Salesians of Don Bosco, pleaded for Religious to return to the traditional apostolate of education. He defined education as "a new aspect of the Gospel's preferential option for the poor," saying that religious orders that had left educational institutions in favor of other ministries for and with the poor should reconsider their decision in light of the potential of education to bring people out of poverty.[34]

The bishops from the United States also espoused a variety of views among themselves. For example, Cardinal Joseph Bernardin counseled against premature judgments about new ways of living consecrated life. He noted that tensions are inevitable in an era of change, and he called for "a broad scope for legitimate diversity."[35] Bishop Francis George, a member of the Missionary Oblates of Mary Immaculate, recognized the "diversity of charisms" in consecrated life, but voiced some concern that individualism sometimes eclipsed the call to holiness. He also noted that "Consecrated persons too trustful of their own experience can begin to assimilate uncritically the imperatives of their culture and gradually lose their ability to be a source of spiritual strength for other men and women struggling to achieve the generosity needed to found Christian families, to defend life in a culture of death, to be faithful to the Gospel in business, the arts and politics."[36]

And Bishop James Timlin acknowledged "many wonderful, beautiful and necessary changes" in religious life since the Second Vatican Council. But he was the most outspoken of the United States bishops, saying that "the last twenty-five years have been devastating to religious life," particularly in the United States. While leaving ample room "for a rich diversity in religious life," Bishop Timlin called for a "refounding and transformation" of religious life and a return to the traditional interpretation of the vows. Apparently alluding to some women Religious who do not attend Mass or receive the sacraments because women are excluded from ordination, he contended that "At the very least, for one to be considered a religious, he or she must be what we euphemistically call a 'practicing Catholic.'" And Bishop Timlin argued that "we must still be clear about what is expected by the church of those who publicly profess to be vowed sons and daughters of the church. We must be determined to chart a clear course for consecrated life. . . . We have dialogued enough. We have experimented enough. . . .

The era of experimentation, or whatever we want to call it, has not been all that successful, and we should honestly and humbly admit it."[37]

Since Cardinal John O'Connor was a co-president of the synod, he submitted a written intervention to the synod secretariat to be included in the published papers of the synod. Cardinal O'Connor observed, in part:

"There can be little question that in overwhelming numbers and in good faith religious all over the world obediently set about, zealously and sincerely pursuing the work of renewal initiated by Vatican II. As in so much of Vatican II's 'aggiornamento,' however, both guidelines and guidance were too frequently lacking. It must be admitted that some bishops seriously failed to instruct their faithful in the documents of Vatican II, and provide firm guidance to religious in effecting reform and renewal. The result was the creation of unfulfillable expectations. On the part of religious, many changes they introduced sincerely believing them to be faithful to Vatican II were ultimately rejected, and, indeed, sincere religious themselves were even criticized for introducing such changes. Obviously, at the same time, some religious abused the occasion for true reform and renewal, in order to accomplish their own objectives, quite different from the objectives of Vatican II. . . ."[38]

John Paul II speaks about religious life

When the pope's apostolic exhortation on consecrated life, *Vita Consecrata*,[39] was released on March 28, 1996, it was greeted with enthusiasm — and relief — by virtually all the Religious in the United States. This warm reception no doubt was due to the fact that the exhortation was extremely positive, and rather than chastising Religious or consecrated persons for any deviation from the norms established by the Church, Pope John Paul II expounded on the reasons behind those norms:

> •Vows: By professing the vows of poverty, chastity, and obedience, consecrated persons make Christ the whole meaning of their lives and try to imitate the way Jesus lived — poor, chaste, and obedient to the Father.
> • Community: Life in community reflects the ecclesial communion of the Church and supports the individuals in their vocations.
> • Spirituality: The spiritual life has primacy in any form of consecrated life. "By its very nature the eucharist is the center of the consecrated life," so the pope urged consecrated persons to share daily in the Eucharist, pray the Lit-

urgy of the Hours, meditate on the Bible individually and in common, renew devotions to the Blessed Virgin Mary — especially the rosary, make monthly retreats, and engage in various spiritual exercises.

• Lifestyle: The Holy Father stressed "the need for fidelity to the founding charism and subsequent spiritual heritage of each institute," and he cited a "pressing need today for every institute to return to the rule, since the rule and constitutions provide a map for the whole journey of discipleship."

• Habit: The habit is a sign of consecration, poverty, and membership in a particular religious family, the pope noted. Citing the Vatican II document *Perfectae Caritatis*, he "strongly" exhorted men and women Religious to wear a habit which should be "suitably adapted to the conditions of time and place."

• Vocations: While some religious institutes may go out of existence because of dwindling numbers, consecrated life as an integral part of the Church will never cease to exist, the pope wrote. And, while new forms of religious life are emerging, the old forms will continue to endure. The pope alluded to dwindling numbers of vocations in Western countries and said that consecrated persons must actively promote vocations and live an exemplary consecrated life that will attract other people "by word and example."

• Education: Since education is "an essential dimension" of the Church's mission, the pope said that consecrated persons can be especially effective in educational activities which lead people to God and empower them to overcome their own poverty. The pope echoed the synod's call for "consecrated persons to take up again, wherever possible, the mission of education in schools of every kind and level and in universities and institutions of higher learning."

• Hierarchy: The pope spoke about one aspect of ecclesial communion as being allegiance to the magisterium of the bishops. "The pastoral initiatives of consecrated persons should be determined and carried out in cordial and open dialogue between bishops and superiors of the different institutes."

• Women: The pope acknowledged the role of women in adding the feminine perspective to the life of the Church and to its pastoral and missionary activity. And, he added that it was "urgent" to make room "for women to participate in different fields and at all levels, including decision-making processes." He particularly praised the contributions consecrated women have made to the Church.

The few negative comments made by the pope were not readily apparent in the predominantly positive exhortation, but he did write about:

• The desire of Religious to become closer to laity can lead to the adoption of a secularized lifestyle or the promotion of human values.

• The authenticity of new forms of consecrated life must be judged by the authority of the Church.

• Formation for new members should take place in community and for a definite time period. Every institute must provide "a precise and systematic description of its plan of continuing formation" of all members during their lifetimes.

• While authority should be "fraternal and spiritual" and involve community members in decision-making, "it should still be remembered that the final word belongs to authority and consequently that authority has the right to see that decisions taken are respected."

• Allegiance of mind and heart to the magisterium of the bishops "must be lived honestly and clearly testified to before the people of God by all consecrated persons, especially those involved in theological research, teaching, publishing, catechesis and the use of the means of social communication."

• Cooperation between consecrated persons and bishops for developing diocesan pastoral life is of "fundamental importance."

• Each institute "should grow and develop in accordance with the spirit of their founders and foundresses, and their own sound traditions," and "follow its own discipline and to keep intact its spiritual and apostolic patrimony."

> • Pastoral initiatives of consecrated persons should be "determined and carried out in cordial and open dialogue between bishops and superiors."
> • Conferences of superiors should "maintain frequent and regular contacts" with the Congregation for Religious as "a sign of their communion with the Holy See."
> • Lack of vocations "must not lead either to discouragement or to the temptation to practice lax and unwise recruitment."
> • Consecrated persons should "foster respect for the person and for human life from conception to its natural end."

It was this pastoral, patient tone that was perhaps the exhortation's greatest strength, but at the same time its greatest weakness. The exhortation was directed to the entire world, and certainly religious life was not in crisis in all the countries of the world. But because the exhortation was so positive and so acceptable, it was interpreted by many as an affirmation of the Religious who ignored, even belittled, the most explicit Church documents as they went about fashioning their own definition of religious life. Mercy Sister Doris Gottemoeller, a past president of the Leadership Conference of Women Religious and a synod auditor, reacted to the exhortation in this way: "Each congregation serves the church and the world in its own distinct way. The exhortation recognizes and affirms this diversity as a testament to the dynamism and vitality of religious life and its ability to change to meet the needs of the people and the times."[40]

What went wrong?

In spite of clear directives from the Church over the past thirty years, many Religious have simply ignored or dismissed these directives as they pursued their own brand of renewal. So, what went wrong? In retrospect, it seems that mistakes were made by all the parties involved in renewal, and there is plenty of blame to be shared.

First of all, the decade of the 1960s was hardly the most stable time for the Church to ask institutes of Religious to evaluate their lifestyle and government structures, particularly in the United States where a massive cultural upheaval was underway. Since institutes of women religious had been run in such an authoritarian fashion before the Council, and sisters had encountered an offensive paternalistic attitude on the part of some clergy and hierarchy, sisters were very susceptible to the tenets of the feminist revolution.

Second, grassroots women Religious had been so overworked that they weren't even able to obtain their professional degrees before being sent to their assignments in the apostolate. How, then, were these women supposed to have the time or the expertise to adequately evaluate all the paperwork coming from Rome? Furthermore, many of the sisters who were being sent to universities for their degrees in the 1960s were influenced by the radical campus politics of that time, as well as by some dissident theologians who were beginning to openly challenge Church teachings. And these were the very women who had leadership roles in their orders.

Third, the directive to religious institutes to rewrite their constitutions even as canon law was being revised was an invitation to disaster, and many institutes succumbed to the temptation of trying to anticipate in their new constitutions what the new code would say about religious life. But even when religious institutes did dutifully write the Vatican for permission to set aside a canon in their new constitutions, it took the Vatican years to reply. And it was not realistic to expect that experiments that had been going on for ten-plus years could quickly be halted or reversed if they did not comply withthe revised *Code of Canon Law* when it was finally issued, for the people involved in these experiments were profoundly changed by their experiences.

Fourth, most American bishops did not involve themselves sufficiently in the renewal process, probably because they did not want to interfere with the autonomy of religious institutes. But many of them did not even familiarize themselves with the new Church guidelines about religious life, so they did not always recognize deviations from those guidelines even when they occurred in their own dioceses.

Finally, and probably most significantly, some women Religious determined that their own "lived experience" was more valid for defining religious life than were any of the directives coming from the Church. These sisters fashioned their own version of renewal, which was then passed along to other sisters in lieu of the official pronouncements coming from Rome.

The chief agent for promoting this Americanized version of renewal was the women superiors' conference, which was recognized by Rome as the official communications link between the sisters in the United States and the Vatican. However, as the next two chapters detail, the superiors' conference eventually evolved into an independent-minded body of sisters more inclined to dictate to Rome the definition of religious life than to take direction from Rome.

5: The LCWR's "Radical Rethink"

"As you well know, the Conference of Major Superiors of Women has undergone a radical process of rethink in the past two years."[1]

Sister Joan deLourdes Leonard, CSJ
LCWR Executive Committee, 1970

Two influential sisters' organizations created in the 1950s initiated many of the needed reforms for sisters; but ironically, these organizations also generated much of the chaos and confusion that thinned the ranks of women Religious, stifled the growth of new vocations, and fermented the revolution in the convents. These organizations were the Sister Formation Conference (today called the Religious Formation Conference, which will be discussed in Chapter Eight) and the Conference of Major Religious Superiors of Women's Institutes (CMSW), today called the Leadership Conference of Women Religious (LCWR). Both groups were established with very noble purposes, and the two organizations effectively served women Religious and the Church for a number of years. But, as is often the case in the United States, good ideas were taken to the extreme, and both organizations apparently led sisters far beyond the reform and renewal that was envisioned by the Second Vatican Council.

The Conference of Major Religious Superiors of Women's Institutes was the most influential organization representing sisters in the United States. As the official superiors' conference recognized by Rome, the conference played a key role in leading renewal in women's religious institutes. However, the brand of renewal promoted by the superiors' conference did not always accurately mirror the renewal mandated by Vatican II. The conference began as a group of mothers superior who joined together in the 1950s to share common problems and ideas about religious life, but it eventually evolved into a far different entity.

In the 1960s, activist sisters in the superiors' conference introduced programming at the group's annual assemblies which promoted a philosophy of religious life that was far more progressive than the renewal envisioned by Vatican II. These activists shaped implementation of the renewal in convents all over the country by conducting a conference-sponsored survey that presented the activists' reform agenda. This survey reached every sister in the United States. Some change-oriented members of the conference also employed questionable political tactics to rewrite the conference's membership requirements and constitution, eventually leading to a split in the organization and repeated conflict with Rome.

In 1971, the conference of women superiors renamed itself the Leadership Conference of Women Religious and began to function as a lobbying organization of professional women who were determined to set their own definition of religious life, based not on spiritual and theological topics, but rather on political and sociological issues. The next two chapters tell the story of that transformation of the women superiors' conference.

Early years of the conference of superiors

During the early 1950s, the Vatican began to encourage superiors of religious institutes to come together in national conferences for the purpose of exchanging information, giving each other support in building up religious life, and coordinating with local bishops, as well as bishops' conferences and the Holy See itself. These conferences were specifically mentioned in the 1965 Vatican II document *Perfectae Caritatis*, and later incorporated into the new 1983 *Code of Canon Law*. The statutes of these organizations need the approval of the Holy See, which alone has the power to erect the conferences. By 1995, 102 countries had these national conferences of Religious,[2] and in his 1996 apostolic exhortation *Vita Consecrata*, Pope John Paul II cited the "significant contribution to communion" made by conferences of superiors, whose principal purpose is "the promotion of the consecrated life within the framework of the church's mission."[3]

Originally, when the Conference of Major Religious Superiors of Women's Institutes and its counterpart for men, the Conference of Major Superiors of Men, were being organized in 1956, it was planned that the two groups be combined as a single Conference of Religious of the United States. Each side was to have its own officers, but the president of the men's section was also to be president of the combined conference. The permanent secretary of the joint conference also was to have been a male Religious. But the women Religious decided they wanted to have their own separate organization that would not be dominated by men, and so the women and men Religious organized into separate conferences. The women's conference was canonically established in 1959, and its statutes were approved by the Holy See in 1962, the same year the Second Vatican Council convened. According to Article I of the statutes:

"The purpose of the Conference, which is to be accomplished through close contact and common endeavor, is: a) To promote the spiritual welfare of the Women Religious of the United States of America; b) To insure an ever-increasing efficacy in their apostolate; c) To effect an ever-closer fraternal cooperation with all religious of the United States of America, with the venerable Hierarchy, with the Clergy, and with Catholic associations; d) To provide a proper and efficient representation with constituted authorities." The patroness of the Conference was "Our Lady under the title of the Immaculate Conception."

Article IV of the statutes pledged "perfect allegiance" to Church hierarchy and "perfect submission" to diocesan authority "as to serve as an example to all." Membership was open only to major superiors who were superiors general or provincial superiors. The conference was broken down into seven geographic regions, each with its own regional chair, vice-chair, and secretary-treasurer elected by the members of that region. The regional officers then formed the twenty-one-member National Executive Committee, which in turn elected from its membership the three national executive officers. Terms of executive officers were three years, with the right of re-election for a consecutive term. The National Executive Committee was charged with managing the affairs of the conference and arranging national meetings. The statutes also allowed for permanent committees made up of conference members.

The early records of the Conference of Major Religious Superiors of Women's Institutes reflect activities such as vocations surveys and discussions of catechetics and common governing issues such as health and finance. As the 1960s progressed, it became apparent that the Second Vatican Council was going to ask religious institutes to renew and update their constitutions and rule books. This anticipation, along with the social, political, and cultural changes of the 1960s — especially the rise of feminism — prompted many women Religious to re-evaluate their role in the Church, and the Conference of Major Religious Superiors of Women's Institutes was both agent and catalyst for this evaluation.

The superiors' conference expanded the scope of its original mandate and went on in the 1970s, '80s, and '90s to engage in nonreligious activities such as pursuing membership in the United Nations as a non-government organization, issuing statements on matters such as labor disputes and the Equal Rights Amendment, and pursuing a strong social-justice agenda almost to the exclusion of spiritual issues. In fact, Benedictine Sister Merle Nolde, co-director of the National Assembly of Women Religious (NAWR) — a small organization of lay and religious women dedicated to a justice agenda — wrote Leadership Conference executive director Sister Lora Ann Quinonez in 1980, complaining that some people were "questioning NAWR's continued existence because LCWR has taken on the justice agenda. . . ."[4]

The evolution of the Conference of Major Religious Superiors of Women's Institutes can be demonstrated rather dramatically by looking at its annual assemblies between 1965 and 1971, when the conference adopted new bylaws and changed its name to the Leadership Conference of Women Religious. Until 1965, the annual assemblies of the women superiors had a predominantly spiritual tone, and much of the assembly time was dedicated to networking between the various institutes of women Religious and addressing issues of common concern to the sisters.

But, as the Second Vatican Council progressed during the early 1960s, it became clear that the Council would call for renewal of religious life. It also became clear that the *Code of Canon Law* approved in 1917 was going to be updated for modern times and revised to reflect many of the decisions of Vatican II. Thus, the national assemblies of the superiors' conference began to reflect an agenda that was more dynamic than topics considered in previous assemblies. Adding to the excitement of the pending changes coming out of the Council was the fact that the chairperson of the women's superiors — Loretto Sister Mary Luke Tobin — had been the only American woman invited to be an observer at Vatican II.

1965 assembly: sisters and the council

The 1965 annual assembly took place just a couple of months before the close of Vatican II, and the prospect of updating canon law and rewriting the constitutions of religious institutes surely influenced the choice of speakers for the meeting. Speakers included Father Paul Boyle, president of the Canon Law Society of America; Redemptorist Father Bernard Haring, an expert consultant to the Second Vatican Council; Jesuit Father Bernard Cooke, a theologian; and Maryknoll Father Eugene Kennedy, a psychologist. (Fathers Cooke and Kennedy eventually left the priesthood. Bernard

Cooke went on to become a member of the board of the activist Call to Action organization.)

Father Boyle raised some eyebrows when he told the assembly that "Whenever an observance of the letter of the law will hinder the attainment of the purpose or spirit of the law, then the letter must fall. The letter is merely a means to an end." He also observed that "In the past sixty years we have witnessed a progressive denuding of religious constitutions, to the point where they are nothing more than cold canonical prescripts." And he said that the "doctrine of experimentation" should be incorporated into revised canon law "as another essential principle which has already been canonized by the Conciliar document."[5]

The proceedings of the assembly published by the major superiors included the main addresses, but the sisters intentionally did not obtain an imprimatur for the book — as they had done in past years — causing considerable consternation at the Vatican,[6] which was accustomed to docile sisters who followed the letter of the law.

The 1965 assembly also approved a petition to be sent to the Congregation for Religious, the pope, and all United States bishops, asking that "Sisters be asked to serve as permanent consultative or acting members of the Sacred Congregation for Religious, of the commission for the revision of canon law and of any post-conciliar commission that may be set up for the implementing of acts of Vatican II in regard to religious."[7] This request eventually was granted for the most part, but in 1965, it was considered to be a very bold statement, especially for women Religious.

1966 assembly: rebuke from Rome

Father Bernard Haring again addressed the 1966 assembly, along with Archbishop William Cousins of Milwaukee; Bishop Gerald V. McDevitt, auxiliary bishop of Philadelphia; sociologist Sister Marie Augusta Neal; and Philip Scharper, who was editor-in-chief of Sheed and Ward, Inc., publishers. Some of these speakers were considered to be uncomfortably progressive on Church-related issues, and Rome began to show some concern over the topics discussed at the women superiors' annual assembly — an event which traditionally had been noncontroversial. About six months after the 1966 assembly, Father Bernard Ransing, an American staff member of the Congregation for Religious and the Vatican's religious advisor to the Conference of Major Religious Superiors of Women's Institutes, wrote the conference's executive director, Sister Emmanuella Brennan, a Sister of the Holy Names of Jesus and Mary, telling her that the apostolic delegate was unhappy with the content of the proceedings of the 1966 assembly.

Father Ransing stressed the need for the conference to "control" the speakers at its assemblies.[8]

In addition, Cardinal Antoniutti, prefect of the Congregation for Religious, eventually wrote the conference's president regarding the 1966 assembly speakers, pointing out the "necessity of choosing carefully the persons who are to address the Conference." He wrote that "A number of doctrinal inaccuracies (if not errors) have been noted in four of the discourses, along with some tendentious attitudes and a marked superficiality in some parts of these same discourses." He pointed out the necessity of getting speakers who were real authorities in their fields and noted for the soundness of their doctrine, and he again reminded the sisters to request an imprimatur from the local bishop for publication of future proceedings.[9]

Again, Rome seemed to react with surprise that the formerly docile sisters were interested in an agenda that had not been dictated to them by the Vatican. Yet Vatican authorities were apparently puzzled over how to handle the increasingly independent American sisters. And as the sisters gradually began to assert themselves, the Vatican fell into the role of reacting after the fact, a role that would continue for many years.

1967 and 1968 assemblies: the Sisters Survey

The topic of the 1967 and 1968 assemblies was the Sisters' Survey, a project of the superiors' conference. The survey was an extensive questionnaire allegedly designed to determine the readiness of American sisters for renewal. However, the survey's critics charged that it also was an indoctrination tool used to introduce radical renewal concepts into convents all over the country. Unlike most surveys that obtain accurate data by questioning a sample of a population, the Sisters' Survey was sent to nearly every active sister in the United States — some 157,000 of them. Chapter Seven of this book examines the survey in depth, and reports the controversial nature of the survey's statements and questions about theology, authority, governance, and lifestyle.

At the 1967 assembly of the superiors' conference, the survey was big news, as the results were just becoming available and being distributed to superiors at the assembly. These results were then used by change-oriented sisters to promote reorganization of the conference. Sister Mary Daniel Turner, who was chair of the conference committee that had prepared and conducted the survey, recommended at the 1967 superiors' assembly that the organization's statutes be revised to reflect the growing desire of sisters for shared decision-making — a conclusion reached by the creators of the Sisters' Survey.[10] (What Sister Mary Daniel didn't tell the assembly was that the eventual revision of the statutes actually would give more power to an elite executive committee.)

The planning committee for the 1967 assembly included Sisters Mary Daniel and Mary Luke Tobin, conference president 1964-67; Sister of Notre Dame de Namur Marie Augusta Neal, a sociologist who prepared the Survey; and Sister Humiliata (Anita) Caspary, who as superior of the Immaculate Heart of Mary community in Los Angeles was engaged in a dispute with Cardinal James McIntyre of Los Angeles about changes in her order's constitution.

This committee revealed something about its own philosophy regarding renewal and relationships with the Vatican through its lineup of invited speakers. Father Paul Boyle was asked to return for the 1967 assembly, and the committee also invited sociologist Father Andrew Greeley. Invited to speak, but not attending, was Christian Brother Gabriel Moran, who eventually would make headlines in the 1970s by declaring that religious orders and Catholic parishes should be dismantled and replaced by "something that is more human, and that builds on qualities other than geography or sexual segregation and institutionalization."[11] Appearing on the program in Brother Moran's place was Jesuit Father Carroll Bourg (who eventually left the priesthood).

At the assembly, Father Bourg encouraged the sisters' independence from the Vatican, saying: "You need to realize that the greatest gift you can give to the Church, the greatest measure of your loyalty, is to become American, to be the religious of the Church as modern American women. To achieve this high and lofty purpose, I think you must become more autonomous, you must be an independent body of women in authority, women of responsibility, more ready to lead than to follow; more disposed to represent to Rome than to be represented by Rome."[12]

At the same 1967 assembly, giving advice quite contrary to Father Bourg, was the conference's religious advisor and staff member of the Congregation for Religious, Father Bernard Ransing. Father Ransing expressed concern that renewal among Religious was getting off track, and he reminded the superiors that the Vatican II documents placed limitations on experimentation: "1) that the purpose, nature and characteristics of the Institute be preserved intact; 2) that any experiments 'contrary to the Common Law . . .' require the permission of the Holy See, before they are put into execution."[13]

The 1968 assembly again took up the topic of the Sisters' Survey, even though some members had requested a more spiritual program. Sister Mary Daniel noted in a 1968 letter to the conference's Executive Committee that perhaps she should resign from the program committee since many members had wanted the national assembly to have a more spiritual tone instead of devoting another assembly to the Sisters' Survey. But she went on to criticize an alternate spiritual program for the 1968 assembly that had been drawn up by other conference officials while she was out of the country, saying it was "so 'other-worldly' in character." She added that, "In a period of 'new humanism' I wonder if the program is not too contrived in order to bring in 'the faith dimension.' "[14] Sister Mary Daniel apparently envisioned that the Survey would be the basis for restructuring the Conference of Major Religious Superiors of Women's Institutes and shaping the renewal in many convents, so she wanted to keep the Survey on the assembly's agenda.

A conference official responded by letter to Sister Mary Daniel, explaining that the best-attended assemblies had been on the subject of prayer, and the program planners were caught between what the members wanted and what Sister Mary Daniel recommended. She suggested that as a compromise, the titles of some of the talks could be changed to reflect the "new humanism," and speakers could be asked to avoid an over-emphasis on the spiritual.[15]

The program finally presented at the 1968 assembly included talks by Jesuit Father Ladislas Orsy, a canon lawyer, and Marist Father Thomas Dubay, a theologian and popular retreat master. But also speaking was militant feminist Mary Daly, author of *The Church and the Second Sex*. In that book Daly had expounded on the second-class status of women in the Church, symbolized by their exclusion from the priesthood. When Mary Daly was in Rome during the Second Vatican Council, she had told nuns that their veils were signs of submission to men.[16] Also on the program for the 1968 assembly was a discussion on "new government structure in religious communities," led by Sister Francis Borgia Rothluebber, Sister Thomas Aquinas (Elizabeth) Carroll, Sister Angelita Myerscough of the Adorers of the Blood of Christ, and Sister Margaret Brennan, all change-oriented sisters who would become presidents of the superiors' conference in the early 1970s.

A good deal of time at the 1968 assembly was again spent on the Sisters' Survey, as well as the idea proposed by the Sisters' Survey committee to restructure the conference. The conference vice-president and chair of the statutes committee reported to the assembly that a draft of revised statutes had been circulated to the total membership of six hundred, but only forty-one members returned the proposed revision with comments. In spite of this apparent lack of interest by the membership in making changes in the statutes, she proposed that the conference hire Booz, Allen and Hamilton consultants to do a study for the conference and recommend changes. She told the assembly that proposed revisions would be submitted to the membership at large for "approval, amendment, etc., prior to any formal vote or decision respecting change."[17] This process did not occur exactly as proposed, for new bylaws eventually were introduced and actually enacted before the national assembly had a chance to vote formally on them.

Resolutions introduced at the 1968 assembly reflected the growing interest of the organization in social action. The resolutions included a proposal that the conference issue a press release supporting the American Civil Liberties Union call for a study of events surrounding the 1968 Democratic National Convention (defeated 194 to 122); and a proposal that the conference invite volunteer representatives to be present at the Baltimore trial of Father Daniel Berrigan, who had been arrested in May for burning draft files at Catonsville, Maryland (defeated 215 to 80).[18]

In February of 1969, the conference's Executive Committee voted to commission Booz, Allen and Hamilton to do a study of the organization, at a cost of $42,000 to $45,000.[19] To pay for the study, each member was to be assessed $.50 for every working sister in her community.[20] Then, in August, just prior to the 1969 assembly, Sister of Charity Mary Omer Downing, conference president, wrote members and told them that the executive committee had decided at its February meeting that regions should not hold regional elections until the Booz, Allen and Hamilton study was finished and the reorganization of the conference had taken place.[21] Reorganization of the conference proceeded even though there had been no clear mandate for change from the membership.

1969 assembly: reorganization of the conference

The September 1969 national assembly in St. Louis, Missouri, was a stormy session. The Booz, Allen and Hamilton report was presented at a general session of the assembly, but not voted on at that time. Causing considerably more controversy was an address by Father Edward Heston, an American canon lawyer and newly-appointed secretary of the Congregation for Religious. He presented six key points for the sisters to consider in renewing their congregations. Father Heston stressed the necessity of: wearing the religious habit, collaboration with the local bishop, community prayer, shared community life, a primacy of the spiritual, and a corporate witness.[22] A superior present at that meeting recalled that Father Heston's talk simply was a reminder of the essentials of religious life as defined by Vatican II and a discreet effort to correct some communities who were going beyond the renewal desired by the Council.

But many of the more change-oriented superiors did not take kindly to

Father Heston's advice, as they saw it as an attempt to slow down the renewal process. Some sisters also thought Father Heston's remarks were designed to gather support for the Congregation for Religious in an ongoing dispute with the Immaculate Heart of Mary Sisters (IHM) of Los Angeles, who had been criticized by Cardinal James McIntyre about radical changes to their constitution and lifestyle that went beyond Vatican decrees and Council documents. Indeed, the same six points made by Father Heston had also been made by the Congregation for Religious in a letter to the Immaculate Heart Sisters. Their case had been appealed to the Congregation for Religious, which came down on the side of Cardinal McIntyre, thus upsetting many of the superiors.

At the end of the assembly, twenty-two resolutions were presented for voting. The first four passed quickly. But resolution number five was that ". . . the CMSW publicly offer support to the IHM Sisters by requesting the Sacred Congregation for Religious allow them to follow their chapter decisions during an extended period of experimentation."

Father Heston warned the assembly that a vote for the resolution would be a vote against the Sacred Congregation. But Sister Angelita Myerscough (who would go on to be elected president in 1970) and Sister Thomas Aquinas (Elizabeth) Carroll (who would be elected vice-president in 1970) called the priest's intervention inappropriate and resumed arguing in support of the resolution.[23] After lengthy debate, during which many members left for home because the hour was late, the resolution garnered a majority of the votes of the 278 sisters still present: 166 voted yes; 90 voted no; and 22 abstained. However, the statutes required 60 percent approval of those present, which would have required 167 votes in favor, so the motion failed by one vote.[24]

Since so much time had been consumed in debate over the Immaculate Heart of Mary resolution, the assembly was not able to vote on the remaining seventeen resolutions. However, a special assembly had been scheduled for February 1970 to present the Booz, Allen and Hamilton report for reorganizing the conference. So, on October 13, 1969, the conference's executive director, Franciscan Sister Mary Claudia Zeller, wrote the membership:

"Because so few members (278) were present for the formal voting on the Resolutions at the annual assembly, I feel that only the first four resolutions which were amended and voted on affirmatively by an almost unanimous decision be considered as finished business. . . . Resolution V as well as the remaining seventeen resolutions need our prayerful consideration until the Special Assembly in February when we shall vote on them."[25]

Sisters in Crisis

Resolution V was the controversial Immaculate Heart of Mary resolution, and Sister Mary Claudia was attempting to bring it up for vote again, reflecting the wishes of some superiors who wanted the conference to go on record supporting the Los Angeles Immaculate Heart of Mary Sisters. However, conference president Sister Mary Omer couldn't accept this endrun around parliamentary procedure. She wrote Sister Mary Claudia on October 22: ". . . I do not think that even I would have the power to say that a Resolution that had been validly voted on would be taken up again. I am afraid this is going to cause a great deal of confusion, and in the past few days it has caused a flood of letters to my office . . . I think it is regrettable that this issue is dividing our membership."[26]

The events of the 1969 assembly did not go unnoticed in the outside world. In an editorial in the October 25, 1969, issue of *Ave Maria*, Holy Cross Father John Reedy, *Ave Maria* editor, criticized the Congregation for Religious and fellow American Holy Cross priest, Father Heston, for his talk at the conference's assembly.

The Congregation for Religious, Father Reedy wrote, had shown "truly extraordinary insensitivity to the exciting progress being made by many communities of American sisters." Father Reedy went on to note that the Congregation for Religious was overreacting to what Father Heston described as "'stacks of mail we have been receiving from very good religious who are complaining about the excesses of renewal programs.'" Father Reedy observed, ". . . it seems a mistake, almost always, to offer leadership by reaction to complaints." Instead, Father Reedy wrote that the Congregation for Religious and Father Heston should have offered ". . . a rousing, encouraging vote of confidence in the tremendously exciting progress which the American sisters have made during the past decade."[27]

After the editorial appeared, the executive director of the superiors' conference, Sister Mary Claudia, wrote Father Reedy, thanking him for the editorial. She also wrote about the "havoc" caused by Father Heston's remarks. She wrote that after the "painful meeting," no one left without feeling "hurt, anxious and demoralized."[28]

Three days later, Father Reedy responded to Sister Mary Claudia, writing that several priests at Notre Dame had argued strongly with Father Heston against his planned presentation. But, "it was like bouncing rocks off the walls of the Vatican." Father Reedy recommended that the sisters not allow confrontation on the issues, but rather, "apply to this authoritative statement [by Father Heston] the same kind of evaluation that a great many conscientious, reverent married couples are using in examining *Humanae Vitae*." He went on to explain that "it seems to me that the situations facing our communities and the conscience of individual religious are so grave today that we simply must evaluate positive 'legislation' in terms of the total demands of charity, justice, reverence for personal dignity of the religious, the state of conscience of the members of our communities." "For myself," Father Reedy wrote, ". . . simple survival and sanity impose on me the obligation to exercise some critical judgment over actions by church authorities which I regard as absurdities."[29]

After the 1969 assembly, a committee was appointed by Sister Mary Omer to recommend a committee structure based on the findings of the Booz, Allen and Hamilton study. That committee recommended a five-member task force to prepare for a special assembly in February of 1970 and to carry out the recommendations Booz, Allen and Hamilton had made.[30]

So, as the eventful 1960s drew to a close, the stage was set for restructuring the superiors' conference, a restructuring that was of little interest to the general membership of the conference. Yet an elite group of change-oriented sisters who were in positions of influence was determined to liberate the conference from Rome's control and create a corporate entity that could exercise the power of women in the Church and in society.

6: The Coup

"The newly-adopted bylaws and title [of the superior's conference] signaled a transformed understanding and appreciation of the *raison d'être* of the conference; not only was it to be a forum for enabling leadership, it was also to become a corporate force for systemic change in Church and society."[1]

Sister Mary Daniel Turner, SNDdeN
Sister Lora Ann Quinonez, SP

As the 1970s dawned, the Conference of Major Religious Superiors of Women's Institutes was about to undergo the transformation from a national group of superiors organized to exchange ideas and to facilitate communication with the Vatican into an organization headed by activist sisters exercising the corporate power of the conference to influence the Church and society at large.

The majority of members of the conference had shown little interest in reorganization, but change-oriented sisters were intent on promoting a new structure that would distance the conference from Rome's control. As we shall see in this chapter, these activist sisters were successful in their quest, for they employed sophisticated political maneuvering and questionable constitutional manipulation to achieve their goal, while the majority of the membership of the conference seemed quite unaware of what was actually transpiring. Nor was Rome aware. In spite of the fact that conferences of superiors depend upon the authority of the Congregation for Religious for their existence, Rome was not consulted about the reorganization, but merely informed after the fact. In the end, the Leadership Conference of Women Religious emerged as a new entity asserting independence from Rome and openly challenging the Church in many areas.

The 1970 special assembly

An unprecedented special assembly of the conference was scheduled for February 23-25, 1970, to consider the Booz, Allen and Hamilton report on reorganizing the conference. But many busy superiors didn't have the time or the money for more than one annual assembly, and interest in restructuring the conference had not been high. Even Father Ransing canceled plans to attend. Nevertheless, the assembly went on as planned and adopted sweeping changes, including: a new purpose for the conference; expanded general membership criteria; expanded geographic regions; a five-member executive committee as committee of the national board; restructuring of the annual assembly; approval of non-superior sisters to serve on special committees; change to election of officers by membership rather than by the national executive committee; and increased dues.[2]

The actions of this 1970 special assembly grew to be quite confusing and controversial, for the official conference interpretation of the meeting was that the organization had voted to dissolve all old structures and build up a new organization from scratch. However, there was considerable controversy over whether the organization had the authority simply to dissolve its old statutes without consulting the Vatican. The 1962 statutes provided that interpretation of the statutes was reserved to the Holy See and that the statutes "may be amended, subject to the subsequent approval of the Holy See, by a two-thirds vote of the members of the National Executive Committee" (Article XV, Sections 1 and 2). The 1962 statutes also allowed for the implementation of bylaws, but those bylaws were to be "not inconsistent with these statutes" (Article XVI, Sec. 1).

The confusion among members was so great that many members simply did not understand what they supposedly had approved at the special assembly. Adding to the confusion and concern of some members was the fact that a new five-member executive committee — made up of the three conference officers and two other sisters appointed by the national board — apparently had assumed sweeping new powers. For example, one of the motions passed at the special assembly directed that a task force on credentials should be appointed by the chairperson and "recommend a definition of membership criteria and should present its recommendations to the executive committee prior to registration for the September [1970] Annual Assembly. This special assembly empowers the executive committee to act on recommendations of this Task Force on Credentials."[3]

In other words, the 1970 special assembly allegedly turned over all decisions about who could join the organization to the new five-member executive committee. And this premise was used to expand membership in the conference beyond major superiors. It is interesting to note that expanding membership beyond major superiors was a total reversal of what the Booz, Allen and Hamilton report had recommended. The management consultants hired by the conference had recommended that since the organization was for major superiors, membership should be limited to canonically defined major superiors if the organization was to have any significance. The report also found that there was too much responsibility in the national executive committee, which isolated members from active participation.[4]

Nevertheless, the task force on organization and coordination of the conference went to work after the February special assembly, and reported on April 2, 1970, that it had finalized an interim organization chart, determined the size and composition of ad hoc and special committees, and appointed chairpersons for all committees.[5] The next day, the task force met with the chairpersons of all interim committees. The report of that meeting indicates new bylaws would be formulated and presented to the membership which would replace the 1962 statutes. Also, the new election procedures supposedly approved by a resolution at the 1970 special assembly would be implemented, and new membership criteria would be approved and adopted by the national board prior to registration for the annual 1970 assembly in September.[6]

The 1962 statutes had directed that each region elect its own chair, vice-chair, and secretary-treasurer. Then those three officers from each of the seven regions made up the twenty-one-member national executive committee. The national executive committee then elected from its own members the three national officers: a chair, vice-chair, and secretary-treasurer. But the new election procedure approved by resolution at the special assembly and put into effect by the national board for the 1970 election provided for popular election of national officers.

This change in method of electing national officers was very significant in light of the fact that the new membership criteria being developed included members from leadership teams in the more change-oriented congregations, which had moved to a team concept rather than the traditional one-superior model. These new members were admitted to the 1970 and 1971 annual assemblies before the national assembly could vote on this change. The official conference explanation was that the special assembly had authorized these actions, but many members remained confused and suspected they had witnessed a *coup d'état*. Thus, when the 1970 regular assembly rolled around in September, there was plenty of commotion and downright ill will, which would be exacerbated at the assembly.

1970 annual assembly: a new image

The statutes committee reported on the progress of the new bylaws, and election of officers took place — the first popular election of officers — using new election methods and new membership criteria allegedly empowered by the February 1970 special assembly. Elected were: chair, Sister Angelita Myerscough, who had been chair of the conference's Canon Law Committee; vice-chair, Sister Thomas Aquinas (Elizabeth) Carroll, who had been chair of the conference's National Sister Formation Committee; and secretary-treasurer, Sister Margaret Brennan, who had been vice-chair of the conference's Sister Formation committee.

The *National Catholic Reporter* described the new officers as a " 'with it' administration," compared to outgoing president Sister Mary Omer, who NCR said "has a reputation as a conservative."[7] Attending the assembly for the first time were observers invited from organizations such as the National Coalition of American Nuns and National Assembly of Women Religious. The NCR quoted Sister Adrian Marie Hofstetter of the National Coalition of American Nuns as saying that "Sister Luke [Tobin, president of the conference 1964-67] was ahead of her time, that now many members of the conference are thinking with her and want to move, not only here, but in their own orders."[8] And *The Southern Cross* of San Diego, California, called the election a clear victory for progressive forces.[9]

An address of the 1970 assembly by Jesuit Father John Haughey seemed to set the tone for the meeting. In his address, Father Haughey, associate editor of *America,* speculated about hypothetical articles he could write based on different interpretations of what he saw at the sisters' assembly.

One article would encourage the superiors' conference to dissolve itself since it was created by the Congregation for Religious as "a device for prolonging the kind of directive authority which has become passé for all but a few benighted souls — those under you who need a mother, and you who need a father to obey or be in tension with." The sisters, he said, had been ignored by bishops and Rome, and "To put it bluntly, you are being made fools of. Until you declare in no uncertain terms that legislation without representation is intolerable, you are still light years away from 1776." If the superior's conference were to be dissolved by Rome, Father Haughey advised the sisters to "join hands with the Women's Liberation movement." He also said an expected encyclical on religious life ". . . will be sprung on you from its surreptitious lair, indistinct origins, fashioned by unknown architects . . . determining for you, what your life as a religious is without benefit of your experience . . . subjugate charism to institution and . . . women to men." And he asked, "Are you ready for a *Humanae Vitae* of the religious life?"[10]

Then, Father Haughey spoke of an article similar to one which he indeed would go on to write in the September 26, 1970, issue of *America*. In that article, Father Haughey wrote that "this year's assembly marked a sharp turning of the corner for CMSW. I have not personally attended anything in the last three years more fraught with significance for the whole American Church. In a word, directive authority is no longer acceptable, unless it comes as a result of having heard out those who are being directed.

"There are several indices of the swift change that has come over this conference in the past year. The national board of officers voted in at this session represented some of the most progressive voices heard from the floor in the past couple years; they are youngish and heavy with postgraduate degrees." Father Haughey also noted that an encyclical on religious life was in the works (which turned out to be not an encyclical, but the apostolic exhortation *Evangelica Testificatio*). He warned that the document "had better reflect something of the understanding of religious life articulated by these 450 major superiors, or there'll be hell to pay."[11]

Father Haughey's remarks at the assembly and his subsequent September 26 article in *America* caused quite a stir among women Religious, and several superiors complained to the conference about them.

One Sister of Charity wrote conference executive director Sister Claudia Zeller, asserting that some sisters did not feel they were represented by the conference described by Father Haughey. She went on to list principles formulated by the sisters of her congregation which she said more accurately defined the attitude of sisters, including: "Assent without reservation to the teaching, the spirit, and the directions of the Second Vatican Council for renewal. . . . Filial and joyful submission to the Holy Father. . . . Fidelity and respect for our Bishop as a concrete expression of our vow of obedience." She also wrote that the "role as religious is distinct from that of the laity" and that renewal does not imply "the indiscriminate introduction of lay customs into religious life."

She continued, "We are bewildered by those religious who question the need for vows. . . .We desire in the matter of religious teaching to hold fast to the integrity of the Catholic Faith which we receive from Scripture, from Tradition and from the Magisterium. . . . We believe that personal opinions are not the fundamental teachings of the faith, and we depend upon the hierarchy to be vigilant and decisive when the personal opinions of some theologians threaten to weaken the faithful."[12]

The "American manifesto"

Another controversy surrounding the 1970 assembly came to be known as "The Statement on American Religious Life in the Seventies," and has been referred to by its detractors as an "American manifesto on religious life." The statement became a major cause of a split within the women superiors' conference after it was introduced on the floor of the 1970 assembly by sisters who wanted the conference to endorse the statement. The statement declared that Rome was not sufficiently open to some of the creative styles of religious life introduced by some American Religious, so the Americans intended to function in a democratic manner and determine their own course of renewal.

The story behind the statement began in 1969. According to a conference memo to the membership, a group of men and women major superiors had been meeting for a year to discuss "the pros and cons of experimentation in small group living." At one of these meetings at the Passionist Retreat House in Warrenton, Missouri, "an atmosphere of real hope and a sense of purpose surfaced among the group in an almost tangible fashion," and the group decided to share their findings. Father Paul Boyle, then president of the Conference of Major Superiors of Men, was contacted, and forty-eight men and women superiors were invited to participate in a seminar in St. Louis September 3, 4, and 5, just days before the Conference of Major Religious Superiors of Women's Institutes had its 1970 annual assembly. That group of men and women superiors wrote a statement which, the memo reported, they felt "may give American Religious some sign of the 'new life' that is developing in the Church."[13]

The statement, appended to the memo, read in part:

> We believe in the primacy of the human person and we affirm that each man or woman has a dignity and freedom that are inviolable. . . . Therefore we deem it destructive if a religious congregation is required to ask a brother or sister to depart, or the congregation itself is asked to abandon its public ecclesial character for the reason that a particular style of life is deemed a priori, incompatible with religious life.
>
> . . . It may well happen that the broad ecclesial role of religious communities will necessitate a revision of the priorities of service within the ecclesiastical institutions of the American Catholic Church.

> . . . Mission and apostolate as expressed in the eccle-
> sial life of religious men and women necessarily require
> that we increasingly engage in secular occupations as we
> search out the 'pressure points of power' that control and
> direct vital areas of human life.
>
> . . . We feel that the Church which terms itself catho-
> lic is capable of assimilating broad developments within
> religious life. We look for the opportunity to speak our
> views to all our fellow Christians, especially those who
> are called to positions of prominent service within the
> Church. We feel the times are critical and issues are ur-
> gent. Because we believe the Spirit is truly alive within
> religious life, we must state that American religious must
> be consulted on any directives that purport to deal with
> them. . . . we shall follow the paths that seem most in har-
> mony with adult Christian living of the Gospel and suit-
> ably responsive to religious living in our age and nation.

Among the fifty Religious — and former Religious — whose names
were appended to the statement were all three women who were elected to
national office in 1970 under the evolving bylaws and wider membership
criteria that had not yet been voted on by the national assembly.[14] A conference press release on the 1970 assembly indicated palpable disappointment that the statement was not approved by the assembly: "The smooth
surface of consensus and unity was ruffled in the final session of the meeting when a statement relative to the CMSW's role in effecting direct communication between American religious and the SCR [Congregation for
Religious] was brought to the floor. The position paper, signed by fifty major
superiors of men and women who had met prior to the CMSW assembly,
was introduced. After a brief, heated discussion, the statement was tabled
indefinitely.

"In opposition to the several sisters who supported the statement and
asked that the CMSW indicate reaction to its philosophy, a number of members rejected any consideration of the statement on the basis that they had
not had sufficient time to study it.

"One pro-statement speaker summarized the assembly's reaction as
suggesting that to this group 'structure is more important than the Spirit'."[15]

Some conference members opposing the statement felt it was a thinly
disguised attempt to gather support for both the group of Los Angeles Immaculate Heart of Mary Sisters who had decided to become laicized rather

94

than bow to Rome, and also for the School Sisters of St. Francis, who were engaged in a similar struggle with Rome over their renewal efforts. Sister Francis Borgia Rothluebber, one of the signers of the statement, was superior of the School Sisters of St. Francis and would go on to become president of the women superiors' conference in 1973.

Following the 1970 assembly, Sister of Mercy Eucharia Malone, chair of the conference's western region, wrote a letter to several fellow conference members, telling them she had made the original objection to having the statement voted on at the assembly because there had been insufficient time to discuss it. She suggested a revised statement that would indicate clearly the conference's relationship with the Church. She wrote: "Whatever Statement, if any, issues from CMSW must include a clear statement of our relationship as religious with the Church. Otherwise, I simply cannot be a part of CMSW. This relationship with the Church seems to be the point on which we are divided. I respect sincerely those who hold another view but I do not see how we can constructively work together for the true renewal of religious life if we hold fundamentally different views on one of the essentials of religious life."[16]

Even though the statement had not gathered enough support to pass the conference's September 1970 assembly, promoters did not wish to see it die, and they were in positions influential enough to see that this did not happen. The November 14, 1970, meeting of the liaison committee for the two conferences of superiors of men and women Religious took up the topic of the statement. The names of all five of the male representatives at that liaison meeting had been appended to the statement: Father Paul Boyle; Mission Father James Fischer; Capuchin Father Finian Kerwin; Jesuit Father Gerald Sheahan; and Christian Brother Augustine Loes. Five of the seven representatives of the women's conference had their names attached to the statement: Sisters Angelita Myerscough, Margaret Brennan, Thomas Aquinas (Elizabeth) Carroll, Francis Borgia Rothluebber, and Rosalie Murphy.[17]

The minutes from the liaison committee meeting report a motion that the statement be sent to all members of the National Conference of Catholic Bishops (NCCB) as "a formulation of a representative trend in American Religious Life today." That motion failed, but the liaison committee did agree to send the statement to the bishops who comprised the National Conference of Catholic Bishop's Liaison Committee with Religious[18] (later named the Commission on Religious Life and Ministry). A cover memo dated November 14, 1970, from the liaison committee of the men's and women's conferences of superiors to the NCCB Liaison Committee with

Religious made clear that the committee members were not acting for all Religious or all superiors. But it explained that the committee of superiors had discussed the advisability of sharing the statement with the bishops to "make known to the Bishops a sample of the thinking of many religious men and women in the United States today." The memo said that "The sentiment of this statement was in part prompted by deep concern that the Congregation for Religious and Secular Institutes is not sufficiently aware of the needs and the strengths of the religious life in the United States and that definite reforms in the constitution and functioning of the Congregation are seriously needed."[19]

The December 1970 issue of *Searching,* the newsletter of the Conference of Major Religious Superiors of Women's Institutes, confirmed that the statement had been discussed by the liaison committee of the two conferences of superiors, and "after much debate it was decided to share the statement with the bishops who are on the Men and Women's Liaison Committee. The Major Superiors felt that it would give the Bishops a sampling of some of the thinking concerning Religious Life in the United States."[20] So, even though the national assembly refused to endorse the statement, the leaders of the superiors' conferences used the authority of their offices to promote the statement that they personally endorsed.

This action caused considerable confusion for the bishops, too. Bishop James Hogan, chair of the bishops' liaison committee with the women superiors' conferences, originally thought that the statement had come from the two superiors' conferences. He wrote in a January 20, 1971, report to the bishops: "As a reaction to the statement 'American Religious Life in the Seventies,' formulated by a group of men and women superiors and furnished to us in November. It did not stem from the CMSW or CMSM — as I felt it did. For me, it contains serious flaws that should not go unchallenged."[21]

Even after the 1970 assembly closed, an effort was made within the women's conference to promote the philosophy in the statement and somehow rally the endorsement of the conference. Sister Angelita Myerscough, newly-elected conference president, informed Bishop Joseph Breitenbeck of the NCCB Liaison Committee that the statement had been distributed at the conference meeting to make it available to all present. She wrote that some members wanted it to be a statement of the conference, but others feared an effort to railroad it through. "I believe many regions may use it for study and for affirmation, and it may be the basis of some future position of CMSW," Sister Angelita wrote.[22]

Indeed, the conference of women's superiors eventually would go on to embrace many of the ideas contained in the statement, as this chapter reports. But the debate over the statement on the floor of the 1970 assembly was a major factor in the splintering of the conference, for it was after the statement was introduced that several mothers superior got together and decided to form a separate organization of sisters because they felt that the superiors' conference was adopting a flawed vision of religious life. That organization, the Consortium Perfectae Caritatis, is discussed in Chapter Fourteen.

The coup is completed

After the 1970 regular assembly, the services of Booz, Allen and Hamilton were terminated by the national board, apparently in a dispute over how many of the Booz, Allen and Hamilton recommendations should actually be incorporated into the new bylaws of the conference. The statutes committee then compiled a draft of the proposed statutes, taken from suggestions of the members, the 1970 annual assembly, and the Booz, Allen and Hamilton report.

But after the statutes committee presented its recommendation to the board, the statutes committee was dissolved by the new national board in early 1971, and the proposed bylaws continued to be transformed under the direction of the national board. The board made recommendations for further revisions of the bylaws and named an ad hoc committee to incorporate the board's suggestions into the new bylaws. Named to that ad hoc committee were: Sister of St. Joseph Joan deLourdes Leonard, Sister Bernadine Pieper of the Congregation of the Humility of Mary; Sister Rosalie Murphy; and conference executive director Sister Claudia Zeller.[23] (Both Sisters Bernadine and Rosalie had been signers of the controversial statement prior to the 1970 assembly in St. Louis.)

The suggestions of the Booz, Allen and Hamilton team evidently were not widely accepted by the national board in its new version of the bylaws. A January 25, 1971, report of the conference's executive director to the National Board noted that "The proposed revision of bylaws and handbook is a complete departure from the tight compartments envisioned by the B.A.H. [Booz, Allen and Hamilton] Report."[24] The executive director had observed earlier that "I am steadily losing respect for the B.A.H. Report. Its greatest service is that it has brought groups together to share, discuss, and in some cases, dialogue."[25] Indeed, the conference acknowledged later that year that some sisters had complained that Booz, Allen and Hamilton had received $40,000 to guide revision of the statutes, but "an incredible number of changes have been made in their work."[26]

The national board not only dissolved the statutes committee, but all other standing committees, too. The February 1971 issue of the conference newsletter *Searching* reported that "In the process of reorganization, the CMSW temporarily discontinued its committee structure in order to begin to build up a new organization."[27]

But this action was not well received by all members of the conference, and some members simply didn't understand what was going on. The chairperson of the defunct statutes committee was so incensed that her committee had been dissolved that she resigned from the conference. Sister of St. Joseph Alice Anita Murphy, also a member of the dissolved statutes committee, wrote Sister Angelita, conference president, in July of 1971, pointing out that her committee's version of the bylaws retained their ecclesial character as a pontifical institute, whereas the newly proposed bylaws which had been "chiseled to its present form" by the ad hoc committee did not. She expressed "deep concern" over the evolving "sociological and civil character" of the conference, with power invested in the national board, executive director, credentials committee, and national executive committee. Sister Alice Anita wrote that few busy superiors had time to figure out what was really happening in the evolving version of the bylaws. She particularly objected to setting a quorum for the national assembly at just one-third of the membership, which would mean that only two-ninths of the members could adopt new bylaws. Sister Alice Anita called for an open discussion of the ad hoc committee's revisions because of the "incredible number of changes" made by that committee.[28]

Other conference members also wrote to express their belief that the new bylaws were unconstitutional because the old statutes were still in effect. Some also pointed out that the juridical existence of the conference depended on approval of the Holy See, and the Holy See would not approve of the conference removing every vestige of dependence on the Church.

Yet this is exactly what happened; the new bylaws constructed by the ad hoc committee defined the conference as more of an independent corporation than an entity created through the authority of the Vatican.

The new bylaws omitted any reference to the conference's connection to the Congregation for Religious, let alone any dependence on, or allegiance to, the Holy See or the hierarchy. Also conspicuously absent was any mention of Our Lady, named the conference patroness in the 1962 statutes. The new bylaws declared that the national executive committee, made up of the three officers and two additional members elected by and from the national board, would "provide the on-going leadership of the work of the LCWR between National Board meetings. . . ."

The basic objectives of the conference listed in Section 3 of the new bylaws included: "To strengthen the leadership service of its members within their congregations and the Church; To provide mutual support to one another; To develop and further understanding of the essential character and meaning of existential role of women religious in a constantly evolving world; To initiate and strengthen relationships with groups concerned with the needs of contemporary man and to exercise the potential of the conference for effecting constructive attitudinal and structural change."

A June 17, 1971, conference memo to members summarized the content of letters received from members regarding concerns about the changes being implemented in the conference. Some of those concerns included: "If [the] Statutes of 1962 are not in effect, who has [the] right to invalidate them? Certainly not the CMSW, whose juridical existence depends upon approval of Holy See"; "Putting By-laws into effect before they are approved by the Assembly is invalid"; and, "Powers vested in the National Board, Executive Committee, Executive Director, Credentials Committee cause great concern."[29]

Former executive directors Sisters Mary Daniel Turner and Lora Ann Quinonez admitted that reassurances by the conference officers about the sweeping changes "did not totally eliminate tensions within the conference. These tensions remained throughout the process of revision and after its completion."[30]

1971 assembly: the Leadership Conference of Women Religious is born

Plans for the 1971 assembly had begun in January with a seminar in Chicago which featured several resource persons, including Father Gregory Baum (who later left the priesthood), Father Richard McBrien, and Father Henri Nouwen of Holland, discussing the assembly topic, "The Church is for the World."[31] Then, each region of the conference was to hold a workshop to discuss the material from the Chicago seminar in order to prepare for the annual assembly.

Fathers Baum, McBrien, and Nouwen also were scheduled to speak at the 1971 assembly. Whether by accident or by design, the choice of speakers for the assembly — as well as the topic itself — discouraged attendance by members who did not accept the change-oriented theology of the speakers. Sister Eucharia Malone, a conference board member, wrote Sister Angelita Myerscough, conference president, about her concerns regarding the program as well as concerns that too many decisions were being made by the five-member executive committee: "I think the content of the September program has disturbed many Sisters. . . . And I think this program is potential for a break within the CMSW." Sister Eucharia further commented that "I think the Executive Committee is making decisions that should first be discussed at the National Board level. We must give serious consideration to the powers of the Executive Committee, those of the National Board and those areas that belong to the membership as a whole."[32]

Sister Claudia Honsberger wrote to Sister Angelita, suggesting that it was time to focus on sisters as Religious women in the Church, and she suggested revamping the program to meet the needs of all superiors.[33]

Dominican Sister Mary Dominic wrote to Sister Angelita that after seeing the proposed program, she would not be attending. The treatment of the assembly theme in the preliminary seminar as well as in questions proposed for regional discussions failed to offer a basis for "fruitful searching" in faith, Sister Mary Dominic concluded.[34]

Another provincial superior wrote that the shape of the program gave her "grave concern," as it focused on what sisters do, not what sisters are, which she said was not the proper perspective on religious life or Christianity. She noted that she would not come unless the program was changed.[35]

But the program was not changed, so the stage was set for considering controversial new conference bylaws at an assembly that was being boycotted by many of the traditional members, because they could not approve of the program or the speakers. It was probably a tactical error for the sisters who were disturbed by the transformation of the conference to stay away from the 1971 meeting, for it was their last chance to influence the direction of the conference.

Like the 1970 assembly, the 1971 assembly also would have additional voting members present under new credentials criteria that had not yet been approved by the national assembly. In a memo to members of the credentials committee, Immaculate Heart of Mary Sister Ann Virginia Bowling explained that the national board had accepted recommendations for changes in credentials in January, so additional members would be allowed to join under the new credentials.[36] The more change-oriented communities surely benefited by this amendment in membership requirements, for traditional communities were holding to the one superior model of authority urged by Rome, while the more change-oriented communities were moving to a team leadership concept, which made several sisters from one community thus eligible for conference membership under the new rules.

But this decision didn't sit well with some members. Sister of Christian Charity Virgina Janson wrote the credentials committee on February 25, 1971, that it was "strange" and "invalid" to already be using new membership criteria that had not yet been approved by the general membership. And, she noted, "the present criteria leave the field wide open for some communities and close it to others," because even small provinces or congregations which were headed by leadership teams had several voting members at the 1970 annual assembly, while larger congregations such as her own that retained the one superior model had only one voting member.[37] (A reading of a 1975 conference directory found as many as eight conference members from the same province of an order.[38] And the trend continues. For example, the 1992 conference directory listed eighty-four members in Region I, encompassing the states of Connecticut, Maine, Massachusetts, New Hampshire, Rhode Island, and Vermont. Of those eighty-four members, nine were from the same address in Massachusetts.)

In response to Sister Virgina Janson, Sister Ann Virginia Bowling wrote that there had not been time at the 1970 assembly to complete deliberations on the credentials. Since so many inquiries were being received about membership, the committee went ahead and expanded the criteria for membership and accepted new members "with genuine confidence that the assembly would agree with their tentative position."[39] The national board also had approved associate membership — voice without vote — for leaders of non-canonical groups such as the National Coalition of American Nuns and the National Assembly of Women Religious, organizations that are profiled in Chapter Thirteen of this book.

Even Rome could not prevail upon the conference's executive committee — Sisters Angelita Myerscough, Thomas Aquinas (Elizabeth) Carroll, Francis Borgia Rothluebber, Margaret Brennan, and Rosalie Murphy — to change the assembly program. On July 21, 1971, Bishop Luigi Raimondi, apostolic delegate to the United States, wrote to the conference president regarding the apostolic exhortation, *Evangelica Testificatio*. Pope Paul VI had issued the exhortation June 29, 1971, in which he reflected on the strengths and weaknesses of renewal in religious institutes since the close of *Vatican II*. Bishop Raimondi wrote the sisters that the Congregation for Religious "urges that national conferences of Religious make this pontifical document the object of particular consideration at their forthcoming assemblies in order to effect the practical application of the teachings of the Holy Father to assure authentic renewal in their institutes."[40]

It is unclear from the minutes of the July 21, 1971, conference executive committee meeting as to whether the Bishop Raimondi letter had been hand-delivered to the conference secretariat in Washington before the meeting convened that day. But the minutes do report that at that meeting, the executive committee decided not to schedule a specific discussion on

Evangelica Testificatio at the assembly. It was sufficient, the minutes concluded, that the topic would come up in discussion in panel reports.[41]

Even if the apostolic delegate's letter had not been seen before the executive committee's meeting that day, there still would have been time to place the exhortation on the agenda of the annual assembly in September. But the exhortation was not placed on the agenda. Not only did the members of the executive committee apparently feel that the exhortation about renewal of religious life was not significant enough to place on the agenda, they also felt no need to let their members know that Rome had made such a request.

Nevertheless, the bishops who represented the NCCB to the superiors' conference wrote in their report on the conference's 1971 assembly that "Since there was scant reference in the assembly to the Apostolic Exhortation to Religious, our Committee injected the message during the liturgy and again at our [liaison committee] meeting."[42]

Just before the 1971 assembly, the superiors' conference national board met on September 4. Minutes of that meeting reveal that the board was very much aware that some members of the conference were questioning the legality of the methods used to expand the membership and implement new bylaws, so the leaders discussed how to handle possible dissent. The minutes reported that "Sister Charitas Marcotte raised the question of the authority of the National Board to approve new CMSW members under criteria not yet accepted by the assembly at large and the possibility of illegal action in the Board's operating under Bylaws which had not received approval of the National Assembly. Everyone agreed that the topics should be given serious consideration to avoid delay and possible unpleasantness during the Assembly."

Then Sister Thomas Aquinas (Elizabeth) Carroll read the motion that had been passed at the February 1970 special assembly, which directed that the task force on credentials should recommend a definition of membership criteria and that the national board was empowered to act on those recommendations. So, the conference officers concluded that they could use the sweeping mandates of the 1970 special assembly as the rationale for their actions. The minutes continue: "Everyone concurred that the acceptance of this motion cleared up any possible misunderstandings regarding the procedure of the National Board and the Credentials Committee. . . ."[43]

The board also was concerned that sisters attending the assembly might attempt to discuss a document titled "History of the CMSW" that had been circulated widely to major superiors and members of the hierarchy. The

"History" traced what the sister-writer called a drastic reversal of policy in the conference and radical restructuring of the statutes, thus leading the conference away from reliance on the Holy See. The document also charged that the new bylaws shifted power away from the superiors and invested that power in the conference secretariat.

But the "History" was not brought up at the 1971 assembly, and the officers attempted to defuse further criticism of their actions in their speeches at the assembly. In her presidential address opening the assembly, Sister Angelita explained that "We have with us at this assembly some members who have come in under the credentials which were approved" by the credentials committee and the national board at its January 1971 meeting. She acknowledged that there "has been some question . . . as to the legality of this." But, she explained that the 1970 special assembly had authorized the credentials committee to continue its work, and that the executive committee was authorized "to proceed on the basis of those credentials for the registration for the Assembly."[44]

Sister Roberta Kuhn of the credentials committee further explained in her report to the assembly that "The membership proposal which had been presented and accepted tentatively at the September meeting last year did not seem to provide adequately for the very rich diversity which is so evident among our membership." Since "broader guidelines were imperative," she said that the credentials committee made proposals to the executive committee, which then incorporated those broader guidelines into the proposed bylaws.[45]

Then Sister Angelita explained away the bylaws crisis by assuring the members that they didn't really have any rights anyway, for all the power of the organization was at the national level: "Strictly, legally as of yet, according to the 1962 statutes, it is only the National Committee, the National Board which has any kind of authority in the conference and until we get those Bylaws voted in by which the Assembly does have authority, this assembly really doesn't have it."[46] So, even though the national board had been operating for over a year under the proposed new bylaws for important matters such as elections and membership, the board invoked a convoluted explanation of the 1962 statutes as justification for its action.

The 1971 assembly went on to ratify the bylaws, though there is some question about the numbers voting. Adoption of the bylaws required approval by two-thirds vote of those present, which would have been 400 in favor, if a CMSW press release claiming 600 members in attendance was correct.[47] The vote reported was 356 in favor, 39 opposed, 2 abstaining.[48] There is no explanation as to where the other 203 members supposedly in attendance were during that vote. And there is no breakdown as to how many of the members voting at the assembly were new members brought in under the broad new membership criteria accepted by the executive committee and implemented before the assembly.

Sister of Notre Dame Mary Elise Krantz, a conference member who objected to the direction being taken by the conference, wrote the Congregation for Religious after the assembly, pointing out that of the 710 total members of the conference, 520 were in attendance at the 1971 assembly. Of those 520, she claimed that 220 were new members.[49]

Sister Mary Elise was head of a coalition of major superiors and other sisters who believed that the conference was straying too far away from the authority of Rome and from the spirit of Vatican II documents. Calling themselves the Consortium Perfectae Caritatis, after the Vatican II document on religious life, *Perfectae Caritatis*, the group already had been in touch with Rome about their concerns. Jesuit Father John Hardon, a theologian who had often consulted for the Consortium, tried to convince the Consortium sisters — and other sisters unhappy with the direction the conference was taking — to confront the conference leadership at the 1971 assembly. However, according to the recollections of Sister Mary Elise, the Congregation for Religious advised the Consortium sisters not to have a public confrontation with conference leaders at that time. Apparently the Congregation for Religious and the traditional sisters thought it would be too unseemly for sisters to be airing their differences in public, but this reticence simply made it easier for the progressives to push through their agenda.

Some moderate members of the conference did try to insert into the bylaws more references and connections to the Congregation for Religious and the authority of the Pope, but these motions were defeated. A last-minute amendment passed 186 to 165, with 5 abstentions, changing the name of the organization to the Leadership Conference of Women Religious.[50] (The parliamentarian ruled that since the name of the organization was a minor matter, only a simple majority vote was required rather than the two-thirds vote required to ratify the bylaws.)

This new name had been suggested at the July 21, 1971, meeting of the conference executive committee, consisting of Sisters Angelita Myerscough, Thomas Aquinas (Elizabeth) Carroll, Francis Borgia Rothluebber, Margaret Brennan, and Rosalie Murphy,[51] and these sisters had a masterfully successful record of getting what they wanted. According to Immaculate Heart of Mary Sister Ann Virginia Bowling, conference executive director at that time, "The whole emphasis was to share power and part of the sharing of power was to get rid of the title 'major superiors.' "[52] Sisters Mary Daniel

Turner and Lora Ann Quinonez, subsequent executive directors, noted that the former name "communicated a negative image to the public: its militaristic and hierarchic connotations needed dispelling."[53] Whatever one's opinion of the titles, the new name of the organization was a much more accurate reflection of the new makeup of the organization, for under the new membership criteria, many members of the conference clearly were not major superiors.

However, the Congregation for Religious did not approve the name until 1974. Sister of Notre Dame de Namur Mary Linscott, a canon lawyer who was a staff member of the Congregation for Religious for several years, explained that the Congregation for Religious was reluctant to approve the name change because there was more involved than simple terminology. First of all, the national conferences were supposed to be made up of major superiors. Secondly, the use of the term "leader" has implications in other languages that it does not have in English (e.g. leader being *fuhrer* in German and *duce* in Italian). Sister Mary explained that "For the congregation [for Religious], 'major superiors' and 'leadership' were not synonymous terms; the use of the one for the other could create confusion and even lead to changes of a more substantial kind, notwithstanding the likelihood that the sisters intended the words to denote the same reality. . . . SCRIS [Congregation for Religious] felt that the substitution of 'leadership' for 'major superiors' could raise problems in an area where clarity was needed. Permission for the change came only after long reflection and on condition that the interpretation of the name was in accord with the provisions and intention of the Second Vatican Council."[54]

Indeed, the Congregation for Religious as well as the National Conference of Catholic Bishops continued to refer to the conference by its original name in official documents until the change was finally approved in 1974. Even then, Rome approved the new name only on the condition that the new title be followed by this sentence: "This title is to be interpreted as: the Conference of Leaders of Congregations of Women Religious of the United States of America."[55]

The Congregation for Religious also insisted on some changes in the new bylaws, including acknowledgment of the authority of the bishops and the Holy See, the relationship of the conference to the Congregation for Religious, and the conference's responsibility to the apostolic delegate.[56] However, the conference executive committee purposely neglected to inform its membership that there were any problems with Rome about the new bylaws. President Sister Thomas Aquinas (Elizabeth) Carroll wrote members on April 24, 1972, that "Up until this time we have not mentioned to you the fact that after Sister Margaret Brennan [conference vice-president] and I presented our Bylaws of the LCWR to Archbishop Mayer and Cardinal Antoniutti [in October of 1971], we had received some negative criticism [from the Congregation for Religious]." Sister Thomas Aquinas wrote that the executive committee had been engaged in correspondence with the Congregation for Religious about several disputed points, including the name change and the fact that the bylaws must be approved by the Holy See before being put into effect. She also wrote that the committee had met twice with the apostolic delegate and continued to communicate by mail. And she told the membership, "You may feel that the whole membership should have known of all these proceedings. Really, there were points so delicate that I felt knowledge of the proceedings by only a few would accomplish more," Sister Thomas Aquinas concluded.[57]

Sister Claudia Honsberger, chairperson of the conference's Region III, fired a letter back to Sister Thomas Aquinas, saying that her region had met on May 16 and discussed the Congregation for Religious points of concern mentioned in the April 24 letter of Sister Thomas Aquinas. Sister Claudia wrote that it was the unanimous decision of Region III that "all future cases, documents or recommendations from the Sacred Congregation should be communicated to the entire membership."[58]

Many other LCWR members were unhappy with the secrecy of the conference's executive committee, as well as the irregular proceedings of the 1971 assembly, which had admitted new members under criteria not approved by the membership and had operated on bylaws not yet approved by either the national assembly or the Congregation for Religious.

Also unhappy were members of elected committees that were dissolved by the national board. After the 1971 assembly, Sister Alice Anita Murphy wrote to conference president Sister Thomas Aquinas, saying that Sister Thomas Aquinas had misused her office by not informing the membership about the Congregation for Religious concerns regarding the bylaws and new title. "The imposition of authoritative procedures imposed on us by this thinking is far in excess of any ever directed by [the Congregation for Religious]," she wrote. Sister Alice Anita also complained that before voting by the assembly, there had been no open discussion of changes made to the proposed bylaws by the ad hoc committee. And she questioned how the conference could proceed to put into use new bylaws which had not yet been approved by the Congregation for Religious.[59]

Sister Thomas Aquinas (Elizabeth) Carroll responded that since it had taken Rome years to confirm the rule of religious congregations in the past, the conference's national board decided to go ahead and implement the new bylaws at the same time they were presented to Rome. Sister Thomas Aquinas tried to justify this action by claiming that this was a common practice by the National Conference of Catholic Bishops whenever it wanted something done by any of the Congregations in Rome or by the pope.[60]

And so, the Conference of Major Religious Superiors of Women's Institutes had transformed itself into the Leadership Conference of Women Religious, and Rome was simply informed after the fact that this metamorphosis had taken place. Some bishops suggested at the November 1971 meeting of the National Conference of Catholic Bishops that since the women superiors' conference had dissolved itself, the bishops should not continue supporting their liaison committee with a group that was defunct. Bishop Floyd Begin asked whether "the mandate of liaison continued, since the Sisters' group to which the committee was accredited no longer exists, but has changed its name, nature, membership and constitution." And Archbishop Paul Leibold said he didn't see how "the liaison committee could have any relationship with a group that no longer exists."[61]

But other bishops convinced their fellow bishops to follow Rome's lead in reacting to the new conference.

For Rome's part, Vatican officials apparently fell into the trap of prolonged "dialogue" until a few minor compromises were made, and eventually Congregation for Religious officials realized they could not put the toothpaste back in the tube, as one superior had observed.

Thus, by means of a political coup, activist sisters succeeded in creating a hybridized double identity for the Leadership Conference of Women Religious: one, as the Vatican-approved official conference of major superiors; and two, as an independent body of leaders of women Religious — many of whom were not major superiors — who were determined to decide their own membership, activities, and goals. Surely this success in confrontation with Rome energized the change-oriented sisters to proceed with their plans to guide renewal of religious life according to the "Statement on American Religious Life in the Seventies," which had been rejected by the superiors' conference in 1970, but unwittingly affirmed in 1971 with approval of the new bylaws.

7: The Many Faces of Indoctrination

"Liberalism is a good thing because it represents a spirit of reform. It is an optimistic outlook expecting meaningful advance. It may not always represent justice, light, and wisdom, but it always tries to do so."[1]

Question 131, Sisters' Survey

The largest project in the history of the Conference of Major Religious Superiors of Women's Institutes — renamed the Leadership Conference of Women Religious — has been a twenty-five-year survey project directed by Sister Marie August Neal, a sociologist. The second stage of that project, a 1967 survey of almost every active sister in the United States, proved to be a major tool for shaping renewal in United States convents and developing the revolutionary new concepts of religious life embraced by many modern Religious. Consequently, the change-oriented leaders lauded the survey as a renewal project that exceeded their wildest expectations, while the survey's detractors have called it a biased instrument with political motives that accomplished the most comprehensive indoctrination of American nuns ever.

One sister who completed the survey observed that if sisters weren't already dissatisfied with religious life before the survey, there were plenty of suggestions in the survey to promote dissatisfaction, including questioning the value of the vows, the authority of superiors, some doctrinal teachings of the Church, and the very significance of religious life. Sisters have told the author that they remember completing the survey and being confused by the statements and questions, many of which really had no one answer. One sister recalled skipping over questions that she felt would indicate disloyalty to the Church. Although some sisters told the author they threw the questionnaire away after they saw its content, most sisters dutifully completed the survey booklet in obedience to their superiors.

Sociologist Sister Patricia Wittberg has observed, "For many, simply completing the survey was a consciousness-raising experience. By asking whether a sister had read a particular modern theologian's writings, for example, or whether she had attended 'meetings of people other than her fellow community members,' the survey legitimated such activities for many respondents who would not otherwise have thought of doing so on their own."[2]

In analyzing the effect of the Sisters Survey on renewal of American sisters, former Leadership Conference executive directors Sisters Mary Daniel Turner and Lora Ann Quinonez have observed that the survey "proved catalytic far beyond what its creators dreamed."[3] And they proudly reported that the results of the survey were used as a basis for proposals for renewal and to help sisters understand what was involved "in living into a new image, in fact a new paradigm, of religious life."[4]

Sister (Thomas Aquinas) Elizabeth Carroll (a member of the Sisters' Survey Committee and conference president in 1971) wrote later that the Sisters' Survey, along with Vatican II, ". . . served to unleash new concepts of what religious life could and should be, and contributed immensely to the creativity and ferment of special chapters all over the country."[5]

What these commentators did not say was that the Sisters' Survey was more than a questionnaire. It was an educational tool used to introduce into every American convent a concept of renewal that had been conceived by an elite group of sisters — a concept of renewal that differed vastly from the guidelines for renewal set forth in the Vatican II documents.

Yet the Sisters' Survey remains a highly esteemed project in the sociological community as a ground-breaking piece of research. James D. Davidson, a sociology professor at Purdue University who has engaged in considerable research on Catholic issues himself, told this author that the Sisters' Survey was not "ideologically loaded or an effort to steer changes in any one direction." Rather, Davidson said, it was "a sincere and competent effort to capture the mood of the time and to provide data that communities could use in their efforts to implement Vatican II. . . . We should be careful not to interpret the survey in light of conditions in today's Church."

Whatever one's opinion of the 1967 Sisters' Survey, it unquestionably stands out as the most extensive effort ever to find out where American Catholic sisters stood on a myriad of issues. Nearly 140,000 sisters took hours to wade through the 649-question, 23-page questionnaire, which was given to every sister in almost every religious institute, with the exception of contemplative institutes. The survey originally was to have been limited to a sampling of sisters, but eventually grew into a much broader project that touched almost every American woman Religious.

The changing sister

The beginnings of the Sisters' Survey can be traced back to the summer of 1964, when ten sisters, ten priests, and forty lay Catholics got together for a week at Grailville, Ohio, to study preliminary drafts of documents coming out of the Second Vatican Council. The drafts had been translated and distributed by a lay organization, so they were not the official Council documents.[6] Among the sisters attending that meeting were Sisters Mary Luke Tobin, then president of the Conference of Major Religious Superiors of Women's Institutes; Mary Daniel Turner, a conference board member and chair of the conference's Sister Formation Committee; Sister of Notre Dame de Namur Margaret Claydon, president of Trinity College, Washington, D.C.; Sister of Charity of the Blessed Virgin Mary, Ann Ida Gannon, president of Mundelein College, Chicago; Sister of Loretto Jacqueline Grennan, president of Webster College, St. Louis; Holy Cross Sister Charles Borromeo (Mary Ellen) Muckenhirn, chair of the theology department at St. Mary's College, Notre Dame, Indiana, and editor of the "Sisters' Forum" for *National Catholic Reporter*; and Sister Marie Augusta Neal, sociologist at Emmanuel College, Boston.[7] (Jacqueline Grennan and Mary Ellen Muckenhirn shortly thereafter left religious life.)

The sisters at that Grailville meeting decided to publish a book about their findings regarding the impact of the coming renewal on sisters. *The Changing Sister*, edited by Sister Charles Borromeo, was published in June of 1965, several months before the council document on religious life, *Perfectae Caritatis,* was published, and more than a year before the blueprint for implementing reform, *Ecclesiae Sanctae.* So, rather than reflecting the final version of the council documents, *The Changing Sister* drew heavily on the writings of Fathers Pierre Teilhard de Chardin, Edward Schillebeeckx, Yves Congar, Karl Rahner, and Bernard Haring. Nine sisters contributed a chapter to the book: Mary Daniel Turner, Marie Augusta Neal, Charles Borromeo (Mary Ellen) Muckenhirn, Holy Cross Sister Elena Malits, Sister of St. Joseph M. Aloysius Schaldenbrand, Loretto Sister Jane Marie Richardson, Immaculate Heart of Mary Sister M. Corita Kent, Franciscan Sister Angelica Seng, and Benedictine Sister Jane Marie Luecke.

After the book was published, and before the 1965 annual assembly of the superiors' conference, the executive committee of the conference appointed a committee of five superiors to conduct research they determined to be necessary for the adaptation and renewal of religious life. Sister Mary Daniel Turner was named chair of that Research Committee on Religious Life. Other superiors appointed to the committee were: Sisters Angelita Myerscough (conference president 1970-71), Thomas Aquinas (Elizabeth) Carroll (conference president 1971-72), Humiliata (Anita) Caspary, and Sister of St. Joseph Isabel Concannon. Sister Mary Luke Tobin (conference president 1964-67) was named an ex officio member.[8] The research committee then selected the nine sister-authors of *The Changing Sister* to be consultants to their committee. These nine sisters also were invited to speak at the August 1965 annual assembly of the Conference of Major Religious Superiors of Women's Institutes, where conference president Sister Mary Luke announced that the research committee had been formed.

The research committee subsequently proposed the idea of conducting a national survey of sisters, ostensibly to determine the readiness of the sisters of the United States for renewal and to decide what direction the planning should take. However, some critics of the Sisters' Survey suggest that the survey actually was designed to determine where the majority of sisters stood on a myriad of issues so that a strategy could be designed for dissuading the sisters from their convictions. Other critics charge that the survey was intended as an indoctrination tool to prepare sisters for the agenda that some of the sister leaders wished to pursue.

There is some evidence to support both charges in the minutes of the meeting of the Research and Study Project on Religious Life that took place in Mequon, Wisconsin, on September 25, 1965.

The minutes make it clear that the idea for the research committee and the survey originated within the leadership of the conference's Sister Formation Committee, chaired by Sister Mary Daniel Turner (who was one of the contributors to *The Changing Sister*). The minutes also allude to the "necessity of permissiveness in regard to experimentation," and suggest that the Sisters' Survey questionnaire must "strive to get at 'attitudes' " and be "educative in purpose."[9] It is important to note that all of these events occurred before the Council decree on the proper renewal of religious life, *Perfectae Caritatis*, was issued on October 28, 1965. *Ecclesiae Sanctae*, the blueprint for implementing *Perfectae Caritatis*, was not issued until August of 1966, so the sisters were not working from the final version of these official council documents. (*Lumen Gentium*, which contained a section about consecrated life in terms of the universal call to holiness had been issued in November of 1964, so that document was available.)

Stage one of the research project was to survey the superiors of the women's religious institutes about personnel, resources and projected ten-year plans. That first stage took place during the summer of 1966, in the form of a questionnaire going out to over four-hundred superiors.

Originally, the research committee had planned for stage two to be a random sample survey of several hundred sisters to find how they felt about change and to get their ideas about what changes ought to be made. But, after seeing the results of the survey of leaders, the board of the Conference of Major Religious Superiors of Women's Institutes decided in early 1967 to survey the entire population of sisters whose leaders belonged to the conference. In sociological circles, it is considered highly unusual to survey an entire population simply to ascertain where the population stands on particular issues; such data can be obtained with a very low margin of error by surveying only a small percentage of a population. This fact gives credence to the argument of survey critics that the survey was intended as an indoctrination tool as well as a tool for comparing orders to each other. In any event, in the spring of 1967, the national Sisters' Survey was sent to 157,000 sisters. An impressive 88 percent of the sisters — 139,691 — completed and returned the Sisters' Survey.[10]

Once the survey got into circulation, controversy arose over the content of the questions and statements in the survey, which seemed to mirror the philosophies of the sisters on the committee who created the survey, rather than the philosophy and theology actually presented in the Council documents. Sister Marie Augusta insisted repeatedly that the survey questions were based on Vatican II documents, but there is more similarity between the content of *The Changing Sister* and the Sisters' Survey than there is between *Perfectae Caritatis* and *Lumen Gentium* and the survey questions.

The essays in *The Changing Sister* frequently carried a revolutionary theme and a heavy new emphasis on the sociological aspects of religious life rather than the spiritual aspects. The writers in *The Changing Sister* also deviated from the long-standing principle that the traditional, primary value of Religious men and women is who they *are* — consecrated persons who witness to the transcendent — and instead placed nearly the entire emphasis on what Religious *do*. And they introduced a new primary mission for Religious — social justice — which they claimed had superiority over the traditional apostolates of Religious, even though those traditional apostolates have consistently encompassed social justice issues.

Sister Marie Augusta had expounded on this principle in a paper presented at the June 1966 Institute on Religious Life in the Modern World when she wrote: "Finally, social justice and charity are the keys for determining the adequacy of a congregation's work. Social justice refers to a condition existing in a society where the rules are such that abiding by them allows the greatest possible freedom for each man to develop his human potential. Many modern communities are far from this ideal. . . . This is the ideal of the Christian community and the goal of religious life."[11]

These new humanistic philosophies eventually would be reflected quite recognizably in many questions or statements in the survey, as we can see from the following examples from *The Changing Sister*. Each example from the book is followed by some of the related questions or statements which subsequently appeared in the 1967 Sisters' Survey, to which the sisters were to indicate their level of agreement or disagreement.

In *The Changing Sister*, Sister Marie Augusta asserted that "the old structure [of religious communities] is no longer relevant to new needs."[12]

> Sisters' Survey: **91**. Every religious community in the spirit of the council must adjust to the changed conditions of the times. This means that no community can continue in the traditional form and be working with the mind of the church.
>
> **99**. I feel that communities of the future should consist of small groups of sisters living a shared life by doing different kinds of work.
>
> **155**. Any organizational structure becomes a deadening weight in time and needs to be revitalized.

In *The Changing Sister*, Sister Charles Borromeo wrote that religious communities of women had been "deforming young persons" for many years and were "rigid and dead forms of a culture bypassed decades ago in the ordinary world."[13] She also introduced some ideas about the vows that would become popular with avant-garde reformers: obedience defined as openness to the Spirit, and one's work being one's prayer.

> Sisters' Survey: **69**. The traditional way of presenting chastity in religious life has allowed for the development of isolation and false mysticism among sisters.
>
> **79**. One of the main characteristics of the new poverty will be openness and liberality of mind, heart, and goods.
>
> **90**. The vow of obedience is a promise to listen to the community as it speaks through many voices.
>
> **401**. In this period of change some have concluded that for their religious order there is little hope of making

the necessary adaptations. This group includes many different views but among them are those who see no hope for change, who see the system as evil, feel that their assignments are frustrating, feel overworked, feel that they lack freedom for professional growth, and feel a lack of warm interpersonal relations in the community.

In *The Changing Sister*, Sister M. Aloysius Schaldenbrand suggested that "Human law, rightly understood, is simply an attempt to express what is due to the person; as an attempt that is never completely successful, moreover, it is always open to completion and correction by due process. Nor does divine law subordinate the person to legal prescription."[14]

Sisters' Survey: **643.** The only purpose of the vows of poverty, chastity, and obedience is to create a community wherein people can effectively channel their human energy to the most immediate realization of the gospel.
644. All authentic law is by its very nature flexible and can be changed by the community in which it is operative.

In *The Changing Sister*, Sister Jane Marie Richardson proclaimed that "Sisters today have the enviable and glorious possibility of standing in the forefront of the Church's renewal. Indeed, their vocation to be human, to be Christian, to be religious demands that they do so. . . . Unless sisters are living in the Church of today, they are not living in the Church at all."[15]

Sisters' Survey: **134.** When I think of social reform, I think of things I believe in so deeply I could dedicate all my efforts to them.
143. Every great step in world history has been accomplished through the inspiration of reformers and creative men.

In *The Changing Sister*, Sister M. Corita Kent, an Immaculate Heart College art professor (who later left religious life as well as the Catholic Church), wrote, "And if our business is to put the always new truth into new wineskins, we need to know the very latest about wineskin making. This means we should be listening to the most experimental (or avant garde or whatever) music, seeing the newest plays and films, reading the latest poems and novels. . . .

"A sister is the same as any other woman. She wants to be beautiful and human and Christian. . . . To the extent that her community prevents her from being beautiful and human and Christian, that community must be remade and remade over and over again."[16]

> Sisters' Survey: **246-251.** Sisters were asked to indicate whether or not they had seen, or had any interest in seeing certain films and television programs. Among those listed were: "Nights of Cabiria," "Wild Strawberries," "La Dolce Vita," "Who's Afraid of Virginia Woolf," "David and Lisa," "Batman," "Man from U.N.C.L.E.," "Bonanza," and "Alfred Hitchcock."

In *The Changing Sister*, Sister M. Angelica Seng wrote that a sister must be in dialogue with her own times by working in inner cities, visiting homes, participating in protests, joining civic causes, challenging priests for more authority in parishes, and getting more involved in parish groups. She wrote, "If the structure, organization and atmosphere of religious institutes do not permit and encourage freedom and initiative in the sisters, then the structure must be changed in view of the needs of our time. . . .

". . . The purpose of the structure of religious communities must be to free the person to respond to the needs of the time."[17]

> Sisters' Survey: **44.** Since Christ speaks to us through the events of our times, sisters cannot be apostolically effective in the modern world unless they understand and respond to social and political conditions.
>
> **49.** I think that sisters who feel called to do so ought to be witnessing to Christ on the picket line and speaking out on controversial issues, a well as performing with professional competence among their lay peers in science labs, at conferences, and on the speaker's platform.
>
> **376-387** asked sisters to indicate if their orders worked, or planned to work, in some of these areas: with drug addicts and alcoholics, racial minorities, war protesters, "mixed communities groups working to reorganize the city in an integrated fashion," "people experimenting with new ways of living in community, i.e., mixed groups of religious and lay members," "groups of people seeking dia-

logue with communists," and "groups in protest against affluence."

In *The Changing Sister*, Sister Jane Marie Luecke declared that ". . . an apostolate in the secular life outside our institutions is also essential if we are to be true to our renewed image. . . ."[18]

> Sisters' Survey: **495.** Do you think all sisters should be allowed to wear contemporary dress at all times?
> **532.** Do you think sisters should be involved in planning and participating in local community events of a civic, artistic, and/or cultural nature?
> **534.** Do you think some sisters in the United States should work in public schools as faculty or staff members?
> **535.** Do you think some sisters in the United States should get involved in civic protest movements?
> **536.** Do you think sisters should be active in the public sector of society?

In *The Changing Sister*, Sister Mary Daniel Turner urged that sisters must be open "to new programs for Christian formation, new techniques for the apostolate, new research and experimentation for implementing the *aggiornamento*. Committed she must be to liturgical reform, to a kerygmatic religious formation of our people, to ecumenical objectives, to social justice and inner-city renewal."[19]

> Sisters' Survey: **504.** Do you feel your religious order is sufficiently engaged in work for the poor?
> **513.** Would you stand up for a sister's right in conscience to speak, write, march, demonstrate, picket, etc. when this conflicts with a higher superior's or a bishop's wishes?
> **524.** Would you want to see forms of hospital administration tried which would be different from the characteristic religious community ownership now most common?
> **525.** Would you like to see basic changes in the parochial school system?

Rome is surprised

The content of the Sister's Survey apparently was a complete surprise to the Vatican until some sisters being surveyed transmitted their concerns to Rome. Shortly after the survey was circulated, Father Bernard Ransing, who was religious advisor from the Congregation for Religious to the Conference of Major Superiors of Women, sent a letter to conference secretary, Sister Rose Emmanuella Brennan, on April 23, 1967. Father Ransing said he was gathering information informally to try to fend off "an inquiry" by the Congregation for Religious about the survey. He asked for immediate information as to who was on the survey committee and who formulated the questions. He reminded the conference secretary that responsibility for renewal was to be with each individual institute, and he indicated the Vatican's concern that the autonomy of each institute would not be preserved if survey results were publicized or used to compare one institute to another.[20]

Subsequent to this letter, the conference leaders seemed concerned about keeping the project secret, and some superiors ordered that the booklets be collected and burned. On May 2, Sister Marie Augusta wrote to superiors, calling in all extra survey booklets, and warning that "use of the instrument by those not understanding its purposes could be serious for unwanted publicity prior to analysis and use for chapters."[21]

That same day, Sister Marie Augusta wrote Sister Mary Luke that Cardinal Egidio Vagnozzi, prefect of the Congregation for Religious, had asked for a copy of the survey. Sister Marie Augusta told Sister Mary Luke that she thought the Cardinal's request as well as Father Ransing's inquiry "have been responses to letters from sisters for whom the questionnaire was a problem."[22]

Sister Mary Luke wrote back to Sister Marie Augusta on May 10, "I suppose it is inevitable that we are being investigated for our questionnaire." "I think it is just as well that we do not have any Bishops, even including Archbishop Dearden, at our meeting [the August 1967 annual assembly at which the survey results would be discussed]. I am hoping one will not be 'appointed' by the Holy See as last year."[23]

Father Ransing again wrote the sisters on June 4, 1967, saying that the Congregation for Religious would be quite unhappy if the survey results were made public. He also pointed out that objections could be made to the way many of the questions were stated, and he observed there was no one answer to some of the questions. And, he indicated again that interpretation of the survey should be left to the communities themselves.[24]

Evaluation: fascism and anomie

However, interpretation of the survey was not left to the communities themselves. Computer printouts that compared an individual community to national totals were made available to superiors,[25] although there was an effort to keep the information within the conference. Sister Mary Daniel Turner, chair of the conference Research Committee on Religious Life that conducted the survey, told the 1967 annual assembly: "The major concern about the survey made during the past two years is the confidentiality of the national totals. National totals and scores are the trust of the Conference. Each member of the CMSW is responsible for guaranteeing that this trust will be respected."[26]

In addition to giving each institute data on how its scores compared to the national totals, a complex interpretation of the scores was provided by Sister Marie Augusta, who had developed complicated, elaborate scales for evaluating the responses of the sisters. At the 1967 annual assembly of the Conference of Major Religious Superiors of Women's Institutes, superiors were given a partial interpretation of survey results, which was subsequently published in the assembly proceedings. In her report to the assembly, Sister Marie Augusta explained that responses to certain groups of questions could identify sisters who had characteristics of "over-submissiveness to legitimate authority along with an aggression against defenseless people, a tendency to superstition, synicism [sic], fascination with power, over-curiosity about sex, and a resistance to looking at one's own inner motivation, plus a pseudo-toughness and a high stress on conventional norms." These folks, Sister Marie Augusta contended, "have a proneness for fascism that is an easy acceptance of arbitrary strong command."[27] A sister was lumped in with the fascists by Sister Marie Augusta's scale if she had agreed with survey statements such as:

> **145.** What youth needs most is strict discipline, rugged determination, and the will to work and fight for family and country.
>
> **160.** Science has its place, but there are many important things that must always be beyond human understanding.
>
> **166.** If people would talk less and work more, everybody would be better off.
>
> **169.** The best teacher or boss is the one who tells us just exactly what is to be done and how to go about it.

Regarding her political pessimism scale, Sister Marie Augusta explained that the political pessimism of sisters was "quite high" because the following items were accepted by more than 50 percent of the sisters:

> **176.** In the past 25 years, this country has moved dangerously close to Socialism.
> **177.** The state of morals in this country is pretty bad, and getting worse.
> **179.** The American Communists are a great danger to this country at the present time.
> **180.** The United States is losing power in the world and this disturbs me a great deal.

She concluded, "The scores suggest a naiveté about the social order that is perhaps a bit high for teaching personnel and indicates a need for more competent teaching of the social sciences in the training programs of novitiates in general."[28]

Another of Sister Marie Augusta's scales was the Anomie Scale. She defined anomie as "an experience of meaninglessness among those who, lacking an enthusiasm for and not understanding or appreciating the new ways, cannot turn to these new ways with spontaneity when their conforming to the old ways has lost its rewards. With no new vision, and a clouding of the old, life loses its zest."[29] "Anomie" was identified by affirmative responses to items such as:

> **118.** With everything so uncertain these days it almost seems as though anything could happen.
> **121.** What is lacking in the world today is the old kind of friendship that lasted for a life time.
> **130.** I often feel that many things our parents stood for are just going to ruin before our very eyes.
> **133.** The trouble with the world today is that most people really don't believe in anything.

Sister Marie Augusta also interpreted her pre-Vatican II and post-Vatican II scales for the 1967 assembly. "A high post-Vatican score can be interpreted to mean that the sisters are oriented to the thinking of Vatican II; a low score on this scale indicate the opposite." Sisters were considered to be "post-Vatican II" if they responded affirmatively to statements such as:[30]

6. I regard the word of God as speaking always and in diverse ways through events, other persons, and my own conscience, as well as through the Bible and the Church's magisterium.

14. I prefer to think of Jesus as our Mediator with the Father, rather than as the Second Person of the Blessed Trinity.

64. If a sister shuns involvement with persons I think she betrays the purpose of her vow of chastity.

76. The drama of renewal will consist largely in laying aside power, ownership, and esteem.

94. Holiness consists in utter self-sacrificing involvement in human needs.

100. It seems to me that sisters should be especially interested in establishing centers where people could come together to experience Christian community through worship, discussion, and the joy of shared activity.

According to a further explanation by Sister Marie Augusta in a memo to the Congregation for Religious, the "post-Vatican II" sisters "expect changes in their style of life, in the orientation of apostolic works, liturgical participation, congregation government. They are eager to participate in the transformation of the world, the taking on of service to the poor in new forms and new places. They are unusually sensitive to the current problems facing the Third World. They want to stay to renew with the Church. At the same time they are much more critical of current conditions in the church and in their community responses to current exigencies." And, the "post-Vatican II" sisters "are better read theologically, read more, are better informed politically and socially, and are more willing to extend their life of service beyond the conventional."[31]

Sisters were considered to be "pre-Vatican II" if they responded affirmatively to statements such as:[32]

5. The mystery of the Trinity is so profound and so central I feel I should humbly accept it as given and not seek to plumb its depths.

12. I sometimes wish I had been alive at the time of Christ rather than now so that I could have really known Him.

33. I like to attend as many Masses as possible each day.

120

72. As long as a sister is personally poor, I think it is good for the community to be financially secure.

95. I feel that the parochial school is still the most effective means for educating Catholics.

97. Personal sanctification comes first, then duties of the apostolate.

312. Christians should look first to the salvation of their souls; then they should be concerned with helping others.

319. The best contribution sisters can make to world problems is to pray about them.

322. I think of heaven as the state in which my soul will rest in blissful possession of the Beatific Vision.

324. What my daily work consists of matters little, since I see it as a way to gain merit for heaven.

The survey creators judged a sister to be "pre-Vatican II" if she preferred reading the work of traditional theologians like Fulton J. Sheen, John Henry Newman, and Thomas à Kempis, rather than contemporary theologians such as Daniel Berrigan, Yves Congar, Hans Kung, Charles A. Curran, Gregory Baum, Gabriel Moran, and Edward Schillebeeckx. And communities were judged to be "nonexperimental" if they did not make available the works of the so-called "post-Vatican II" theologians.[33]

Sister Marie Augusta explained in her memo to the Congregation for Religious that pre-Vatican II sisters "are upset by the changes, do not want to evaluate the current effectiveness of their modes of service, are more concerned with saving their own souls than in helping in the renewal of the world, prefer a life apart, see the changes as detrimental to a spiritual life, do not want changes in life styles, are satisfied with current service to the poor and the witness their life gives to poverty, and are quite satisfied with a slower pace of change." And, she declared that a pre-Vatican II orientation in a Church that had moved into a post-Vatican II era showed a disrespect for spiritual things as well as "a tendency to define the holy in terms of the old, the traditional, and even harmful to the degree that what is held on to is harmful."

Sister Marie Augusta even suggested that these "pre-Vatican II" sisters were responsible for much of the friction about renewal in congregations and that these sisters gave "witness to the irrelevancy of religious life." She wrote that the only way to stem departures from religious life was to "give evidence of genuine support for sincere efforts to realize the gospel in modern ways. Without this support the efforts are going to be turned to manifestations of frustration, anomie, and indifference."[34]

In 1968, Sister Marie Augusta told a workshop sponsored by the Canon Law Society of America that the reading recommendations made by religious superiors were a key factor in understanding the philosophy of a particular religious community. She reported that of the 410 superiors questioned in a preliminary survey before the Sisters' Survey, 222 superiors had recommended a "mixed" reading range to their sisters. Only 55 out of the 410 superiors recommended readings that "if digested would have allowed the sisters to develop a real awareness of what was going on in the world and what was happening in the Church," according to Sister Marie Augusta. Thus, she concluded, "The Sister's Survey confirmed our hypotheses that one of the most critical variables separating religious communities able to respond creatively to change from those involved with problems of ambivalence and confusion is the reading and viewing preferences of the sisters." And these enlightened sisters who read contemporary theologians, Sister Marie Augusta contended, "were better able to realize that the Church was passing through a period of radical transition and could rejoice in and celebrate the process." Her conclusion, naturally, was that "the Survey indicates and suggests strongly a reform of reading and of viewing habits."[35]

Here again, even though the vast majority of superiors were steering a middle course in approaching the "new theology," and some 355 out of 410 superiors were not enthused about all the theologians touted by the survey committee, the powers that be in the Conference of Major Religious Superiors of Women's Institutes were telling superiors that if they were to get with the renewal program, they had to reject pre-Vatican II thinkers entirely and get their sisters immersed in the work of other theologians, some of whom were considered to be quite controversial at that time.

Sociologist Gene Burns observed that "The Sisters' Survey was, however, one of many activities within CMSW that increased commitment to a feminist, antihierarchial worldview.

"The CMSW Research Committee, which conducted the survey, was quite visible within the organization in the late 1960s, providing reports on the progress and meaning of the survey and articulating a radical view of religious life."[36]

The conference leadership was pushing the agenda of the Sisters' Survey committee so hard that the survey was the main topic again at the 1968 assembly, even though many superiors had asked that the assembly return to a more spiritual topic. And, the results of the Sisters' Survey were used

by the survey committee to push for revising the conference statutes supposedly to give more power to the membership in the conference, because
the survey results indicated that sisters wanted to play a more active role in
decision making.[37] (As the last chapter detailed, the revised conference bylaws actually gave more power to the executive committee, not to the general membership.)

The Sisters' Survey results apparently were used in a variety of ways.
Sister Claudia Zeller, CMSW executive secretary, wrote Sister Marie Augusta on October 17, 1969, suggesting that the survey results be used to
identify sisters with expertise who might serve on CMSW committees since
the CMSW had opened up committee membership to non-superiors.[38] Unfortunately — or perhaps fortunately — the individual survey responses
were anonymous, and so individuals could not be identified, even though
the conference secretariat apparently hoped to locate politically correct sisters through the survey.

Nevertheless, the indoctrination of sisters apparently was somewhat
successful, for the Sisters' Survey was used in a good number of renewal
chapters, where many of its proposals, along with of the ideas of some of
the "post-Vatican II" theologians, were incorporated into chapter decrees,
even though many of those ideas and proposals clearly were contrary to
documents coming out of the Second Vatican Council, not to mention canon
law and the intrinsic rights of members of those institutes.

The Autumn 1968 issue of the *Sister Formation Bulletin*, published
by the Sister Formation Committee of the Conference of Major Religious
Superiors of Women's Institutes, gives some indication of the impact of
the Sisters' Survey on chapters and constitutions. A report from a Sister
Formation Conference workshop at Woodstock, Maryland, in the summer
of 1968 contained the following recommendations regarding the survey:
"5. Each congregation should know its CMSW Sisters' Survey profile
and develop its formation and renewal programs accordingly." And, "6.
In view of the question of authoritarianism raised by this Survey and keeping in mind the thrust of conciliar theology, each congregation should
create governmental structures to incorporate: a) genuine decentraliza-
tion of authority, b) actual adherence to the principle of subsidiarity, c)
room for personal freedom and responsibility."[39] While the suggestions in
number six sound quite reasonable, even necessary, in actuality sisters
used these very terms to justify the total deconstruction of their institutes,
where authority was all but abolished, the concept of subsidiarity was
distorted to mean democracy, and personal responsibility decayed into
individualism.

Critics of the survey

Dominican Sister Elizabeth McDonough, a canon lawyer, has observed that "Critics of [Sister Marie Augusta] Neal's work point to survey questions formulated in qualitative language, to information reported in questionable categories, and to Neal's apparently subjective interpretations expressed in her follow-up memos as being especially problematic. The surveys engendered ever more controversy as findings originally proposed as an information base on resources for renewal began to function instead as LCWR's [the superiors' conference] single central source for pursing social-justice agendas, for questioning ecclesiastical authority, and for picking up the pace of renewal. Indeed, the quarter-century survey project that coincided with the postconciliar constitutional revision in women's institutes may arguably be the single most significant factor that can account for the systematic and progressive deconstruction evident among so many institutes of women religious today."[40]

Sister Elizabeth also has suggested that "In addition to problems with the instrument, interpretation, agenda, etc., the 'Sisters' Survey' study may have fallen into two aberrations that are common with such surveys, namely of: (1) becoming the basic decision maker for renewal and of (2) being confused with renewal itself. That is to say, either the survey itself was the decision maker about what happened next or those responsible for the survey made the decisions about what happened next. . . . The systematic and progressive deconstruction of conventual religious life for women in America may have been a consciously programmed occurrence or it may have been orchestrated by persons relatively unaware of fundamentals in the theology, history, evolution and structure of religious life."[41]

In an April 4, 1990, retrospective lecture at St. Michael's College in Colchester, Vermont, Sister Marie Augusta expounded on her ideas about ecclesiastical authority and what she had ordained to be the new mission of the Church — social justice. This lecture, "The Church, Women and Society," was characterized by Sister Marie Augusta as a "challenge to patriarchy," and her remarks offered many insights into the person who constructed and interpreted the Sisters' Survey.

Sister Marie Augusta said that the pastoral patterns of the Church in First World countries "are now dysfunctional for its new mission to bring the Good News to the poor, that is to the newly migrating peoples of the world." She contended that the Church is having difficulty implementing this new mission to migrating people because it is hierarchical and patriarchal. "The solution of the social problems associated with its mission

124

today, however, calls for a democratic structure modeled on a community of peers rather than on the ancient traditional structure of an extended family ruled by a patriarch," Sister Marie Augusta said. And, she suggested that this lack of democracy in the Church leads its members to reject the sacraments: ". . . A tradition that does not speak to the experience of the people, or which provides power over others to the advantage of some at the expense of exploiting the remainder of the population, engenders alienation and anomie in the society and disbelief in the sacraments of the Church."[42]

Indeed, Sister Marie Augusta's stated goal of democratizing the Catholic Church and liberating women is quite evident throughout the Sisters' Survey. She obviously found many supporters of like mind in the leadership of the Conference of Major Religious Superiors of Women's Institutes, for this revolutionary philosophy was promulgated to almost every Catholic sister through the Sisters' Survey. This philosophy was then used as the ideal by many communities of women Religious in rewriting their constitutions to prepare for post-Vatican II renewal.

Surely, communities of women Religious are still experiencing the consequences of that 1964 Grailville meeting where a small group of people formulated this new ecclesiology and philosophy of religious life and packaged it as a legitimate interpretation of how the Second Vatican Council wanted Religious to renew, even before the final version of the official Council documents on religious life were released. Every major study of religious life done in the 1990s has found that religious communities which embraced the philosophy of democracy and liberation set forth in the Sisters' Survey have experienced diminishing membership, loss of corporate identity, fracturing of community, and an uncertain future.

Yet, in spite of these facts, the Leadership Conference of Women Religious continued to praise the impact of the Sisters' Survey on women Religious nearly thirty years later. In her 1995 conference report, conference executive director Sister Margaret Cafferty, a sister of the Presentation of the Blessed Virgin Mary, wrote that "The Sisters' Survey, undertaken at the request of LCWR, played a decisive role in readying United States religious institutes for renewal and thus helped to shape the United States church that emerged from Vatican Council II." And, she continued, "the learnings from the study helped guide religious institutes through the first difficult years of renewal, providing valuable insights for each participating institute about its own strengths and weaknesses. The study also led the conference to change its name and revise its organizational structure, in keeping with the values of renewal." But apparently the survey didn't sufficiently liberate women, for Sister Margaret also observed, "While teaching the essential equality of all, the church continues to alienate women."[43]

Lay "change agents"

Certainly, sisters, priests, and theologians were not solely responsible for the indoctrination of Religious during the turbulent time of renewal. Lay people also got in on the act. Religious institutes began to consult lay people for their help in writing new constitutions and formulating chapter decrees in the 1960s. Lay consultants also were called upon to give workshops for Religious to prepare them for renewal. Some religious institutes were very selective in choosing such workshops, but unfortunately, too many Religious bought into the "anything goes" attitude prevalent during the 1960s.

One of these laymen who worked frequently with Religious during the 1960s and 1970s is psychologist William Coulson. Coulson earned a Ph.D. in philosophy from the University of Notre Dame and a Ph.D. in counseling psychology from the University of California. For many years he was an associate of Carl R. Rogers and Abraham H. Maslow at the Western Behavioral Sciences Institute in LaJolla, California, where he conducted workshops on "therapy for normals," also known as values clarification. Coulson has recanted his association with this humanistic psychological movement and now regrets the influence he had on the many Religious he encountered.

In an interview with the author,[44] Coulson recalled that "There were literally dozens of [religious] orders that asked us to do what we called basic encounter groups at the time." The encounter group was another name for sensitivity training, but Coulson and Rogers changed the name when sensitivity training started to have negative connotations. Coulson said he did most of the workshops for Religious because he was "the resident Catholic." Among the orders booking the workshops were the Immaculate Heart of Mary Sisters of Los Angeles, the Dominicans of San Raphael, Sisters of Providence of Seattle, Mercy Sisters of Burlingame, and Madames of the Sacred Heart of San Francisco and San Diego. Coulson blames his workshops for the demise of the Los Angeles Immaculate Heart of Mary order and for the movement among many orders to close schools and other institutions.

"Our job was to facilitate change — we were change agents," Coulson said. "Our job was to be, as Rogers later wrote, revolutionaries. It became a very deliberate act." Coulson said that in 1966 he did a pilot program with the Los Angeles Immaculate Heart of Mary community. "That went so swimmingly, it was agreed to bring us in to do workshops for every participant in the chapter the next summer. We were often doing that, but in no case more concertedly than with the IHMs."

Coulson said that in their sensitivity training workshops, Religious weren't allowed "happy talk or holy talk," even if they came into the session sensing no real dissatisfaction in their lives. Instead, the participants were pushed "to be real," and Coulson explained, in those days, "to be real in a psychological exercise is to be miserable. If you're not miserable, we'll try to find a way to get you to confess that you are."

By the early 1970s, Coulson said his group was doing "land office business" in the summer training of facilitators for Rogerian human potentials workshops — encounter groups. "We trained many thousands from more than thirty-five countries. Catholic religious were the largest single vocation group coming to the summer conferences held at the University of California San Diego campus in LaJolla.

"We trained hundreds of Catholic religious women and men as what we called facilitators," and designed the workshops so that the material could be taught in the facilitators' home communities, Coulson said. "But we didn't have official standing. We thought what we were doing was immanently human. It turned out to be all too human, because one of the things we could achieve was that we freed everybody from local doctrine. They were no longer constrained by rules because we persuaded them to make their own rules for themselves. Each individual would follow now his own life. Each individual had direct access to God, and this was through self-consultation. . . . We freed them from the constraints of doctrine. . . .

"When we freed them from Catholic doctrine, Catholic religion, there were no more certitudes available to them, and it allowed their impulses to bubble to the surface." And those impulses often were not compatible with religious life, or even with the Catholic faith, Coulson later concluded. "Jesuits of the Northwest province stopped their young men from coming to LaJolla because they saw that these young men had become just exactly what Rogers said they should become: quiet revolutionaries, subversives. It is not the case that we didn't believe in institutions. We believed only in our own. So, it was stupid for the Church to allow this to happen because it was inviting the enemy in. We were the Trojan horse."

Coulson said that consultants like him and Carl Rogers and numerous others who worked with Religious during the renewal period did not have a good grasp of what the Church was all about. He said they were opposed to an institutional approach, because they thought it was coercive. Their own program had no structure, and because people found it exciting to be part of that kind of experience, many Religious came to believe that it was best not to have any structure in their community life either. "We persuaded a whole raft of Catholic communities to try openness, and the predictable thing happened; they fell apart," he said.

Coulson said organizational development specialists had the same access to religious orders that he and his sensitivity training colleagues had. He feels the influence of organizational development specialists was not as destructive to religious life as was his influence, but was still destructive because it promoted democracy in all institutions. The Catholic Church is vulnerable to that kind of effort, Coulson said, because it is not democratic and was not designed to be democratic. Coulson said this type of training is still going on among Religious in programs like enneagram and intensive journal workshops. (The enneagram is supposedly a system that defines nine personality types. Enneagram workshops allegedly examine the enneagram in light of these personality types, intertwined with nine faces of God within creation, as well as nine devils or personal demons with their own will and intellect.[45])

Coulson continued: "Everybody likes to play psychiatrist. And the best way to play psychiatrist is to not have to bother going to medical school and residency, but rather to go to a weekend workshop and become an amateur psychiatrist. We clinical psychologists are in a sense semi-professional psychiatrists. And nuns and priests who do psychologically-oriented workshops and give questionnaires on things like how do you feel about this or that — they are amateurs, rank amateur psychiatrists. And you're getting exactly the kind of damage that you would predict."

Rogers and Coulson found the unfortunate result of all this psychological workshopping "therapy for normals" has been that many Catholic Religious have suffered great pain, distress, frustration, anger, loneliness, self-depreciation, and lack of trust. "We now have Catholic organizations, religious communities, which seem dedicated to seeding the whole American church with such [negative] experiences of community for no rational reason, except that it remains politically correct," Coulson explained. "It's really irrational, the net effect of what I call TMP — Too Much Psychology." He added that some Religious persist in this folly for the sake of revenge. Rather than admitting they have made mistakes, they persist because they want company in their misery.

Coulson said that it was politically correct in the 1960s to say that pre-Vatican II ways were overly structured and authoritarian, but he now believes that is not necessarily the case. "The human spirit calls for containment," he said. "No life is possible except under authority." He said that young men and women are not attracted to the structureless life that has evolved in many religious communities, but there are plenty of good models of religious life still around. "It would make no sense to say religious life is dying," Coulson said. "What's dying is the American experiment with the '60s. And let it go, I say. There is no call for keeping the '60s alive; it's over."

Enneagrams, goddesses, and other Aquarian things

Even though the 1960s and 1970s are over, many programs that seem to belong to the "Age of Aquarius" still are being promoted by and for Religious. Rather than deepening the theological knowledge or spiritual understanding of the Religious, many of these programs appear to be New Age experiences that would do little to orient a sister toward a deeper spiritual life or a better understanding of Catholic theology. Yet religious orders seem willing to pay for their members to attend these programs and even encourage attendance. For example, a 1993 brochure entitled "Opportunities for Growth Loretto Community" and circulated to Loretto sisters promoted the following programs:

"Zen Meditation Weekend/Week with Ama Samy, S.J." A Grailville program at the Loveland, Ohio, location, described as: "This silent retreat will offer time for quiet meditation and reflection, including sitting meditation, samu (work practice) and individual consultation. Fr. Samy, a Zen master from Madras, India, studied under the Dai-Roshi Yamada Koun in Japan."

"Creation Spirituality 5-Day Retreat" at Omega Institute, Rhinebeck, New York. Description: "Matthew Fox and Friends of Creation Spirituality weave the perennial wisdom of the world's great religions with medieval mysticism, earth-honoring spiritualities, transpersonal psychology, ecology, feminism, social justice, and other threads into a tapestry that has inspired spiritual seekers worldwide." (Matthew Fox was then a Dominican priest who had been silenced for a time by the Vatican for his questionable writings and preachings and his affiliation with a self-proclaimed witch named Starhawk. Fox was eventually removed from his order and has since left the priesthood and the Catholic Church, becoming an Episcopal priest in 1994.)

"Varieties of Feminist Voices in Theology," "Womanist Spirit, Womanist Witness," and "Ecofeminist Theology in Global Perspective" at the Pacific School of Religion, Berkeley, California.

"The Institute for Deep Ecology Education 2-Week Summer School: Applied Deep Ecology." At Shenoa Retreat Center in Philo, California, one could opt for staying in a cabin for the two weeks at $650, or camping for $390. The housing fee was in addition to the $750 tuition. Described as:

Sisters in Crisis

"The Summer School will explore both the insights and educational techniques emerging from within the deep ecology movement and focus on their application to the practical work of social change."

"Introduction to the New Cosmology" at Genesis Farm, Blairstown, New Jersey. Description: "The New Cosmology offers an inspiring and challenging way of viewing the universe and the human's role within it. To help familiarize students with its content and language, Genesis Farm offers an intensive 5 day introductory course designed to explore the concepts of the New Cosmology, to identify and answer difficult questions, and to explore and internalize a creative personal response."

Also available at Genesis Farm for $1,500 was "An experiential 6-week program, exploring the New Cosmology and Bioregionalism, and their practical implications for our lives. This intensive program emphasizes hands-on experience with natural foods cooking, art and ritual, gardening and wild foods, and field trips. Guest presenters will share reflections and life experiences around weekly themes."

In 1992, one could travel to the Sisters of Charity of Nazareth retreat center in Nazareth, Kentucky, for "Enneagram: Co-Dependency," presented by Dominican Sister Maria Beesing, focusing on "the insights of Enneagram on the experience of co-dependency."

Also at Nazareth, one could attend a weekend program presented by Rev. Kharma Udaka Kanromon, Osho., a "Zen priest in the Rinzai Zen tradition." The program promised: "We will explore the basic Zen Teachings of selfless love and intuitive wisdom and how this relates to the pressures we face in the temporal world. We will practice some of the traditional forms of Zen meditation that are essential for opening our hearts and realizing ultimate truth." Attendees were urged to bring "meditation cushions/benches and mats" and "comfortable clothing in subdued colors."

The April 1992 issue of *Update*, a publication of the Leadership Conference of Women Religious, carried news of a program titled "A Circle of Women: Women's Spirituality and the Healing of the Earth." The program, sponsored by the Passionist nuns of Clarks Summit, Pennsylvania, was promoted "For women religious to reflect on the challenges in an ecological age and an invitation to respond creatively to the deepest intuitions of connection and interrelationship with the entire communion of life."

More recently, sisters could participate in a nine-month sabbatical from September 1996 through May 1997 at Wholistic Growth Resources, operated by the Franciscan Sisters of Little Falls, Minnesota. Promotional material promised that this "transformational journey" would include activities such as: group process, body therapy, enneagram, parental synthesis, sound therapy, ritual, psychosynthesis, foods, feminine spirituality, T'ai Chi Chih, prayer forms, and more. The nine-month program was recommended for sisters dealing with stress due to burn-out, unresolved grief or loss, abuse, transition, or unemployment.[46]

In his book, *Catholics and the New Age*, Jesuit Father Mitch Pacwa analyzes many of these New Age programs, which he was involved in himself as a young Jesuit, including I Ching (Chinese fortune-telling), enneagram, Eastern meditation, and astrology. He concludes that: "The more we live our faith and understand it, the better we can discern what is true and false about NAM [New Age Movement]. Today the weak link is the lack of understanding of our faith. We need to shore up our knowledge of Scripture, church history, theology, and Christian morals. Yet this knowledge should never be disassociated from living the faith, making it strong in our personal lives.

"Because our faith holds together so well, it can integrate science far better than NAM's creation of new mythologies."[47]

Regarding the new emphasis on social justice and ecology among many Religious, Father Albert DiIanni, a theologian and vicar general of the Society of Mary from 1985 to 1993, observed in 1994 that, while Religious have historically and rightly cared for the poor, their primary duty is to love God. He argued that a new theology of religious life has replaced the traditional philosophy of religious congregations that used to consider striving for personal holiness primary, and ministering to one's neighbor, secondary. Father DiIanni wrote that:

> . . . some peace and justice workers, in a way similar to [Karl] Marx, have lost sight of the deep meaning of Christianity as well as confidence in the Resurrection. Partly due to a lack of faith in other worldly and eschatological realities, they have found it necessary to find a totally earthly locus for their passion. . . . They continue to use God-language and to quote the Scriptures, but on their lips such language often seems a mythic overlay, a symbolic vehicle for motivating people to become engaged in the more important task of social, economic, and ecological reform.
>
> They speak frequently of the need to "build up the kingdom" and insist that "salvation must begin on earth" but have only lip-service for the eschatological aspects of the Kingdom and salvation. They are more at home with

social action and politics than with piety, with prayer of petition, with praise of the Lord. They espouse most of the liberal or radical social causes of the day, criticizing neo-conservatism as escapism and remain quite silent on moral issues such as abortion. They tend to shy away from the "mere sacramental ministry" and at times translate liturgy into a political statement.[48]

This philosophy described by Father DiIanni is in part a legacy of the Sisters' Survey, which ordained the primary mission of religious life to be social justice. And this theme of Religious as primary agents of social and political change was carried forward through various educational efforts, including the influential Sister Formation Movement, which is discussed in the next chapter.

8: The Re-Education of Sister Lucy

"It is difficult to overemphasize the seminal importance of
Sister Formation in the changing of American nuns. For many
the SFC initiated a conceptual shift in theology and spirituality
. . . and grounded still other, more radical, conceptual shifts."[1]
The Transformation of American Catholic Sisters

Like the Conference of Major Religious Superiors of Women's Institutes, the Sister Formation Conference had a noble beginning and was instrumental in promoting needed reforms among women Religious. But, like
the conference of superiors, the Sister Formation Movement evolved beyond its original purpose — promoting better education for sisters before
they were sent out into their apostolates. The Sister Formation Movement
went on to foster training for sisters that would introduce them to leftist
theologies and radical feminist concepts of religious life which were foreign to the guidelines of Vatican II. Thus, the Sister Formation Movement
eventually contributed to the indoctrination of sisters and the deconstruction
of women's religious institutes in the United States.

Educating Sister Lucy

Holy Cross Sister Madeleva Wolff, who was president of Saint Mary's
College at Notre Dame, Indiana, from 1934 to 1961, was one of the pio-
neers of the Sister Formation Movement. Sister Madeleva had recognized
the educational problems of sisters for many years. Not only were young

sisters being placed in professional positions before they were adequately prepared, but the orders were having a hard time coming up with money for educating the growing number of sisters. Sister Madeleva also saw the need to train teachers of theology, but neither Religious nor lay women were admitted to graduate theology programs at that time.[2]

Sister Madeleva took matters into her own hands and established a School of Sacred Theology at Saint Mary's College in 1943. The graduate school of theology offered the master's or doctorate degree to sisters and lay women and became a model for Regina Mundi, a pontifical institute for sisters which opened in Rome in 1953. The Saint Mary's School of Sacred Theology operated for twenty-four years, educating theology teachers — mostly sisters — for high schools, colleges, and formation programs within congregations of sisters. The program was closed in 1967 for financial reasons, and because Catholic universities finally were opening up graduate theology programs to women.[3]

Also during the 1940s, Sister Madeleva and several other concerned parties repeatedly had asked the National Catholic Educational Association (NCEA) to establish a section for teacher education. After a 1948 NCEA Midwest College and University Department panel discussion on teacher preparation and the education of sisters, a teacher education section of the National Catholic Educational Association was officially set up. The following year, at the 1949 NCEA annual meeting, Sister Madeleva presented a paper, later published as "The Education of Sister Lucy," which had a major impact.

Sister Madeleva's paper suggested that young sisters who were going to be teachers should receive their baccalaureate degree and teacher certification prior to final profession of vows and prior to being assigned to full-time teaching. She acknowledged the problems in trying to attain this ideal — the expense involved in educating a sister before she made a decision to stay in the community and take her final vows, and the growing pressure for sisters to staff parochial schools — but she insisted that "if we cannot afford to prepare our young sisters for the work of our communities, we should not accept them at all. We should direct them to communities that will prepare them."[4] Sister Madeleva's paper proved to be a major impetus for establishing the Sister Formation Conference as a committee within the College and University Department of the Teacher Education Section of the NCEA.[5]

Initially, the Sister Formation Conference was founded to promote the education and professional certification of sisters before they were assigned as teachers, nurses, and social workers. This original purpose was a tremendous benefit to the sisters who then started to receive adequate preparation for their work assignments, and it also gave a needed boost to the reputation of Catholic institutions where the sisters worked. During the 1950s, approximately one-hundred-fifty religious institutes established degree programs for their sisters, variously called juniorates or motherhouse colleges. National Sister Formation programs open to sisters from any religious institute were offered at various sites during the summer months.

In addition, religious institutes that already operated four-year colleges often welcomed sisters from other congregations, where the sisters were educated alongside lay women, but Sister Formation leaders tended to prefer that the sisters be separated from lay students. And so, some specific Sister Formation colleges were born. Seattle University opened a College of Sister Formation in 1958 that had equal status with other Seattle University colleges. The university provided faculty and facilities until Providence Heights College was finished in 1960 and staffed by Sisters of Charity of Providence.[6]

Another Sister Formation College, Marillac College in St. Louis, Missouri, run by the Daughters of Charity, had originally been an extension program of DePaul University, opening in 1937. In 1955, Marillac Junior College became a corporate junior college of St. Louis University. Then, in 1957, Marillac became an independent four-year liberal arts college exclusively for sisters. In the 1959-60 academic year, the thirty-four faculty members represented fifteen different religious communities. Daughter of Charity Sister Bertrande Meyers, president of Marillac, had been one of the promoters of sister education for years and served on the National Sister Formation Committee. By 1963, Marillac enrolled three hundred fifty students from twenty-five religious congregations. Daughters of Charity made up about two-thirds of the student body in 1963, and took their novitiate year between the freshman and sophomore years of study, thus comprising a five-year program. Student sisters from other orders usually entered Marillac in the sophomore year and lived off campus in their own juniorates under the supervision of their own orders to preserve the distinctive spirituality of each order.[7] (Canon law required that the novitiate year be spent in one's own religious institution.) By 1966, there were sisters from thirty-five different orders at Marillac, outnumbering the Daughters of Charity by more than two to one.

Dissent at Catholic universities

Not all sisters attended Sister Formation schools or colleges conducted by their own orders. Beginning in the 1950s, it became increasingly common for sisters to attend various Catholic universities, particularly for graduate degrees. Some of these sisters went full time, but many studied only during the summer months, and it was quite common to see more Religious than laity on the campuses of some Catholic universities during the summer session. In general, superiors felt comfortable sending their young Religious off to study at Catholic institutions in the company of Religious from other institutes.

However, this feeling of comfort began to dissipate during the turbulent 1960s, when many sisters were radicalized by their professors and fellow students at Catholic colleges and universities. Superiors say that some of their sisters even lost their faith when they were sent off to Catholic universities to study. The situation was viewed so seriously by some superiors that they started to enroll their young sisters in state colleges and universities, where they received little to no theology training, but at least the sisters weren't exposed to some of the Catholic theologians who, in the 1960s, began to attack the magisterium, loosely interpret Vatican II documents, and dissent from Church teaching.

The most publicized example of this theological dissent during the 1960s, and very likely the incident which set the stage for ongoing public dissent from Church teachings, was an unprecedented statement of opposition to Pope Paul's encyclical *Humanae Vitae*. Father Charles Curran, a theology professor at Catholic University, led a group of theologians, philosophers, and canon lawyers who disagreed with Paul VI's condemnation of birth control and criticized the pope's views on the authority of the Church.[8]

Among the names appearing on an August 14, 1968, *National Catholic Reporter* page entitled "Signers of Statement Disagreeing with Encyclical" (*Humanae Vitae*) were, in addition to Father Curran: (former) Jesuit Father Daniel Maguire, who was among nine priest faculty members from Catholic University who signed the statement; and Father Bernard Haring and Benedictine Father Godfrey Diekmann, both of whom would go on to teach at Catholic University in the 1970s. Priest signers from the University of Notre Dame included Benedictine Father Aidan Kavanaugh. Father Richard McBrien, who was at Gregorian University in Rome when he signed the statement of dissent, went on to become chairman of the Theology Department at Notre Dame.

Also among the prominent signers of the statement of dissent were (former) Jesuit Father Bernard Cooke, chairman of the Theology Department at Marquette University; Father Peter Riga of La Salle College; Christian Brother Paul K. Hennessy, of Iona College, New Rochelle, New York;

and Christian Brother Gabriel Moran, from Manhattan College. Among the fourteen priests from Fordham University whose names were on the statement was Jesuit Father Christopher Mooney, chairman of the Fordham Theology Department. Also appearing in the statement of dissent were the names of five priests from each of the faculties of Loyola University, Chicago; St. Mary's Seminary and University in Baltimore; and Woodstock College in Maryland.[9] (Note that many of these men had been or would be featured speakers at the national assemblies of the Conference of Major Religious Superiors of Women's Institutes/Leadership Conference of Women Religious.) Priests, Religious, and lay faculty from numerous other Catholic colleges and universities also signed the statement of dissent.

This example gives some indication about the state of confusion reigning in the theology departments of some of the Catholic universities during the 1960s and 1970s, regarding the teachings and authority of the Church. And this atmosphere of dissent permeated other departments in the very Catholic universities that were charged with the higher education of sisters during the same years that women Religious were grappling with issues of authority when rewriting their constitutions.

From professional to spiritual formation

The Sister Formation Movement was affected by this atmosphere of questioning Church teachings and authority. In addition to the specialized Sister Formation colleges like Marillac and Providence Heights, many ad hoc programs eventually were offered under the umbrella of the Sister Formation Movement. As the 1960s progressed, the scope of Sister Formation programs expanded beyond strictly professional preparation and started to include more of the spiritual formation of sisters.

This expansion of the Sister Formation programs caused considerable controversy, since canon law directed that spiritual formation of Religious was to be under the supervision of their own superiors, who were familiar with the spirit and charism of their own institutes. (This concern eventually led the Congregation for Religious to insist that the Sister Formation Movement be placed under the control of the Conference of Major Religious Superiors of Women's Institutes in 1964.) Some superiors clearly felt that Sister Formation programs should be kept within their own congregations, and they bumped heads with Sister Formation leaders who believed that such small programs were academically inferior and financially impossible. (Historian Philip Gleason has noted that by 1960, ninety-three of these juniorate colleges had fewer than fifty-five students, and only three of those ninety-three were accredited.[10]) Consequently, some superiors refused to get involved in the Sister Formation Movement because they felt it was a danger to religious life. Others embraced it enthusiastically.

One of the aspects of the expanding Sister Formation programs that worried some superiors and some Church officials was the theological and spiritual content, some of which seemed designed to re-educate Sister Lucy in the latest theological, sociological, psychological — and eventually New Age — fads. Certainly, many Sister Formation courses presented very solid, orthodox teaching from some of the finest theologians and professors of the time. And the *Sister Formation [SF] Bulletin* also contained some excellent articles. But the *Bulletin* consistently presented the most contemporary theological thought, much of which was controversial and speculative at that time. While this level of theological inquiry would be stimulating and appropriate for well-prepared theology students, most young sisters had little or no training in theology, and even older sisters often had fewer courses in theology than in spiritual life. As a result, some of the *Bulletin* articles were not critically assessed by the sisters who read them, which caused considerable confusion and misinterpretation.

The *SF Bulletin*, which was widely read by nuns and reached a peak circulation of eleven thousand, often published the first English translation of the writings of controversial European theologians. Appearing regularly was the work of Jesuit Father Karl Rahner, Redemptorist Father Bernard Haring, and Dominican Father Edward Schillebeeckx. A *Time* magazine education writer observed in 1964 that the Sister Formation courses and *Bulletin* "sometimes offer more avante-garde theology than most seminaries for priests allow."[11] Franciscan Sister Angelyn Dries observed that "During the 1950's and '60's, many authors who were excerpted in the *Bulletin* were influential among American progressive groups: J. LeClerq, P. Grelot, L. Bouyer, Chenu, and Congar."[12] Much of this contemporary theology was eagerly consumed by the sisters who encountered it, and the *Bulletin* was praised for bringing this new theology to the American sisters.

Unfortunately, many sisters simply did not have the training necessary to distinguish between groundbreaking — although legitimate — theological inquiry and outright theological speculation which was sometimes presented as dogma. Even thirty years after the Vatican Council closed, trained theologians with doctoral degrees were still trying to sort out and understand some of the complex theological concepts espoused by many of those theologians whose work appeared in the *Bulletin* regularly.

Significantly, many of the sisters who took Sister Formation courses and followed the *Bulletin* closely were the very sisters who were in leadership positions in their congregations and responsible for the training of younger sisters. In some convents, the *Bulletin* was the designated reading material during meals. So, virtually every sister came into contact with the material in the *Bulletin*, but not every sister had the theological background to put all the articles in the *Bulletin* into the proper context, especially during an era when there was so much speculation about what was happening or would happen at the Second Vatican Council.

The *SF Bulletin* also was a showcase for the writing of American sisters, some of whom were beginning to reflect the women's liberation agenda and question the meaning of the vows, the importance of community, and the role of authority, as evidenced in the previous chapters of this book.

For example, in the Autumn 1966 *SF Bulletin*, Sister Formation executive secretary Sister of Charity Rose Dominic Gabisch observed after a trip to Europe that "The religious women of Germany seem to be eager to stop making minor adaptations; they would prefer a radical use of contemporary theology to acquire an entirely new view of religious life."[13]

In the same issue, Sister Rose Dominic summarized a September 1966 colloquium on "World Apostolate of Women Religious" at Louvain, reporting that the entire conference adopted the conclusions of the English-speaking group: That if obstacles to religious fulfillment are to be removed, "extensive — and in some cases, revolutionary — experimentation will be essential. . . . This response will entail immediate and extensive experimentation in various forms of the 'community without walls.' "[14] This interpretation of renewal was far more radical than the renewal actually mandated by the Second Vatican Council, which never suggested religious orders undertake revolutionary experimentation or community life without walls. Nevertheless, this interpretation of renewal was set forth in the *Bulletin* as normative.

In a lengthy article in the Summer 1967 *SF Bulletin,* Sister of the Holy Names of Jesus and Mary, Mary Audrey Kopp, discussed "The Renewed Nuns: Collegial Christians." In the article, Sister Mary Audrey wrote that the modes of authority in religious life were dysfunctional and even heretical, and she wrote of "our split-level convent, about to nail up a sign reading, 'Condemned for human occupancy.' "[15] Congregation of the Mission Father James W. Richardson wrote a letter of concern to the *Bulletin* editor, Sister of Notre Dame de Namur Joan Bland, about that article, noting that Sister Mary Audrey was quite correct in calling for abandoning authoritarianism in religious life, but she had been "excessive in excluding jurisdictional power from the Church" and in saying that obedience is simply a response to a group decision summed up and expressed by an elected spokesperson.[16]

However, Sister Formation leaders didn't seem to share Father Richardson's concern, as Sister Rose Emmanuella Brennan, executive secretary of the conference of major superiors, who was a former Sister Formation regional chairperson, wrote Sister Mary Audrey, telling her the article was "excellent," and she suggested that Sister Mary Audrey's article become a major theme for Sister Formation discussions during the coming year. Sister Rose Emmanuella dismissed Father Richardson's comments by saying he was just showing interest in the sisters.[17] (Apparently even this support was not strong enough and change was not fast enough for Sister Mary Audrey, for she left her order in 1969 and founded a noncanonical organization called Sisters For Christian Community. That same year, she also co-founded the National Coalition of American Nuns with School Sister of Notre Dame Margaret Ellen Traxler, which is profiled in Chapter Thirteen.)

Another influential leader of Sister Formation, Sister Ritamary Bradley of the Congregation of the Humility of Mary, edited the *Sister Formation Bulletin* from its inception in 1954 until 1964. She was largely responsible for determining its content. She observed in the Summer 1964 *Bulletin* that "not everyone agreed with all that was going into print in the *Bulletin* recently." She went on to suggest that one of the roles of the publication was to "stimulate leadership in assuring that the clarified notions of 'liberty of conscience' and 'religious liberty' be used without admixture of unworthy ends and without cowardice. . . ." She also called for a "negative" role for future publications of the *Bulletin*: "that of keeping the literature about Sisters from regressing into being 'spiritual' in an isolated sense; that of preventing the intellectual formation of Sisters from being only 'theological,' thereby thwarting the properly human development in which the rest is rooted."[18]

When she wrote those words, even Sister Ritamary probably could not have predicted just how human the intellectual formation of sisters would become in the years that followed and how far "liberty of conscience" took many sisters in the deconstruction of their institutes. (Sister Ritamary eventually left her congregation and joined Lillanna Kopp in the noncanonical Sisters For Christian Community and also became a leader of the National Coalition of American Nuns.)

Psychology, politics, and many opinions

Just as some of the *Sister Formation Bulletin* offerings were quite orthodox and solid, many of the Sister Formation programs and courses certainly were theologically and philosophically strong. But, like some of the offerings in the *Bulletin*, some of the Sister Formation programs and courses eventually proved to be controversial.

With a grant from the Ford Foundation, a group of fifteen sister educators met at Everett, Washington, in 1956 to devise what came to be known as the "Everett Curriculum." This curriculum stressed "the study of psychology, sociology, political science and current events, subjects usually not part of normal school training with its heavy emphasis on teacher-training courses."[19] While the idea behind the curriculum may have been quite solid, one sister who had experience with the Everett Curriculum has noted that it was valuable to have courses in the social sciences, but the curriculum did not provide for adequate theological and spiritual education. So, the training of the sisters swung from one extreme of being too spiritually-oriented and inadequately professional, to the other extreme of emphasis on the professional to the detriment of the spiritual.

Starting in 1958, a series of summer workshops for Sister Formation personnel convened at Marquette University. There, superiors and directresses of formation learned about how to apply the Everett Curriculum to individual formation programs of religious communities.[20] But, after the first year, when over one hundred sisters from thirty-seven religious communities attended, the emphasis on professional training changed. According to one sister historian, "Discussion of what was important and changing in sister education allowed the emphasis of the Marquette Workshops to change dramatically in the next years. . . . Perhaps only someone who attended all SFC-sponsored conferences and workshops could see how all the activities led to one goal — that of better understanding the changing face of religious life and thus the need to change formation programs."[21]

Thus, the Sister Formation Movement was evolving past its original goal of establishing better professional preparation for sisters and instead getting directly involved in structuring the spiritual formation of sisters. Moreover, by entering into this area of spiritual formation that had traditionally been handled strictly within individual religious institutes, the Sister Formation Movement intruded on the autonomy of individual religious institutes. In effect, Sister Formation leaders thus began to exert an inordinate influence on the very structure of individual congregations, but at the same time had very little guidance or oversight from the official Church. And this was occurring at the very time that religious institutes were engaged in rewriting their constitutions.

For example, the changing nature of religious life was a topic open to wide interpretations in the late 1950s and early 1960s, and the Marquette workshop participants apparently were exposed to a myriad of opinions, depending on who was teaching in the program. Several of the sisters teaching in the Marquette workshops held a radical view of religious life that was based on humanistic psychology and leftist politics, and clearly they wanted those concepts to be injected into the professional and spiritual formation of sisters. Sister Ritamary Bradley regularly taught in the Marquette summer workshops, as did Sister of St. Joseph Annette Walter, Sister Formation executive secretary for several years and a frequent lecturer on psychology. Sister Annette remained a member of her order until her death, but she also held membership in the noncanonical Sisters For Christian Community (even though "one cannot simultaneously hold membership in a canonical religious institute and in a non-canonical group," according to the Vatican Congregation for Religious[22]). Sister Annette also went on to become a leader in the National Coalition of American Nuns.

Other sisters who taught in the Marquette Sister Formation programs also would go on to openly challenge Church teaching and authority. Two of these teachers were Sister Thomas Aquinas (Elizabeth) Carroll and Sister M. Humiliata (Anita) Caspary. Sister Thomas Aquinas had been on the Sister Formation executive committee and would go on to become president of the conference of major superiors at their stormy 1971 assembly, when the major superiors changed their name to the Leadership Conference of Women Religious. Sister Thomas Aquinas eventually joined the staff of the Center of Concern, where for many years she led efforts to promote ordination of women and passage of the Equal Rights Amendment. Sister Humiliata (Anita) Caspary had been a Sister Formation regional chairperson. In 1970, Anita Caspary led over three-hundred members of her Immaculate Heart of Mary order in asking for dispensation from their vows because Cardinal James McIntyre of Los Angeles and the Vatican's Congregation for Religious did not approve of changes the sisters made in their constitution and lifestyle (described in Chapter Eleven).

Other regular faculty members of the Sister Formation Marquette summer workshops included Reverend François Houtart, director of the Center for Socio-Religious Research, Brussels, Belgium; Dr. David Riesman, Department of Social Relations, Harvard University; Rabbi Marc Tanenbaum, director of the American Jewish Committee, New York City; Jesuit Father Renato Poblete, S.J., director of the Research Center in Religious Sociology, Santiago, Chile; and Monsignor Ivan D. Illich, director of the Centers for Intercultural Formation at Cuernavaca, Mexico, and Petropolis, Brazil.[23]

In a January 9, 1971, article in *America*, Monsignor Illich conveyed his philosophy about education when he suggested that a Religious who teaches "will either become the victim of other people's insights, remain within the present system of schooling, insist on being a classroom-teacher and thus lose his vocation as an educator of the poor; or he will recognize his unique position among teachers, use his freedom to liberate education from schools and himself become an educator of his colleagues." [24]

The Sister Formation Movement also heavily promoted other programs such as the Eleventh Annual Institute on Religious and Sacerdotal Vocations at Fordham University in the summer of 1961. The Spring 1961 *Bulletin* urged mistresses of novices, postulants, and juniors, as well as superiors, to attend the program, whose featured speakers were Sister Annette Walter, Father Charles Curran, and Jesuit Father Daniel Berrigan.[25]

In a 1994 essay on the Sister Formation Movement, Franciscan Sister Mary Lea Schneider of Cardinal Stritch College noted: "This search for excellence and relevance exemplified in theological studies continued in all facets of the [Sister Formation] Conference. Under its second executive secretary, Sr. Annette Walters, S.S.J./S.F.C.C. (1960-1964), the conference continued to expand its vision and its range of activities. There was growing awareness of the social and political issues fermenting in the United States and abroad and a realisation [sic] that sisters needed to become involved in systemic social change." Sister Mary Lea concluded that "The wisdom gained in the decades-long process of self-discovery as professional women in the church-in-the-world is a gift for the church if it will accept it. Whatever the future, there will be no turning back from the direction now taken."[26]

The leadership network

At the insistence of the Vatican Congregation for Religious, the Sister Formation Conference became a committee of the major superiors in 1964, but not without a great deal of turmoil. Executive secretary Sister Annette Walter and *Bulletin* editor Sister Ritamary Bradley bitterly resisted the move, since Sister Formation had been virtually autonomous under the National Catholic Educational Association. But that very autonomy had concerned the Congregation for Religious so much that its secretary, Archbishop Paul Philippe, a Dominican, ordered the Sister Formation Conference to become a committee of the major superiors. Archbishop Philippe told the national committee of the major superiors and the officers of the Sister Formation Conference that formation of sisters was one of the duties of major superiors, and the superiors could not let formation be out of their control.[27] The new National Sister Formation Committee was directed by a board of six voting members elected from the membership of the conference of major superiors and six non-voting consultants elected from the Sister Formation Conference.[28]

Sisters in Crisis

But under the major superiors, Sister Formation would move even further away from its original purpose, since the superiors' organization itself was in a process of evolution, indeed some would say, even revolution. The Sister Formation Movement would also prove to have been an effective training ground for sister/administrators who would move into leadership roles in the transformed major superiors' organization. The leadership of both sisters' organizations had evolved from the busy mother superiors and novice directresses of the 1950s who had little time for conference work, to highly educated professional administrators of the 1960s and 1970s, who had decreasing responsibilities in their own congregations, and plenty of experience in marketing, networking, and politics. These modern leaders also were skilled in identifying and grooming like-minded successors, and many of the same sisters simply recycled into different leadership positions in the two organizations.

These same women also frequently helped determine the reading matter offered to sisters during the years of renewal, thus significantly shaping the information available to sisters. For example, in 1964, the advisory board of *Sponsa Regis*, a monthly spiritual magazine for sisters (later named *Sisters Today*), included several sisters who were leaders in Sister Formation and/or the major superiors' conference. Among them were: Sisters Ritamary Bradley, Annette Walter, Immaculate Heart of Mary Sister Mary Emil Penet, and Franciscan Sister M. Emmanuel Collins, all leaders in Sister Formation; Sister of Loretto Mary Florence Wolff, a Sister Formation leader and major superiors' executive secretary from 1960 to 1963; Sister M. Rose Emmanuella Brennan, a Sister Formation regional chairman and executive secretary for the major superiors from 1964 to 1969; and Sister Mary Francine Zeller, midwest regional chairman of Sister Formation who became president of the major superiors in 1974.[29]

Also in the 1960s, during the renewal years, the *National Catholic Reporter* published a "Sisters Forum," which was planned and written by many of these sister leaders and edited by Sister M. Charles Borromeo (Maryellen) Muckenhirn. Before she left religious life, Muckenhirn also edited *The Changing Sister*, which became the basis for the controversial 1967 Sisters' Survey. The minutes of a 1965 meeting of the major superiors' Research and Study Project on Religious Life indicate that the sisters considered the "Sisters Forum" to be "an organ for 'grass roots thinking.' " The minutes also alluded to the "invaluable role that the Forum has played and will continue to play for the renewal of Sisters in the U.S.A." And, it was suggested that the "Sisters Forum" make "use of documentation and reports of experimentation to give flesh and blood to the topics raised."

144

Also reflected in the minutes was the "problem of getting the less 'progressive' position convincingly written." And, since there didn't seem to be too many "less progressive" folks in their circle, the suggestion was made that "a perceptive person not in agreement [with the less progressive position] could do a good presentation."[30]

Under the major superiors of women, the Sister Formation Committee went on to endorse programs for sisters that were quite controversial, such as the 1967 "Collegial Weekend" at Barat College, Lake Forest, Illinois, promoted in the Winter 1967 issue of the *Sister Formation Bulletin*. At these weekends, sisters could hear, among other speakers, Father Charles Curran of Catholic University talk about "The New Morality." (The following summer, Father Curran would lead the dissent from the papal encyclical, *Humanae Vitae*.)

At another 1967 "Collegial Weekend" at Barat, sisters were invited to join priests, brothers, and lay people for a program on "The Cosmic Christ of St. Paul and the Omega Point of Teilhard de Chardin." A workshop at Marquette University cited in the Winter 1966 *Bulletin* was "designed to serve the National Sister Formation Committee's purpose of providing philosophical insights into the social science and practical demonstrations of social projects." Included in that program, which promised investigation of "the new knowledge of person and society," was "study of Teilhard de Chardin.[31]

These programs were recommended by the Sister Formation Conference even though the work of Jesuit Father Pierre Teilhard de Chardin was still under a monitum, or warning, from the Vatican Congregation of the Holy Office because of confusion that might be caused by "Teilhardism."[32] Earlier, Cardinal Egidia Vagnozzi, apostolic delegate to the United States, had warned against placing Teilhard de Chardin's works in seminary libraries.[33] This kind of censorship may seem strange to contemporary Catholics, especially since Teilhard de Chardin's work has been more moderately interpreted in the last decade of the twentieth century than it was in the 1950s and 1960s. But it was still a common practice in the 1960s for the Church to employ such means to try to protect Catholics from doctrinal error. (It was not until 1966 that the Congregation for the Doctrine of the Faith lifted the penalty of excommunication for Catholics who read, possessed, or sold a book that was on the Index of Prohibited Books.) Regardless of what anyone might think of the work of Teilhard de Chardin, the point is that the Sister Formation Conference — the committee of the superior's conference that was supposed to be overseeing and coordinating the formation of sisters — was obviously unconcerned about Vatican monitums.

Sisters in Crisis

Also advertised in the Winter 1966 issue of the *Bulletin* were "Traveling Workshops" under the sponsorship of the National Catholic Conference for Interracial Justice. Among the traveling faculty were Sisters Mary Audrey (Lillanna) Kopp and Mary Peter (Margaret Ellen) Traxler. It was out of their base at the National Catholic Conference for Interracial Justice in Chicago that Sisters Mary Audrey and Mary Peter founded the militant National Coalition of American Nuns. And the two sisters obviously had more on their minds than interracial justice when their team covered over thirty-thousand miles throughout twenty-eight states in a fifteen-month period.[34]

Lillanna Kopp (the former Sister Mary Audrey) would later write: "From city-to-city, state-to-state, and coast-to-coast our race relations team traveled with a double agenda. We prayed that we might somehow make a small gain toward bettering race relations. We'll really never know. But that our gatherings made an impact on American Sister Renewal, we have no doubt. During them, American sisters envisioned together wholly new religious life models for the 21st century, and they are working still to make them a reality. Our mutural [sic] concern for genuine change in sisterhoods was so intense, it lighted a prairie fire of determination, a grassroots revolution among sisters."[35]

Sister (Mary Peter) Margaret Ellen Traxler acknowledged that she and Sister Mary Audrey successfully recruited eleven hundred sisters for their National Coalition of American Nuns while they were doing the traveling workshops for the National Catholic Conference for Interracial Justice. "All you had to do was mention the coalition [National Coalition of American Nuns] and they signed up. You didn't even have to ask them,"[36] Sister Mary Peter related. These workshops, which also functioned as a recruiting front for the National Coalition of American Nuns, were promoted in the *Bulletin* by the Sister Formation Conference, a committee of the major superiors' conference.

"Highly recommended resource material"

The Sister Formation Conference regained its autonomy in 1970, while the Conference of Major Religious Superiors of Women's Institutes was being transformed into the Leadership Conference of Women Religious. The December 17, 1970, report of the superiors' conference's Ad Hoc Committee on the Agenda indicated that, in the opinion of the ad hoc committee, the Sister Formation Conference had no operative affiliation with the major superiors of women.[37]

It is unclear why the Vatican's Congregation for Religious allowed this dissociation to happen, since the Congregation for Religious had originally insisted that the Sister Formation Conference be placed under the major superiors of women. The action apparently was a *fait accompli* about which the Vatican was not consulted, just like the move to dissolve the original structure of the women superiors' conference; the Vatican was simply informed after the action took place.

With its autonomy, the Sister Formation Conference was even less inhibited.

By 1974, the conference was calling for the ordination of women.[38] In 1975, the conference was promoting a "Futureshop on Formation" at the Mercy Generalate in Bethesda. The September 1975 issue of *In-formation* — the publication that replaced the *Bulletin* — listed "highly recommended resource material" for the Futureshop, including "Lifestyle," described as "a reflection/action workbook for those seeking greater freedom in their style of living and dying." On the "Futureshop" program were the films "Meditation: Yoga and Other Spiritual Trips," "Universities: Tearing Down the Ivy," and "Multiple Man." Speakers included Dominican Sister Nadine Foley, who was a leader in the women's ordination movement. (Sister Nadine would go on to become president of the Leadership Conference of Women Religious in 1988.) Participants in "Futureshop" then returned to their communities to conduct "mini-Futureshops."[39]

A mimeographed report from "Futureshop" predicted trends for the 1980s: "Personal self-development and aspiration of members of an organization will take gradual priority over organizational conveniences, order, efficiency, and expenditures for profit." And, "Increasing demand for participation is replacing the old authoritarianism or executive power. A growth in anti-authoritarianism will continue, resulting in greater alienation from outmoded institutions. . . ."[40] This prediction was quite accurate, for women Religious did become increasingly focused on individualism and alienated from their institutions, outmoded or not.

By 1978, *In-formation* was promoting programs such as enneagram workshops, presenting the "Sufi System of nine personality types in the context of prayer and discernment. A useful tool for getting in touch with ego fixations." Also being pushed in the Easter 1978 *In-formation* was a program at Mundelein College in Chicago, called "An Institute in Creation Centered Spirituality For Those Who Believe Holiness is Holness." "Good reading" recommended by the newsletter included *Jesus and Freedom* and *Christian Education for Liberation and Other Upsetting Ideas*.[41]

During the mid-1970s the Sister Formation Conference also endorsed ongoing workshops taught by an activist sister. The May 1976 issue of *In-formation* promoted "Bread Broken/Life Shared," a workshop given by Sister of St. Joseph Dorothy Donnelly, an associate professor of historical theology at the Jesuit School of Theology at Berkeley, California.[42] Sister Dorothy also had been one of the speakers at the first Women's Ordination Conference in 1975, and had taken over the presidency of the National Coalition of American Nuns from Sister Margaret Ellen Traxler in 1973.

The Sister Formation Conference continued to undergo a complete transformation from its original purpose, reflecting a growing feminist agenda and urging support for left-wing groups. In 1976, the Sister Formation Conference became a member of the National Catholic Coalition for the Equal Rights Amendment, and *In-formation* contained a progress report on "Priests for Equality," a group of priests organized by Jesuit Father William Callahan, to support women's ordination.[43]

In 1976, the Sister Formation Conference changed its name to Religious Formation Conference, a name change that accommodated new categories of membership, including men. A 1995 brochure of the Religious Formation Conference indicated approximately eleven hundred members from about four hundred eighty religious communities of men and women in the United States, Canada, Europe, Asia, Africa, Australia, and the West Indies. Auxiliary membership was available to campus ministers, continuing education groups, vicars for Religious, etc.

It indeed is ironic that the organization that did so much good in promoting the necessary education of sisters also helped foster and propagate some questionable renewal programs and theologies variously described as avant-garde and speculative. It is significant that this effort by the Sister Formation Conference was being made at the very same time that institutes of women Religious were engaged in rewriting their constitutions, and setting a course for renewal as directed by the Second Vatican Council. In fact, the Sister Formation Conference sponsored renewal workshops to train sisters for effecting renewal in their own communities. Thus, when sisters were re-educated or misinformed in sloppy, speculative, or downright erroneous courses, they often carried this misinformation back to their congregations, where it was disseminated as truth, resulting in the great confusion of many sisters and the general detriment of their religious institutes. In many cases, rather than promoting the actual teachings of the Second Vatican Council, the Sister Formation Movement instead helped spread misinformation and false interpretation of the Council documents which resulted in the chaos in women's orders described in the next chapter.

9: How Did Feminists Gain Control?

"Every element, every assumption, every custom, every jot and tittle of the rule, no matter how longstanding and sacrosanct, became refreshingly suspect, tiringly suspect. Here was a social scouring of immense proportions, one of the most total in social history, perhaps."[1]

Sister Joan Chittister, OSB

Many sisters who did not favor deviation from the essential elements of religious life attempted to steer their orders along the pathway defined by the Vatican II documents and by the various statements and documents coming out of Rome. However, these sisters were often reprimanded or belittled for being old-fashioned or unwilling to accept change when they expressed concern about many of the radical transformations being introduced rapidly into their communities. So, if many sisters were not in favor of unmitigated change, how did some of these changes get approved by their orders? How did progressive feminists get elected to positions of authority in congregations that are populated by a majority of women who are decidedly not at all inclined toward the gender feminists' agenda?

Skilled organizers and vulnerable institutions

The answers to these questions seem to follow the same patterns. As we have seen, religious institutes of women were badly in need of updating and reforming by the time Vatican II called for renewal. Since many orders were in this weakened condition, they were vulnerable to take-over by activists determined to modernize their communities. The problem was not with modernization — that was a necessity long overdue. The problem was that the renewal desired and promoted by some Religious was not what Vatican II had envisioned and subsequently mandated; rather it was excessive reform created by individuals who saw renewal as an opportunity to liberate sisters from male oppression and to forward some specific sociopolitical agendas at the expense of the spiritual aspects of religious life. Not surprisingly, the cultural upheaval of the 1960s offered the perfect setting for this quiet revolution in religious life.

Often the sisters who were being groomed for leadership roles were sent on for higher education or continuing formation programs, which brought these sisters into contact with questionable theologies and revolutionary views on how religious life should be transformed. Many of these sisters also became knowledgeable about community organization and political action, and they learned how to promote with great skill their desired agenda, especially among women who were primarily teachers, nurses, and social workers with little political acumen. Furthermore, the average sister was too trusting that superiors would always make the right decisions and that all institute members would respect those decisions. Thus, the activist sisters, who often were the most educated sisters in their orders, were able to push through the reforms they wanted.

Sister Maureen Fiedler, who transferred to the Loretto Sisters from the Sisters of Mercy because she "wanted to be part of a women's community challenging the church from within ecclesial structures,"[2] wrote about the importance of political savvy when it came to affecting change in religious institutes: "The spring and summer of 1968 introduced me to an important skill: political organizing. Those of us who wanted fundamental change in community structures held late night meetings in basements, developed phone networks to keep allies informed, and learned the importance of setting agendas, preparing proposals in advance, and determining who would speak most effectively for our point of view."[3]

Obviously, the average sister who was preoccupied with her job and prayer life did not have time for such political networking, nor did she develop the skills to recognize or counteract political maneuvering when it occurred in her community.H

Also influencing women Religious in the 1960s was the concept of liberation theology, which had its roots in Latin America. The liberation theology movement emphasized the Christian commitment to the poor and criticized "sinful structures" within society. Many orders of women Religious had generously responded to Pope John XXIII's 1961 request for American Religious to send missionaries to Latin America. When some of these American sisters rotated back home to their congregations, they brought with them an experience — and belief — in liberation theology. And liberation theology's emphasis on liberating the poor and oppressed connected readily to the emerging tide of feminism and the desire of some women to liberate themselves from what they saw as male domination of the Church.

Mercy Sister Janet Ruffing has explained that "Feminist theology is liberation theology done from the perspective of women's experiences."[4] But, a 1984-86 study of liberation theology by the Vatican's Congregation for the Doctrine of the Faith expressed serious reservations about some aspects of the liberation theology movement, including elements of Marxism and a narrow understanding of the term liberation.

This liberation theme also dovetailed with a growing philosophy among some Religious in the 1960s that social justice — not spirituality — should be the foundation of religious life. This emphasis on liberation and social justice, almost to the exclusion of spirituality, was contained in the Sisters' Survey and is reflected in many constitutions and decrees written during the 1960s and 1970s. Sister Marie Augusta Neal, creator of the Sisters' Survey, observed in 1990 that "the work of the sisters on their constitutions focused . . . on the implementation of the new agenda calling for a critical social analysis of existing political, economic and social systems . . . even the structures of the church itself."[5] A preoccupation with working with the poor also explains why many congregations withdrew their sisters from Catholic schools where sisters perceived that many of the students tended to come from the middle class or the wealthy.

Unfortunately, some sisters did not grasp the Vatican II message that renewal included figuring out ways to address these pressing social issues while at the same time preserving the heritage, nature, and work of the religious institute. Certainly, some orders renewed in just this fashion, but too many sisters felt they had to discard the traditions and apostolate of their institute in order to become modern Religious attuned to the needs of the world.

Election maneuvering

This transformation of many orders of women Religious often occurred while the majority of the sisters in that order were hundreds of miles away from their motherhouses, doing the jobs they were assigned to do. Many sisters also lacked information about Vatican II documents and other legislation about religious life because this data was not made available to the sisters by their superiors; rather the sisters were often given only an interpretation of the document by a superior. Sisters tended not to question this practice, because they had always trusted their superiors previously, and it did not occur to them to seek out and read the original Vatican II documents and other legislation themselves. Most sisters simply did not realize anything was amiss until it was too late to do anything about the situation.

One Sister of St. Joseph, who had been a teacher and principal for several years in a Catholic school her order staffed in another state, said she didn't notice what had happened in her congregation until she received an assignment that brought her back to the motherhouse. Only after she returned to the motherhouse did she realize that the leadership in her order had been taken over by gender feminists who resisted direction from the Vatican while pursuing a model of religious life quite foreign to the majority of sisters in the order.

Sisters also began to see maneuvering in election processes for chapter delegates and for officers of their congregations.

Chapters are general meetings of a religious order usually held about every three to five years for the purpose of electing leaders and determining important business of the community, such as constitutional changes. Delegates to the chapter are elected by sisters in the community, but the selection process for delegates differs from congregation to congregation. Canon law provides that all vowed members of a religious institute have "active voice" — the right to participate in governance by voting. Professed members also have "passive voice" — the right to run for election to office. Chapter delegates usually elect officers of the institute. All elections are supposed to be secret, according to canon law, but some sisters from various institutes have reported elections by telephone and by numbered ballots which would reveal who was casting the vote.

Direct election of superiors had not been the past practice of most religious institutes before Vatican II, but generally sisters felt they had adequate input in choosing superiors and making their wishes known to the chapter, and these rights are guaranteed by canon law. Generally, too, sisters felt they could elect delegates to the chapter who would be aware of the common good of the community, and thus represent the nature, spirit, and character of the institute at the chapter meetings.

This changed in many communities when leadership teams came into existence after Vatican II. Often that team — or a committee appointed by the leadership team — acts as a nominating committee, determines the election process, runs the election, as well as plans and conducts the chapter.

The result in some orders is that the same leaders simply play musical chairs year after year in the various leadership positions, with very little chance of new players being admitted to the game. (Indeed, leadership teams themselves are canonically questionable, as canon law directs that personal authority resides in a superior; however, some constitutions of women Religious empower a superior to act only in concert with her council or leadership team.)

In many congregations which have a large proportion of elderly, the vote of the elderly sisters is diluted considerably when voting is done by age blocks, for blocks of elderly usually have more numbers in them than blocks of younger sisters. Some of these blocks may be determined by years in the community, and some may be determined by place of residence.

For example, one general chapter set up voting blocks of sisters according to their years in religious life in this way: 50 and over; 45-49; 40-44; 35-39; 30-34; 25-29; 20-24; 15-19; 10-14; and less than 10 years.[6] Obviously, the age blocks that have the largest numbers have less representation than those blocks with small numbers. This may have been a fairly even distribution in 1969, when this particular model was used, but as the median age of sisters has risen to the upper 60s, the elderly have less representation when voting is done this way.

Determining voting blocks by living units, as some orders do, still dilutes the vote of the elderly, as the elderly tend to live in retirement communities of twenty or more sisters. When voting by living units, such a large community of elderly might have the same representation as a smaller unit of younger sisters (which may be a combination of several households) of perhaps only six or seven.

Commenting on this practice, a Sister of St. Joseph who is a member of her provincial leadership team explained that the elderly have a shorter future in the community than do the younger members, so it is appropriate for the younger sisters who will be around for many more years to have a greater voice. Thus, some religious institutes believe it is logical to dilute the voting power of the retired members, and this explains how some of the constitutional changes in religious institutes were effected, even though most of the elderly sisters did not endorse those changes.

Another issue is group dynamics. Once the chapter meeting convenes, sisters report that often a group psychology is at work where delegates are pressured to come around to support the politically correct viewpoint. Often the sisters who are skilled in group dynamics are able to manipulate those who are less sophisticated.

Another difficulty at the chapters is that delegates often feel intimidated by their more vocal colleagues. Holy Cross Sister Rose Eileen Masterman wrote of her order's 1973 chapter that "certain minority groups in Chapter can manage to turn the thinking of many other sincere capitulants [delegates]."[7] Admittedly, after Vatican II, there were some immovable sisters who wanted no changes at all, not even those mandated by Rome. But even sisters who were eager to follow Rome's directives often found themselves being derided by others for being too "conservative" or resistant to change or behind the times or indoctrinated by patriarchy.

In 1977, eighty-eight sisters from one province sent a letter to the members of their general chapter about their concerns regarding several issues, including the lack of regulations about a habit, a weak formation program, a wasteful and multi-layered bureaucracy, and questionable provincial-chapter decisions. The sisters expressed their consternation that chapter delegates seemed to represent in chapter not the common good of the majority of sisters, but rather their own opinions.[8]

A friend of Sister Rose Eileen Masterman wrote her on November 15, 1980, with information about her own provincial chapter meeting. The sister wrote Sister Rose Eileen that she was afraid to sign her name lest the letter would fall into the wrong hands, and she had the letter hand-carried by a mutual friend because she had reason to believe her mail was being tampered with. The sister sent a transcript of an audio-tape of her provincial meeting in August of 1980. In the transcript, a leader explains to the chapter that the comments of the pope that Religious should wear a habit were merely opinion and not directives, so secular dress for the sisters was permissible. (The superior did not address the fact that canon law directs that the pope is the highest ecclesiastical superior of any Religious, and Religious owe him their obedience; nor did she admit that canon law directs that all Religious must wear religious garb.) And when a sister at the meeting complained that she was having a hard time reconciling *Perfectae Caritatis* and the statements of the pope with the actual practices of her order, since the order seemed to just pick and choose what it wished, the superior replied that she could not address the sister's concerns without having specific examples.

The letter writer concluded: "There were delegates in the Chapter at the time experimentation was supposed to begin who tried hard to get it set up properly and the more powerful and domineering ones ignored them and ramrodded everything the way they wanted it and left the majority of us suffering ever since. That chapter is referred to by some as the INFAMOUS ONE! During the past 10 years the majority seems to have joined the powerful ones because they couldn't beat them, it was easier to join them."[9]

With few exceptions, most religious institutes of women had trained their sisters (before Vatican II) to be docile and unquestionably obedient, so when a superior suggested changes that the sisters might not have agreed with, they were not inclined to vote against the superior's wishes. Nor were they inclined even to question what the superior was suggesting. Sisters in general trusted their superiors implicitly, and they usually felt that the superior never would misinform them. Indeed, one sister recalls that when sweeping changes were being promoted in her own congregation which went far beyond the guidelines of Vatican II, a well-liked superior exploited her leadership position by making the rounds to each of the elderly sisters, lobbying for the changes. Because the elderly sisters trusted this superior and wanted to please her, many of them went along with her wishes without really understanding, analyzing, or agreeing with the proposed changes.

A priest Religious who has observed the chapter meetings of several religious orders as well as his own, has noted a certain "psychology of large meetings" in chapters. He reported that this psychology builds up so that individuals want to be upbeat, politically correct, with the times, and they are reluctant to vote "no," especially when proposed changes are cloaked in pleasant terms.

This psychology of large meetings also was reported by a sister who attended a recent chapter meeting of her institute. Everyone present at the chapter meeting — including non-delegates and lay persons who were not members of the institute and did not have the right to vote — was given a color-coded card to indicate "pro" or "con" on matters considered by the chapter. A "straw vote" was taken, in which everyone present was invited to hold up her card, indicating her opinion on the issues. Then, the meeting was adjourned for a coffee break — and for lobbying efforts — and after the break, the delegates then cast the actual vote by holding up the appropriate card. While on the surface this process seems to be a congenial exercise in consensus building, in actual practice it was an effort to pressure delegates to vote for the majority position of those casting the straw vote, even though some of those people did not have voting rights and did not even belong to the institute.

Sister (Thomas Aquinas) Elizabeth Carroll, former superior of the Sisters of Mercy of Pittsburgh (and member of the Sisters' Survey Committee and 1972 president of the Leadership Conference of Women Religious), wrote that her order's special renewal chapter "completely altered almost all the accidentals of our life together." And, "In the end, we had almost total unanimity from the delegates on the final decision. Unfortunately less than ten percent of the congregation immediately shared in this excitement, struggle and agreement."[10]

Sisters in Crisis

When fewer than ten percent of the sisters in a religious institute are happy with the chapter decisions of an order, how well is the common good of a congregation represented?

Additionally, some of the pre-chapter exercises which allegedly "prepare" members of the institute for the upcoming chapter are quite questionable. Some of those preparation sessions, as well as some of the processes orchestrated by facilitators during chapter meetings, have become highly sophisticated psychological exercises that suggest the possibility of thought reform and manipulation rather than the guarantee by canon law that all members of the institute must have free input into the chapter. In fact, "facilitating" chapter meetings has become a burgeoning industry, particularly among former sisters, who have had firsthand experience in chapters. These "consultants" find themselves in high demand, and some are quite skilled at seeing to it that chapters arrive at conclusions preordained by the people who have hired the consultant.

In a 1994 article in *Review for Religious*, Jesuit Father David Coughlan, a consultant on organizational development, discussed one chilling model of conducting an assembly or a chapter of a religious institute that conjures up images of cult-like intimidation.

Father Coughlan spoke of "targeting" individuals and the need to arouse "guilt" or "anxiety" in delegates in order to accomplish goals. He outlined the process of change, describing the first stage as "unfreezing," or creating the motivation in members to change. This is the most difficult stage of the process, Father Coughlan explained, because "for effective unfreezing to occur the following elements must be present: 1) the present state is somewhat disconfirmed; 2) sufficient anxiety or guilt is aroused because some goals will not be met or standards not be achieved; 3) sufficient 'psychological safety' is provided to make it unnecessary for the target individuals or teams to psychologically defend themselves because the disconfirming information is too threatening or the anxiety or guilt is too high." The essence of effective unfreezing, Father Coughlan wrote, is "a balancing of enough disconfirmation to arouse a sufficient level of anxiety or guilt and to provide enough support, direction, and help so that the system feels sufficiently safe to confront and act on the problem." Some Religious, he observed, will exhibit denial and try to avoid change or to remain on the edge of change. "In religious life, many have opted to remain in this mode and have in effect opted out of the contemporary developments of religious life."

The second stage of the process described by Father Coughlan is "changing." Once people are "unfrozen," they are more likely to pay attention to information, ideas, suggestions, and orders and are more active problem solvers "because they are uncomfortable." The final stage is "refreezing," which Father Coughlan wrote is "more about ensuring the change survives than about creating stability."[11]

Invalid chapter meetings?

Canon law designates that only professed members of a religious institute have the right to participate in governance of the institute. They formerly did this by voting for chapter delegates and by making suggestions to the chapter. Now some religious institutes have adopted what they call "total participation," which means every sister supposedly actually "participates" in the chapter, and each sister can choose her degree of participation. While total participation sounds quite democratic on paper, this participation may range from praying for the success of the chapter, to serving on planning committees, or to acting as a chapter delegate. The canonical problem with this model is that the chapter delegates are thus self-appointed, and sisters unable to serve as delegate thus have no voice.

As canonist Sister Elizabeth McDonough explained in her *Review for Religious* "Canonical Counsel" column, this total participation model tends "to minimize or to eliminate entirely even the possibility of 'active' participation by members who happen to be elderly or ill or stationed at a distance or unable to serve on committees and attend numerous meetings. This, in turn, results in arbitrary curtailment or elimination of the acquired right of these members to participate in the governance of their institute in a juridic manner. Since those who are elderly or ill currently often comprise a large portion of the membership of religious institutes, a significant number of religious in institutes and provinces are actually subtly disenfranchised by these supposedly 'full' participation methods of conducting chapters."

Sister Elizabeth added that each Religious has the canonical right to submit specific proposals to the chapter. However, some religious institutes establish procedures in which a steering committee attempts to bring sisters to a "prechapter consensus," and the chapter simply rubber stamps the consensus that had been hammered out before the meeting. Sister Elizabeth cautioned that such practices "cannot validly or legally be enacted and implemented if these procedures totally eliminate the possibility of an individual religious actually submitting matters to the chapters."[12] Yet, Medical Mission Sister Catherine M. Harmer, a consultant and facilitator for religious chapters, observed in 1994 that "so many chapters now use consensus that actual voting is not common any more."[13]

Jesuit Father Richard A. Hill, a canon lawyer, has expressed similar concerns about the freedom and validity of the consensus style of election that has been used in some women's institutes. Father Hill wrote in *Review for Religious* that sometimes pre-chapter committees consider themselves empowered to create election procedures. This is not valid, Father Hill wrote, for "the election procedures most recently approved by a general chapter are to be followed." Of course, chapter decisions are subject to canon law, and he warned that any process that inhibits the rights of individual Religious to participate in governance renders an election invalid, and invalidly elected superiors cannot act validly on any subsequent matters of the religious institute. While presenting slates of candidates to a chapter is licit, Father Hill wrote, "it is never allowed that the members of the chapter are obligated to limit their votes to these preselected members of the community." In addition, he stressed that votes of each member must be secret, and he wrote: "It is my opinion, but only my personal opinion, that presenting slates of candidates or teams, rather than conducting distinct elections of superiors and of individual councilors, illegitimately restricts the active voice of the members of the community or of the chapter, quite apart from its unsavory similarity to civil elections in some parts of the world.

"Predetermining candidates for office by means of a pre-chapter process of arriving at consensus or discernment, as it is sometimes called, may very well curtail or even deny the eligibility of many members to be elected. When this is done by persuading certain persons to forego their eligibility, their passive voice, in the interest of consensus or unity, the freedom and even the secrecy of a subsequent election has to be called into serious question."[14]

Who belongs?

Another canonical problem turning up at chapter meetings is that some religious communities started to allow so-called associate members or co-members — lay people who want to be closely associated with the spirituality and work of the institute — to participate in chapter meetings or to serve on committees that impact the governance of an institute. However, canon law precludes anyone other than a vowed member from participating directly in the governance of an institute. Yet, Sisters of Mercy associate, Karen Schwarz, observed in 1991 that "Many co-members live or affiliate with sisters in congregational living groups. . . . Some co-members serve on congregational committees, many work in congregational ministries and sit on boards of congregationally sponsored institutions, and most attend and participate in congregational meetings. Many participate in congregational discernment. . . ."

". . . These new forms, however, are not without their problems. . . . It is difficult for some sisters to feel comfortable with nonvowed members, especially with women in married or committed relationships with men. . . . Some sisters feel threatened as associates/co-members are included in congregational business. Many fear that the associates/co-members will be gone tomorrow, after having made unwise decisions about already short congregational assets and taking private congregational information with them."[15]

Some sisters also resent funds from their congregation being used for individual projects of co-members or associates which may be worthwhile, but are totally unrelated to religious life, such as building houses for Habitat for Humanity. Also of concern to some sisters is the alleged transferring of congregational funds to lay co-members in anticipation of the possibility that some members of the congregation may eventually decide to form noncanonical communities, and thus already have a funding base in place that would not have to be approved by the Vatican. Many sisters also resent the employment of large numbers of lay co-members or associates by a congregation when there are sisters within the institute who could fill the position given to the lay person with less expenditure of congregational funds.

In addition to allowing lay associate members some voice in congregational governance, some women's institutes also have placed associates or co-members in leadership roles. Canon law requires that only a vowed Religious may be a superior, but that canon is circumvented by using other titles, such as coordinator.

The outgoing president of the Leadership Conference of Women Religious told the Conference's annual assembly in 1995 that "We seem to be clear that associates participate with vowed members in spirituality and mission. Tensions arise, however, when some of us believe that associates should participate in our internal forum, having equal access with vowed members to decision making about our lives together without having the same accountability to live the consequences."[16]

While the connection of associates to a religious institute may have some benefits for all involved, the associate category nevertheless carries with it the possibility of blurring the distinction between religious life and non-vowed secular life. Pope John Paul II referred to this concern in his 1996 apostolic exhortation *Vita Consecrata,* when he wrote that integrating lay associates into a religious institute "should always be done in such a way that the identity of the institute in its internal life is not harmed."[17] Still, religious institutes of women who are in decline seem to believe their associate programs will insure survival of the order, even though the order no longer is able to attract vowed members. However, this attitude betrays a basic misunderstanding of the nature of religious life, as associate members can never be considered actual members of a religious institute.

Father David F. O'Connor, canon lawyer and a priest of the Missionary Servants of the Most Holy Trinity, wrote that ". . . Lay volunteers, associates or affiliates are not members of the institute. It is misleading to apply that term to them. They have none of the rights or obligations of members in the institute. . . . It seems best not to speak of them as members but only as volunteers, associates, affiliates, or some similar term."[18] However, religious institutes of women seem oblivious to this fact, for Vincentian Father David Nygren, a psychologist, found in a 1988 survey of seven hundred forty leaders of religious institutes that seventy percent of the female leaders were "adapting their membership to include full or partial membership by laity."[19]

The Loretto Sisters were the first to use the term co-member, starting that program in 1970. In announcing the new Loretto program, the *Trans-Sister* newsletter defined the co-membership category as a new form of membership in a congregation that extends affiliation to women who want to be associated with the congregation's mission, but do not want to accept the canonical restrictions of a vowed Religious.[20] The first four applicants for Loretto co-membership were two former nuns and two current Loretto nuns who were seeking dispensation from their vows.[21]

The Congregation for Religious continues to express discomfort about the nature of the co-member program of the Sisters of Loretto, including a concern that the Loretto Sisters may be trying to create a new form of religious life by integrating the co-members so intimately into their institute. In November of 1995, the undersecretary of the Congregation for Religious wrote Loretto president Sister Mary Ann Coyle about a "continued concern regarding the involvement of the Loretto Co-Members in the life of the Congregation. . . . Our concern is caused by the involvement of co-members in community living situations, in the community groups and in the General Assembly. Actually the norm quoted [by Sister Mary Ann from the Loretto procedures book in an earlier letter] reserving canonical and financial matters to the Sisters of Loretto does not seem adequate as a recognition that co-members do not have a right to participate in the governance of the religious institute."[22]

The bitter fruit of renewal chapters

Certainly, through their renewal chapters and various experiments, some religious institutes managed to effect a version of renewal fully in compliance with the Vatican II documents and other pertinent legislation. But too many institutes apparently exceeded the limits of valid experimentation, and brought confusion and chaos when they discarded so many of their former practices and traditions and even the basic purposes for their institutes, and then put very little in place to fill the gap.

In writing about "The Democratization of Religious Life" in 1970, Jesuit Father Thomas J. Casey observed: "Old structures have been abolished and little social support remains to underlay the religious life. Religious communities increasingly resemble boarding houses rather than communities. . . . Change is one thing, but change that proceeds at an unreasonable pace or that substitutes nothing reasonable for what it has destroyed can hardly be considered progress.

". . . So far more adeptness has been shown in destroying all forms and structures, in abolishing traditional symbols and expressions, than in creating new and viable ones. One therefore legitimately suspects that fundamental values in the religious life are under attack. . . ."[23]

Canonist Father David O'Connor wrote in 1990 that Religious were not adequately prepared for the renewal period: "They lacked, frequently, a sense of history — an understanding of what had gone before. Their theological acumen was often too minimal or outrightly deficient. Psychologically, they were forced out of a rigid and tightly-controlled lifestyle into a new-found freedom that appeared, at times, to overwhelm many of them in a variety of ways. Some of their brothers and sisters escaped from the confusion and instability of the times and sought dispensations. Change in the church became a way of life. It took place while the west, especially North America, was going through its own cultural and social revolution. It soured many on institutions, structures, authority, law and order."[24]

10: The Deconstruction of Ministry, Community, and Prayer

"Making religion a career logically calls for a 'religious form of life,' i.e., one in which the principal structures and practices give witness to what transcends the world."[1]

Sister Mary Anne Huddleston, IHM

The souring of many women Religious "on institutions, structures, authority, law and order" described at the end of the last chapter by Father O'Connor profoundly affected the lives of women Religious, even more than their male counterparts, for, with the exception of brothers, the men Religious had the identity of the priesthood to sustain and anchor them. But women Religious suffered a significant identity crisis, a crisis that affected every aspect of their lives, from their spiritual life to their community life to their apostolic life.

Institutes of active women Religious are supposed to have specific apostolates undertaken in the name of the Church. And, as Father O'Connor has written, "The exercise of the apostolate by religious is never entirely a private and personal ministry. It is always, in some sense, a public and corporate one." Further, "Religious are always to be subject to their own superiors and to the local bishop in the exercise of all forms of the external apostolate."[2] (Canon 674 states: "Apostolic action, to be exercised in the name and by the mandate of the Church, is to be carried out in its communion.")

The breakdown of ministry

Traditionally, the apostolates of religious orders were performed within the framework of Catholic institutions. Many sisters were Catholic school teachers; some worked in health care; some in social services; and some in parishes and diocesan programs. However, under the influence of the feminist movement and some of the other social movements of the 1960s, some sisters began to believe that they were simply preaching to the choir by teaching Catholic children in Catholic schools or by being confined behind the walls of Catholic institutions, even though many of the people they served in those institutions indeed were victims of poverty, prejudice, and oppression. Many sisters felt their time would be better spent working with adults or children who were not enrolled in Catholic schools. Some of these sisters even felt that to be true evangelizers, sisters were called to work among the nonbelievers, the poor, the afflicted, and the addicted (as suggested by the Sisters' Survey).

Certainly the ministry of women Religious needed to be better adapted to the needs of the times, and many women Religious really had little knowledge about the needs of the forgotten members of society. The problem was, some sisters seemed to be convinced they had to deconstruct their religious institutes in order to serve the poor, and some felt that their institutes could not serve both the Catholic population and the poor and non-Catholic population at the same time. Others felt that their energies were better spent on ministries they identified themselves, rather than on a corporate ministry adopted by the institute.

Sister Joan Chittister, who was president of the Leadership Conference of Women Religious 1976-77, explained this new philosophy of religious life in this way: "For all practical purposes, the task that most [religious] communities came to this country to do had — with the ascension of John F. Kennedy to the presidency of the United States — been completed. Through the school system, the faith had been preserved in a strange land; Catholics had been inserted into a Protestant culture; the church had a tightly organized catechetical base and major institutional system. But whole new pockets of poor and oppressed people have arisen in this society and women Religious are attempting to start all over again with the same bias toward the poor of this generation." Somehow, Sister Joan rationalized that the poor could be helped only by the deconstruction of the traditional forms of religious life. She wrote that in order for Religious to serve the poor, ". . . we have to put a lot of things down: so-called religious garb, institutionalism, withdrawal, a common apostolate in favor of corporate commitments to global issues of peace, poverty, hunger, minority concerns, human rights and the equality of women."[3] However, history has proved that women Religious can very effectively serve the oppressed within the structure of their institute, as Mother Teresa's Missionaries of Charity have demonstrated. Additionally, sociologists have observed that organizations are usually better able to perform their services from a strong corporate base.[4]

Sister Joan's philosophy has been echoed by other women Religious who answered the legitimate call of Vatican II to make religious life less authoritarian, but rather than implementing reasonable reforms, they threw off all semblance of authority and eventually discarded most of the traditions of their religious institutes, even the reasonable ones, including the apostolate that the institute had always performed. Gone with the structure and traditions was the specific end or purpose of the institute, even though Vatican II decrees stressed that the purpose of the institute must be preserved.

One sister in a teaching order recalled that in the late 1960s and early 1970s her community went to a policy called "open placement." Previously, sisters had received their September teaching assignments as late as August and often had little time to prepare themselves to travel to assigned duties about which they had no input whatsoever. Nor did they always have sufficient notice to familiarize themselves with new text books or prepare themselves for classes they may not ever have taught before. So, the new open placement policy was welcomed by the sisters. With the new policy, assignments were agreed upon in consultation between the sister and her superiors, and then the sister was "missioned" to her area of ministry.

This sister felt that this new concept worked quite well, and the sisters enjoyed and appreciated having some input regarding which assignments they felt competent to undertake, while still adhering to their vows of obedience. However, before long, this scenario of consultation soon deteriorated into sisters "doing their own thing" without consulting superiors. Since the mission of the congregation was education, some sisters undertook work which they rationalized was educational, such as selling encyclopedias, working on political campaigns, and working in travel agencies. And superiors did not stand in their way. This sister observed, "We have a saying in our congregation to describe our so-called 'freedom.' It is said that if a sister decides that going to hell might be fulfilling for her, the leadership will pay her way, generously, and never check on her again!"

College English professor Sister Marcella Marie Holloway, a Sister of St.

Joseph, voiced her concern about such excesses and abuses in a 1974 article in *Liguorian* magazine. She wrote of her admiration for a sister colleague who stayed to teach because she felt obligated to do so after her community supported her education to obtain graduate degrees. But she also wrote about other sister-teachers who were searching endlessly for other careers, and living off the working sisters in the community while they conducted this search. "For us who remain [in teaching], it is often difficult to reconcile a Sister's release for study, for training in a specific area, and then her coming home to announce after six years that 'teaching is not her thing' and so another release period of training for another kind of work, ad infinitum."[5]

Indeed, Catholic sisters are the most educated group of women in the United States, probably even in the world. But how much of that education is now obtained to serve the needs of the Church or of society or of the sisters' religious institutes? And, while the professional interests of sisters may change over time, just as the needs of society change, are there some jobs that are not suitable for Religious, who through their public vows and membership in canonical religious institutes, are representatives of the Catholic Church?

A 1980 *Our Sunday Visitor* article enumerated some of the professions nuns were engaged in at that time: a Daughter of Charity headed the secular American Hospital Association, and a sister in Vermont was a public school principal. Sisters in Arizona and Rhode Island were state representatives, and a Sister of Charity of the Blessed Virgin Mary was mayor of Dubuque, Iowa.[6] (The 1917 *Code of Canon Law* allowed Religious to hold political office with appropriate permissions. However, the 1983 code contains a generic prohibition against Religious holding public office which involves civil jurisdiction.)

Today, sisters are engaged in even more diverse occupations, which raises the question of how such diversity can reflect a corporate apostolate that serves the Church. For example, among the occupations listed for sisters in the 1993-94 Sisters of Loretto (a teaching order) directory were: public school teacher; teacher and cosmetologist; receptionist for Apple Computer; public school computer specialist; farm worker ministry; self-employed family counselor; oncology program manager at a Baptist hospital; fund-raiser for Save our Cumberland Mountains; clinical psychologist; staff attorney for legal aid society; self-employed law librarian; organizational and financial consultant; certified enneagram consultant; public library employee; therapeutic touch practitioner; area manager for World Book Educational Products; and self-employed insurance executive. One Loretto sister even listed her occupation as "resisting patriarchy."

Sisters in Crisis

School Sister of Notre Dame Margaret Ellen (Mary Peter) Traxler (a founder of the National Coalition of American Nuns) noted that "In 1965, when I began work in another province of my community and worked at an independent agency, our community directory showed that I was only one of several Notre Dame Sisters working thus. Now, 20 years later, our community directory shows hundreds of our sisters working apart from the formal institutions of convent and church."[7]

Ironically, along with this trend for sisters to self-select their jobs, there also was a devaluing of "domestic" work done by sisters. Even though some sisters preferred to be the "home-makers" for the order, supervising the kitchen and laundry and attending to all of the other details necessary for operating an institution, this concept of service was no longer acceptable to some institutes of women Religious. Instead, lay people were hired for domestic tasks, and young women who were not academically suited for, or personally interested in, higher education degrees were turned away as potential members of many orders.

The trend of sisters self-selecting their jobs also impacted those sisters who wished to continue doing the traditional work of their institutes. For, often a religious institute had to withdraw its sisters from a school or hospital or social service institution since it could make no guarantee that enough sisters would make themselves available to staff the positions. Complex financial and demographic factors — some of which were linked to a shortage of sisters — also forced the closing of many Catholic institutions where sisters traditionally worked. Thus, even sisters who wished to remain in their traditional apostolates often found themselves without a place to work because their institute had withdrawn from or sold the institution traditionally staffed by that order.

Sisters — many of whom were middle-aged or approaching retirement age — thus found themselves in the entirely new position of having to seek and apply for jobs, not to mention having to find living quarters, since the jobs available were not always within commuting distance of a convent, even if the sister could find a convent still open and with any empty rooms. Consequently, many sisters became alienated from their institutes simply because of distance.

This new wrinkle raised another problem for the sisters — unemployment — a phenomenon never before experienced by nuns.

Mercy Sister Georgine M. Scarpino, a research consultant and former employment director for the Job Training Partnership Act Program, reported in 1988 that unemployment among sisters exceeded the national unemployment rate.[8] This is indeed an ironic situation when most administrators of Catholic institutions would be delighted to have a sister on staff. But, there is a problem of matching the open position with the qualifications — and desires — of available sisters. It is a fact, too, that unlike unemployed lay persons, an unemployed sister usually can maintain a roof over her head and food on her table through the support of her community. So sisters often do not feel the same financial pressures as lay persons to take jobs which may not fit their ideal of what "the Spirit" is calling them to do.

One other difficulty encountered by Religious choosing individual ministries is their income tax status. When Religious were engaged in the work of their institutes in Church-related positions, they were exempt from income tax. However, when Religious moved into jobs with secular entities, they no longer automatically enjoyed that tax-exempt status, even when assigned to those jobs by their orders. The federal government has tended to apply the tax laws much more strictly in the last several years, and many court rulings on the taxability of clergy and Religious have occurred since 1979. Furthermore, tax lawyers warn that as more and more members of a religious institute choose secular occupations, the tax-exempt status of the institute itself is placed in jeopardy. One potential outcome of having a large number of members employed outside Catholic institutions is that the religious institute could be interpreted as being in the "business" of loaning employees. If this determination is made by the government and upheld in the courts, then the institute could be taxed on the profits of that "business."[9]

Perhaps the most significant and ominous result of the trend for sisters to determine their own work is that their religious institutes lost their corporate identity when they opted for this occupational diversity.

According to the largest study ever done of American Religious, this lack of corporate identity has had a huge impact on the ability of religious institutes to sustain the loyalty of Religious and to attract new vocations. Sister of St. Joseph Miriam Ukeritis and Vincentian Father David Nygren, both psychologists, spent three years gathering and analyzing data from 10,000 men and women Religious from 816 congregations that had a total of 121,000 members. In September of 1992 they released the results of that study, called "Future of Religious Orders in the United States" (FORUS). Regarding corporate identity, they concluded that orders which do not have a clearly defined mission do not attract new members. And, an emphasis on individual ministry has "eclipsed the symbolism of and statement previously made by corporate commitments."

This individualism also impacted the relationship of the Religious to her institute and to the Catholic Church, the study found: "Many religious have migrated to the periphery of their congregation, often living lives that reflect significant ministerial contributions but which have little to do with their congregations or religious life." Thus, "The loss of conviction about the vows, lack of clarity about the role of religious, reactance [sic] to authority, lack of corporate mission and ministry, and disillusionment with leadership pose significant threats to the future of religious life."[10] The FORUS study found that orders which appear to be rebounding or stabilizing have carefully reinstated monastic practices and a sense of clarity regarding their life and work.

Community life disintegrates

As this diversity in apostolates and trend toward open placement became widespread in some religious institutes, community life was inevitably affected. When Religious shared a community apostolate, they lived with other members of their community in large or small groups. Living in community, they shared a common life, meals together, the daily Eucharist, common prayer, and an ongoing relationship with the sisters in their community. Sisters living apart from their community indeed were rare exceptions, and a concerted effort was made to keep those sisters in frequent contact with their order.

However, when sisters within congregations began to choose diverse ministries, daily schedules varied considerably, and it became more common for sisters to live closer to their work. Indeed, many sisters took jobs in locations where their religious institute did not even have a presence, so they began to live alone, with sisters of other religious institutes, or with lay people.

Some sisters moved away from their communities even when their institute maintained a convent in the same city because they did not want to continue living a common life. Immaculate Heart of Mary Sister Sandra Schneiders calls this phenomenon "psychological-spiritual." According to Sister Sandra, "As religious become more aware of the uniqueness of personality and of the different needs an individual has at various stages of human growth and spiritual development, they are less hesitant to recognize that lifestyle is an important factor in mental and spiritual health. . . . Increasing numbers of religious have good personal and spiritual reasons for choosing lifestyles other than the traditional one, at least at certain periods of their lives, and they will increasingly insist that those choices be honoured."[11]

Prior to Vatican II, it is true that most religious institutes did not pay much attention to the psychological or social needs of members, and sisters who were burned out or unable to cope with the demands of common life were usually sent off on retreat for a week or just told to pray about their difficulties. But there is a great deal of middle ground between ignoring the psychological and social needs of a sister and giving sisters complete *carte blanche* to select their own style of life. Religious institutes can exercise sensitivity toward the changing needs of their members while still expecting those members to adhere to certain standards of the institute. This penchant displayed by some Religious to "do their own thing" surely has alienated some lay persons who also grow weary of their lifestyles from time to time. However, few lay people feel that they can justify leaving a spouse and children behind whenever they feel the need for more private space. And few lay persons can afford individual residences for all the members of their family.

Sisters often have little choice about where they live. Many communities have sold most of their property for a variety of legitimate reasons: they needed the money; their numbers had dwindled and they didn't need the space; the old buildings were too expensive to maintain; or they felt it somehow was not a proper witness to poverty to own buildings. But some other philosophies also motivated sisters to sell off their property, some of them based on a strange interpretation of religious life.

For example, Sister Dorothy Vidulich indicated that owning property somehow inhibited the sisters' ability to pursue their ministry. She wrote that her congregation, the Sisters of St. Joseph of Peace, was committed to work for justice locally and globally, so: "Sensitive to the need to divest ourselves of excess property, we sold our motherhouse with its acres of land. . . ."[12] Sister of Mercy Doris Gottemoeller (president of the Leadership Conference of Women in Religious 1993-94) felt that the only acceptable reason for keeping institutions was to serve the poor: "If sponsorship of institutions is to continue to be a way to realize the mission of religious life, it must be because we are able to enlist them as powerful instruments on the side of the poor, to alter the oppressive structures in society which perpetuate poverty."[13]

Some of this "alienation of property," as it is referred to in canon law, was done without the necessary permissions of higher Church authority. Current canon law requires that property owned by church entities, including religious institutes, cannot be sold without Vatican approval if the property is valued at more than three million dollars. (This figure was unrealistically lower in the 1960s and 1970s, when many Church institutions were sold or converted to secular entities.) The reason behind requiring these permissions is to safeguard Church property, much of which has been acquired by religious institutes operating as official representatives of the

Church, and often has been acquired through the donations of the faithful who expect religious institutions to operate in service to the Church. Vatican approval to alienate property usually is given only with the concurrence of the local bishop.

In the 1960s and 1970s a number of the institutions owned by religious orders were converted to secular entities in order to obtain additional funding for those institutions. However, many of the religious orders which reorganized their corporate apostolates, giving up corporate control of their institutions to lay-dominated boards, relied on a controversial interpretation of canon law set forth by Monsignor John J. McGrath, a professor of canon law at Catholic University who became president of Saint Mary's College at Notre Dame, Indiana, in 1968.

In his 1968 book, *Catholic Institutions in the United States: Canonical and Civil Law Status,* which was published by Catholic University, Monsignor McGrath contended that schools and hospitals that were separately incorporated from the religious institutes that owned them were not subject to canon law. According to a 1990 article in *The Jurist,* the publication of the Canon Law Department of Catholic University:

"The McGrath thesis was relied upon by ecclesiastical entities such as religious orders which operated universities, colleges, and hospitals to secularize them in order to obtain government funding. Such secularization threatened the Catholic character of these institutions and the canonical safeguarding of millions of dollars of church property. The Holy See, through the Congregation for Catholic Education and the Congregation for Religious and Secular Institutes, protested that the McGrath thesis was never considered valid and had never been accepted. Meanwhile, Dr. Adam J. Maida, now Archbishop of Detroit [later named Cardinal in 1995], also a civil and canon lawyer, adopted a contrary position in *Ownership, Control and Sponsorship of Catholic Institutions: A Practical Guide* [published by the Pennsylvania Catholic Conference in 1975]. The momentous issues of canon and civil law here raised have yet to be resolved satisfactorily."[14] Indeed, many properties owned by women's religious orders were disposed of or secularized under the "McGrath thesis" without ecclesial approval.

Disposing of motherhouses, convents, schools, hospitals, and other institutions was, in some cases, obviously the only prudent course a religious institute could take, especially given the dire financial straits of some orders. But, there are sisters who contend that their orders sold off property in a subversive effort to cut all ties with past traditions of the order and a heavy-handed way to force sisters into small living units and away from like-minded individuals who might unify to protest the actions of the leadership. (And some lay people whose families contributed to acquiring or building those properties interpret these sales as a betrayal of their investment in the future of the Church.)

Divestiture of property also meant that many sisters could not find a convent of their own congregation to live in, even if they wanted to live in community, which many of the sisters did desire. Even today, some middle-aged or younger sisters accept jobs in their orders' retirement centers because that is the only vestige of community life left in their congregations. Unfortunately, some sisters are forced to live alone because the sisters in their community live in small, self-selected groups, and no one has selected them. It is indeed ironic that some sisters are not welcome in communities of their own institute, especially when some of the leaders who forced this lifestyle on their communities were the very ones to complain that the all-male Church hierarchy oppressed women by being exclusive.

As Sister Joan Chittister explained: "Now we live in self-selected groups where interests and schedules and needs match and we come together as a large group at the priory time and again throughout the year for liturgy, for community projects, for celebration, for discussion, for education, for retreat, for chapter concerns, for parties."[15] And Sister Sandra Schneiders defines community as "the psycho-socio-spiritual unity of minds and hearts in Christ," and she contends that ". . . there are religious who, in terms of lifestyle, live singly, but who are living fully in community because of the intensity of their felt belonging and participation in the life of the congregation."[16]

As one sister observed, these models of religious life resemble more the lifestyle of sorority sisters than religious sisters.

Certainly, these are not the definitions of community life according to canon law, the Vatican II documents, or pronouncements coming from Rome. Canon 665 states: "Observing a common life, religious are to live in their own religious house and not be absent from it without the permission of their superior." A 1994 letter from the Congregation for Religious and approved by the pope, entitled "Fraternal Life in Community," summarized the Church teaching on community life for Religious. The letter stressed that community life — physically living together in common — is essential to the identity of Religious. The Congregation for Religious cited a "culture of individualism" that weakened the ideal of life in common and commitment to community projects. In a true fraternal community, the document said, each member contributes to sharing, understanding and mutual help, and supporting other members of the community on a day-to-day basis: "Religious community is the place where the daily and patient passage from 'me' to 'us' takes place, from my commitment to a commitment entrusted to the community, from seeking 'my things' to seeking 'the things of Christ.' " And, the document concluded, each institute must have a common mission, with its members conducting works proper to that institute. But, "Should there be institutes in which, unfortunately, the majority of members no longer live in community, such institutes would no longer be able to be considered true religious institutes."[17] However, many religious women in the United States ignore these clear directives and continue to follow their own wishes, apparently with impunity.

New ways to pray

Along with the disintegration of community life came the deterioration of prayer life for many sisters. Certainly some of the renewal efforts in prayer life were valuable and enriched the spiritual lives of the sisters. Some communities designed community prayer to be less rote recitation and more meaningful, with appropriate connections to liturgy and Scripture. There was a new emphasis on personal prayer. Unfortunately, some communities offered so much flexibility to their members that some sisters felt no obligation to continue community prayer of any kind, and some even absented themselves from the daily community Eucharist. Then, as living arrangements and jobs became more diverse in many religious institutes, community prayer really went by the wayside, and some sisters even eschewed personal prayer, claiming that their work was their prayer.

While some sisters no doubt are very conscientious about prayer, many have had difficulty sustaining their prayer life without community support. Some sisters have told the author that they are much more inclined to pray if a particular time is set aside each day for prayer, and the Religious can pray in the presence of other members of their community. One sister observed that she was much more inclined to get up at 5:30 a.m. to go to morning prayer when the whole community was expected to do so, than after morning prayer was made optional. She said she often told herself that since few other sisters were rising at that early hour to pray, it was perfectly acceptable for her to sleep in, too. The problem was, she said, she did not find time in her day for prayer when she did sleep in, and her spiritual life suffered.

Many communities make no provision at all for personal or group prayer. One Sister of St. Joseph who lives alone observed that her community provides no guidelines to its members regarding prayer. Nor does the order provide for regularly scheduled spiritual events for the members who live away from community. She did say, however, that many of the sisters who live alone do arrange to get together occasionally for prayer groups, aerobics, or potluck dinners.

Some sisters even refuse to attend Mass because they resent the all-male priesthood. In a 1991 address to the Leadership Conference of Women Religious, Benedictine Sister Mary Collins, a theology professor at Catholic University, observed: "In my judgment as a student of liturgical performance, the crux of the troubled relationship American women religious have with the Roman Catholic Church is clear. It is centered in contemporary Catholic eucharistic praxis. . . .

". . . As we pass through this decade of the 1990s, matters related to women and the eucharist promise only to become more publicly conflicted. . . .

". . . Who among you sees as insignificant the alienation of the sisters who chose to remain members of your communities but who no longer participate in any eucharistic liturgy? 'I am no longer part of the institutional church,' they say. And they identify eucharistic liturgy as part of the system of power and privilege they reject."[18]

Loretto Sister Ann Patrick Ware has noted that "There are increasing numbers of women religious who quietly celebrate the eucharist or participate in such a celebration out of the public eye. There are many who have prepared themselves theologically for ordination. There are Sisters who refuse to take part in Catholic rites as inherently sexist in nature."[19] And Mary Jo Leddy, a former Canadian Sister of Our Lady of Sion, has observed that the sacraments of reconciliation and the Eucharist ". . . have never seemed more problematic, especially to female religious. Women are realizing how much these liberating sacraments have also served to reinforce a patriarchal structure in the church. This experience has moved some women to develop their own rituals of cleansing and celebration."[20]

However, in *Vita Consecrata* Pope John Paul II wrote that "By its very nature the eucharist is at the center of the consecrated life, both for individuals and for communities. It is the daily viaticum and source of the spiritual life for the individual and for the institute."[21] And, the Congregation for Religious document "Fraternal Life in Community" stressed that prayer in common has always been considered the foundation of all community life. Therefore, it said, all Religious "must remain strongly convinced that community is built up starting from the liturgy, especially from celebration of the eucharist and the other sacraments." The document noted that "religious community is regulated by a rhythmic horarium to give determined times to prayer and especially so that one can learn to give time to God (*vacare Deo*)."[22]

Re-interpreting the vows

The "Fraternal Life in Community" document also observed that one of the fruits of renewal was that religious communities became less formalistic and less authoritarian. However, this reaction against rigid structures had a downside too, for some Religious and some institutes did not adjust well to new concepts of freedom and personal responsibility. The Congregation for Religious observed in the "Fraternal Life" document: "As a result, a certain number of communities have been led to live with no one in charge, while other communities make all decisions collegially. All of this brings with it the danger, not merely hypothetical, of a complete breakdown of community life; it tends to give priority to individual paths and simultaneously to blur the function of authority — a function which is both necessary for the growth of fraternal life in community and for the spiritual journey of the consecrated person."[23]

Even though canon law requires that Religious live in a house of their institute under the authority of a legitimate superior, some religious communities actually do function as if no one were in charge. As one sister observed, in practice, many religious communities have less structure than a family or even a sorority. Often in a religious house there is a person called a coordinator, but in effect the coordinator is merely a communications person who passes along information. Sister Marie Augusta Neal reported that in 1982, seventy-five percent of women's religious institutes already had some or all living units without a local superior.[24]

An earlier LCWR survey reported in 1977 that "The role of authority is seen as a service role exercised within the community rather than from above," and "There is a more mature acceptance of obedience as a positive orientation of one's life to the will of the father and as a commitment to engage with others in a search for the expression of that will."[25] Tensions reported by the survey which were a result of these changes in the practice of authority included: less articulate members allowing themselves to be manipulated by the more vocal; confusion about locus of authority; polarization between liberal and conservative members; measures of accountability being somewhat undeveloped; authority sometimes eroding, especially at the local level, leaving the group to just drift; fewer persons willing to accept leadership; and individualism causing tension.[26]

Many of these problems also were cited in the FORUS study some fifteen years later. In fact, the FORUS study contended that authority in religious life is the most pressing question for Religious to solve, and that the effectiveness of leaders is inhibited by a lack of respect for authority, both local and Church-wide. The study also found that there is little structure to consensual decision-making by Religious and that the concept of a personal call to individual ministry has a higher priority for many Religious than does the mission of their religious congregation.[27]

With this struggle over the concept of authority, the vows took on strange new meanings quite foreign to the understanding of the vows that most women Religious had originally professed. The vow of obedience often came to be interpreted as the practice of the community "discerning" what would be done, and then the superior simply ratifying the decision. Frequently, obedience was defined as responding to "the Spirit." But the problem with this concept was that each individual was thus in control of what "the Spirit" directed. The result for some Religious, according to the FORUS study, was that "the dynamics of individualism and 'inner authority' have come to dominate over any notion of vocation that entails either obedience or even discernment of the will of God in the context of a congregational commitment."[28]

Likewise, poverty came to be interpreted diversely and seemed to have little connection to the tradition of foregoing private ownership of property and living a lifestyle based on spiritual values rather than material goods. The new definitions of poverty ranged from making oneself available to other people, to engaging in open dialogue, to working for redistribution of wealth, to stewarding the earth's resources, to divesting religious institutes of their buildings and property. Sister Sandra Schneiders offered an unusual generic definition: "Religious poverty is an evangelically inspired and structured relationship to material creation which involves owning well, using well, and suffering well for the purpose of transforming human existence, our own included."[29]

The FORUS study found that while most religious congregations proclaim a mission to serve the poor, "a significant number of religious feel no personal commitment" to this mission,[30] and "the impulse to generosity among some religious is being eclipsed by self-preoccupation, psychological decompensation, stark individualism and a lessening of the willingness to sacrifice."[31]

Immaculate Heart of Mary Sister Mary Anne Huddleston wrote in 1993 that potential members of religious institutes of women are confused and put off not only by the wide range of occupations that sisters pursue, but also by the diverse lifestyles of sisters that sometimes give little witness to poverty: "While some members reside in huge motherhouse complexes, some (few these days) live in small groups in well-worn parish convents. While some live individually and simply in studio apartments, others live in twos or alone in more comfortable houses, apartments, or condominia complete with the state-of-the-art audio-visual systems, and canine or feline pets."[32]

Breaking the habit

Of all the aspects of religious life for women, the issue of the habit has caused some of the most heated debates. While many sisters dismiss the habit simply as a minor detail regarding what clothing one chooses to wear, controversy over the habit touches on far deeper issues.

The habit identifies the Religious as a vowed member of a particular religious institute which is empowered to exercise its apostolate in the name of the Church. The religious habit also serves as a visible sign of poverty. However, the insistence by Rome on the habit and the subsequent refusal by some Religious to wear the habit is not just a dispute about clothing — it is a dispute about authority. Sociologist Gene Burns has noted that the controversy over the habit was "somewhat symbolic in the minds of both sisters and the SCR [Congregation for Religious] of the ultimate locus of authority over renewal."[33] In spite of the fact that Rome has been equally insistent that male Religious and clergy wear a habit or clerical dress — as recently as 1995 — some feminists claim that patriarchial structures in the Church require the habit in order to keep women in their place, as subordinates to men. (It must be noted that, historically, women Religious have been much more attentive to wearing religious garb than have been male Religious.) So, the refusal of some sisters to wear a habit is their declaration of independence from patriarchal authority, as explained by author Marcelle Bernstein in *The Nuns*:

"The churchmen who want their daughters in religion to be veiled and robed insist they do so to protect them, to preserve their modesty and chastity as much as to make them a sign of God in the world. But it is surely significant that in other societies where women are so treated, covered up and hidden from sight, it is not done out of any kind of respect but because they are scarcely seen as people in their own right. They are the property of men, and in a masculine society they are second-class citizens. No wonder the overwhelming reaction of nuns who have abandoned the habit has been that for the first time they feel they have achieved liberty."[34]

The habit issue takes on added dimensions of importance because the style of habit — or lack of habit — frequently reflects a religious person's (or order's) attitude about accepting the authority of the Church hierarchy. The style of habit also can reveal how seriously an order has pursued the renewal outlined by Vatican II. For example, a few institutes of women

Religious still wear shoe-length, voluminous habits and elaborate veils that completely engulf the face. This style of religious garb hardly reflects the directives of the popes and Vatican II to modernize and simplify the habit, and one might legitimately wonder if such orders have followed Church directives to renew other aspects of their lives. On the other hand, sisters who wear secular clothing rather than a religious habit appear either ignorant of Church teachings requiring Religious to wear distinguishable religious garb, or else they feel no obligation to adhere to that teaching.

The Church is very clear in declaring the necessity of a religious habit. The directive is found in canon law, *Perfectae Caritatis, Ecclesiae Sanctae, Evangelica Testificatio*, the exhortations of several popes, and numerous other documents emanating from the Vatican. Canon lawyer Sister Elizabeth McDonough observed in 1992 that "No sound interpretations of conciliar and postconciliar legal texts even suggest that wholesale abandonment of simple, identifiable garb for religious was (or is) intended."[35]

In early 1972, Cardinal John Krol, president of the NCCB, received a letter from Archbishop Luigi Raimondi, apostolic delegate to the United States, which Cardinal Krol in turn sent to all U.S. bishops. The letter called attention to the fact that "religious, men and women, in ever-increasing numbers, are abandoning the religious habit and also any distinctive external sign." The Raimondi letter contained a letter from Cardinal Antoniutti, prefect of the Congregation for Religious, which stated: ". . . the religious habit has been considered by the Second Vatican Council as a sign of consecration for those who have embraced in a public way the state of perfection of the evangelical counsels. . . .

". . . Religious institutes, in their general chapters, may, and in some cases, ought to, modify the traditional habit in accord with practical requirements and the needs of hygiene, but they may not abolish it altogether or leave it to the judgment of individual sisters."[36]

The Antoniutti letter also stated that secular clothes could be permitted by competent superiors for sisters to whom the habit would constitute an impediment or obstacle in certain activities, but even then the dress should be in some way different from the clearly secular.

Cardinal Antoniutti elaborated on this point in a February 5, 1972, response to an inquiry by Bishop Leo A. Pursley of Fort Wayne-South Bend: "In regard to the Religious Habit, as you are aware, various Institutes have taken liberties far beyond what was ever intended by the Council. And if they say that Rome has approved their wearing of contemporary secular dress, they should be challenged to show proof of this. . . . Never has any positive approval been given to laying aside the Religious Habit. Neither has such a provision been passed over in silence, unless, in some rare case, through an oversight. Nor does 'silence give consent' as some have contended, who presume that because they have heard nothing from this Sacred Congregation, their Interim Constitutions are approved. . . .

". . . We would ask you to continue your insistence on the habit, Your Excellency. As you know, it is not only your right but your duty, in keeping with the Motu Proprio 'Ecclesiae Sanctae.' "[37]

In spite of these clear directives, some women Religious still insisted the topic was open to debate. Sister Thomas Aquinas (Elizabeth) Carroll, president of the Leadership Conference of Women Religious 1971-72 and general director of the Sisters of Mercy of Pittsburgh, wrote the members of her order on February 21, 1972, that Archbishop Raimondi's letter was "not a legal document and was not promulgated to the religious congregations." She told her sisters that to put to rest any conscience problems they might have with the letter, she was continuing to authorize the sisters to wear either "modified habit, recognizable symbol, or purely secular clothes conformable to the 'poverty, simplicity and modesty proper to the religious state.' " She called for an end to "mutual condemnations" regarding clothing, and said it would be "impertinent to establish any form of clothing as an essential of a life dedicated to the following of Christ." Instead, she said that the sisters' diversity of dress should be used as means of personal development and growth in charity.[38]

The next day, Sister Thomas Aquinas sent a similar memo to members of the Leadership Conference, in which she criticized the Raimondi letter as an attempt to interfere in the lives of sisters, to curtail the power of the general chapters, and to return to a pre-Vatican II model of authority and obedience. She reminded the sisters that "we are dealing with a letter; it does not purport to be a law." And in a convoluted explanation of the new understanding of obedience, Sister Thomas Aquinas wrote that "This circumstance imposes upon religious the burden of greater discernment, greater freedom before the Spirit and greater courage in trusting their own decisions. Even obedience must be purified, converted from a simple docility to every rule proclaimed into the great Christian obligation of finding the Will of the Father. . . ."[39]

The habit was such an emotional topic among sisters that most bishops simply avoided the issue. Clearly, some bishops feared that if they insisted that sisters wear the habit, the sisters would simply depart from their dioceses, leaving many Catholic institutions unstaffed at a time when demand for the services of Catholic institutions was at an all-time high. Indeed, Bishop Vincent Waters, bishop of Raleigh, North Carolina, from 1945 until his death in 1974, saw many sisters leave his diocese when he insisted that they wear a recognizable habit while working in the diocese. Bishop Leo A. Pursley, Bishop of Fort Wayne-South Bend until his retirement in 1976, was the only other bishop to take a firm stand publicly during the turbulent 1960s and 1970s, though many bishops no doubt agonized over the situation privately. In February of 1972, Bishop Pursley wrote Cardinal John Wright: "Apparently I am the only anti-Women's Liberation member of the U.S. Hierarchy to join Bishop Waters in his one-man crusade. It is likely that Sisters leaving this Diocese will be promptly signed up by another [diocese], like free agents in pro football. This is collegiality? Why not stand together behind our own votes at Vatican II?"[40]

Abandonment of the habit may also have been encouraged by some bishops, according to 1976 correspondence from the Vatican. In a January 27, 1976, letter to all pontifical nuncios and delegates, Cardinal Sebastiano Baggio, Prefect of the Sacred Congregation for Bishops, wrote that Church norms regarding the dress of priests and Religious "have been largely neglected and even attacked, under evasive doctrinal and pastoral motives, with serious and harmful effects, among which are the embarrassment and confusion of the faithful. But what constitutes the motive of my present letter is the painful evidence that such self-will has not rarely had its source in the bishops themselves and has been encouraged by their example, if not directly by their formal expression, as in the cases of communities of women impelled by some bishops to abandon the religious habit."[41]

Subsequently, Archbishop Jean Jadot, Apostolic Delegate to the United States, wrote Cardinal Joseph Bernardin, then president of the National Conference of Catholic Bishops, asking Cardinal Bernardin to pass along his letter to all United States bishops. Archbishop Jadot wrote, in part: "Cardinal Baggio has noticed that in some cases the arbitrary rejection of appropriate attire for priests and religious can be traced to bishops who have tolerated abuses or who have not given the proper example by their own choice of clothing. It has even been reported that some bishops have directly advised religious communities of women in their dioceses to abandon the religious habit."[42]

In spite of such definitive statements, confusion about the habit continued. A Washington, D.C. priest reported in 1979 that when he showed some sisters a copy of *Origins* in which the Pope was quoted as saying that Religious should wear some kind of habit, the sisters responded that "(a) the Holy Father was misquoted and never said this, and (b) that their Mother General had written to them saying that this particular wish on his part did not apply to them, going so far as to say that this particular reference was countermanded later on by another statement saying that he [the pope] did not mean what he said. . . ."[43]

In May of 1983, the Congregation for Religious had a confrontational meeting in Rome with leaders of the Leadership Conference of Women Religious over the habit issue. A *National Catholic Reporter* article said that the Congregation for Religious had accused American women superiors of deviating from Vatican II directives, canon law, and statements of the pope regarding religious garb. The Leadership Conference contingent, headed by its president, Sister of Charity Helen Flaherty, "countered that requiring distinctive garb would cause 'serious polarization in communities, a loss in members (including some leaders of communities) and a weakening of the authority and credibility of the institutional church.' " And, the Leadership Conference delegation insisted "that an 'evolution' had taken place among women religious in this country, and they could no longer accept laws about dress as 'binding in conscience.'

"Vatican authorities then reminded the American superiors that their authority came from 'the church,' not from their communities. They added that the revised constitutions of some U.S. religious communities seemed to confuse 'the process of decision-making with the definition of the vow of obedience.' "

NCR also reported that an unnamed source present at the Rome meeting felt that "the real issue behind the religious garb focus . . . was Vatican control over essential aspects of American religious life.

"Sister Catherine Pinkerton, a sister of St. Joseph of Carondelet [sic], also at the meeting, said the Vatican representatives understandably were presenting a traditional theology of religious life, while the Americans were open to a variety of theologies."[44] Sister Catherine was the Leadership Conference of Women Religious 1983 president-elect, and had been chairperson of the National Assembly of Women Religious from 1973 to 1975. (She actually was a member of the Sisters of St. Joseph of Cleveland, not Carondelet.)

With their leaders making such statements, women Religious were confused and misinformed on the habit issue. Several sisters told the author that they sincerely felt they were following the directives of Vatican II and being obedient to the pope and their orders when they switched to lay clothing. Some of those sisters were very surprised when they finally read *Perfectae Caritatis* or *Evangelica Testificatio* or *Ecclesiae Sanctae*, or heard one of the pope's statement on the habit.

One Sister of Mercy was happily wearing secular clothing when she accepted a job in a diocese where the bishop required Religious to wear a habit when they were at work in a diocesan institution. She said she went back to wearing her modified habit, and was amazed to see that the habit made a positive difference in her work. She then sought out the Church documents on religious life, discovered that the habit is mandatory, and has been wearing the modified habit ever since. Other sisters tell similar stories, and some sisters have even devised their own modified habits because their religious institutes do not designate a design for a modified habit.

Vatican officials no doubt have contributed, perhaps unknowingly, to confusion over the requirement for religious garb, for the Vatican has approved constitutions for some religious orders that include very vague statements on the dress of the institute's members, statements which are open to wide interpretation. For example, this statement on religious garb is from a constitution approved by Rome for a large congregation of American women Religious: "Our dress . . . simple and modest and appropriate to women consecrated to the service of the Lord, identifies us as religious in the Church. It is worn with the symbol of the Congregation or some other religious symbol." As one sister reported, this "other religious symbol" in her order was a pin with a butterfly. Sisters confirm that constitutions are often written in these general terms so that, while Rome might give the sisters the benefit of the doubt about such vague language, the sisters can then interpret the constitution in the broadest possible terms. This technique of vague and general language also is employed for other topics in constitutions which are much more important than the habit issue.

What did the bishops think?

During the 1970s, when constitutions and rule books were being rewritten, there was some effort by the United States bishops to address some of these various problems in the religious life of the sisters, but it seems that the bishops' concerns were not passed along to sisters by their leadership.

In 1971, Bishop James Hogan, chairman of the NCCB Liaison Committee with the Conference of Major Religious Superiors of Women's Institutes, wrote all bishops to ask if they had any issues they wanted to be brought to the attention of the sisters. Then, at the April 25, 1971, meeting of his liaison committee with the liaison committee of the superiors' conference, Bishop Hogan presented each member of the superiors' conference committee with a document in which he had collated the remarks of the fifty-five bishops who had responded to his letter. These remarks included:

• The bishops were concerned over "confusion, tension, anxiety and disunity in some congregations," which had a negative impact on vocations and caused sisters to depart because the congregations changed so much.

- "Many bishops are persuaded that, in good faith, misinterpretation of Vatican II's documents crept in," and that Vatican II documents are very clear on the essentials of religious life.
- Bishops could not respond to the Conference's request that they support the chapter decrees of religious institutes when such decrees "were deemed to be at variance with the mind of the Church."
- Bishops were concerned that the writings of some sisters had "a negative attitude toward and inordinate criticism of the Holy See."
- The bishops had difficulty justifying requests for larger salaries, apartments, cars, and clothing, given the sisters' vow of poverty.
- The bishops were "not happy with growth of extra-community residences," which resulted in fragmentation and lay resentment.
- Bishops were unhappy with congregations opening new houses and undertaking new apostolic works without consulting the local bishop.
- Bishops were concerned that some congregations belittled and criticized the important work of the teaching sister.[45]

Sister Angelita Myerscough, president of the Conference of Major Religious Superiors of Women's Institutes, responded to Bishop Hogan that "In order to facilitate further dialogue and to widen the input from CMSW a bit more, we are circulating the pages among the members of our National Board (about twenty members)."[46] But the concerns of the bishops apparently went only as far as the twenty-member national board and were not passed along to the members of the superiors' conference. Sister Angelita in fact directed the national board not to distribute the bishops' comments in their regions. She observed in an April 28, 1971, letter to the members of the conference's national board and liaison committee with bishops that ". . . in no sense was this compilation [of bishops' comments] prepared for wide distribution or publication, but simply as an instrument for dialogue among our CMSW committee members and the Bishops' Liaison Committee. Hence we are limited in its distribution at the time, and I would ask you not to send it out in the regions. If the Bishops were to prepare something for that kind of circulation, I am sure they would want to put it into a somewhat different form."[47]

However, Bishop Hogan obviously had intended for the bishops' comments to be passed along to all the members of the conference. After the September 1971 annual assembly of the Conference of Major Religious Superiors of Women's Institutes, which Bishop Hogan attended, he made a report to the National Conference of Catholic Bishops. In his report, Bishop Hogan observed: "It does not appear that the relative concerns of some 55 bishops submitted to the Sisters in Detroit last April [at the Liaison Committee meeting] evoked subsequent discussion."[48]

These transformations made by institutes of women Religious impacted the sisters greatly, but also had a tremendous effect on Church-sponsored institutions, as well, and the bishops continued to agonize over them. But the bishops were slow in learning that the superiors' conference was not inclined to take their concerns seriously enough even to pass the bishops' comments along to the membership of the conference.

In 1973, Bishop Hogan wrote Conference executive director Sister Mary Daniel Turner about replies to another questionnaire he had sent bishops. He wrote that "the following points continue to be elements of concern." Among the issues of concern to the bishops:

- Free placement where sisters were permitted to find their own work lessened stability and made it impossible for the community to maintain a commitment to a specific work in a diocese or parish.
- Regarding the sisters' leaving Catholic schools, the bishops said they didn't minimize the sisters' intense concern for the poor and oppressed, but they wondered how Christian leaders could be trained for the social apostolate if the sisters left the Catholic schools.
- "In the light of some experimentation regarding life style and government, have some communities defacto moved into the status of Secular Institutes?"
- Bishops were not always informed about who was performing what apostolate in their dioceses; and
- "Bishops continue to express their solidarity with Vatican II and the Holy Father in asking for some significant external sign manifesting Religious commitment."

Bishop Hogan wrote that he hoped the bishops' concerns could be discussed at the Leadership Conference's annual assembly in August and at the bishops' annual meeting in November.[49]

However, the author found no evidence that the entire membership of the superiors' conference or the majority of grass-roots sisters ever were informed that some bishops had raised these concerns, for the leaders of the conference were intent on pursing the course of renewal they had defined. The following chapter presents two examples of self-styled renewal of women's religious institutes which had tragic results for both the sisters in those institutes and for the Church in general.

11: Communities vs. the Hierarchy: The IHMs and the School Sisters of St. Francis

"We set out to push back the boundaries of religious life."[1]
Anita Caspary
Former superior, Immaculate Heart of Mary Sisters
Los Angeles, California

The chaos experienced by many religious orders during the renewal years can be understood more easily by looking at two specific examples: the Immaculate Heart of Mary Sisters of Los Angeles, and the School Sisters of St. Francis of Milwaukee. These religious institutes made headlines in the 1960s and early '70s because of their self-styled approaches to renewal and subsequent clashes with Church authorities over their renewal decisions. Other religious institutes of women watched these communities closely, and the ultimate disposition of these conflicts with Rome eventually affected other communities of women Religious quite profoundly. In turn, the Catholic institutions traditionally staffed by sisters were also impacted dramatically.

The IHMs and Cardinal McIntyre

The Immaculate Heart of Mary conflict with Cardinal James McIntyre of Los Angeles during the late 1960s was widely reported by the press and caused much consternation among women Religious. The major difficulty with the whole situation was that few people knew all the facts, and much misinformation was circulated. The prevailing piece of misinformation — carried by journals such as *Time* and *Newsweek* — was that the Immaculate Heart of Mary Sisters were dutifully complying with the directives of Vatican II to renew their order. But, alas, according to the politically correct story, Cardinal McIntyre, described by *Newsweek* as "an old guard standard-bearer of the Roman Catholic hierarchy,"[2] would not allow the sisters to modernize according to Vatican II directives. Backing him up was Congregation for Religious prefect Cardinal Ildebrando Antoniutti, described by *Newsweek* as "the aging misogynist who jealously guards Catholicism's monastic traditions."[3]

The whole sticky situation was finally resolved in 1970, when Anita Caspary, formerly Sister Humiliata, the Immaculate Heart of Mary superior, led approximately 315 of the Immaculate Heart of Mary Sisters out of the order into a lay organization called the Immaculate Heart Community, leaving behind about fifty Immaculate Heart of Mary Sisters who wanted to retain their canonical status as a religious institute in the Catholic Church. The whole affair was a traumatic situation for all involved, but it was hardly the fault of an intransigent hierarchy determined to preserve the pre-Vatican II model of religious life, as the secular press and much of the Catholic press reported.

So, what really happened?

Like many other religious institutes, the Immaculate Heart of Mary Sisters went far beyond the guidelines set out by Vatican II and subsequent Church documents relative to religious life. Heavily influenced by the women's liberation movement and the popular psychology of the 1960s, the institute had declared optional virtually all of its past traditions and practices, including common prayer, community life, the religious habit, the corporate apostolate of education, and the shared Eucharist. When Cardinal James McIntyre of Los Angeles told the order that these innovations did not adhere to the Vatican II guidelines for renewal of religious institutes, the sisters appealed to Rome, which came down on the side of Cardinal McIntyre. The sisters skillfully solicited support from sympathetic American Religious and laity and some members of the women superiors' conference, claiming that Cardinal McIntyre and Rome were trying to prevent them from following the Vatican II mandate to update.

Support for the sisters was plentiful, including support from sectors of the secular and Catholic press, which depicted the Immaculate Heart of Mary Sisters as obedient daughters of the Church who were being prevented from renewing their order by a misogynist hierarchy. But Rome and Cardinal McIntyre did not back down from the position that the essentials of religious life could not be changed. Subsequently, eighty percent of the sisters chose to leave the order rather than accede to the renewal guidelines of the Church. Thus, the Immaculate Heart of Mary Sisters of Los Angeles became a *cause celebre* during the very time most other religious institutes were rewriting their constitutions.

The IHM chapter decrees

The October 1967 Immaculate Heart of Mary chapter decrees provide solid evidence of how much the sisters were influenced by the women's liberation movement. One can also detect in the decrees a heavy emphasis on individualism similar to the world view that psychologist William Coulson said his "Training for Normals" workshops provided the Immaculate Heart of Mary Sisters. Part of this world view is set out in the these sentences from the prologue to the Immaculate Heart of Mary 1967 chapter decrees: "Women, perhaps especially dedicated women, insist on the latitude to serve, to work, to decide according to their own lights. Our community's history . . . speaks of our readiness to abandon dying forms in order to pursue living reality. It expresses, also, our willingness to seek human validity rather than some spurious supernaturalism.

"Women around the world, young and old, are playing decisive roles in public life, changing their world, developing new life styles. What is significant about this new power for women is not that it will always be for the good, nor that it will always edify, but that there can be no reversing of it now. Women who want to serve and who are capable of service have already given evidence that they can no longer uncritically accept the judgment of others as to where and how that service ought to be extended. American religious women want to be in the mainstream of this new, potentially fruitful, and inevitable bid for self-determination by women."[4]

The chapter decrees followed the same pattern as the prologue, including these declarations: "every humanizing work would seem to be a proper apostolate for us"; "participation in the temporal order calls for a new style of communal existence — one which will not rigidly separate us by customs, cloister, or clothing from those we serve"; and "Our religious obedience consists not in passive submission but in cooperative interaction with other members of the community." Community was defined to have "no fixed pattern or structure nor even a permanent involvement in one type or manner of work."[5]

News reports indicated the chapter decrees gave Immaculate Heart of

Mary Sisters the freedom to choose the type of work they wanted to do and removed the requirement of having a local superior at each local convent. Those local convents also were given wide discretion in government and community prayer schedules. And, individual sisters were free to choose their own style of clothing, whether it be a religious habit or lay clothing.

Cardinal McIntyre subsequently told the Immaculate Heart of Mary Sisters that the Council documents and other legislation required them to wear some kind of religious habit, to have daily prayer in common, and to continue the work of their institute, which was education. The Congregation for Religious backed up Cardinal McIntyre, issuing a letter on February 21, 1968, explaining that the purpose of an institute must be kept intact, and it cited the purpose of the Immaculate Heart of Mary Institute from its own constitution as: "The specific end is to labor for the salvation of souls through the work of Catholic education. . . ." The Congregation for Religious letter also stated that every community of Immaculate Heart of Mary Sisters should meet daily for some kind of common prayer, at the very least by attending Mass together. And the letter reaffirmed the authority of the local bishop over the works of the apostolate of a religious institute. Additionally, the letter confirmed that lay clothing for Religious was not permitted under *Perfectae Caritatis,* canon law, or *Ecclesiae Sanctae.*[6]

Clearly these guidelines were nothing new, and fully in accordance with Vatican II directives on renewal. However, the press painted a picture of obedient sisters just trying to go along with what the Council had decreed, but then being forced back into a pre-Vatican II mold by a conservative hierarchy. And many Religious from other orders, as well as many lay people who were not sufficiently familiar with the Vatican II documents, bought into this whole scenario that the Immaculate Heart of Mary nuns were being persecuted for merely being obedient to Church directives.

Anita Caspary admitted that the main issue that caused the controversy with Cardinal McIntyre was the issue of the sisters' lifestyle. As Sister Dorothy Vidulich wrote in 1995, Anita Caspary and her followers "had rejected a life pattern of community that had to conform to a *Code of Canon Law* issued by male clerics of another culture."[7] And, because the sisters did not wish to conform their lifestyle to canon law and directives from Rome concerning life in community, prayer in common, religious garb, and collaboration with diocesan authority, Cardinal McIntyre felt he could not allow the sisters to continue teaching in diocesan schools. Needless to say, this had a tremendous impact on Los Angeles Catholic schools, for in 1967 the Immaculate Heart of Mary Sisters had 197 teachers in 28 grade schools and 8 high schools in the Archdiocese of Los Angeles.[8]

Sisters in Crisis

Naturally this was a situation being watched closely by Catholics all over the country. Bishops in other dioceses whose parochial schools were overflowing with "baby boom" children worried about what they would do if they lost their teaching sisters. Parents worried about the Catholic schools and the sisters being there to teach their children and to model reverence for the Catholic Church and its doctrine. And other religious institutes watched with fascination for clues about how the Immaculate Heart of Mary renewal would affect them and the direction of renewal in their communities. In reality, many other orders of women Religious were considering or had already passed chapter decrees similar to the Immaculate Heart of Mary Sisters, but few bishops had raised any protest over decrees that went beyond Church guidelines. Some United States bishops apparently were not too familiar themselves with Vatican II documents on religious life, some were confused about the bishop's role relative to Religious in his diocese, and some bishops even quietly applauded the sisters' efforts to test the limits of Rome's patience. Probably most bishops feared a mass exodus of sisters from Catholic schools, hospitals, and social service agencies if the bishops appeared to be interfering in the sisters' renewal efforts.

Support for the sisters

So, all Catholic eyes were on Los Angeles, and the press had a field day with the situation, which dragged on into 1970. Headlines appeared like: "McIntyre to oust 200 updating nuns,"[9] "13 Jesuits praise L.A. nuns' renewal,"[10] "Vatican rules against IHM nuns on changes opposed by McIntyre,"[11] "3,000 sisters support IHMs,"[12] "Immaculate Heart Sisters — Hemlines and Humbug,"[13] and "Battling for 'Nuns' Rights."[14] A sympathetic editorial in *Ave Maria* concluded that "It is unfortunate that this controversy has clouded the announcement of the Immaculate Heart Sisters' response to the spirit of the Council."[15] A *Commonweal* editorial opined: "Our first impulse, and undoubtedly the impulse of many, is to counsel the IHMs to stop playing diplomatic games with their Cardinal and Rome, and just walk out. But there is reason to be hesitant about this impulse. Rome should be given the chance to open itself to reason and protest." The editors then called for a letter-writing crusade to protest the treatment of the Immaculate Heart of Mary Sisters.[16]

America editors called on United States bishops to intervene with Rome on behalf of the Immaculate Heart of Mary Sisters to allow completion of their renewal program and thus win "a degree of flexibility" with the Congregation for Religious. The *America* editorial did admit that a "literal interpretation" of the Church documents on religious life backed up the position of the Congregation for Religious; but the *America* editor also declared that "A more liberal, more empirical approach to the subject provides the Immaculate Heart Sisters with a strong case as well."[17]

Behind the scenes, sisters who supported the Immaculate Heart of Mary vision of renewal were hard at work to garner support for them, knowing that the outcome of the Immaculate Heart of Mary case would impact renewal in their own communities. In January of 1968, Sister Mary Omer Downing, president of the Conference of Major Religious Superiors of Women's Institutes, consulted Father Edward Heston at the Congregation for Religious about the Immaculate Heart of Mary situation, and he advised the conference not to make a public statement since not all aspects of the case were known to them. So, in January, the conference executive committee voted not to make a statement.

On February 12, Sister Thomas Aquinas (Elizabeth) Carroll — superior of the Sisters of Mercy of Pittsburgh and a member of the Sisters' Survey Committee of the Conference of Major Religious Superiors of Women's Institutes — wrote Sister Mary Omer asking for a conference statement supporting the Immaculate Heart of Mary Sisters.[18] Sister Mary Omer polled the executive committee again, and still, two-thirds of the executive committee voted "no." She then wrote the executive committee, telling them they did not have a complete picture of the situation, and asked the superiors to try to dissuade other superiors from making a public statement.[19] Failing to get the support of the conference board, Sister Thomas Aquinas wrote her own letter to the pope regarding the Immaculate Heart of Mary Sisters.[20] And conference executive secretary Sister Rose Emmanuella Brennan teamed up with Father Boniface Wittenbrink, a Missionary Oblate of Mary Immaculate who was executive secretary of the Conference of Major Superiors of Men, to write the apostolic delegate on March 19, complaining about the treatment of the Immaculate Heart of Mary Sisters and expressing concern that their two conferences had not been consulted by Rome about the situation.[21]

Meanwhile, in February of 1968, Sister Francis Borgia Rothluebber, superior general of the School Sisters of St. Francis in Milwaukee, organized an archdiocesan council of major superiors in Milwaukee. One of the first actions of the Milwaukee council was to issue a statement of support for the Los Angeles Immaculate Heart of Mary Sisters.[22] Of course, Sister Francis Borgia was in the midst of leading her own congregation on a path of renewal very similar to that of the Immaculate Heart of Mary Sisters, so she had a vested interest in the outcome of their case.

Sisters in Crisis

In March of 1968, Loretto Sister Jane Marie Richardson and Sister of St. Joseph Mary Schaldenbrand (both writers for *The Changing Sister* and consultants to the Sisters' Survey Committee), drew up a statement of support for the Immaculate Heart of Mary Sisters and circulated it to convents, garnering about three-thousand signatures.[23] A similar petition drive was organized by a lay group. Sister Mary Schaldenbrand told the *National Catholic Reporter*, "It seems to me that if we allow this kind of ruling to stand we collaborate with an exercise of authority which is abusive and which undermines the authority of the Church. . . . I hope it gets to the point of nonviolent resistance." Sister Mary seemed particularly put out that Cardinal McIntyre expected sisters to wear an identifiable habit, which she, herself, did not do. And she warned that she would leave religious life if she were ordered to wear a habit, which she said "segregated" sisters from society.[24]

On April 15, 1968, the president of the superiors' conference, Sister Mary Omer, wrote the conference members and enclosed an April 4 statement from the Congregation for Religious on the Immaculate Heart of Mary case. The Congregation for Religious letter expressed surprise that so much publicity had been stirred up around points which were not open to question, such as the necessity for a habit, community prayer, and close collaboration with diocesan authority. The letter observed that "The appeals, letters, and petitions circulated on behalf of the Sisters of the Immaculate Heart of Mary give the impression of having been requested and solicited. Many of these present identical texts, along the lines of form letters, suggesting a campaign organized by one central office. . . .

". . . One would be tempted to conclude that many of those who have undertaken to send letters etc. have not read the Council decrees attentively or even the norms issued by the Holy See."[25]

The community splits

In late April 1968, the Congregation for Religious appointed a four-member visitation team made up of three American bishops and a priest, to look into the Immaculate Heart of Mary controversy. That team reported that there already was a split within the Immaculate Heart of Mary order over the chapter decrees. The team directed that Immaculate Heart of Mary Sisters were to decide between the two groups — Sister Anita Caspary and those who supported the controversial 1967 chapter decrees, or sisters who wanted to follow the original Immaculate Heart of Mary constitutions, under the direction of Sister Eileen MacDonald. (Over one hundred Immaculate Heart of Mary Sisters chose neither option, and left their order during this time of turmoil.) The Congregation for Religious team issued a decree that Sister Anita's group would be "given a reasonable time, taking account of the points already made known to them, to experiment, to reflect and to come to definitive decisions concerning their rule of life to be submitted to the Holy See."[26]

As 1969 passed, it became clear that neither the Congregation for Religious nor the Immaculate Heart of Mary Sisters aligned with Sister Anita Caspary would back down. In August 1969, Sister Margaret Ellen Traxler and Sister Mary Audrey Kopp founded the National Coalition of American Nuns "to protest the interference by men in the internal affairs of the sisters"[27] — an obvious reference to the Immaculate Heart of Mary situation. And in September, the annual assembly of the Conference of Major Religious Superiors of Women's Institutes debated a resolution to support Sister Anita's group in its dispute with the hierarchy. That resolution failed by one vote, even though Sisters Angelita Myerscough and Thomas Aquinas (Elizabeth) Carroll (both members of the Sisters' Survey Committee) lobbied hard to get the assembly to approve the resolution. After the assembly, some conference members tried to keep the issue alive, and Sister Rosalie Murphy, a member of the 1970 conference executive committee, sent a letter to conference members soliciting signatures of superiors for a petition to the Congregation for Religious.[28]

In February of 1970, 315 Immaculate Heart of Mary Sisters announced that they would seek dispensation from their vows and establish an independent community of lay women, the Immaculate Heart Community, under the leadership of Anita Caspary. Predictably, many press accounts reported that the sisters were forced out of their order by Church authorities, even though the decision was made by the women themselves not to accept the Church authority regarding their renewal decisions. (Clearly, this was not an easy decision for many of the sisters who left the canonical group, but some sisters followed Anita Caspary out of a sense of loyalty and because they had been convinced that their chapter decrees were valid.) Financial settlements later worked out deeded Immaculate Heart College, Immaculate Heart of Mary High School, Queen of the Valley Hospital, and a retreat center to Anita Caspary's lay group.[29] (This lay group, called the Immaculate Heart Community, now includes married couples as well as men and women of different faiths who "make an annual commitment of 'time, talents and treasure' " to the organization.[30]) The approximately fifty Immaculate Heart of Mary Sisters who chose to remain canonical and accept the Congregation for Religious guidelines were awarded the esteem of the Church, but virtually nothing in material assets.

"An entirely new manner of religious life"

While the Immaculate Heart of Mary controversy was brewing in California, a similar situation was developing in the midwest in a far larger community, the School Sisters of St. Francis, who numbered about 2,800 sisters, with the generalate in Milwaukee. Sister Francis Borgia Rothluebber was elected superior general of the School Sisters of St. Francis in 1966. Also in 1966, the School Sisters of St. Francis chapter meeting produced "Response in Faith," to be the experimental rule of the community, which replaced the order's 1964 constitution.

Some of the changes instituted in the 1966 decrees were quite radical for that time, especially considering that sisters had previously lived in a tightly controlled atmosphere that offered little opportunity for personal decision-making or responsibility and were ill-prepared for the task of reforming their institute. As Sister Francis Borgia told the 1969 meeting of the Canon Law Society of America, the sisters' 1966 chapter decrees had included the following innovations: sisters moved from convents to self-selected small group living situations; local superiors were removed from even large group settings; time spent in community became optional; prayer took on a free form; the order's traditional mission of Catholic education became optional; open placement became common; and the formation program for new members became quite unstructured.[31]

In short, the School Sisters of St. Francis were on the same road to renewal that had been taken by the Immaculate Heart of Mary Sisters in Los Angeles. However, the outcome of their story is somewhat different from the IHM story. This ill-conceived brand of renewal also had disastrous consequences for the institute, but the School Sisters encountered no resistance to their renewal program from the local hierarchy. To the contrary, the School Sisters apparently had strong allies in influential positions, both in the hierarchy and in the men's and women's superiors' conferences, for an effort by the Congregation for Religious to correct the aberrations in the sisters' renewal evaporated. And Sister Francis Borgia went on to be elected vice-president of the Leadership Conference of Women Religious in 1972, becoming president of the conference in 1973, a not-so-subtle indication that leaders of many other institutes of women Religious applauded the example of the School Sisters of St. Francis.

In her October 1969 presentation at the annual convention of the Canon Law Society of America, Sister Francis Borgia made it clear that her community was forging a new definition of religious life. She explained that ". . . within the forms and structures of the old, an entirely new manner of religious life is developing."

Sister Francis Borgia defined religious life from a humanistic viewpoint, saying that "religious life is based on a respect for person." She also reduced the concept of authority to a pragmatic level: "The primary authority in religious life is fellowship authority. All authority is concerned with deepening the quality of life." Sister Francis Borgia was correct when she contended that ". . . a new texture, a whole new manner of living has come into being." But she neglected to mention that this new manner of living did not conform to her institute's charism and apostolate or to the needs of the sisters, let alone the Church teachings on religious life. Of course, Sister Francis Borgia had addressed the issue of Church legislation about religious life when, in her speech, she dismissed the requirement that religious institutes maintain the nature and end of their institute. She related, "A canonist asked recently whether we were abiding by our primary and secondary purposes. Such a separation no longer seems valid."[32]

According to a former School Sister of St. Francis, Sister Francis Borgia was not alone in pushing for this unmitigated new style of life, for a group within the School Sisters of St. Francis was promoting experimentation even broader than Sister Francis Borgia was advocating. In fact, this former School Sister felt that Sister Francis Borgia succeeded in getting elected in 1966 because she was more moderate than others in the community who were promoting a much more radical feminist agenda.

Turmoil in the school sisters

Many School Sisters of St. Francis were unhappy with the ensuing style of renewal in their congregation, and some contacted the Vatican about their concerns. Thus, in 1969 the Vatican ordered an apostolic visitation to the community to investigate reported abuses. Meanwhile, as the order was awaiting the results of the apostolic visitation, the School Sisters' own chaplain gave the sisters his insights on their renewal experience at their August 1969 chapter meeting. Father Donald N. Weber, a priest of the Archdiocese of Milwaukee, had been the sisters' chaplain for fourteen years. His address is quoted here almost in its entirety, as it provides a detailed picture of the havoc this unregulated renewal visited on the institute.

> Sisters, I am very grateful for this opportunity to speak to the General Chapter. . . . I approach this assignment with great humility and with much trepidation. It is a very difficult thing to counsel those you love. I need say little of my affection for the School Sisters of St. Francis. If my record of service and dedication during these fourteen years has

not proven my devotion and feeling, there is little that I can say now that would do so. And I'm sure the record will show that I have not attempted to interfere in the administration of your community.

I feel that I am in an enviable position though. Not only have I had the opportunity of seeing a previous lifestyle in this convent but I also lived with you during the transition period and would hope that I could help you evaluate the situation which now exists. . . .

. . . I have had opportunity to speak to many members of your community in the course of these years. I feel positively sure that I am reporting the feelings of a great percentage of your community. We are concerned particularly with the events of the past three years especially since Vatican II has instructed religious communities to engage in adaptation and renewal. What I say may sound very negative and yet I would be of no service to you were I to be dishonest. I refuse to be so; I will strive to be completely objective, just and truthful. It is a terrible choice to decide whether to tell you what you may want to hear or what I truly believe!

I have seen a large number of Sisters particularly this summer. For example, since the announcement of the [apostolic] visitation, I have calculated that I have seen more than thirty people, each for an hour or more even though I was on vacation for two-and-one-half weeks. I have seen more people from outside [other convents] than from within this [mother]house. Perhaps these people have been of a certain common mentality, but all of them have displayed deep anxiety, mistrust of administration, insecurity, fear. . . .

There is no question in my mind that everything that has transpired in these years has been motivated with deepest sincerity by those who have been making the decisions. To the extent that I understand the documents of the Church regarding adaptation and renewal I feel that you have succeeded to some degree in many areas, but may I honestly say that in the most basic principles which seems to be the full thrust of the documents there is much to be desired. I speak of the spiritual life and the inner ascetics of religious life. I see here little evidence of renewal or adaptation.

May I present to you now some of the specific comments that have been made to me by the Sisters who have approached me during these years. I believe these comments are accurate, truthful, and I agree with their positive criticism for the most part. In matters where I disagree I will certainly point out this difference. Sisters continue to complain that the whole emphasis on the renewal has been placed on the exterior and on life-styles and life-habits, that there has been little done to really further, strengthen, deepen, and broaden the interior life of the religious.

Prayer-life has almost been destroyed. Many Sisters as well as myself are fed up with the constant retort that your life can be your prayer. Our lives always were our prayer, Sisters, but there was within them in the past something that brought us much closer to God because we set aside a certain time, a certain spirit, and a certain place, and a certain way that we involved ourselves in conversation with Him in answer to the request of the Lord. . . . I honestly believe that the basic reason of our failure today is our lack of prayer. We're not on our knees, we're afraid to bend our knee, or to visit the home of our Lord. We are indifferent to the Mass and the Sacraments and the place of adoration. I fully agree with those who believe that we will never be blessed unless we remain men and women of prayer. . . .

It appears to me that your congregation is in turmoil and great confusion because of the varied and different interpretations of adaptation and renewal. I would publicly go on record that I think those who would see their renewal begin in the spiritual life, to be closer to the truth than those who chose some other vein.

While you have made a great thrust for the external, the exterior, the outside world, I feel there has been a breakdown in your communal worship, in your communal prayer, in your community life, in your formation program, in the effectiveness of the apostolates for which you were instituted. It appears that there is a certain unconcern for the real needs of a large group of Sisters. Your older Sisters are tremendously insecure. They are distrustful of your administration, they have no confidence, actually they seem to have little love for the people they should love most. Perhaps you have caused this. They would tell me by the hour how their real needs have not been met, how they feel that this very Chapter is concerned about things which are not the true needs of the community.

A great bulk of the Sisters seem never to have understood the "Response in Faith" [the chapter decrees] and while I personally believe that it is a beautiful manifesto yet I can well understand that it is not in the language that most of your Sisters understand and it is not complete in itself. To me it seems like a beautiful preamble for something that should follow, for some guidelines and some directions. While we are not here endorsing the legalistic approach or putting undue emphasis on moral theology or canon law, yet it would seem that for an organization to prosper and to come to its fullest fruition there must be some guidance and authority within the structure.

I feel that a completely permissive administration cannot be effective and successful. It is true that mature women should make their own decisions and should not need many commandments, yet the fact is that there has been little deliberate gradualism to bring them to this level. It has been forced upon people overnight; they cannot mature that quickly. From my experience in the family life apostolate I have learned that the maturation process is one which takes years. If Sisters have been kept in a certain shelter for many years (which may have been correct in its time) we cannot expect them to prudently, wisely, discreetly make the decisions that are necessary by forcing this freedom and liberty upon them overnight. I think they have a right to receive some suggestions and guidelines. I do not endorse a completely permissive administration. The business world, the military and government do not exist on completely permissive structures.

It has been repeated to me frequently that the Sisters do not feel that this Chapter nor some of the provincial Chapters are truly representative of the rank and file of the community. They are distrustful of the means that have been used to bring people to the role of delegate. They say they are not all astute students of political science. I cannot overlook the fact that with the mean age of 53 in your community you have only four North American voting representative who are that age or older.

The sisters point out that there seems to have been a systematic elimination of sisters who hold to orthodoxy from positions of influence and authority within the community and we need only look down the list of names and recognize that there is much validity in their complaint. Sisters seem to refuse the concept of "No Superiors." Cardinal Suenens at Notre Dame pointed out that " every community needs policy making and policy taking." A group must gather and make the decisions and someone must implement them.

It is their opinion too that many innovations are extreme and radical and these innovations have been placed upon them, and upon the community, under the guise of experimentation. That experimentation has actually been misused may be a very accurate judgment. There seems to be little evaluation of experiments.

While there has been much lip service in respect to the dignity of the human person, yet persons are being hurt right and left. The numbers of people that I have seen in recent months who have been left stranded or without assignments, or voted out of residence or told to go places where they felt they need not go, is just astounding. Freedom has been extended to some but others seem to have little of it. Even those who may need certain therapeutic assistance or rehabilitation are indelibly hurt in the procedures that are used to bring about this type of attention. Sometimes there seems to be a lack of true charity. We speak fine phrases of love, but we do not live it.

While to a great extent there has been creativity displaced within the congregation, yet there seems to be a lack of creativity in using the resources of people who have rich knowledge through experience and though previous authority. When leaving office they are immediately shelved and no honest and legitimate recourse has been made to the talents that they have used for years previously. . . .

There seems to be an insufficient communication amongst the members of the congregation. Major decisions are forwarded to them but much of the true family happenings of the community are not made known. When their opinions are sought they have alleged that previously the decisions have often been made. Communiqués are sent from the Chapters and some of the preparatory committees but oftentimes because of the involvement of many people, communication does not filter down the line to those who face the public on the firing front. There seems to be much dissatisfaction with press releases and the public image of the community.

Many Sisters feel that there is a certain subtle ridicule of all the past without the proper interpretation given; that the past may have been very proper and correct in its own time. Sisters do not seem convinced that the ideals of their founders are being held to in a sacred way nor renewed with the proper change and adaptation that is now necessary. I have never quite understood what this means, but they say that the whole concept of Franciscanism seems to be by the boards.

It's a difficult thing to interpret fully the meaning of the vows today. The spirit of poverty seems to be flouted in a million ways. Obedience is only to be exercised when certain demands are to be forced upon subjects. Discretion and modesty that protects chastity seems to be needed.

I find no confidence in the formation program. It has gone through a series of experiments and has dissolved into verily nothing. No true challenge of denial and dedication is offered. If reports are true, candidates are so screened that even the twelve apostles wouldn't pass the test. There seems to be no welcome extended to people who are not sophisticated intellectuals. Domestic work is not at all appreciated.

There seems to be constant criticism of the apostolates to which the community is now directing itself and with the innuendo that the parochial school system is dying. Even Father Greeley has greater hope for it if we commit ourselves to stay at it and try to correct its problems. Cardinal Suenens said: "Stay where you are! If you are a teacher continue to teach and try to become a better teacher; it you are a nurse, try to be a better nurse. Do not be in the street all the time."

I find, Sisters, constant criticism about the matters of small group living artificially arranged. It seems to be an exclusive, selective way of surrounding oneself with companionship which satisfies itself in a spirit of secularism. The spirit of the world seems to have shown itself forcibly in apartment living. I am interested in what percentage of recent defections in the congregation have previously had exposure to apartment living? . . . The Sisters seem greatly disturbed by your evacuation of convents.

Criticism continues on the lay attire, the denial of Christian witness of a religious woman to the people of God. It seems that even in charity our lay people have a right to see some identification. I believe that 85 percent of these lay people would prefer some modern form, but that it be a religious habit with a religious veil. Suenens again says that "the concept of a sign or witness implies identity." I do not believe that most of our laity are pleased with the modern image.

Many sisters seem to resent that some are obliged to contract for their jobs and others do lay labor while the true work of the sisterhoods remains wanting. Some do whatever form of work they want to do instead of answering the needs that the Church defines.

And this I so regret to say, Sisters. I hear from priests and Sisters everywhere of a spirit of hostility toward priests which has developed. I do not intend to whitewash the responsibility of priests — the "bum deal" you have received from some in the past and still in the present. But let's remember that this relationship often resulted from training given by sisters to sisters. They were trained to "remain far away from priests — only contact them on a strictly professional level," etc.

There is a fear amongst sisters that all roots are going to be sold. And I hear reported that the sale of buildings is being contemplated. This breeds insecurity in sisters with the accusation by some that money from the sales will be used by indiscreet women who are hardly mature in their use of money.

Sisters detect an apparent deception in listing defections. It may be normal that one province would lose ten percent in less than three years, but I would suggest a close evaluation. There seems to be little concern about defections. Really, people are leaving for different reasons than soon after Vatican II. Now they say that they do not want to be identified with the image of modern religious life. They say this is not what they came to the convent for. They allege that there are no principles, no ideals and truly good women are leaving now. I am very curious, too, at this moment in history — how many members of this congregation have married priests?

Many sisters speak of an over-exaggerated spirit of feminism being foisted upon the community. They are not ready to buy this whole doctrine. They find serious problems in accepting this approach which the congregation is making to society. Don't worry, sisters, that we don't know that you are women — we certainly do!

Some sisters object strenuously to indignant and disrespectful letters sent to church and civil authorities on certain social issues. They feel that there is an over-emphasis on social sciences at the expense of the spiritual. They do not feel that the image of the School Sisters of St. Francis nor the root problems are satisfied by this religious avocation.

Very many sisters criticize the amount of liquor consumed, the smoking and even the dating and dancing done by some. They find it fully inconsistent with the ideals for the Christian life of women living in religious community — and I fully agree!

Please realize sisters, that I have not had time to illustrate or prove all my contentions. But I will be available during this chapter session and thereafter to discuss and to offer testimony. There are some limitations as to what I can reveal because I am bound by certain confidences which I will not break. But to the extent that I can reveal, I would be willing to illustrate. I'm sure that you and I both know the truth!

I found these comments not only from older sisters, but from a certain number of middle age and from some young who have chosen to discuss their problems. I find that they in no way want a blanket endorsement of the past or a retrogression to a form of life of the past. Yet, they do not feel that they suffered greatly from any subjection in the past. They feel that they were persons and were treated as persons with a discipline that was good in its time. They look to the present and the future and they have hopes as you do, but they seem to insist that the future be guided by principles of *Perfectae Caritatis* and the motu proprio *Ecclesiae Sanctae* and subsequent exhortations of the Holy Father and the Sacred Congregation for Religious. It seems that diligent and attentive study must be given to these decrees. And while you have fulfilled certain of their recommendations, yet much is to be done.

I believe with an honest, sincere and loving conviction that the work of this chapter and all subsequent chapters should be directed along this line in answering the needs of your people, and not diverting your interests to areas that do not demand attention at this hour. There may be a time, sisters, when in God's grace, the religious woman will be able to focus out completely and give herself to a work of the world in a different way than in the past. But I think this would have to be done with a certain gradualism, and can in no way be done with extremism and reactionism.

Once again — I can only serve you by being honest, and this I have tried to be, Sisters. Whether I am right or wrong, I ask that you consider what I have said, because I have said it out of knowledge of you and out of a deep, genuine love for you. And I thank you for your indulgence.[33]

Father Weber had intended for his presentation to the chapter meeting to be confidential, but some sisters who were present at the chapter, as well as some who were not there, requested a transcript of the talk. In the interest of accuracy, Father Weber made a transcript available only to School Sisters of St. Francis. A note from Father Weber on that transcript indicated that his remarks to the sisters had been the most difficult action of his years as a priest. He also noted that his conclusions had been collaborated by hundreds of interviews over the years.

A sister speaks up

One year after the 1969 chapter meeting at which Father Weber spoke, another document was produced that gives the insights of a sister who had lived through the renewal process. This document was written by Franciscan Sister M. Clemens, who was mother general of the School Sisters of St. Francis from 1960 to 1966. She had refused to be considered for re-election at the 1966 School Sisters of St. Francis election which elected Sister Francis Borgia. Sister M. Clemens's statement is dated June 1970, and was circulated to several people, including a staff member of the Congregation for Religious. It is quoted here in its entirety:

> In the name of the Father and of the Son and of the Holy Spirit, I am writing these lines so that after I am gone, everyone will know how I felt about the events and occurrences in the Congregation that took place after the Election 1966. God alone knows how much I have suffered in seeing that spirit which Mothers Alexia, Alfons, Stanislaus, and Corona held so sacred, disregarded and destroyed.
>
> The most crushing burden of this four-year ordeal has been the growing disregard for the legitimate authority of the Church in regard to the religious renewal proposed by the Vatican II Council as implemented by the Sacred Congregation for Religious. None of the documents of the Council nor the addresses given at various times by the Holy Father and members of the Sacred Congregation for Religious have been made known and available to the Sisters. Therefore, most of the Sisters do not know the directives of the Sacred Congregation for an authentic renewal. Those who have read these documents have searched for them in sources outside our community. There has been a flagrant disregard of ecclesiastical directives with reference to the celebration of the liturgy. There has been vocal opposition, such as "We are tired of being governed by men." This is hardly the language of those obedient to the Church — a virtue most highly prized by our foundresses — Mothers Alexia and Alfons.
>
> Within the community, the worst innovation was the

manner in which respect for the priesthood deteriorated. This lack of respect is absolutely contrary to that which the Sisters have been taught since the foundation of the Congregation. Mother Alexia's dying words were, "Respect the priesthood." Now, that respect is gone. Because of his firm stand against abuses, the Chaplain, the Reverend Donald N. Weber, a zealous, pious, holy priest, deeply interested in our community, has been treated shamefully. This grieves me to the core of my being. How can we expect God's blessing when we dishonor his ministers. Through this our loved community has lost its spirit of loving and humble service to the Church.

Along with this spirit of loving service, this Mary-like spirit, our Sisters, influenced by the derisive comments prevalent today, have set aside many practices of Marian devotion, such as the Rosary. The rhythms of the Hail Mary are no longer the distinctive cadence that sanctifies the daily tasks.

The next destructive force introduced has been the "living out" form of community life, in which the Sisters left their convent home to rent apartments in which to live with companions of their own choice. This took away our wonderful community spirit of sharing temporal and spiritual blessings with all of God's children and especially with the members of our religious family. There is much talk about love, love, love, but the more talk there is, the less love I see manifested. We never had so many "superiors" but yet when we need something, we are sent from one to another before we receive an answer to our request.

I cannot understand why the Sisters, a considerable number of them, were asked to go out and look for a job, while right here in the Motherhouse, more and more lay persons are hired. Why have a number of our Sisters gone to work in other health care units when their services are greatly needed in our own hospitals and nursing home? I cannot understand why our community was forced into such complicated business procedures in the handling of funds, whereas formerly such matters were conducted simply and beautifully in a spirit of communal sharing. The equating of a Sister's service with that of a hired employee on an eight-hour-a-day schedule is hardly valid in view of the community practice of freeing the Sisters for intervals of prayer during the work day.

Of course, I do not condemn all the changes, for many enable the Sisters to serve God and their fellow men in a better manner, but the implementation of these took place too rapidly. For instance, the change in regard to the habit has been a source of confusion. At first, the directive was the colors were to be black, white, blue, or gray and that the style of the dress was according to a specific pattern. But before one could realize what was happening, completely lay attire was introduced by a few Sisters. Now, it is really unbelievable how many outfits some Sisters have — and in what styles and colors! Surely, earrings and necklaces are not needed. Fancy hair-dos, wigs, and makeup scandalize many whom the Sisters expect to lead to Christ. For what purpose are the Sisters doing this? I cannot understand their intent in adopting current fashions. Their dresses are simply too short and too tight. Modesty is considered outmoded by a considerable number of Sisters. They consider slacks and shorts as suitable attire in which to appear in public. The TAU cross on a chain was substituted for the crucifix at the time of the change in habit. A number of the Sisters neither wear this or the smaller pin, subsequently adopted. Thus, in lay attire, the identity of the Sister is concealed.

With this lack of restraint in dress, the Sisters can go freely to places of entertainment formerly considered unsuitable for religious women. The result has been a "night life" with the consequent late hours. Taking the needed sleep the next morning has interfered with the celebration of the Eucharist. These Sisters have been heard to say that "Sunday is enough." Prayer is no longer the core and center of the life of the Sisters. Devotion to the Blessed Sacrament has declined. The practice of perpetual adoration, inaugurated by Mother Alfons in 1917, has been curtailed because of the scarcity of "adorers."

The celebration in the community of important events has always been a festive occasion. But these festivities have taken on a different tone with the introduction of hard liquor and the practice of smoking. This has led to the formation of the habits of smoking and excessive drinking by individual Sisters. The liturgical rites at the time of entrance and the profession of vows are now subject to the will and caprice of the individuals desiring member-ship in the Congregation. In some instances, these sacred rites have been conducted in such a way as to be the ob-ject of ridicule. Ecclesiastical directives for the celebra-tion of the Eucharist have been ignored. There is no for-mation of those admitted in the authentic form of religious life. It is difficult to ascertain how many young women are in formation — even where they are. All of a sudden, one or sometimes two or three pronounce vows.

Previous to 1966, our aging and infirm Sisters were assured of a home and the loving care of their fellow Sis-ters. This is no longer their expectation. Despite the need for additional living quarters for our retired and semi-re-tired Sisters, presently both the Rockford and the Omaha Provincial Houses are for sale. Little provision is being made for those Sisters who have devoted their lives in the service of Christ in the Church. Priests have opened par-ish convents to these Sisters in some instances, because they had no place to reside. In at least one Province, the practice has been adopted of placing Sisters in need of nursing care in outside nursing homes.

There has been almost a complete reversal of the phi-losophy of service to the Church in parish schools and Confraternity of Christian [Doctrine] classes in order to accept positions in the public school system and other civic activities, which are more to the individual Sister's liking. At the same time, the Sisters are withdrawing from ser-vice to the sick, their own Sisters as well as lay persons. The worth of a Sister is now equated with the monetary remuneration she receives "on the job," and her value in community is measured by the nature and quality of her education and her professional competency. There is much discussion about the dignity of the human person but an evident disregard of the grace of God at work in a voca-tion to the religious life.

The "increasing trend toward secularization," men-

tioned by Cardinal Antoniutti in his address to major superiors has been the affliction — the burden of these last
years of my life." The statement is signed, "Mother M.
Clemens, O.S.F." [34]

Note that Mother Clemens was not a reactionary opposed to change,
but she wanted that change to be guided by Vatican II documents on renewal, which she observed had not been passed along to the sisters.

The Vatican reacts

Two months after Mother Clemens wrote her statement, Cardinal
Antoniutti, prefect of the Congregation for Religious, wrote Sister Francis
Borgia on August 17, 1970, with the Vatican's response to the apostolic
visitation of the School Sisters of St. Francis. He wrote that the Congregation for Religious was pleased with many elements of the sisters' renewal,
including pioneering efforts in race relations and a concern for the poor.
However, Cardinal Antoniutti cited "Uncontrolled experimentation . . . allegedly in the name of the Renewal" that was not based on the documents
of Vatican II or the teachings of the Church. He cited in particular "an exaggerated cult of freedom," "a tendency to nullify authority on all levels," and
"considerable 'secularism.' " Regarding the mission of the School Sisters
of St. Francis to teach, Cardinal Antoniutti wrote: ". . . the special end of
your Congregation seems to have been relegated to a subordinate place and
to have given way to a wide-open apostolate, which is no longer a matter of
corporate commitment to the Church, or even to the Community, as Religious Life should be, but of personal commitment to whatever type of activity appeals to the individual."

Cardinal Antoniutti alluded to "a large number" of School Sisters of St.
Francis who wanted to live a true religious life, but were subjected to pressures and even threats to give up their ideals. He ended by suggesting that if
some sisters did not feel that the needs of the Church and the world could
be well served in the religious state as defined by the Church, those sisters
were free to pursue their goals and new lifestyle as lay persons: ". . . we
would raise no objection to their following their convictions, but not inside
the Religious State. It is altogether unjust to remain in this [religious] State,
harming it from within for those who wish to preserve it and live it. If
experimentation in another life-style is to be carried on it should be developed separately and on its own, not to the detriment of a State recognized
and esteemed by the Church." [35]

As with the situation involving the Immaculate Heart of Mary Sisters, a great deal of activity ensued to gather support for the School Sisters of St. Francis, especially among Religious who wanted to test Rome's limits in their push for unlimited experimentation. This activity included the informal meeting of selected members of the conferences of major superiors of women and of men — and others of like mind, including Anita Caspary — that took place September 3, 4, and 5 in St. Louis just prior to the 1970 annual assembly of the Conference of Major Religious Superiors of Women's Institutes (which was discussed in Chapter Six). Some sisters believe that this informal meeting was called specifically to garner support for Sister Francis Borgia, especially since Anita Caspary had failed to persuade the Congregation for Religious to allow unlimited experimentation for the Los Angeles Immaculate Heart of Mary Sisters. That informal 1970 meeting issued the famous "Statement" or "Manifesto" on religious life, and at least one section of the Statement seemed to relate to Cardinal Antoniutti's August 17 letter to Sister Francis Borgia. That part of the statement read: "Therefore we deem it destructive if a religious congregation is required to ask a brother or sister to depart, or the congregation itself is asked to abandon its public ecclesial character for the reason that a particular style of life is deemed a priori, incompatible with religious life."

The *National Catholic Reporter* published Cardinal Antoniutti's letter and quoted Sister Francis Borgia as saying that there had been some "mistakes and some excessive applications." But, she continued, "I happen to believe what we're doing is authentic religious life. We'll try to communicate this to Rome."[36]

The School Sisters continued along the renewal path they had set in 1966, but not without efforts by dissenting sisters to prompt Rome to intervene in what they considered to be a destructive path. A former School Sister reported that several School Sisters confronted Sister Francis Borgia in late 1971 about the fact that she had not shared with the community a document she had received from Rome about the conclusions of the apostolic visitation. Receiving no satisfaction from Sister Francis Borgia on the issue, five of the School Sisters flew to Rome to meet with the Congregation for Religious about the situation. The sisters were received graciously by the Congregation for Religious, which gave a sympathetic ear to their concerns. But still, nothing official transpired.

On October 22, 1972, a contingent of School Sisters sent a letter to all School Sisters of St. Francis, with copies to several bishops and the Congregation for Religious. In the letter, the sisters stated that a number of sisters in their institute wanted to maintain their corporate apostolate of teaching, as well as community life and prayer. These sisters cited the solution offered at the end of Cardinal Antoniutti's letter and suggested that "secularizing communities" conduct private polls as to whether sisters wished to live religious life as defined by the Church, or whether they would prefer a form of lay apostolate that would also be of service to the Church. The group suggested, "This would have a double effect of giving them [the lay group] ecclesiastical recognition and hopefully an opportunity of serving the Church as an organization of dedicated lay people; and it would free those thousands of sisters in the United States who are willing and ready to be religious according to the vowed commitment they made as the Church understands Religious Life to be in our age as in any age." The sisters ended their letter by asking the Holy See to resolve the problem.[37]

Again, Catholics watched the situation with great interest to see what precedent would be set. Many people speculated that the School Sisters of St. Francis would split into two groups — noncanonical and canonical — as did the Immaculate Heart of Mary Sisters. Bishops, priests, and parents were fearful that action by Rome would result in a sudden loss of School Sisters of St. Francis from Catholic schools that already were experiencing teacher shortages, much like the Immaculate Heart of Mary experience in California, but on a far larger scale. And sisters who wanted to support the Church's official version of religious life were painfully aware that in the Immaculate Heart of Mary case, the sisters who decided to remain canonical and under the direction of the Congregation for Religious, came away from the deal stripped of their order's institutions and almost penniless.

Apparently the School Sisters of St. Francis had strong allies in influential positions, for Rome made no further public move to alter the course of the sisters' renewal. Sister Francis Borgia possessed considerable personal popularity, and Rome probably had reason to fear that she would be viewed as a martyr if she were reprimanded or her decisions were curtailed by Church authorities. Given the outcome of the Los Angeles Immaculate Heart of Mary experience, Rome also probably feared a mass exodus of sisters to noncanonical status, which would have had a greater impact on Church institutions since the School Sisters numbered well over two-thousand members at that time. But predictably, Rome's decision not to interfere in the direction being taken by the School Sisters gave a green light to other sisters who had been contemplating a similar pattern of change in their own institutes.

Eventually, in 1981, a handful of School Sisters of St. Francis who continued to be unhappy with the direction of renewal in their order left the School Sisters of St. Francis and re-established themselves in Davenport, Iowa, as a new religious order, the Franciscan Sisters of Christ the Divine

Teacher, with Sister Bernadette Counihan as superior. Some sisters who also were unhappy with the form of renewal in their order opted to stay with the School Sisters of St. Francis to work for renewal of their order from within.

The School Sisters of St. Francis, who had about 2,800 members in 1965, had 1,000 fewer members by 1995. In 1995, Sister Francis Borgia Rothluebber asked for and was granted dispensation from her vows as a Religious after writing a controversial book, *Nobody Owns Me*. According to a book review in *Review for Religious*, "In *Nobody Owns Me* Rothluebber explores the issue of celibate sexuality — or, more accurately, celibate genitality — through the fictional journal of a 41-year-old woman religious."[38]

While these are two very specific examples of the chaos of renewal, these examples are quite representative of the experience of not all, but certainly many women Religious in a variety of orders in this country. Poorly-conceived renewal programs were imposed on sisters who were not well prepared for massive change. And when that change did come, it was not introduced at a reasonable, incremental pace so that the sisters could assess the experiments and gradually assimilate the positive elements into their constitutions, as Vatican II had directed. Rather, sisters who had been accustomed to having every detail of their lives spelled out for them abruptly found themselves in a "free-form" community. In these sweeping renewal programs, sisters suddenly were expected to make decisions that had always been pre-determined for them: where they would work and live; what work they would perform; whom they would live with; what they would wear; when and how they would pray. In the case of the Immaculate Heart of Mary Sisters and the School Sisters of St. Francis, media-savvy, charismatic leaders promoted this extreme version of renewal in the name of the Church, and they succeeded in convincing a good many people that they were in the vanguard of Religious eager to respond to the call of Vatican II, but being impeded unfairly by aging Vatican chauvinists who wanted to keep women in a subordinate role.

The results of this self-styled, unlimited renewal have been devastating for many communities of women Religious. Ironically, it has been quite common for some of the sisters who pushed most vehemently for excessive change in their orders to eventually depart from their communities, consigning to the remaining sisters a legacy of turmoil created by the very sisters who left their orders. The result of all this turmoil was abandonment of apostolates, polarization within communities, confusion of the faithful, and a significant increase in departures from religious life. This chaos also impacted the vocations picture so dramatically that in 1983, the pope gave a specific charge to United States bishops to study religious life to try and determine why so few young people were entering religious institutes and why so many Church institutions were forced to close their doors. That study is reported in the next chapter.

12: The Quinn Commission Examines Religious Life

"Information does not always result in either wisdom or understanding."[1]

Sister Margaret Cafferty, PBVM
Executive Director
Leadership Conference of Women Religious

As the numbers of men and women Religious in the United States continued to decline because of death, departure, and the dearth of new vocations, the Vatican became more and more alarmed about the state of religious life in the United States. Consequently, in 1983 Pope John Paul II asked the bishops of the United States to undertake a study of religious life in this country to try to determine why this decline was occurring. The pope also asked the Congregation for Religious to summarize the Church teachings on religious life in a document which the bishops could use as a reference in their study.

This papally-mandated study of religious life and the accompanying document were met with considerable resistance by many Religious, particularly some sisters who were openly hostile, accusing the pope of trying to return religious orders to the pre-Vatican II authoritarian model of religious life. Most organizations of sisters, such as the National Assembly Religious Women, also openly opposed the study. As the three-year study progressed and bishops held meetings around the country to hear what Religious had to say, sisters who were engaged in re-writing the definition of religious life in their own terms seized the opportunity to educate Rome and the bishops about these "new paradigms" of religious life they had created through their "lived experience." Anger by some Religious over the Vatican chastisement of American sisters who had signed a 1984 abortion rights statement in the *New York Times* further inflamed some change-oriented sisters, as did the insistence by Rome that Mercy Sister Agnes Mary Mansour could not remain a sister while directing a state government office that disbursed funds for abortions. And some of these sisters made it abundantly clear that Rome and the bishops had nothing of value to say to them.

When all was said and done, the study of religious life in the United States accomplished little more than emphasizing the polarization that had occurred in religious institutes and the Church's inability to deal with the crisis in religious life. The commission of bishops conducting the study concluded, incredibly, that religious life was in generally good shape with the exception of a few minor problems. But grass-roots Religious charged that the commission heard only what it wanted to hear from leaders who were out of touch with their memberships. Furthermore, bishops who were concerned about airing dirty laundry in public, or who did not want to alienate their diocesan workforces, were reluctant to ask hard questions or make specific demands on Religious, even though part of the pope's charge was for the bishops to instruct errant Religious about the essentials of religious life. In the end, the United States bishops seemed to accept the recommendation of one of their number that they simply do nothing until the turn of the century, hoping that the whole mess somehow would work itself out. Here is that story.

Pope John Paul II creates the Quinn Commission

On Easter Sunday of 1983, Pope John Paul II wrote the bishops of the United States about his concern over "the marked decline in recent years in the numbers of young people seeking to enter religious life, particularly in the case of institutes of apostolic life." The pope asked the bishops to conduct a study to determine the reasons for the declining numbers of Religious, a decline which he said placed an undue burden on Religious who try "to continue manifold services without adequate numbers," thus resulting in "a consequent risk to their health and spiritual vitality."

Pope John Paul also asked the bishops to "render special pastoral service to the religious of your dioceses and your country" by "proclaiming anew to all the people of God the church's teaching on consecrated life." The pope observed that the teachings on consecrated life were set out in *Lumen Gentium, Perfectae Caritatis,* and *Evangelica Testificatio,* in addresses of himself and his predecessor, Paul VI, as well as in the new *Code of Canon Law.* And he summarized what he called "basic elements" of religious life, including public vows, stable community life, fidelity to charisms and sound traditions, corporate apostolate, personal and liturgical prayer, public witness, and government by religious authority. The pope observed that fidelity to these elements "guarantees the strength of religious life and grounds our hope for its future growth."

The pope appointed Archbishop John Quinn of San Francisco to head a commission to oversee this study by the bishops. Also appointed as other members of the commission were Archbishop Thomas Kelly of Louisville, a Dominican, and Bishop Raymond Lessard of Savannah. The pope asked that the bishops consult with a number of Religious, to profit from their insights. He added that the commission would work in union with the Congregation for Religious and follow "a document of guidelines which the congregation is making available to them" and to all the bishops.[2]

The pope's April 3 letter was not released to the general public until June 22. When it was released, it was accompanied by the "document of guidelines" for the bishops, to which the pope had referred in his letter. This document was titled *Essential Elements in Church Teaching on Religious Life.* The document, prepared by the Congregation for Religious, noted that superiors, chapters, and bishops had asked the Congregation "for directives as they assess the recent past and look toward the future." And it observed that the renewal of religious life had had mixed results: ". . . these institutes have been dealing with sudden shifts in their own internal situations; rising median age, fewer vocations, diminishing numbers, pluriformity of lifestyle and works, and frequently insecurity regarding identity. The result has been an understandably mixed experience with many positive aspects and some which raise important questions.

"Now, with the ending of the period of special experimentation mandated by *Ecclesiae Sanctae II,* many religious institutes dedicated to the works of the apostolate are reviewing their experience."[3]

The *Essential Elements* document, then, was to be used as a guide for evaluating the renewal experience. Certainly the document broke no new ground, but drew frequently and heavily on the Vatican II documents cited by the pope and on several papal exhortations and addresses, as well as the new *Code of Canon Law,* which had been released on January 25, 1983, and would go into effect November 27, 1983. But clearly, the renewal efforts of many religious institutes in the United States did not conform to those guidelines for a variety of reasons that have been discussed in this book.

Consequently, the establishment of the Quinn Commission by the Holy Father and the subsequent issuance of *Essential Elements* angered and concerned many Religious. Some Religious considered the appointment of the Quinn Commission to be an undeserved inquisition by patriarchal authority. Others felt that American Religious were being singled out by the Vatican for undue criticism of their renewal efforts, since no other country had received the same mandate. And some Religious tried to discredit the *Essential Elements* document, saying it did not have proper authority because it was not signed by the pope. Others resented the fact that the document was prepared without any consultation with the Religious of this country.

The Agnes Mary Mansour affair

The timing of the Vatican-mandated commission also was viewed with alarm, particularly by some sisters, because just one month before the Quinn Commission was announced, Sister of Mercy Agnes Mary Mansour had requested dispensation from her vows after months of negotiations with the Vatican about her political appointment as Director of Social Services for the State of Michigan. Archbishop Edmund Szoka of Detroit had directed Sister Agnes Mary to take a clear stand against Medicaid payments for abortion or else resign the state position, as he felt the situation presented scandal and confusion. When Sister Agnes Mary did not do so, Archbishop Szoka told the Sisters of Mercy Detroit provincial leadership team on February 23, 1983, that Sister Agnes Mary did not have his permission to remain in the position, and he directed the Mercy superiors to inform Sister Agnes Mary that she must resign from the state job. (At that time, canon law required that a Religious needed the permission of the local bishop to hold political office. The new *Code of Canon Law*, which went into effect November 27, 1983, has a generic prohibition against Religious holding public office at all.)

On March 4, 1983, Archbishop Szoka met again with the provincial leadership team, which acknowledged that Sister Agnes Mary needed the archbishop's permission to retain the position. But still the Mercy leaders did not issue any directive to Sister Agnes Mary, contending that the archbishop's directive did not have to be followed if "a greater good was involved." In her state confirmation hearing on March 8, Sister Agnes Mary testified that she was opposed to abortion but could tolerate Medicaid funding for abortion through the Department of Social Services. On March 10,

Archbishop Szoka contacted the Vatican, reporting that "Catholic people are confused, disturbed and dismayed by the spectacle of a Catholic nun being in the position of director of a department which pays for abortions and refusing to state her opposition to such payments."

The apostolic delegate, Archbishop Pio Laghi, instructed Sister Theresa Kane, president of the Sisters of Mercy of the Union, to require Sister Agnes Mary to submit her resignation as director of the Social Services Department. On April 11, Sister Theresa Kane requested a formal reconsideration of the decision reached by the Congregation for Religious. The Congregation for Religious then appointed Bishop Anthony Bevilacqua (who was chair of the United States Bishops' Canonical Affairs Committee) as the Vatican's ad hoc delegate for the Mansour case. The Congregation issued a letter on April 16, reporting that the pope had directed Bishop Bevilacqua "to approach Sister Agnes Mary Mansour directly and to require, in the name of the Holy See and by virtue of her vow of obedience, that she immediately resign as director" of the Department of Social Services.

On May 9, 1983, Bishop Bevilacqua met with Sister Agnes Mary and explained to her that if she refused to resign from her state job, the canonical process of imposed secularization would be initiated. At that May 9 meeting, Sister Agnes Mary requested dispensation from her vows rather than resign her state job or have the canonical process of secularization be initiated.[4]

Sister Agnes Mary and the Mercy leaders contended that the process had been unfair and that insufficient dialogue had taken place. Thus the Agnes Mary Mansour case became a rallying point for sisters who felt that the Vatican was unfairly wielding patriarchal power over a woman who was sincerely committed to helping poor women. She was even referred to in terms of martyrdom.

Few sisters seemed to recognize that the Mansour case also was a power struggle between the hierarchy and the leaders of the Mercy Sisters at the provincial and national levels, who had refused to comply with the directives of the local bishop or the Holy See. In a press release, NETWORK (a lobbying group composed mainly of sisters), revealed the extent to which individualism had been enshrined as the locus of authority for some women Religious. The press release on the Mansour case expressed NETWORK's support of "the individual's right to act on the dictates of conscience in pursuit of the public good." The press release cited "authoritarian exercise of administrative power on the part of Vatican officials and their representatives," and affirmed "the right to individual and corporate dissent within ecclesial as well as political structures."[5]

The National Assembly of Religious Women and the National Coalition of American Nuns issued a joint press release on the Mansour case that contended the "Roman Congregation for Religious in their fear of losing 'authority' has ignored the principle of freedom of conscience." The press release asked that women protest on Pentecost Sunday, 1983, "as a visible witness to the arrogant use of power in a male dominated church."[6] Joining in a small protest outside St. Matthew Cathedral in Washington, D.C., were Sister Theresa Kane, Sister Dorothy Vidulich, and Ruth McDonough Fitzpatrick (executive director of the Women's Ordination Conference and a representative of the National Assembly of Religious Women). Sister Donna Quinn, president of the National Coalition of American Nuns, protested outside the Holy Name Cathedral in Chicago. Sister Donna was later quoted in *Ms.* magazine: "The Pope's order of obedience without consulting the administrative team, without due process, 'tramples on who we are as women religious in the United States'."[7] And, the *Ms.* writer, Mary Kay Blakely, described in the article's credit line as a "recovering Catholic," added her own opinion: "Will the Pope know, now, that a slowly smoldering brushfire is moving toward the Vatican? I hope so. If he thought, though, that forcing out Sister Mansour solved the 'little sister' problem in America, then Mansour is right: the Pope doesn't understand the American people, and he doesn't understand the American nun."[8]

So, it was in the middle of this volatile situation that Archbishop Quinn was beginning his work on the papally-mandated study of religious life in the United States.

Educating the bishops

Archbishop Quinn appointed a committee of Religious to assist his commission. But some Religious were unhappy with the committee's make-up, suggesting that its members represented only the left wing of the political spectrum of Religious in the United States. Some were concerned that the heavy representation of the two superiors' conferences on the committee would result in study conclusions based on the opinions of the conference leaders — opinions which sought no input from the thousands of grassroots men and women Religious.

Appointed to the committee were: School Sister of Notre Dame Clare Fitzgerald (a past-president of the Leadership Conference of Women Religious, 1980-81); Sister of St. Joseph Bette Moslander (past president of the Leadership Conference of Women Religious, 1981-82); Daughter of Charity Sister Teresa Piro; Sister of Province Alexa Suelzer; Franciscan Father Alan McCoy (past president of the Conference of Major Superiors of Men);

and Xaverian Brother Thomas More Page (a former executive director of the Conference of Major Superiors of Men).

In order to discuss the work of their commission as soon as possible with Religious, Archbishop Kelly attended the annual assembly of the Conference of Major Superiors of Men on August 8, 1983, and Archbishop Quinn met with the women superiors at their assembly on August 16. News reports of those two meetings indicate that the pope's mandated study and the accompanying document did not sit well with some of the major superiors, even though the bishop members of the commission had hastened to reassure Religious about the intent of the study. Concerns raised by the male superiors included the fear that the commission represented "Roman interventionism" and had been "set up as a watchdog agency to deal with religious who stray from Church norms." But other male superiors indicated support for the commission, with one even observing that a stricter definition of religious life could help end confusion among the laity about the role of Religious.[9]

In a panel discussion at the meeting of male superiors, Bishop Kelly said he felt that many bishops had stayed away from what was happening in religious life because most bishops felt they didn't understand religious life very well. "If there is anything that's going to come out of this study and the mandate that is given to the bishops," Bishop Kelly said, "it is precisely that they will come to understand religious life, be able to articulate it and, as the mandate is on them, to preach the values of religious life to the churches they serve."[10]

At a news conference after he had spoken at a closed session of the assembly of women superiors, Archbishop Quinn said he had a positive experience at the session, but "sensed real anxiety on the part of the sisters about whether the Vatican's directives will be interpreted 'blindly or with flexibility.' " Sister of Charity Helen Flaherty, president of the Leadership Conference of Women Religious, told the news conference that most major superiors did not agree with the Vatican's emphasis on the negative aspects of the decline in vocations and they did not link that decline to the secularization of religious life. "We see the decline as a positive part of the trend toward greater participation by the laity in the ministry of the Church," Sister Helen said. "It's not a numbers game. We want to get away from that." Sister Helen described Archbishop Quinn's appearance at a closed session of the conference assembly as "lively and candid."[11]

Former conference executive directors Sisters Mary Daniel Turner and Lora Ann Quinonez were more descriptive of the conference assembly's reception of Archbishop Quinn in their book *The Transformation of Ameri-*

can Catholic Sisters. They wrote that "One member after another voiced her dismay at Pope John Paul II's mandate for a review of religious life in the United States."[12] Further, "From microphones scattered throughout the hall, voice after voice placed ministry, the work for justice and peace, and deep involvement in the mission of the church in the world at the core of religious identity. Repudiating the characterization of religious life in *Essential Elements* as alien to the experience of American sisters, they held up the truth of their own experience. . . . Their words held a consistent message: no one, not even church officials, and nothing, not even ecclesiastical pronouncements, will divert them from that quest. They trust themselves and they trust their journey. Their destination they are willing to discover in the process."[13]

Members of the National Assembly of Religious Women, meeting immediately after the women superiors, were equally unrestrained in their assessment of the appointment of the Quinn Commission. The Assembly's national coordinator, Dominican Sister Marjorie Tuite, said that "What we are seeing today is an escalating pattern of oppression against women religious by Rome. It amounts to a witch hunt." Assembly board member Sister of Charity Barbara Aires observed that sisters needed to rally together to protect their renewal efforts: "We sweated, suffered and died in our congregations. We're past that. We won't go through that upheaval again!"[14]

Sister Margaret Ellen Traxler of the National Coalition of American Nuns also reacted angrily to the Quinn Commission and *Essential Elements*. She was quoted as saying: "I observe that in the United States Rome is cutting itself off. When the pope speaks, he's speaking from another world," and "the feeling of the American Sisters is that nobody is going to turn us around."[15]

In fact, this "Vatican-initiated investigation of 'religious life' in the United States" prompted Sister Margaret Ellen and several other sisters to collect a book of essays "to let the investigating commission know what renewal of religious life in the post-Vatican II church has meant to us."[16] The work of these sisters, many of whom were active members of the National Coalition of American Nuns, was funded by an anonymous donor as well as the Sisters of Loretto and the Sisters of the Mercy of the Union, and published as *Midwives of the Future*.

In November of 1983, Sister Bette Moslander addressed the fall meeting of the National Conference of Catholic Bishops. A past president of the Leadership Conference of Women Religious, she was one of the six Religious named to the advisory committee for the Quinn Commission. Sister Bette discussed the hopes and concerns of women Religious regarding the bishops' study of religious life, indicating that the sisters intended to be on the speaking end of the dialogue, not on the listening end.

The sisters' hopes were, according to Sister Bette: 1) that the bishops would allow sisters to "share with you as we would with brothers and friends"; 2) that through such sharing "we might dispel some of the confusion and negative judgments that have accompanied the changes of the past 20 years"; and 3) "that in this process the whole church in the United States will be enriched by a deeper understanding as the people of God in this country and in this time."

The concerns of the women Religious expressed by Sister Bette were: 1) "We are concerned lest this study promote division and polarization within our religious communities and among the various religious congregations. . . . The heavy imposition of a narrow and fundamentalist interpretation of the 'Essential Elements' document or a simplistic application of the document to all religious communities without respect for the unique charisms or diverse experiences of the communities may fragment religious communities and bring immense pain and suffering"; 2) "We are concerned lest the study become preoccupied with in-house self-examination and divert us from the very grave needs of our people and of the world"; and 3) "Last, we are concerned lest women in our country look upon this study as another painful example of the inability of the clerical church to receive and honor the experience of women as full members of the church."[17]

At that same November 1983 meeting of the bishops, Archbishop Quinn shared some of his reflections on the pope's mandate for the bishops to study religious life in the United States. Archbishop Quinn observed that the pope was asking the bishops to render pastoral service to Religious, which was not to be construed as interfering in the internal business of the religious institutes. ". . . By reason of the apostolic structure of the Church, bishops have a responsibility for religious life in their churches," he said, and he stressed that "*Essential Elements* is a compilation from conciliar and other magisterial documents and from the new *Code of Canon Law*," and that these sources should be consulted in interpreting the document. He told the bishops they were not asked to condemn, but rather "to invite those relatively few among the larger number of faithful religious who may be living in conflict with the Church's norms or teaching, to walk together with us anew the journey of conversion."[18]

In spite of Archbishop Quinn's public optimism, some United States bishops apparently had misgivings about the pope's intentions and about the *Essential Elements* document. Some of those concerns were documented by Archbishop Quinn in a December 21, 1983, report.

Archbishop Quinn wrote that, "While the attitude of the bishops was basically positive, there were certain fears and apprehensions which are shared also by religious." Some bishops expressed the fear that the pope's mandate would imply the right of bishops to interfere in the internal affairs of religious institutes. Others feared that the pope wanted religious life to revert to a pre-Vatican II model, and some thought that the pope intended to monasticize all forms of religious life. Archbishop Quinn observed that "One of the weaknesses is the fact that most of the bishops are not well acquainted with *Perfectae Caritatis, Evangelica Testificatio,* or *Mutuae Relationes* [a 1978 document from the Congregations for Religious and for Bishops that gave doctrinal background and practical norms for cooperation between Religious and the hierarchy], or other such documents of the Magisterium pertaining to religious life."

A second weakness identified by Archbishop Quinn was "the fact that most bishops have little understanding of religious life and still less understanding of what has taken place in religious life since the Council. Thus in this matter there is a wide gap in understanding between religious and bishops. . . . On the other hand many religious do not understand the problems and outlook of the bishops."

Archbishop Quinn concluded that most Religious loved the Church and wanted to cooperate with the bishops. He wrote that there were "some individual religious and some groups of religious who give cause for concern. But I think it would be a mistake to make them the focus of our efforts at this time." He advocated, rather, that the moderate Religious be strengthened and encouraged in order to lessen the influence of "the extreme left and the extreme right." The "radical" Religious were losing some of their influence, Archbishop Quinn wrote, and direct confrontation "with the left runs the risk of restoring them to a position of greater importance than they merit."[19]

By spring of 1984, the Quinn Commission had been at work for almost a year, and Religious were continuing to let Rome and the United States bishops know that they did not take kindly to the pope's mandated study of religious life. A March 19, 1984, article in *Newsweek* quoted Archbishop Rembert Weakland of Milwaukee, a Benedictine, as saying, "The Vatican's Congregation for Religious and the American sisters are at total odds." The same article quoted Servants of Mary Sister Sean Fox, described by *Newsweek* as a divorce lawyer in Oak Park, Illinois: "The American bishops, she believes, are 'walking a tightrope' between Rome and the sisters. They'll want to tread lightly, she adds, 'because they might lose their work force.'" The article concluded that "many American sisters now say they will refuse all Vatican efforts to revive traditional convent life. Sister Lora Ann Quinonez, executive director of the LCWR [Leadership Conference of Women Religious], believes the church should recognize that sisters in apostolic orders 'are called to ministry, not community.' "[20]

It is interesting to note that the executive director of the superiors' conference perceived community and ministry as being mutually exclusive, whereas the classical understanding of religious life has always been that community enables ministry.

Hostile elites, silent grassroots

The bishops forged ahead, and during 1984 many of them initiated "listening sessions" in their dioceses, in which the bishops invited Religious to dialogue with them about their experiences in religious life. The bishops then were to make an interim report about these sessions to Archbishop Quinn before the bishops met again in November of 1984.

In some — or perhaps many — dioceses, there appears to have been little effort to engage grassroots Religious in the process at all. On the other hand, a number of high-profile Religious gathered during the summer of 1984 to speak at two formal programs about the meaning and implications of the pope's charge to the United States bishops to study religious life, and some of them were openly hostile.

The first program was a conference at Boston College June 20 through 22, 1984. At that conference, a number of speakers were featured, including Sister Margaret Brennan, who had been president of the Leadership Conference of Women Religious 1972-73; Jesuit Fathers James Hennesey and John Padberg; Franciscan Father Richard Rohr; and Claretian Father John Lozano. Sister Marie Augusta Neal, creator of the Sisters' Survey, sounded her familiar theme when she told the conference that "peace, poverty and human rights are the central concerns of the committed Christian," and that religious institutes had been "endeavoring to be obedient to this mandate to participate in the righting of the wrongs of injustice."[21]

However, Archbishop John Whealon of Hartford told that same gathering that as one of few remaining United States bishops who had attended the Second Vatican Council, he could confirm that the developments in religious life being discussed at the meeting were "not in the least, foreseen by the United States bishops at Vatican II." Rather, he said those developments resulted from sociological trends in society rather than from Vatican II. Archbishop Whealon also observed that the presentations at that meeting "did not express the viewpoints of all United States religious," as more than half of the leaders of religious institutes in his diocese had told him that the papal letter and the ten essentials did represent their view of religious life and their lived experience over the past twenty years. But the voice of those satisfied Religious had not been heard during the gathering, the archbishop commented. And, he expressed his chagrin that "I saw this conference as not a constructive, positive, happy meeting . . . because so much of the conference was given to criticism (indeed 'resentment' was one verb used) of the Roman congregation [for Religious] and Roman document [*Essential Elements*]. Major applause here was given to anti-document protests."[22]

The second program was a lecture series at the University of San Francisco during the summer of 1984. Among the speakers was Sister Helen Flaherty, a past president of the Leadership Conference of Women Religious (1982-83), who stressed the American emphasis on democracy, even in ecclesial matters: "There is strong reason to believe that the church of the future is the church rising from below, not imposed from the top. . . . Modeling participative and corporate authority will have a particularly powerful, prophetic impact on this country because, as we know, high value is placed on rights, due process and individual freedom."[23]

On September 10, 1984, two months before the U. S. Bishops' fall meeting, the administrative board of the Consortium Perfectae Caritatis sent Archbishop Quinn and the other bishops a letter expressing concerns they wanted the Quinn Commission to address. The Consortium was a group of traditional sisters who had banded together in 1971 because they believed that the Leadership Conference of Women Religious was moving away from the definition of religious life approved by the Holy See. In their letter, the Consortium stated: 1) that *Essential Elements* had not been communicated to "a great number of individual religious in the United States"; 2) "that several general chapters have been held since the publication of the *Essential Elements* without any reference whatsoever to the existence of this document"; 3) that the pope would not receive a report from the commission that would clearly indicate "the seriousness of the condition of religious life in the United States; that the voice of many in leadership positions will not communicate the lived reality of the large number of religious who are prevented from living out their vowed commitment to the Holy Father as their highest superior"; and 4) that the present state of religious life fails to inspire vocations.[24]

The Consortium sisters also asked the bishops several questions in their letter:

• Would Religious "continue to be prevented from community prayer life, corporate apostolate, authentic community living, personal and corporate poverty, and identifiable public witness through religious apparel" because of the absence of an authority structure required by the Church?

• Would the "Holy Father hear the voices of the many religious who are suffering because their leaders will not follow the guidelines for authentic renewal mandated by our Holy Father? And what will be done to help them in their powerlessness?"

The sisters further asked the bishops to "investigate the dioceses where our Holy Father's letter to the Bishops and the *Essential Elements* have not been circulated," to follow the study of *Essential Elements* with a survey to ascertain the commitment of each Religious to living out *Essential Elements*, and to establish and extend canonical approval to a new conference of major superiors of women Religious, to which members who implemented *Essential Elements* could belong.[25] (This latter suggestion indeed became a reality eight years later, as detailed in Chapter Fourteen.)

The *New York Times* ad

Then, on October 7, 1984, the Sunday designated by the United States Bishops as "Respect Life Sunday," a $30,000 ad appeared in the *New York Times* headlined "A Diversity of Opinion Regarding Abortion Exists Among Committed Catholics." The full-page ad was sponsored by Catholics For A Free Choice, Inc., and included a "Catholic Statement on Pluralism and Abortion." The statement began: "Continued confusion and polarization within the Catholic community on the subject of abortion prompt us to issue this statement. Statements of recent popes and of the Catholic hierarchy have condemned the direct termination of pre-natal life as morally wrong in all instances. There is the mistaken belief in American society that this is the only legitimate Catholic position. In fact, a diversity of opinions regarding abortion exists among committed Catholics:"[26]

Included in the published list of the approximately one-hundred people who endorsed the ad were twenty-six women Religious,[27] two religious brothers, one religious priest, and one diocesan priest.

In late November, the Vatican sent letters to all the institutes of the Religious involved and directed them to tell those Religious to publicly retract their support of the statement or face expulsion from their religious institutes. Most institutes and Religious initially refused, but eventually agreements were reached between the Vatican and all the Religious except for Sisters of Notre Dame de Namur Barbara Ferraro and Patricia Hussey, who eventually resigned from their order four years later.[28]

When the November 1984 meeting of the United States Bishops convened, again there was ongoing turmoil surrounding sisters, and the polarization among women Religious was even more obvious.

At the bishops' meeting, Archbishop Quinn reported that seventy percent of the diocesan bishops had made interim reports on the listening sessions. He gave a summary he had compiled from those reports, which discussed some of the strengths and weaknesses discovered in the past twenty years of renewal.

Strengths included: effort to return to the spirit and charism of the founder; deepening of the life of prayer; greater integration of the community, spiritual, and apostolic dimension of religious life; growing sense of solidarity with the church; greater maturity of candidates entering religious life; appreciation of the feminine; and more mature understanding of the vow of obedience.

Weaknesses, which he said almost all bishops agreed on, included: decline in numbers entering; loss in membership; necessity of leaving traditional works and institutions; tensions across generations; rejection and hostility toward Religious by some bishops, priests, and lay people because of changes in religious life; and growing financial problems. Some bishops also found that: congregations had lost their identity, and hence numbers, by abandoning uniform religious garb and a uniform style of community life; a sense of the cross has been lost; there was an overemphasis on the individual and on the women's movement; and that authority was not properly recognized and respected either within the community or in the Church at large.[29]

Archbishop Quinn told the bishops that their study of religious life was just in the initial stages, and that after data had been collected and collated, it would be submitted to experts in theology, church history, psychology, and cultural anthropology for "reflection and reaction." He reported on his visit to Rome the previous month (October 1984), during which the commission members discussed their progress with the Congregation for Religious. He said that the congregation affirmed that the *Essential Elements* document should be interpreted in light of its source documents and that "it is not the intent of the document to monasticize religious life." Archbishop Quinn proposed that the bishops spend time at their next meeting, in June of 1985, coming to a common understanding of the five points that generated the most interest at the 1984 listening sessions: 1) community life; 2) religious obedience; 3) structures of authority; 4) public witness and religious identity; and 5) consecration and mission.

Then, Archbishop Quinn asked that after that June 1985 meeting the bishops would invite Religious to dialogue about those major themes by answering three questions:

"1. How do the religious understand these issues and how do they feel they are fulfilling the expectations of the church in living these points?
"2. How do the bishops understand these issues? How do they see religious in actual fact fulfilling the expectations of the church in their dioceses?
"3. "Where there are difference in understanding, how can these be resolved in a peaceful, non-threatening and loving way which will build up the body of Christ and promote religious life?"[30]

A "don't ask, don't tell" policy?

Apparently a number of bishops went on to distribute these three questions to some or all Religious in their dioceses. But the questions were criticized by some Religious as unbalanced, in that they did not solicit the opinion of Religious about what abuses and excesses had occurred in their institutes, nor did the questions invite Religious to address concerns they had about polarization in their communities and what they considered to be rejection of Church authority and teachings. The questions also did not offer the opportunity to address in a significant manner the five main points of interest that Archbishop Quinn said had come out of the listening sessions.

At any rate, many bishops seem to have made a diligent effort to respond to Archbishop Quinn's plan. But the listening sessions, dialogues, and openness of bishops and Religious varied from diocese to diocese, resulting in a very uneven experience. Many Religious were not invited to any such meetings at all, and in fact, some Religious didn't even know such listening sessions were going on. Some diocesan meetings were conducted by Religious themselves at the direction of the local bishop. Often, these Religious had a predetermined agenda that did not coincide with the points the bishops wanted to be addressed. Some Religious even looked upon the meetings as their opportunity to instruct the bishops and Rome about their own version of religious life, and they simply never entertained the notion that they had made any mistakes in renewal or had anything to learn from — much less obligation to adhere to — the Church teachings summarized in *Essential Elements*. And some meetings apparently were dominated by the most vocal faction and offered little opportunity for input from grassroots Religious. One sister reported that at the state-wide meeting she attended, speakers from the Leadership Conference of Women Religious dominated the meeting. She said she was disappointed because Religious were invited to discuss the issues on "essential elements" of religious life, but instead the discussion seemed to center on "injustices and sufferings" of women Religious during the past ten years.

225

Sisters in Crisis

Marist Father Thomas Dubay, a theologian, found that some Religious were asked to reflect only on the positive results of renewal, and were instructed not to mention any negative results or problem areas. He wrote Archbishop Quinn:

"Another source of disillusionment with the current study of religious life is the questionnaire and the diocesan meetings. One of the former which I received told us expressly not to mention negative developments in our institutes but to report what we have found to be favorable happenings since Vatican II. This is an almost incredible rigging of results, and it can give only a rosy picture to the Holy See. The evidence I have indicates that religious across the country have experienced in diocesan meetings a similar slanting." (Father Dubay had indicated earlier in his letter that as a retreat master on the road for many years, he had met and counseled thousands of Religious and usually received about seventy-five letters a month from Religious. He wrote that most of the Religious he heard from were "on the middle and left of the opinion spectrum." He said he heard "little from the far right, presumably because they consider me too liberal.") He continued:

"The study consequently is not representative of all of us. We could not without impoliteness express our real views, and thus despite the meetings, thousands of us remain unheard and unrepresented in any effective way. Rome, therefore, will receive an optimistic report that, a.) most American religious are quite happy with what has happened in their congregations; b.) we have no grave problems, for we mentioned none — indeed we were told not to mention them; c.) contrary reports to Rome are consequently unfounded, reactionary, and thus to be disregarded.

"The questionnaire likewise did not raise the Holy Father's chief concern: why the great drop in religious vocations? Could it be that secularized congregations are embarrassed at how poorly they are doing, while those who gladly accept Vatican II and canon law are attracting goodly numbers, sometimes very large numbers? For this statement I can offer specific documentation should you wish it. Young men and women are voting with their feet. And it is clear where they are going and where the future of religious life lies."[31]

A different perspective on the diocesan sessions was presented by Archbishop John Whealon in a 1984 letter to Pope John Paul II. (Each bishop was directed to write a letter to the pope, expressing the results of his diocesan sessions and indicating his conclusions about the condition of religious life in his diocese.) Archbishop Whealon's letter also gives some insights into the dilemma of bishops and the distress of some Religious.

226

Archbishop Whealon reported that he had visited with either the provincial or council or community of the ten religious institutes which had provincial houses in the Archdiocese of Hartford. Of those ten institutes, Archbishop Whealon wrote that seven institutes — four of women and three of men — perceived that the ten essentials of religious life named by the pope in his 1983 letter to United States bishops described the way they were living religious life. Most of those seven communities had already had their constitutions approved by Rome, the archbishop wrote.

The three remaining communities — all women's institutes — "experienced renewal in a different way," according to Archbishop Whealon. They had "experienced the reduction of centralized and local authority in favor of a more collegial approach and openness to difference in the individual apostolates; a willingness to permit smaller groups to live apart from the larger community and the replacement of religious garb with simple secular dress." In all three communities, the archbishop noted, a minority had retained their religious garb.

He then shared six conclusions with the pope: "1) We have today in the U.S.A. two sharply different approaches to religious life. The one approach follows the ten essentials; the other approach follows some of the ten essentials but has adopted a noticeably more democratic approach to authority, work, living arrangements and religious garb. 2) These two approaches are irreconcilable. There is a painful division between the two groups and a more painful division within a community in which the leadership and most younger members have followed a progressive approach to renewal while most of the older members have remained conservative. 3) Some, not all, conservative communities are growing. The more progressive — our largest communities of women — are showing no growth. 4) Because of these two different approaches to religious life there is widespread confusion about the identity of religious life. 5) The progressive group include many of our best, brightest, most dedicated religious. Their life style and works of religion are to the credit of their community and Church. That they are not growing in numbers is cause for lamentation. 6) The progressive group is confirmed that its approach to renewal will be judged as not valid and they will loose [sic] their status as religious in the Church. One answer to this is that they have already effectively converted the community to the status of a secular institute."

Archbishop Whealon then suggested two possibilities for dealing with what he called the "extraordinarily complex" situation:

"1) Following the Gamaliel principle, do nothing. In fifteen years — a brief time in the life of the Church — the picture will be much more clear.

At the end of the century a decision can be made. 2) Designate the religious following the ten essentials, including individuals in progressive communities, as religious of strict observance and designate the others by a different terminology. The conservatives in progressive communities should be given special consideration."

Archbishop Whealon wrote that in the long run, there probably would be little difference in the two courses of action he recommended. But, he added that his second suggestion — to designate the two types of Religious by different titles — would help identify the Religious in the Church and would encourage religious vocations.[32]

Consultants consider the problem

In October of 1986, the Quinn Commission presented its 152-page final report to Rome. That report was given in summary form to the United States bishops at their November 1986 meeting, and subsequently published in *Origins*. The process for arriving at the final report had continued past the gathering of data at the listening sessions. That data was given to forty people, identified by Archbishop Quinn as experts in a variety of fields. The experts then met and wrote a core report. That core report was given to seventeen bishops who were asked to react to the report and to get the reaction of priests, Religious and laity in their dioceses.

Some insight into the opinion of the approximately forty consultants who worked with the Quinn Commission may be found in the book *The Crisis in Religious Vocations*. The book contains sixteen of the thirty-four essays written by those consultants and which accompanied the Quinn Commission report to the Vatican. The consultants were given data which included 1980s research by the Center for Applied Research in the Apostolate at Georgetown University, published as *Religious Life in the United States: The Experience of Men's Communities*. Significantly, the book serving as a data source on sisters was *Catholic Sisters in Transition: From the 1960s to the 1980s,* by Sister Marie Augusta Neal, creator of the Sisters' Survey. Based on their study of that data, the consultants then were asked to submit a paper based on these two questions: "Why did religious leave their congregations?" and "Why are young people not entering in greater numbers?"

Here is a very brief synopsis of what some of these expert consultants had to say. It is apparent in some of their comments that the Sister Agnes Mary Mansour case and the controversy over the *New York Times* abortion rights statement had an appreciable impact on many Religious. And, some of the consultants seem to concur that American Religious had more reason to instruct Rome than to learn anything from Rome.

Jesuit Father John Padberg, director of the Institute of Jesuit Sources in St. Louis and president of the International Conference of Catholic Theological Institutes, opined that lack of vocations was due to: 1) loss of corporate identity; 2) external regulations (imposed by Rome); 3) disillusionment with actions of Church officials; 4) disillusionment with outmoded structures and activities of religious communities; 5) alienation caused by some of the present teachings of the Church, e.g. ordination of women; 6) concern over how social justice can be practiced in religious life. Father Padberg concluded that recommendations about religious life "will have to be made in the context of what makes up this American people in an American tradition."[33]

Sister of Charity Mary Ann Donovan, a professor of historical theology at the Jesuit School of Theology, Berkeley, concluded that religious life had become less attractive because of 1) the emerging lay role; 2) the "institutional face of the church" which is "often hardened by clericalism and the accompanying patriarchalism which is destructive of healthy relationships"; 3) "the current situation of women religious in the church," i.e. the process of approving constitutions of congregations, the handling of cases such as the Religious who signed the *New York Times* abortion rights ad, and "the papal intervention in apostolic religious life in the United States." She concluded: "Our task is to enable the laity to assume their rightful role in the church and to be content with our smaller numbers. It is my conviction that a reduction in numbers does not constitute a crisis of vocations, but rather is God's unique gift to the American church today."[34]

Dominican Sister Mary Ewens, associate director of the Cushwa Center for the Study of American Catholicism at the University of Notre Dame, observed that "The signs of the times need to be studied not only by religious communities, but also by their bishops and members of the curia. . . .

"A closer affiliation with the church and its hierarchy through entrance into religious life will not attract zealous young women if the church is seen to transgress basic human rights, to eschew due process, to violate freedom of conscience, to treat women like second-class citizens, and to summarily dismiss from their communities sisters whose work for the poor and study of the gospel imperative take them into the political arena."[35]

Dominican Sister Donna Markham, a psychologist who founded the Dominican Consultation Center in Detroit and who would be elected president of the Leadership Conference of Women Religious in 1991, concluded: "Compassionate understanding, non-judgmental respect, and support of all members [of religious congregations] whose varying ways of giving expression to their religious commitment co-exist within the institution of religious life today are crucial."[36]

Sisters in Crisis

Sister of St. Joseph Rose McDermott, a canon lawyer and vicar for Religious, observed that "Church authorities should be careful to avoid stifling the variety of gifts and the prophetic utterance of religious in the church." Sister Rose said that institutes of women Religious "are moving away from pre-conciliar structures and norms which never adequately conveyed their gift and potential to the church. As women take their proper place in society, they cannot be denied it in a church that teaches the fundamental equality of persons and justice in the world. Charisms, the gifts of the Spirit, are carried in fragile earthen vessels. The authorities of the church must trust the generous, searching response of religious to the gifts of God in the midst of transition, confusion, misunderstanding, and misplaced zeal."[37]

"Religious life in the United States is in good condition"

The final report of the Quinn Commission sidestepped the whole area of bishops' "proclaiming anew to all the people of God the church's teaching on consecrated life," as the pope had directed in his letter. Instead, the report concentrated on the other part of the pope's charge by supposedly identifying the reasons for the decline in the number of vocations in the United States:

1. Cultural factors, such as new attitudes about freedom, authority, sexuality, the role of women, etc.
2. The impact of Vatican II, which called the laity to holiness and stressed the importance of lay ministry and the social dimensions of the Gospel.
3. Developments in the Church in the United States, including:
    a. movement of Catholics into the mainstream of American society
    b. movement of Catholics to the suburbs
    c. the rise of the women's movement
4. Impact of all the above on religious communities, i.e., the expanding economy made more vocational options available to women, and the civil rights movement changed the focus of many Religious to service to the world by promoting justice and human rights.
5. Experiences which had affected personal choices, including:
    a. an identity crisis for Religious resulting in blurred corporate identity
    b. Religious too dependent on structures left religious life when those structures were diminished
    c. Religious lacked the necessary public witness to attract vocations
    d. careful screening processes diminished the number of aspirants accepted

e. the requirement of celibacy and permanence dissuaded some
people from a vocation.

The report admitted that the role of superiors was an issue of concern, and there needed to be "a correct synthesis of the consultative and collegial approach with a correct understanding of personal authority in religious life." And, it cited "certain tensions which exist between some religious and the Holy See," as well as "some individuals and some groups which give cause for concern and do not appear to fulfill the ideals of religious life." But the report made no promises or proposals to address those issues, and concluded, ". . . our three years' work leads us to believe that in general religious life in the United States is in good condition."[38]

So, in an effort to steer a middle course and to avoid confrontation with feminist sisters, the Quinn Commission accomplished very little, and Father Dubay's prediction that the commission would whitewash the state of religious life in the United States seems to have been fulfilled. While the Quinn Commission did initiate some interaction between Religious and bishops that would not have occurred otherwise, the work of the commission appears to have reached no important conclusions and had little impact on religious life in the United States. As Sister Margaret Cafferty, executive director of the Leadership Conference of Women Religious, observed in 1993: "For Religious, the greatest benefit of the work of the Quinn Commission was the dialogue it generated, not the Commission's final report."[39] It was as if the "Gamaliel principle" recommendation of Archbishop Whealon to simply do nothing was unanimously adopted by most bishops and accepted by Rome. Furthermore, the issuance of *Essential Elements* seemed to have only further polarized those Religious who had sought to follow the teachings of Rome from those who considered such teachings to be without real authority and open to wide interpretation and dialogue. Within religious institutes which have members of both persuasions, life has been very difficult.

A final wrap-up meeting involving the Quinn Commission took place in Rome in early March of 1989, and included Pope John Paul II, Vatican officials, and thirty-five United States bishops. At that meeting, there were some subtle hints that the Vatican was not completely pleased with the outcome of the American bishops' study on religious life, either. Cardinal Jean Jerome Hamer, a Dominican who was prefect of the Congregation for Religious, reminded the bishops that a bishop is "responsible not only for the apostolate of men and women religious (regarding their schools, their hospitals, catechesis, parish assistance, etc.) but also, to a certain extent, for their religious life as such. That is, he must oversee their observance of chastity, poverty and obedience; their fraternal life in community; the witness they must bear to God before the people of God; and their fidelity to their distinct charism, which ought to place its stamp on all religious life."

Cardinal Hamer commended the bishops for their work on the study of religious life, but he reminded them that their attention to religious life should be ongoing as part of their pastoral office. "This pastoral service of religious life must be not only pursued, but intensified," Cardinal Hamer said. "We must exercise it within the framework of the actual situation of the church in the United States."[40]

Barely three weeks after that Rome meeting with the thirty-five United States bishops, Pope John Paul II wrote all United States bishops on March 29, 1989. In that letter, he thanked the bishops for their response to his request for the study of religious life in the United States, and he observed that the bishops had "generally been positive about the state of religious life in your dioceses." But he also pointed out that the Quinn Commission had reported on only two stages of the bishops' work — listening and dialogue. The pope reminded bishops that he had directed them to perform "special pastoral service," which should not be temporary, and he urged them to meet on a regular basis with the Religious in their dioceses. And, he wrote that Religious "must be constantly exhorted to remain faithful to the church's mission and teaching.

"In your role as bishops you have the responsibility to teach all your people, including men and women religious. Related to that teaching office is the need and obligation to present a sound theological exposition of religious life." The pope chided "tendencies to excessive self-fulfillment and autonomy in living, working and decision making" and said "serious work must be done on the charisms, community life and vowed life." He said that "The substitution of a management model of authority for a government model is not the answer" to correcting past abuses of authority. "Management may be useful in producing products, but the purpose of government in religious life is to safeguard the charism and stimulate its growth." And, he reminded bishops of the public character of religious life: "Because religious are public persons in the church, their own obligation — as men and women who follow the obedient Christ — is to reflect accurately and clearly the teaching of the church. When necessary, you and their superiors must remind them of this reality."[41]

In spite of this clear instruction from the Holy Father and the Congregation for Religious, the American hierarchy has not been inclined to confront Religious who clearly do not reflect the teaching of the Church, and in fact often publicly reject Church teaching. This reticence is somewhat understandable when one considers the strident nature of some of the most outspoken and hostile sisters, and the fact that these sisters know how to use the media to their advantage. Most bishops probably have nightmares about headlines screaming: "Local Bishop Demands That Sisters Attend Mass on Sundays" or "Day-care Center for Poor Mothers Closes After Bishop Forces Nun To Resign From Her Order" or "Catholic Sisters Boldly Resist Bishop's Heavyhanded Effort to Regulate Their Lives."

In addition to being media-savvy, activist sisters also are politically astute, and they have created organizations which project the image that these groups speak for the majority of sisters, so it indeed is difficult to know where the majority of sisters stand on issues. The next chapter examines some of the organizations in which sisters have been influential and analyzes the impact of these groups on the public image of sisters, as well as the influence of these groups on religious life in the United States.

13: The Ideological Transformation of Sisters' Organizations

"We have waited in vain for American nuns to speak out through their regular organizations. . . . But I have really had it because nobody speaks out. And this is what the coalition means to do."[1]

Sister Margaret Ellen Traxler, SSND
Foundress, National Coalition of
American Nuns

Many people rarely encounter a Catholic sister unless a sister happens to be working in a local parish. Thus the image of contemporary women Religious often is shaped by media reports about organizations which involve sisters. But this media image is often quite distorted, for the most vocal organizations of Catholic sisters don't represent the average sister. Rather, these organizations are preoccupied with promoting feminist causes and confronting ecclesial authorities in order to remake the Church.

While these organizations may grab the headlines, they do not represent or serve the sizable percentage of women Religious who adhere to their vows, are loyal to the Church, and continue to serve the Church and society in a variety of ways. Nevertheless, to understand the complete picture of how the crisis in women's religious communities has developed, it is important to examine these organizations and the effect these groups have had on the sisters themselves, the public perception of sisters, and the image of the Church.

Leadership Conference of Women Religious

The Leadership Conference of Women Religious has remained the most prominent and influential organization of sisters in the United States, even though many of its activities have been very controversial. In the years since the conference transformed itself in 1971 (as detailed in Chapters Five and Six), the organization's philosophy has alternated between ignoring directives from Rome and challenging Church authorities in an effort to promote a women's liberation agenda. The result has been a widening of the chasm between activist sisters who believe it is their destiny to challenge patriarchal Church authority, and traditional sisters who accept the teachings of the Church on religious life as they have been stated by the Vatican II documents and other church legislation. Many of the traditional orders of sisters have withdrawn from membership in the Leadership Conference.

While the conference has retained Vatican approval, the Vatican also gave its approval in 1992 to another superiors' conference of women, the Council of Major Superiors of Women Religious, which based its statutes on the essential elements of religious life set forth in 1983 by the pope. This move by Rome to recognize an alternate superiors' conference was unprecedented, and undoubtedly was a signal that the Vatican wanted to encourage women Religious who espouse loyalty to the Church. The erection of the new superiors' conference may also have been a signal that Vatican authorities had grown weary of dealing with an organization of women Religious which continually ignored or challenged the authority of the Church. (See next chapter.)

The Leadership Conference of Women Religious actually is made up of approximately nine hundred sisters who hold leadership positions in their communities. Although the Leadership Conference often claims to speak for all sisters in the United States, in reality the conference is empowered only to speak for its membership of nine hundred. The other eighty-nine thousand grassroots sisters have no input into conference policies and no vote for conference officers.

The LCWR's claim that it speaks for all nuns has resulted in confusion and resentment among grassroots sisters when the conference, or the conference's twenty-member board, take public stands in the name of all sisters without actually polling those sisters about their opinions. For example, in 1993, the twenty-member board of the Leadership Conference issued a response to the *lineamenta* which had been issued by the synod secretariat to gather input for the 1994 synod on consecrated life. In that statement, the twenty-member conference board contended: "We therefore believe that we speak for all women in the church when we ask to be included in the formal sessions of the synod in order to speak for ourselves and for the future of the religious life for women."[2]

Similarly, confusion and resentment sometimes occurred when the entire membership of the Leadership Conference did not participate in or support some of the organization's more controversial positions and activities. Some controversies arose because of actions or decisions of the group's twenty-member board or one of the group's officers or committees, often resulting in the public perception that these leaders had the approval of the membership when this was not necessarily the case. Conference executive directors Sisters Mary Daniel Turner (1972-78) and Lora Quinonez (1978-86) have observed that generally, the membership of the LCWR was ambivalent about feminism and tended to be more interested in religious life and social-justice issues. And, some members regularly cautioned the conference about promoting women's issues. Yet, the former executive directors noted, the conference leadership had a far stronger "commitment to name and battle sexism wherever it occurred."[3]

Thus, some of the controversies generated by the Leadership Conference actually involved the conference as a whole, while others reflected on the conference, but really were never sanctioned by the membership. Here is a very brief summary of some conference activities since 1971, which provides a few examples of those controversies, many of them centered on the women's liberation theme.

In 1972, Sister Francis Borgia Rothluebber was chosen vice-president (and thus president-elect for 1973) of the Leadership Conference. Sister Francis Borgia had been engaged in an ongoing dispute with the Vatican over renewal changes in her order, so her election was widely read as a message to the Vatican that American sisters stood in solidarity behind her. At the 1972 conference assembly, canon lawyer Clara Henning (the first woman to receive a canon law degree from Catholic University) proposed a single sisterhood of all Catholic women to struggle for women's liberation in a talk subtitled "Religious Communities as Providential Gift for the Liberation of Women." She also suggested bringing class-action suits against the Church in both civil and church courts and staging an economic boycott against parish churches.[4]

Archbishop Helder Camara of Brazil, an outspoken proponent of liberation theology, addressed the 1973 annual assembly. His address, as well as the presentations of outgoing conference president Sister Margaret

Brennan and incoming president Sister Francis Borgia Rothluebber all were based on liberation themes.[5]

In the mid-1970s, the conference's Ecclesial Role of Women Committee produced a monograph on the Equal Rights Amendment and the ordination of women, as well as a "consciousness-raising" kit, *Focus on Women*, which was a "collection of booklets for group reflections on sex-role stereotyping, symbol and myth as vehicles of sexism, women and God, and the economic status of women."[6]

In 1974, the conference published *Widening the Dialogue*, a critique of *Evangelica Testificatio*, the 1971 papal exhortation evaluating the strengths and weaknesses of the ongoing renewal of religious life. According to former conference executive directors Sisters Mary Daniel Turner and Lora Ann Quinonez, the tenor of the book was that *Evangelica Testificatio* was just the first word in what should be an ongoing dialogue about religious life rather than a authoritative Church statement about the issues.[7] Also in 1974, a resolution approved by the conference annual assembly stated that "all ministries in the church be open to women," which was understood to mean ordination of women as priests, according to the *National Catholic Reporter*.[8]

When the first Women's Ordination Conference was being organized in 1975, conference president Sister Francine Zeller appointed Sister Nadine Foley, who was a member of the Leadership Conference Ecclesial Role of Women Committee, as a liaison person to the group organizing the ordination conference. The Leadership Conference subsequently received a letter from the Congregation for Religious, directing the conference to disssociate itself from the Women's Ordination Conference. Then-executive director Sister Mary Daniel Turner wrote later that Sister Francine took the issue up with the Leadership Conference executive committee, and with the approval and support of the conference board, she refused to dissociate the conference from the women's ordination group.[9] In fact, Sister Nadine went on to become coordinator of the organizing task force for the ordination conference. Also during the 1970s, the national board of the conference voted to join the National Organization for Women boycott of convention sites in states that had not ratified the Equal Rights Amendment.[10]

A Contemporary Theology Project was launched in 1976 that resulted in some controversial conference publications which carried a heavy women's liberation theme, emphasized individualism, and attempted to justify some of the renewal efforts that had been questioned by the Vatican. The first publication, *Steps in the Journey*, published in 1979, offered a history of the project and contained data gathered at various workshops and gatherings on topics such as authority and obedience, social justice, and mutuality and culture.

Sisters in Crisis

Starting Points: Six Essays Based on the Experience of U.S. Women Religious, published in 1980, carried essays reflecting on that "lived experience" of women Religious since 1965. The introduction to *Starting Points* explained that "women religious are increasingly willing to trust their experience as a locus of God's revelation and, therefore, as a valid base for making judgments and choices."[11] Essay titles included "The Changing Mission of Religious Life" by Sister Doris Gottemoeller, "Towards a Theology of Religious Obedience" by Sister Sandra Schneiders, and "On Becoming Religious" by Sister Mary Daniel Turner.

Claiming Our Truth, published in 1988, was the third publication of the Contemporary Theology Project, and was a collection of papers discussing the questions: "What is the world?", "Who do we say God is?", and "Who do we say we are?" Included in this book were the essays "Women's Center: Incarnational Spirituality," "A World Church and Christian Feminism," and "What's at Stake: Women Religious Naming Ourselves Women." Sister Nadine Foley, editor, observed in the introduction that for women Religious, "there is an evident convergence around their sense of identity, particularly their claiming themselves as women and grappling with God images and symbols to fit their emerging self-awareness."[12] Sisters Mary Daniel Turner and Lora Quinonez noted that in the two latter publications, the sisters were reluctant to suggest that there was only one valid theology of religious life.[13]

In 1977, the Leadership Conference drew a rebuke from the Committee for Pro-Life Activities of the National Conference of Catholic Bishops. The Leadership Conference had published a booklet entitled "Choose Life" in response to the bishops' Pastoral Plan for Pro-Life Activities. However, Monsignor James McHugh (later named bishop), director of the bishops' pro-life committee, sent a letter to all the bishops, warning them that the booklet was "ambiguous in regard to the moral prohibition of abortion" and too preoccupied with broadening the context of concern for the quality of life. He further charged that the booklet's public policy position on abortion was counterproductive to the policies of the bishops.[14] Sister Mary Daniel Turner, Leadership Conference executive director, then wrote all members, directing them to ask their bishops for "precise concerns" about the "Choose Life" document, and she provided them with material to give to the local media if the press had carried the National Catholic News Service story about Monsignor McHugh's objections. The documentation accompanying Sister Mary Daniel's letter suggested that "There is evidence that McHugh's analysis and critique violates principles of logic . . . employs accusatory language . . . adopts subjective and argumentative style and denies the obvious."[15]

At the 1977 annual assembly, conference president Sister Joan Chittister tried to justify the movement of sisters from their traditional apostolates into individual ministries, explaining: "The old vision of religious life says that the purpose of religious life is to be a labor force to do institutional work. There is a new vision rising that says the purpose of religious life is to be a leaven in society. . . ."[16]

In 1979, the conference came under heavy criticism from many fronts because of the actions of its president, Sister Theresa Kane. As conference president, she was selected to represent women Religious when Pope John Paul II visited the United States. Sister Theresa was to greet the pope when he spoke to five-thousand nuns gathered at the National Shrine of the Immaculate Conception in Washington, D.C., on October 7. However, in the context of her greeting, Sister Theresa also plugged women's ordination when she said, in part, ". . . the church in its struggle to be faithful to its call for reverence and dignity for all persons must respond by providing the possibility of women as persons being included in all ministries of the church."[17]

Sister Theresa's remarks were considered by many to be in particularly poor taste since the pope had just days before reiterated the Church's official position that women could not be ordained. Many sisters also felt that as Leadership Conference president and representative of all American sisters at the papal event, Sister Theresa should have kept her personal opinions to herself. In four months, the conference office received five-thousand letters reflecting a variety of opinions about the president's action.

Sister Theresa subsequently wrote all conference members, confirming that the officers were "conscious that directions taken by LCWR might be a cause of discomfort for some of our members." And, she asked members who were considering terminating their memberships to "dialogue" with board members, officers, or the executive director before making a decision about leaving the conference.[18]

One sister wrote in the *National Catholic Reporter* letters section that the LCWR president "did not have the right to make the impression that she spoke for the majority of sisters in the United States. As representing the Leadership Conference of Women Religious, neither did she have the right to voice her personal views."[19] The Sisters of St. Francis of the Martyr St. George took out a large display ad in the *Washington Post* on October 12 to apologize to the pope. The ad read:

"We, who most likely speak for the large majority of religious women in the United States, apologize to his Holiness, Pope John Paul II for the public rudeness shown him by Sister Theresa Kane, R.S.M., this past Sunday in Washington, D.C.

Sisters in Crisis

"One does not treat any foreign guest by attempting to correct him publicly before the world. Yet, for those who accept the Catholic premise, a person with no teaching office in the church does not presume to correct the one to whom the whole flock was commissioned by Christ.

"Sister Theresa was not only impertinent to the Holy Father, but she has also offended the millions of us who love him and gladly accept his teaching."[20]

One month after Sister Theresa's "greeting" of the pope, the Leadership Conference attended a regularly scheduled meeting at the Congregation for Religious, a meeting that apparently was quite strained, according to a conference memo to members. Executive director Sister Lora Ann Quinonez reported to conference members that the November 5, 1979, meeting in Rome evidenced "clear differences of understanding and belief between the LCWR representatives and several SCRIS [Congregation for Religious] members." She cited areas of disagreement, including the diversity, concept, and image of church; and the nature of authority and obedience. In reflecting on the meeting, Sister Lora Ann told members, "There is no question that we are coming from diametrically different concepts of church and, therefore, of authority, of obedience and fidelity, of the nature and role of law/legislation, of decision-making, of dissent." And, she remarked on a collision of cultures in which "certain actions labeled dissent, disloyalty, disobedience, by one group will be seen as dialogic, faithful, and responsible by the other."[21]

In 1982, the LCWR held a joint annual assembly with the Conference of Major Superiors of Men. Five of the sisters had been asked to be extraordinary eucharistic ministers of the wine at the joint liturgy, but the celebrant, Archbishop Pio Laghi, apostolic delegate, would not allow the extraordinary eucharistic ministers when there were plenty of priests available to distribute the bread and wine.[22] His directive was fully consistent with Church regulations on extraordinary eucharistic ministers, but apparently the assigned sisters were not informed until they went forward to get the wine and were turned away. The issue thus was interpreted as clerical insensitivity toward women. Sister Mary Daniel Turner described the incident as "a massive psychological jolt to the membership" that had impacts "ranging from deep anger and pain to bewilderment, fear, denial, and a sense of urgency that action be taken in response. That experience brought home publicly the exclusion of women from realities which are deeply formative in our lives, and . . . brought us face to face with our great vulnerabilities."[23]

At the 1984 annual assembly the conference agreed to create panels of canon lawyers, theologians, and administrators to help sisters "experiencing difficulties with ecclesiastical authorities." The Sister Agnes Mary Mansour case had played itself out in the media during the preceding months, and the work of the Quinn Commission was in full swing. Also, just a few days before the assembly convened, the Vatican had intervened in a matter involving the leadership of the European province of the School Sisters of St. Francis. Regarding the creation of the panels, newly-elected president Sister Margaret Cafferty explained: "We live in a time now of dialogue and clarification about how United States sisters live out the life-style and commitments we believe the spirit calls us to. While other segments of the world church may question what they see, we claim the validity of our lived experience, and offer our critics a record of fidelity."[24]

In 1985, the conference invited Mercy Sister Margaret Farley to be a featured speaker at its annual assembly. Sister Margaret was one of the Religious who had signed *The New York Times* 1984 statement sponsored by Catholics for a Free Choice which claimed there was more than one legitimate Catholic position on abortion, and she had not yet resolved her position with the Vatican. The National Conference of Catholic Bishops and the Vatican asked the conference to withdraw its invitation to Sister Margaret, but conference officers refused to do so. Consequently, Archbishops John Quinn and Pio Laghi, apostolic delegate, who had been scheduled to speak at the assembly, canceled their appearances at the meeting.

At the 1989 Leadership Conference joint assembly with the Conference of Major Superiors of Men, several "Transformative Elements for Religious Life in the Future" were developed. These ten elements then were published in brochure form and discussed by various regions of the conference over the next few years. In 1995, the brochure on transformative elements was reprinted and continued to be circulated. An explanation in the brochure indicated that five of the elements had not received wide "affirmation" of the Religious attending the 1989 assembly that had developed the list of elements, but the conference leadership was continuing to promote all ten elements. The 1995 brochure explained that, "Over the intervening years, the conferences' various regions and religious institutes have found reflection and work on these elements helpful in their endeavors to move religious life into the future." Among the more startling concepts in the brochure is number eight, which articulates a unique new definition of religious life: "In 2010 religious communities will be characterized by inclusivity and intentionality. These communities may include persons of different ages, genders, cultures, races and sexual orientation. They may include persons who are lay or cleric, married or single, as well as vowed and/or unvowed members. They will have a core group and persons with temporary and permanent commitments.

"These communities will be ecumenical, possibly interfaith; faith sharing will be constitutive of the quality of life in this context of expanded membership. Such inclusivity will necessitate a new understanding of membership and a language to accompany it.

"Religious life still includes religious congregations of permanently vowed members."

Virtually every study of religious life done in the last two decades has concluded that this "vision" of religious communities is so inclusive that it would lead to conditions that have no boundaries, and thus neutralize the impact of religious orders and cause them to lose their identity as a group.[25] However, the leaders of the Leadership Conference of Women Religious persist in directing their energies toward the liberation of women and the oppressed, rather than the issues central to the very meaning of religious life, issues which include social justice for all people. Among the six goals and objectives the conference designated for 1989-94 were: "To develop structures of solidarity with women in order to work for the liberation of women through the transformation of social and ecclesial structures and relationships." And, "To effect action for justice leading to systemic change locally and globally in order to bring about harmony among people in communion with the earth."[26]

In 1995, the women's liberation theme was extended another five years in one of the 1995-99 Leadership Conference goals: "We will work for the liberation of all oppressed people, especially women, through the transformation of social, economic, and ecclesial structures and relationships."[27]

The theme for the 1996 Leadership Conference annual assembly in Atlanta was nonviolence, reflecting the conference's continuing priority of placing socio-political issues ahead of spiritual issues or the very pressing structural issues confronting institutes of women Religious. In planning for the assembly, the conference office announced that "current and former LCWR members will reflect on their leadership during a time when their institute or its members were victims of violence. The four panelist will reflect on physical violence suffered by members as well as the violence that results from conflicts with ecclesiastical authorities, social institutions, and the media." Workshops covered issues such as the global relationships in the platform from the 1995 Beijing women's conference, relationships with the media, relationships affected by gender and sexual orientation, and relationships with the earth. One of the two keynote speakers was Sister of St. Joseph Helen Prejean, author of *Dead Man Walking*, a book that chronicled Sister Helen's experience of counseling death-row inmates.[28] The other keynoter was Reverend Renita J. Weems, a Protestant minister and an assistant professor of Old Testament studies at Vanderbilt Divinity School.[29] Reverend Weems is the author of *Battered Love: Marriage, Sex and Violence in the Hebrew Prophets; Just a Sister Away: A Womanist Vision of Women's Relationships in the Bible;* and *I Asked for Intimacy.*

National Assembly of Women Religious

In addition to the superior's conference, several other organizations of Catholic sisters sprang up in the 1960s and early '70s. Though none of these organizations had the same influence as the Leadership Conference of Women Religious, these groups nevertheless reflected many of the issues affecting sisters during the renewal years and even to the present time. They also gravitated toward a confrontational approach with Rome and a principal agenda of women's liberation in the Church and in society. The emergence of many of these groups prompted *Time* magazine to comment in 1972 that "U.S. nuns have organized their reform activities in a proliferation of groups that bear a marked similarity to secular Women's Lib federations."[30] Though some of these organizations purported to speak for mainstream sisters, and the media often portrayed these groups as representative of modern American sisters, none of them ever achieved the support or sympathy of a significant number of sisters. These groups also frequently shared overlapping memberships, for many activist sisters participated in several of these groups at the same time.

The National Assembly of Women Religious (NAWR), which later changed its name to the National Assembly of Religious Women (NARW) after it opened its membership to lay people, started as a grassroots organization of sisters. The concept of such an organization was born in 1968 at the First International Conference of Councils and Senates of Women Religious. At that meeting in Portland, Maine, four-hundred sisters from twenty-three diocesan sisters' councils discussed how the newly-formed sisters' councils could most effectively function. A subsequent 1969 meeting in Chicago attracted about fifteen hundred sisters. Featured speakers included Brother Gabriel Moran and Sister Margaret Ellen Traxler, founder of the National Coalition of American Nuns. At that 1969 Chicago meeting, a task force was appointed to draw up plans for a national body of American sisters.

Then, on April 19, 1970, around 1,300 sisters,[31] less than half the number that had been expected by the task force,[32] met in Cleveland and voted to form the National Assembly of Women Religious. (There were about 161,000 sisters in the country at that time.) The organization was designed to be a counterpart to the newly-formed National Federation of Priests' Councils organized by Monsignor Jack Egan of Chicago. The ultimate goal of the organization was to represent nuns on a national pastoral council affiliated with the United States Catholic Conference. However, the United States bishops never did approve the idea for a national pastoral council.

Sister Ethne Kennedy of the Society of Helpers, task force chairperson, became the first chairperson/coordinator of the organization. The rationale for the new organization reflected the quite reasonable desire for sisters to network with one another and to take a more active role in Church affairs:

"Sisters feel a need for corporate identity, a voice to express their stands on issues of concern to the church in the world. Sisters want top-level communications with one another to share research, personnel, facilities, vision. Sisters ask to be inserted into the ecclesial process of decision-making, to participate from the grass roots with bishops, priests, and lay men and women, so that the creative insights of women religious can influence Church thinking and action."[33]

In actual practice, however, the National Assembly became more involved in controversial issues than its original purpose had indicated. Some flavor of the organization was evident at the April 1970 meeting in the keynote address by Sister Francis Borgia Rothluebber, president of the School Sisters of St. Francis, who at that time was engaged in a dispute with the Vatican about questionable renewal practices in her own community. Sister Francis Borgia told the first meeting that the Church and Religious had a tendency to be static, and there was "too great a security in the status quo, or in authority, or in rule-keeping, or in any inflexible structures . . . all hostile to the future, to hope, to being present today."[34] Sister Marie Augusta Neal, creator of the Sisters' Survey, also spoke. Resolutions passed by the 1970 assembly included support for: the grape boycott, new forms of Christian community, and the former Immaculate Heart of Mary Sisters of Los Angeles who left religious life rather than comply with Vatican definitions of renewal.

Membership in the National Assembly grew from 43 sisters' councils and 2,029 individual or associate members in 1970 to 75 councils and 4,567 individuals or associates in 1971.[35] Then, in 1972, the organization's House of Delegates discarded the national assembly's original purpose of facilitating networking between American sisters and instead picked up the power and liberation theme that the Leadership Conference of Women Religious had adopted. The organization's new "vision-goal" became: "A ministry of justice by the continuous use of our organized power to effect local and national policy for the liberation of all peoples from oppression, to work actively to promote respect for all human life, and to insure effective participation of people in decisions which affect their lives."[36] This abrupt change in direction effected by the House of Delegates apparently impacted membership numbers, for between 1971 and 1972, the organization lost 10 councils and 1,600 individual or associate members.[37] Finances also became an issue of concern. The group's January 1972 newsletter, *Probe*, announced the organization's debt of $4,537.

The August, 1974, meeting of the NAWR in St. Louis drew approximately six hundred sisters.[38] Assembly speakers included Cesar Chavez, a replacement speaker for Dorothy Day, "who announced at the last minute that sisters didn't need her because they knew everything already."[39] Chavez told the meeting that since April of 1973, more nuns than labor leaders had been jailed on the picket lines of the farm workers' strike. Joseph Holland of the Center of Concern "urged the nuns to study the socialism of Karl Marx as an alternative to capitalism, to join the labor movement as still 'the hardest fighter for justice' in industrial society, and to support the women's liberation movement in the context of a broader socialist struggle."[40]

In October of 1974, Sacred Heart Sister Maggie Fisher, the organization's director of development and finance, wrote the Knights of Columbus, asking to speak to the K of C board about funding. Even though membership stood at 2,893 individuals and associates, and 99 sisters' councils in 1974,[41] Sister Maggie wrote: "We represent 90,000 sisters who have chosen to remain in religious life and to continue to serve the Church in this hour of need."[42]

At the 1975 convention in San Francisco, ordination of women jumped into the spotlight. The *National Catholic Reporter* headlined its article on the convention: "NAWR: Power in church sisters' aim."[43] The article reported that newly elected president, Sister of St. Joseph Kathleen Keating, went on record as saying that women should have the same option as men to seek ordination. The outgoing president, Sister Catherine Pinkerton, told NCR that communities of sisters had gone through "a massive wrenching" after Vatican II. "'We had to spill blood,' Pinkerton told NCR, 'but we didn't disband our communities to do that. We changed our forms of government, lifestyles, prayer forms, corporate commitments. . . .'"[44]

The 1976 assembly was so controversial that the organization's membership figures fell dramatically after that event, though even at its peak membership in 1971, the National Assembly of Women Religious never attracted more than three percent of American sisters. The *National Catholic Reporter* ran a front-page photo and article about the 1976 assembly, which included an "unfinished liturgy" performed by Sister of Mercy Mary Reilly and two lay women, Anita Caspary (formerly Sister Humiliata, superior of the Immaculate Heart of Mary Sisters of Los Angeles), and Mary Beckman of the Catholic Charities Social Action Office in Brooklyn.[45] *Commonweal* magazine, under the headline "Aborted Liturgy," explained that the three women proceeded through the Liturgy of the Word; the Preparation of the Gifts; Eucharistic Prayer; "Holy, Holy, Holy"; and the prayer prior to the Consecration, then became silent. "After a pause, a delegate seized the microphone, and referring to women's inability to complete the Eucharistic celebration, said: 'I hope you are all as disturbed by this as I am.'" The *Commonweal* article reported that some sisters present approved of the action, including Sister Maggie Fisher, who observed that the demonstration would lead women to consider the injustice of being excluded from ordination. However, another sister present was quoted as saying, "I wouldn't want to be part of an effort to go beyond the boundaries of our authorized liturgy."[46]

More controversy arose in 1977 when the NAWR convention meeting in New Orleans passed an affirmation of Sister of Mercy Elizabeth Candon.[47] Sister Elizabeth was Vermont state secretary for human services. When the United States Supreme Court ruled that states were not required to make Medicaid payments for abortion, Sister Elizabeth was quoted by Vermont newspapers as saying that although she was personally opposed to abortion, she favored continuing state abortion payments for the poor. Bishop John Marshall of Burlington, Vermont, countered in a letter to Vermont Catholics that Sister Elizabeth's action was "confusing, misleading and scandalous," and he pointed out that "these free-will decisions can place her outside the sacramental life of the Roman Catholic Church and deprive her of her good standing as a member of a religious community in that church."[48]

National Assembly of Women Religious officials claimed the affirmation of Sister Elizabeth was not supporting abortion, but rather standing with a sister who had been threatened with excommunication. The resolution said, in part: "Be it resolved that NAWR affirms Sister Elizabeth Candon, secretary of Human Services of the State of Vermont, through a letter of support of her stand regarding the equal access of all women to legal rights. . . ."[49] However, many people did not interpret this affirmation so innocently. Archbishop Philip Hannan of New Orleans, in whose diocese the meeting took place, called the affirmation "absolutely deplorable, contrary to Catholic doctrine and completely illogical."[50]

Several members of the National Assembly of Women Religious also took issue with the action, and some questioned the process that resulted in the resolution. The Sisters' Conference of the Diocese of Peoria wrote Sister Maggie Fisher, asking for a clarification of the organization's position on Sister Elizabeth Candon. The Peoria conference's secretary wrote: "We are experiencing a division among our membership as to our participation in a membership in NAWR."[51] The Council of Women Religious from the Archdiocese of Omaha wrote Sister Kathleen Keating, president of NAWR, alleging that "pressure was exerted to influence the voting" on the resolution affirming Sister Elizabeth Candon. The Omaha council observed that since the media treated the Candon resolution not as an issue of justice, but rather as support of abortion, "the public image of NAWR and of women religious suffered a setback."[52]

The executive director of the advisory council of Religious from Portland, Maine, also wrote Sister Kathleen to express her council's uneasiness about the voting process at the 1977 assembly. She said that resolutions should be sent to delegates well in advance of the meeting, and she observed that "there is more to Christianity than just changing the social order."[53] And some individual members expressed concern that delegates at the 1977 assembly felt they were manipulated, and that assembly leaders prematurely closed discussion on a resolution presented by the National Council of Catholic Women because the assembly leaders were disturbed that the National Council of Catholic Women did not support the Equal Rights Amendment.

In January of 1978, Sister Kathleen received a letter from the president of the Senate of Religious Women of the Diocese of Cleveland. The president explained that her council was withholding renewal of its membership in NAWR until some issues were resolved. She asked that Sister Kathleen visit Cleveland to address these issues: 1) lack of accountability of NAWR to local councils when presenting a national image of sisters; 2) decision-making process which didn't provide for collegiality and consensus between the national and local regions; 3) confusion as to the constituency with which NAWR identified itself; 4) the image of sisters NAWR presented to the national media; 5) "liberal jargon" that did not reflect depth of thought; 6) and the tendency "to come off as anti-life." The writer indicated that her council felt that support of the unborn was a higher priority than supporting one sister.[54]

The number of sisters councils belonging to the NAWR slipped from eighty-two in 1977 to sixty-seven in 1978.[55] Several individual sisters also terminated or did not renew their memberships in NAWR because the Candon resolution appeared to give the organization a pro-choice position. For some sisters who were already embarrassed by the "uncompleted Mass," the Candon affirmation was the last straw.

In 1978, the National Assembly of Women Religious extended full membership to lay women, but even this move did not serve to bolster dwindling membership. The individual membership numbers dropped from 2,291 in 1978 to 1,548 in 1979.[56] By 1980, individual membership stood at 1,400, with only 23 sisters' councils still belonging.[57] Not only had the NAWR lost its focus as a grassroots organization for the average sister, it also had taken on an agenda that was not supported by most sisters, even the most progressive sisters.

The corresponding secretary for the Sisters Council of the Diocese of Grand Island, Nebraska, wrote Sister Kathleen Keating on March 14, 1978, expressing the concern of the Grand Island sisters about the direction of the organization. "We find it imperative that the National Association make a clear statement concerning its opposition to abortion under any circumstance," the sisters wrote. They also expressed their opposition "to opening NAWR to lay women, as this is not in conjunction with the original purpose of NAWR." And they asked that the agenda of the summer 1978 meeting include re-evaluation of the group's goals. "We feel that social justice has received undue emphasis to the exclusion of such Gospel-oriented ministries as evangelization, reaching out to the unchurched, fostering spiritual growth, religious vocations, Catholic education, and healing of the sick."[58]

Finances became even more of a problem as membership declined and the organization's agenda became difficult for most sisters to support, but the leaders forged ahead, convinced of their mission. NAWR development director Sister Maggie Fisher wrote to Loretto Sister Elizabeth Dyer, chairperson of the Loretto Six Percent Committee, asking for money from the Loretto order (which was obtained — $500 in 1978[59] and $1,000 in 1981[60]). Sister Maggie wrote: ". . . we have been taking some real risks over the past year. We have stood with many persons in opposition to official, safe, taboo issues. And we have felt the results . . . several sisters councils and many individuals have found us just too radical. Some think we should be focusing on evangelization and the development of spirituality. We've done just too much in the area of social justice. . . .

"We have now lost the possibility of going to most Catholic church groups for funds, for some of the reasons I cited above."[61]

In spite of declining membership and the accompanying loss of funds, the leaders of NAWR demonstrated no inclination to heed the concerns of their constituents. The corresponding secretary of the sisters' council of Grand Island, Nebraska, wrote again in 1980, seeming to express the disillusionment of many sisters. She explained that her council was not renewing its membership because the "whole thrust of NAWR has changed." The letter criticized the opening of membership to lay persons, as well as changing voting procedures so that "group representatives are overwhelmed by the voting power of the individual members." The assembly had lost its "leadership and vibrancy as an organization for women religious," she wrote.[62]

At the NAWR 1980 annual meeting in Milwaukee the *National Catholic Reporter* observed that "Separate liturgies were held during the conference to accommodate women who will not participate in liturgies presided over by males as long as females are excluded from ordination."[63] Elected president of the board in 1980 was Sister Marjorie Tuite, a founder of NAWR who had strongly influenced the social justice and feminist direction of the organization.

In 1982, the group further distanced itself from its original purpose as a grassroots organization for American sisters when it transposed the last two words in its title to become the National Assembly of Religious Women. As *Probe,* the organization's newsletter, explained, the name was changed " 'to concretize inclusiveness and the bonding of women' and as an indication of unwillingness to participate in the strategy of dividing Catholic women against each other."[64] Sister Catherine Pinkerton, a NAWR founder and leader who went on to become president of the Leadership Conference of Women Religious in 1983, observed later that the change in name helped the organization find a more profound level in the women's movement and "enriched us all by being the vehicle for uniting women of various cultures, races, ethnicities and differing faith dimensions, and developing as a result processes and programs which focus on inclusivity and equality."[65] By 1983, one-third of the organization's membership were lay women.

The 1984 annual conference in August attracted 225 participants, one-quarter of whom were lay women, according to an article in the *National Catholic Register*. The *Register* reported that at the meeting, Sister Theresa Kane, former president of the LCWR, "called for feminist liturgies, 'new rituals of Eucharist,' where women can remember each other's stories of pain and oppression." While Sister Theresa advocated nonviolence, NARW board member Ada Maria Isasi-Diaz disagreed, saying "I want to be aggressive about taking power. This talk of non-violence is problematic." Another board member, Maureen Reiff, declared that "The institution [Catholic Church] is dying and the Vatican is making desperate moves in its throes of death."[66]

Later in 1984, many members of NARW and its president, Sister Marjorie Tuite signed the October 7 statement in *The New York Times* headlined: "A Diversity of Opinion Regarding Abortion Exists Among Committed Catholics."[67] The Vatican had instructed religious institutes to demand a retraction from Religious who signed the statement, and to begin the dismissal procedure against Religious who refused to retract. Some sisters still were in a state of "dialogue" over the incident when a subsequent "Declaration of Solidarity" statement appeared in *The New York Times*, March 2, 1986. This statement invited sympathizers to write the Vatican Congregation for Religious to protest disciplinary actions against Religious who had signed the 1984 statement, and it, too, bore the names of NARW members. The 1986 declaration also called on the National Conference of Catholic Bishops to "protect and defend the right of Catholic religious, scholars and activists to speak out on controversial issues of public policy freely, fully and without reprisal."[68]

In lieu of a national conference in 1986, the organization sponsored an interfaith women's conference in Chicago: "Women of Faith: Same Journey, Different Paths." In 1992, the NARW national conference attracted about five hundred women, including fifty teenagers, to Spokane, Washington. "This conference was to be a counter-conference to the Columbus celebration," according to Sister of Mercy Maureen O'Sullivan writing in *Probe*. She observed that "all the conference's ritual garments, the Great Hoop and the Dream Catcher were made in nearby forest ceremonies."[69] The 1993 conference was not held so that NARW could give "support and solidarity to the Women-Church/ Convergence Conference."[70]

NARW was one of about twenty-five feminist organizations making up the Women-Church Convergence. *The New York Times* religion writer Peter Steinfels has described Women-Church as originally "a movement founded by Roman Catholic feminists as an outgrowth of their blocked efforts to get the church to ordain women as priests." And he observed "the movement's drift toward a kind of free-style Unitarianism, a creedless faith in an undefined divinity expressed in a profusion of rituals as well as in politically liberal good works."[71] According to a Women-Church Conference planner, Dominican Sister Jamie Phelps, the April 16-18, 1993, Women-Church Conference in Albuquerque, New Mexico, was organized around six "threads": Native-American, African-American, Asian-American, Hispanic, Euro-American, and lesbian/bisexual.[72] There was no Catholic Mass celebrated at the conference, but rather "in an attempt to appeal to everyone and offend no one, rituals, prayers, and worship services focused on an undefined deity."[73]

By 1994, NARW leaders were sending out signals that the end may be near for the organization that had evolved into an entity far different than the idea envisioned by the four hundred sisters who met in Maine in 1968 to create a national organization for the ordinary nun. In January of 1995, the board sent out nearly fifteen hundred letters to former members, seeking input about the future of the organization. The Winter 1995 issue of *Probe* announced that elections to the board had been suspended, and it suggested the possibility that the organization should be disbanded. But the newsletter still promoted a national conference in July of 1995 to celebrate the twenty-fifth anniversary of NAWR/NARW, and a registration blank for the event was published in the newsletter.

Included in that Winter 1995 issue of *Probe* was a new mission statement written at the February 10-12, 1995, board meeting: "The National Assembly of Religious Women (NARW) is diverse women of faith, creatively networking across barriers of race, gender, class and sexual orientation. NARW, rooted in the catholic tradition, provides critique and analysis of social issues, education and organizing for action. NARW is committed to mutuality, diversity and making connections between prophetic vision and systemic change."[74]

The Summer 1995 and final issue of *Probe* brought the news that the National Assembly of Religious Women was being dissolved by its national coordinating team. The organization was about $20,000 in debt and unable to attract substantial membership, support, or even enthusiasm for the twenty-fifth anniversary celebration. The national coordinating team attributed the demise of the organization to several factors, including decline in funding by religious communities, and the proliferation of other grassroots organizations with a similar or related focus that competed for funds and members.[75]

National Coalition of American Nuns

The stated primary purpose of the National Coalition of American Nuns (NCAN), is "women's liberation."[76] NCAN was started in 1969 in Chicago by Sister Margaret Ellen (Mary Peter) Traxler and Sister Mary Audrey (Lillanna) Kopp. Both Lillanna Kopp and Sister Margaret Ellen were staff members of the National Catholic Conference for Interracial Justice in Chicago during the 1960s, and it was out of that organization that they developed NCAN in 1969.

Sister Margaret Ellen told the *National Catholic Reporter* that it was easy to attract sisters to her organization, for "The first concern of these sisters is obviously that they don't want their communities interfered with on the part of bishops, or the bishops for religious, or Rome." Among the examples of hierarchical interference she cited were the dispute between Cardinal James McIntyre and the Immaculate Heart of Mary Sisters of Los Angeles, and the apostolic visitation of the School Sisters of St. Francis in Milwaukee. The article also quoted *Trans-Sister*, the newsletter representing the coalition at that time, as saying that the NCAN organization would help nuns defend themselves "against those who would interfere with the internal and/or renewal we alone must and can evolve in our communities."[77]

Also in 1969, Sister Mary Audrey Kopp left her religious order and resumed her baptismal name of Lillanna. She went on to found the noncanonical group Sisters For Christian Community in 1970. Kopp had been influential in the Sister Formation Conference, and she and some other former Sister Formation Conference leaders eventually became directors of NCAN: longtime Sister Formation executive secretary, Sister Annette Walters, and former sister Ritamary Bradley, who was longtime *Sister Formation Bulletin* editor.

Like the National Assembly of Women Religious, the National Coalition of American Nuns was not successful in attracting a significant number of American sisters — at the most, two percent of all sisters, according to NCAN's own estimates. But NCAN members tended to be politically savvy, organizationally astute, very aggressive, and extremely vocal. And, they knew how to get press coverage for their activities and their positions, even though only a handful of nuns were involved. Apparently NCAN leaders had considered becoming a part of the National Assembly of Women Religious at one time. Sister Dorothy Donnelly wrote in 1970 that NCAN could become a part of the National Assembly of Women Religious if the National Assembly "gives the Coalition the chance for necessary fast and completely honest freedom of speech."[78] However, there must not have been a meeting of the minds, for the two groups never did merge.

In 1970, NCAN launched an all-out drive for women's ordination, and hosted the first three organizational meetings of the Women's Ordination Conference. In 1971, the organization set 1976 as a cut-off year for granting full priesthood for women. If this did not happen, NCAN declared it would call upon "the universal sisterhood of women" to boycott church collection baskets by placing only straws in the baskets as a symbol that "we will no longer pay for the straws for the bricks Pharoah mandates."[79]

In 1973, NCAN criticized canon law, calling it "rule without the consent of the governed." The organization also contested "the non-authority of the (non) Sacred Congregation for (against) Religious."[80] The 1976 NCAN medal of honor was awarded to Anita Caspary, the former superior of the Immaculate Heart of Mary Sisters of Los Angeles who led the majority of her order into noncanonical status rather than accede to the guidelines for renewal set forth by Rome.[81] In 1977, NCAN called for the decriminalization of prostitution so that prostitutes could receive retirement benefits and health insurance, and it reaffirmed commitment to passage of the Equal Rights Amendment. In 1978, NCAN endorsed the statement of the Catholic Coalition for Gay Civil Rights, and it protested "sexist language" in the liturgy. In 1979, the group voiced support for Bella Abzug.[82]

NCAN went on record opposing the Hatch Amendment in 1982, thus taking a position contrary to the National Conference of Catholic Bishops, which had endorsed the bill. The Hatch Amendment would have given states the right to determine whether abortion would be legal, and was eventually defeated in the United States Senate. That same year, four NCAN members went on the "Phil Donahue Show" to expound on their position on "the right to choose": Sisters Ann Patrick Ware, Margaret Ellen Traxler, and Donna Quinn; and Deborah Barrett, a member of Sisters For Christian Community.

Reflecting on negative responses to the NCAN's position on abortion, Sister Ann Patrick later wrote in *Ms.* magazine: ". . . the virulence of those in opposition to women having choice over their pregnancies cannot be overestimated. None of the constraints of civil discourse seems to apply when this subject is discussed. In fact, one may make the case that a certain 'holy fanaticism' takes over and makes them even more intolerant and dangerous. Charity, the end-all and be-all of the Christian faith, in these hearts is dead for all except fetuses."[83]

When the new 1983 *Code of Canon Law* was issued, NCAN voiced opposition to the long-standing Church requirement that constitutions of religious institutes be submitted to Rome for approval. NCAN also rejected the mandate from the Congregation for Religious to end experimentation. Instead, NCAN issued a statement that read, in part: "We are suspicious of moves toward imposing religious garb, which reintroduces elitist distinctions, and of requiring 'superiors' in every community as the ultimate decision makers, which destroys collegiality. We feel impelled to resist these moves and by so doing to call the church to the realization of its own ideals." The statement also called on women Religious to accept full responsibility for regulations in their own communities, even if that meant taking noncanonical status because of lack of Church approval.[84]

In 1984, seven NCAN board members were among the Religious and lay persons who signed the controversial abortion rights statement in *The New York Times* sponsored by Catholics for a Free Choice: Sisters Margaret Ellen Traxler; Ann Patrick Ware; Donna Quinn, (past-president); Maureen Fiedler; and Jeannine Gramick. Lay members of the NCAN board who signed the statement included Elisabeth Schussler Fiorenza (then a theology professor at the University of Notre Dame) and Frances Kissling, director of Catholics for a Free Choice.[85] After the Vatican instructed Religious who signed the statement to issue public retractions, Sister Donna Quinn told *Time* magazine that "We believe we have the right to speak out when we have a differing opinion, and this is something European men do not understand."[86] In 1986, NCAN gave its "national medal of honor" to Frances Kissling, founder of Catholics for a Free Choice, "for her prophetic leadership in reclaiming for women the decision-making for their own bodies."[87]

The January 1986 NCAN newsletter called on retired Catholic bishops to ordain women to the priesthood, since, NCAN reasoned, the retired bishops had nothing to lose, "not promotion to positions of higher jurisdiction, nor to a red hat."[88] In 1987, NCAN endorsed "individual choice" in sexual ethics, saying that "individuals should be allowed to make their own decisions in the area of homosexuality. . . . Individuals have a right to choose how they fulfill the divine command to love one another."[89]

NCAN celebrated its twenty-fifth anniversary in October 1994 in Rome with picketing in St. Peter's Square and a "Sisters Synod" during the World Synod of Bishops, which was meeting on the topic of consecrated life. The NCAN newsletter announced that members were invited to join the protest in St. Peter's Square to demonstrate their message of "Enough already, of 'big daddy-o's' who have all decision-making in the Church."[90] Sponsors of the Sisters Synod included Catholics for a Free Choice; 8th Day Center for Justice, Women's Issues; Corpus Association of Married Priests, Seattle; New Ways Ministry; Institute of Women Today; Catholics Speak Out, Quixote Center; the Women's Office of the Sisters of Charity of Chicago; and the BVM Network for Women's Issues of California.[91] According to an NCAN newsletter, the Rome event was attended by five NCAN board members and five lay women, including Professor Margaret Susan Thompson of Syracuse University. The board members were Sister of St. Joseph Anne Mary Dooley; Dominican Sisters Michelle Olley and Donna Quinn; and Sisters Margaret Ellen Traxler and Jeannine Gramick.[92] Six members of the group carried banners across the piazza while singing "We shall not be silenced." Since such demonstrations are prohibited by local law, Italian police confiscated two of the three banners and briefly detained the demonstrators at the police station.[93] In 1996, NCAN joined the We Are Church coalition, profiled later in this chapter.

In spite of this attention in the media, the fact is that NCAN has represented the views of very few American sisters over its nearly thirty years of existence. NCAN claims to have about eighteen-hundred members, but only a handful of NCAN supporters show up at NCAN-orchestrated events like the demonstration during the 1994 synod. It is relevant to note that the NCAN membership figure is worldwide, and membership is open to any person, Religious or lay. So, contrary to what its name implies, the National

Coalition of American Nuns is really not a group of American nuns; it is an international organization composed of women Religious as well as lay men and women. As with the National Assembly of Women Religious, the NCAN's radical views have unfairly impugned the image and reputation of many American women Religious who support the authority and teachings of the Catholic Church and do not share NCAN's militant agenda.

NETWORK

NETWORK is a Washington, D.C., lobbying organization controlled by sisters and defined as "a national task force to facilitate the process of political education and action for American religious women and their organizations in ministry for social justice."[94] It was started in 1971 by several individuals, including Sister Marjorie Tuite of the National Assembly of Women Religious and Sister Margaret Cafferty, who was president of the Leadership Conference of Women Religious 1984-85 and became its executive director in 1992. NETWORK was endorsed in 1972 by a Leadership Conference resolution.

Dominican Sister Carol Coston was executive director of NETWORK for many years, and traveled extensively to give workshops for nuns on the legislative and political process. Several former presidents of the Leadership Conference of Women Religious have served on NETWORK's board or staff at one time or another, including: Sisters Mary Luke Tobin (conference president 1964-67), Bette Moslander (conference president 1981-82), Catherine Pinkerton (conference president 1983-84, chairperson of the National Assembly of Women Religious 1973-75, who became a full-time lobbyist for NETWORK), Margaret Cafferty (conference president 1984-85 and Leadership Conference executive director 1993-present), and Immaculate Heart of Mary Sister Carol Quigley (president 1986-87).

NETWORK's early lobbying involved efforts to: cut off funds for the Vietnam War, reduce foreign aid to countries violating human rights, reduce the defense budget, increase social services funding, support the Equal Rights Amendment, raise the federal minimum wage, and establish an independent public corporation to provide legal services for the poor.[95] But NETWORK also has been heavily involved in women's liberation issues. In 1975, congresswoman Bella Abzug told three hundred sister members of NETWORK who were meeting in Washington that "We may not have been at the last supper, but you can be damned sure we'll be at the next one."[96] In 1983, NETWORK stood firmly behind Sister Agnes Mary Mansour in the dispute with the Vatican over her appointment as director of Social Services for the State of Michigan.

Sisters in Crisis

NETWORK continues to be closely allied with the Leadership Conference of Women Religious and regularly sponsors a NETWORK booth at meetings of Church-reform organizations such as the Women's Ordination Conference and Call to Action.[97] Even though NETWORK is primarily controlled by women Religious, its membership is open to any interested individuals. The organization claimed to have about ten-thousand members in 1994.

Women's Ordination Conference

The Women's Ordination Conference (WOC) is not a sisters' organization, but sisters — many of whom were also active in the Leadership Conference of Women Religious, the National Assembly of Women Religious, and the National Coalition of American Nuns — have been instrumental in sustaining it. As noted already, the National Coalition of American Nuns fostered the beginnings of the Women's Ordination Conference, which was established in 1975. Sister Mary Luke Tobin, who was president of the Conference of Major Religious Superiors of Women's Institutes from 1964 to 1967, was an influential member of the WOC task force. Even though Archbishop Augustine Mayer, secretary of the Congregation for Religious, asked the Leadership Conference of Women Religious not to be associated with the first Women's Ordination Conference meeting in Detroit in 1975, Sister Mary Daniel Turner, executive director of the Leadership Conference, was a major presenter, along with Sister Marjorie Tuite of the National Assembly of Women Religious. Also speaking were Sister Marie Augusta Neal (creator of the Sisters' Survey), talking on "Models for Future Priesthood"; Sister (Thomas Aquinas) Elizabeth Carroll (a former Sister Formation Conference leader and president of the Leadership Conference 1971-72), talking on " 'The Proper Place' of Women in the Church"; Mercy Sister Margaret Farley, on "The Moral Imperatives for the Ordination of Women"; and Sister Anne Carr, a Sister of Charity of the Blessed Virgin Mary, speaking on "The Church in Process: Engendering the Future."[98] Priests addressing the conference included Fathers William Callahan, Carroll Stuhlmueller, and Richard McBrien.[99]

Among those making public endorsements of the 1975 WOC conference were some of the past or future presidents of the Leadership Conference of Women Religious, including Sister Angelita Myerscough, president 1970-71; Sister Francine Zeller, president 1974-75; and Sister Theresa Kane, elected president in 1979. The National Assembly of Women Religious and several provinces or orders of sisters also offered their endorsement, including the Sisters of Loretto, Sisters of St. Joseph of Cleveland, and the general council of the Adrian Dominican Sisters.[100]

The WOC established an office in the Quixote Peace and Justice Center in 1977, with Ruth McDonough Fitzpatrick (a co-member of the Sisters of Loretto) as the first staff person. The second major meeting of the WOC in 1978 drew about one-thousand people, and was endorsed by the executive committee of the Leadership Conference of Women Religious. In a letter to the WOC's Sister Mary Luke Tobin, Leadership Conference executive director Sister Mary Daniel wrote, ". . . the executive committee feels we would be doing the LCWR and the entire Church a disservice if we fail to be associated with the upcoming meeting." For good measure, Sister Mary Daniel enclosed an LCWR check for $100 for the WOC.[101]

In 1984, the WOC honored Sister Theresa Kane as a "prophetic figure" because of her 1979 public challenge to Pope John Paul II on the subject of women's ordination. Feminist theologian Elisabeth Schussler Fiorenza was similarly honored for "working for equality within church and society."[102] According to news reports, only about fifty people attended that awards ceremony. Attendance was not large at the WOC tenth anniversary meeting in St. Louis in 1985, either, as that meeting reportedly drew about two hundred people.[103]

Apparently the WOC ran into financial difficulty over the years, for in a July 1995 letter to "Dear WOC Friend," WOC national coordinator Ruth McDonough Fitzpatrick begged for donations. She wrote: "We survive by one pay check at a time because of your checks that keep coming into our mail box one at a time. We need to keep this office thriving and the staff paid on a timely basis. . . .

"We are on an incredible spiritual journey. Our struggle for structural change, a new feminist priestly ministry and social justice is often very difficult, and so political."

Fitzpatrick implored, "We need money not only to help with office expenses but also to bring people with meager funds to the November [WOC] meeting. . . .

"Once again we urgently appeal to you to make the most generous contribution possible to enable WOC to move into the 21st Century."

If the Women's Ordination Conference does survive into the third millennium, it may be as a splintered organization. The November 10-12, 1995, national WOC meeting — the first national meeting in ten years — drew about one thousand participants although planners had expected about three thousand. There was speculation that some WOC supporters did not attend because they feared reprisals from Catholic employers since Pope John Paul II had ordered an end to discussion about women's ordination in his May 1994 apostolic letter, *Ordinatio Sacerdotalis*.[104] (Mercy Sister Carmel

McEnroy had been fired April 26, 1995, from her tenured position at St. Meinrad Seminary in Indiana because of her public advocacy for women's ordination.)

Indeed, there were plenty of fireworks at the WOC national meeting, but not because of the pope's letter. Rather, a power struggle between factions of the WOC became quite evident. One faction, represented by Professor Diana Hayes of the Theology Department of Georgetown University and Professor Elisabeth Schussler Fiorenza of Harvard Divinity School (author of *Discipleship of Equals: A Critical, Feminist Ekklesia-logy of Liberation*) advocated dropping their goal of ordination in favor of reconstructing the Catholic Church. Schussler Fiorenza argued that the gospel vision of equality cannot be realized in a male-dominated church based on a Roman imperial model.[105] WOC board member Karen Schwarz was quoted as saying: "WOC will demonstrate that the mere ordination of women does not solve anything. Nothing short of major deconstruction of clericalism, patriarchy and hierarchy will do."[106]

Peter Steinfels of *The New York Times* reported that "The meeting's planners presented an elaborate program proposing that the group's goal should now be a 'discipleship of equals,' a concept of a church without hierarchy, and without priests ordained for life and bestowed with special power to administer sacraments.

"This model of the church is associated more with New Testament times, with the radical wing of the Protestant Reformation and with movements like the Quakers rather than with Catholicism."[107]

The other WOC faction was represented by WOC board members Sisters Maureen Fiedler and Jeannine Gramick. Sister Maureen observed, "I love the ideal of a discipleship of equals, but if it means we don't seek ordination in the Roman Catholic church, I don't buy one syllable of it." Sister Jeannine said that the WOC mission statements of 1991 and 1994 incorporated the vision of "discipleship of equals" but also included the goal of "ordination to a renewed priestly ministry." Sister Jeannine had written meeting coordinator, Loretto Sister Agnes Ann Schum, in May of 1995 about her concern that meeting planners were moving to an "either-or" model. Silvia Cancio, president of the WOC board, acknowledged that the board had agreed the meeting would include both options, but the meeting had taken on "a life of its own."[108]

One month after the tumultuous national meeting, WOC national coordinator Ruth McDonough Fitzpatrick resigned, saying the WOC board had violated her contract by interfering with her ability to manage the affairs of the WOC office. She also said she felt she was being made "the scapegoat for the financial deficit of the WOC Gathering '95," estimated by the *National Catholic Reporter* to be around $100,000.[109] A 1996 mailing from new national coordinator Andrea Johnson solicited new members to keep alive the discussion of women's ordination and to "help birth a more inclusive church."

Mary's Pence

Mary's Pence is an organization that also includes lay women, but it has been supported primarily by Catholic sisters.[110] Mary's Pence was incorporated in 1987 as a feminist alternative to Peter's Pence, the traditional collection for support of the Vatican. The idea behind Mary's Pence is to provide an agency for Catholic donation that is independent of hierarchical control. According to one of the founders of Mary's Pence, feminist theologian Rosemary Radford Ruether, "This allows Catholics who are distressed and alienated by the way the institutional Church is using it resources to channel their contributions into a Catholic fund that will support the sort of empowerment of women and poor people that is closer to the liberation model of church."[111]

Some of the projects that have received grants from Mary's Pence include health, nutrition, counseling, education, and shelter programs for women and children. Mary's Pence also has given grants to women for attending theological seminaries, helped fund a support group for "women facing burn-out from work in service to human and community needs," and provided seed money for a New Ways ministry "project of organizing Catholic lesbians to develop a consciousness-raising and support group."[112]

Several sisters who have served on the Mary's Pence board are recognizable names from some of the other sisters' organizations cited above. They include Dominican Sisters Kaye Ashe (of the National Assembly of Religious Women) and Carol Coston (of NETWORK); Sister Mary Luke Tobin (former president of the Conference of Major Religious Superiors of Women's Institutes and formerly active in NETWORK and Center of Concern); Sister Amata Miller (of NETWORK); and Sister Margaret Ellen Traxler (of the National Coalition of American Nuns). Ruether also has served on the board of Mary's Pence, as has historian Margaret Susan Thompson (of the National Coalition of American Nuns).

Call to Action

Call to Action is a Church reform organization based in Chicago, with affiliated local groups in about twenty-four states as of 1996.[113] The organization has a variety of supporters, about thirty percent being women Religious.[114] These women Religious involved in Call to Action are among the most visible proponents of the reforms being promoted by the group. Regular speakers at the Call to Action conferences include Sisters Joan Chittister and Theresa Kane, both former presidents of the Leadership Conference of Women Religious, as well as Sisters Sandra Schneiders and Maureen Fiedler, Franciscan Sister Fran Ferder, Immaculate Heart of Mary Sister Nancy Sylvester of NETWORK, and Sister of St. Joseph Christine Schenk of FutureChurch.

Call to Action draws its name from an October 1976 meeting in Detroit sponsored by the United States Bishops as part of the American bicentennial celebration. Sister Margaret Cafferty, president of the Leadership Conference of Women Religious in 1984-85 and executive director of the conference since 1992, planned and coordinated the 1976 "A Call to Action" conference for the bishops.[115] However, the similarity between that 1976 event sponsored by the bishops and the contemporary Call to Action organization is in name only. Before the 1976 conference took place, the late Cardinal Joseph Bernardin, then president of the National Conference of Catholic Bishops, called the conference "an effort to consult the church at large in the United States on a broad range of issues relating to justice in the church and society." But the conference seemed to take on a life of its own, for some of the 1,350 delegates approached the conference determined to promote their own special interests. (Some of the conference facilitators and group chairpersons — including some leaders of women Religious — had also attended the first Women's Ordination Conference in 1975, titled "Women in Future Priesthood Now: A Call for Action," and they took the women's ordination agenda to the 1976 conference sponsored by the bishops.) By what some conference observers called a manipulation of the political process, several controversial resolutions were approved by the body of delegates, which reportedly passed every resolution that came out of committee. After the conference, Cardinal Bernardin observed:

> First, in retrospect, it seems that too much was attempted. Any one of the eight large topics considered [humankind, personhood, nationhood, ethnicity and race, the church, neighborhood, the family and work] would have provided more than enough work for the limited time available. All of them together overwhelmed the conference. The result was haste and a determination to formulate recommendations on complex matters without adequate reflection, discussion and consideration of different points of view.

Second, special interest groups advocating particular causes seemed to play a disproportionate role. These groups had a right to be present and make their views known. However, their actual role went beyond this and, in my judgment and that of others, dominated the conference as a whole. The result was a process and a number of recommendations which were not representative of the church in this country and which paid too little attention to other legitimate interests and concerns.[116]

The recommendations from the conference were lengthy and wide-ranging, covering every one of the eight topics addressed. Many of the recommendations were well-reasoned and within the authority of the bishops to address, such as appropriate training of leaders involved in family ministry, availability of Natural Family Planning classes, and fostering of vocations to the priesthood. But, there also were some more controversial recommendations well beyond the authority of a bishops' conference, including:

The local church must be involved in the selection of bishops and pastors.

That the National Conference of Catholic Bishops take affirmative action to respectfully petition the Holy Father . . . to allow married men to be ordained to the priesthood and that they also initiate dialogue on this topic with such national groups as National Federation of Priests' Councils, Corpus, Fellowship and Padres.

That the National Conference of Catholic Bishops initiate dialogue with Rome to . . . allow women to be ordained to the diaconate and priesthood.

That the church, bishops, priests, religious, laity affirm their commitment to the validity of personal sexual fulfillment in married life while at the same time engaging in continuing dialogue with each other and with other persons who are expressing their sexuality in a variety of lifestyles on matters related to the human and spiritual significance of human sexuality.

That the church in the United States acknowledge that it is living in a state of conflict and anguish arising from tension between the common understanding of church teaching on contraception and the current practice of many

Catholics, and that this state of conflict produces intense pastoral and human problems which, in justice, the church is obliged to face.

The American bishops should use the present pastoral leadership to affirm more clearly the right and responsibility of married people to form their own consciences and to discern what is morally appropriate within the context of their marriage in view of historic church teaching including *Humanae Vitae,* and contemporary theological reflection, biological and social scientific research; and those factors influencing the spiritual and emotional qualities of their marital and family lives. . . ."

That the church leaders publicly address the request of the divorced who have remarried to receive, under certain conditions, the sacraments of the church.[117]

In response to the recommendations, a 1977 statement by the United States Bishops noted that some of the recommendations departed from official Church positions, specifically recommendations related to contraception, homosexual activity, divorce, priestly celibacy, and ordination of women. But, the statement also pointed out that all recommendations were being referred for study to committees of the USCC and the NCCB and that implementation of appropriate recommendations would be considered.[118] This ended the formal relationship of the United States Bishops with the "A Call to Action" conference. But some people dedicated to Church reform instead saw this event as a beginning, not an end.

According to the Call to Action newsletter *Churchwatch*, "The 800,000 people who fed ideas into Detroit [in 1976], and the delegates who voted there, trusted that the bishops really wanted to listen to them. So they raised issues of reform in the church as well as justice in society. Many bishops didn't want to hear about church reform. The resolutions were not acted upon.

"Chicago-based Call to Action was organized the following year by people who didn't want the Detroit issues to die. Many of those issues — women's ordination, hearing lay people's experiences on sexual issues, a lay voice in decision-making, multicultural leadership — are still on 'our' agenda and are reiterated in our Call for Reform in the Catholic Church. Most of all, the process of listening to the people begun in Detroit is the way we want our church to do business again!"[119]

An Ash Wednesday 1990 ad in *The New York Times* titled "A Call for

Reform in the Catholic Church" carried the Call to Action platform, which was reaffirmed by Call to Action in 1996 after the Pope and the Congregation for the Doctrine of the Faith stressed in 1994 and 1995 that the matter of women's ordination was not open to debate. Call to Action announced in the December 1995-January 1996 issue of its newspaper that "CTA and FutureChurch are launching a 1996 National Dialogue on the priest shortage crisis and the availability for ordination of qualified, spirit-called women and married men." Some other issues still being promoted in that platform included popular election of bishops; return of resigned priests to ministry; consultation with the laity on sexual issues; more dialogue, academic freedom and due process; and financial openness by the Church.

Call to Action bills itself as an organization of mainstream Catholics, but its positions have been extreme on many issues. Call to Action founded and coordinates an umbrella organization called Catholic Organizations for Renewal (although some of these organizations are Catholic in name only and have an ecumenical membership). Among the member groups of that coalition are: Catholics For Free Choice, Catholics Speak Out (Quixote Center), Celibacy Is The Issue, Chicago Catholic Women, Conference for Catholic Lesbians, Dignity/USA, FutureChurch, Friends of Creation Spirituality (Matthew Fox), Friends of Vatican III on Church and Democracy, Loretto Women's Network, National Coalition of American Nuns, New Ways Ministry, and Women's Ordination Conference.[120] Most of these organizations also are involved in the We Are Church movement, which is coordinated by Sister Maureen Fiedler.

The November 15-17, 1996, Call to Action national conference was moved to Detroit from its usual site in Chicago. According to a Call to Action report, the Hyatt Regency O'Hare Hotel in Chicago canceled its contract with Call to Action in order to rent space to a more lucrative client. In an effort to make lemonade out of lemons, the conference planners boasted that the Detroit site was even more appropriate than Chicago because Detroit had been the site of the original Call to Action conference. The casual reader may well have inferred from conference promotional material that the 1996 conference was somehow linked to the 1976 conference which had been sponsored by the bishops: "We gather in Detroit on hallowed ground: Cobo Hall, site of the original United States Bishops' Call to Action conference in Fall, 1976. We celebrate the 20th anniversary of the historic event when 1,351 lay, religious and clergy delegates, appointed by their local bishops, voted for an inclusive church, open to women and married priests, with shared decision-making and greater social justice."[121]

At the 1996 Call to Action conference in Detroit, the group's annual award was presented to the women Religious of the United States, who, according to conference promotional material, "have played a key role in bringing the U.S. Church to a new threshold of renewal in 1996."[122]

We Are Church

We Are Church is a coalition of groups which organized in 1996 to attempt to gather the signatures of at least one-million Catholics to promote democracy and broad reforms in the Catholic Church. The coalition was modeled after the 1995 national petition drives in Germany and Austria that called for ordination of women, optional priestly celibacy, and a voice for the laity in choosing hierarchy and defining Church doctrine. Most groups in the We Are Church coalition are made up of lay persons as well as some Religious and priests, but sisters are heavily involved, with Sister Maureen Fiedler serving as national coordinator of the We Are Church campaign.

The reforms called for by We Are Church are very similar to the Call to Action platform: lay participation in selecting pastors and bishops; ordination of women to the diaconate and the priesthood; optional celibacy for priests; primacy of pastoral care over canon law; respect for "primacy of conscience in all moral decision making" (i.e. on sexual issues); and a Church welcome for "those who are divorced and remarried, married priests, theologians and others who exercise freedom of speech."

We Are Church billed itself as a project of the Women's Ordination Conference in conjunction with Catholics Speak Out. Organizations involved in the national task force coordinating the campaign were: Association for the Rights of Catholics in the Church; Call to Action; CORPUS, the National Association for a Married Priesthood; Dignity USA; Federation of Christian Ministries; New Ways Ministry; Priests for Equality; and Pax Christi Maine. Co-sponsoring groups included: Catholics For Free Choice; Chicago Catholic Women; Loretto Women's Network (made up of Loretto sisters and co-members); and National Coalition of American Nuns. As noted above, many of these Church-reform organizations have overlapping memberships, and some are "paper organizations" which have only a handful of active members, but consider any person on a mailing list to be a member.

Most of the groups involved in We Are Church also are members of the Catholic Organizations for Renewal coalition, founded and coordinated by Call to Action. Catholic Organizations for Renewal bills itself as a "collective Catholic voice" which "generates successful coalition efforts like a signature ad about contraception that helped neutralize Vatican lobbying at the [1995] Cairo population conference."[123]

Archbishop Anthony Pilla of Cleveland, president of the National Conference of Catholic Bishops, observed that the We Are Church referendum challenged long-standing church teaching and ignored the views of Catholics who do not agree with the opinions of the sponsoring groups, since the referendum asked only for agreement. He also pointed out that being Catholic means sharing a common religious heritage and moral vision. "It is not something purely subjective, radically private and self-constructed. It is a system of religious teachings and moral imperatives which are to be freely embraced and faithfully handed on to the next generation."[124]

Yet, some sisters who are in the forefront of the We Are Church movement have expressed their certitude that they are more qualified than the official Church to interpret the movement of the Holy Spirit and that even definitive Church doctrine should be open to question, or endless "dialogue." Loretto Sister Virginia Williams, who took it upon herself to try to gather the signatures of Loretto sisters in the state of Missouri for the We Are Church petition, told the *St. Louis Post Dispatch* that the We Are Church campaign was "a public way to let 'good Catholics' who differ with the Vatican on some issues know they are not isolated. . . .

"We want to give heart to many to practice their faith. . . . The Holy Spirit moves at will. We cannot box the Spirit in, or out. Everyone who is a child of God, female or male has a mandate to be open to the movement of the Spirit."[125]

We Are Church national coordinator, Sister Maureen Fiedler, observed that the referendum "will make church reform and renewal a household word in the United States. . . ."[126]

Through these various groups, the most visible and vocal American sisters have professed a vision of the Catholic Church and of religious life that is in sharp contrast to actual Church teaching and to the desire of the majority of women Religious to use their feminine gifts to build up the Church. Additionally, these high-profile sisters have shown their disdain for Church authority and for the reputation of their own religious institutes. They have made it clear that they have a great deal to tell the Church, but the Church has nothing of value to tell them. As a result, the image of every American sisters has suffered considerably. Rather than giving sisters a corporate presence and a voice in the affairs of the Church, these organizations have further delineated the differences between sisters who accept the authority of the Church and those who reject it. Even the prestigious Leadership Conference of Women Religious fell into this destructive pattern and saw its membership split into two groups, as the next chapter relates.

14: The Leadership Conference Splits

"Both CMSM [Conference of Major Superiors of Men] and LCWR [Leadership Conference of Women Religious] are on record as seeing clearly that at least in the countries of the western democracies, the pattern of religious life that has prevailed for several centuries has, for all practical purposes, served its purpose and is passing away."[1]

Sister Elizabeth Johnson, CSJ

The organizations of sisters that were discussed in the last chapter shared a very activist vision of religious life, and they felt the definition of religious life should come from their own "lived experience" rather than from Rome. But there were many other sisters — and superiors — who were concerned about the direction renewal was taking in communities which drastically altered not only their lifestyles and the mission of their institutes, but also the entire concept of what religious life meant. In many cases, their concerns centered around a tendency by the change-oriented sisters to redefine religious life in light of the American experience and to apply the American concept of democracy to their relationship with the Church, the hierarchy and with Rome. This polarization between the change-oriented and traditional sisters caused a split in the superiors' conference that fermented for twenty-two years before an alternate superiors' conference for traditional sisters was recognized by Rome in 1992.

An April 11, 1970, article in *America* magazine observed that two different positions on religious life were beginning to emerge among women

Religious: one group who accepted the essential elements of religious life as defined by the Church, and another group who wanted the definition of religious life to come from themselves rather than from Rome. The *America* article noted that a new phenomenon was occurring in the American Catholic Church — women Religious were beginning to join together in national organizations. "The phenomenon says something about the turbulence within contemporary Roman Catholicism. It says even more about the Americanization of religious life and is an interesting testimony to the new assertiveness of modern woman," wrote Jesuit Father John C. Haughey.

In writing about the Conference of Major Religious Superiors of Women's Institutes, Father Haughey observed: "The conference is beginning to fill up with the superiors elected and formed by the renewal processes of their own congregations. . . . Two different positions on the meaning of religious life are beginning to emerge. One of these is quite content with the essential characteristics of religious life that have been spelled out by the Sacred Congregation for Religious. The other could, in general, be described as less certain about definitions that do not come from the religious themselves."[2] Father Haughey came down solidly on the side of the sisters who wanted to create their own definition of religious life.

This polarity in the very philosophy of religious life was articulated clearly at the 1970 annual assembly of the Conference of Major Religious Superiors of Women's Institutes, particularly when some superiors attempted to have the assembly endorse the "Statement on Religious Life in the 1970s" that had been formulated by an informal group of women and men Religious just prior to the conference assembly. That statement contended that American Religious need to function under a democratic system, and therefore American Religious could not continue to automatically accept directives coming from Rome. The statement also put the Vatican on notice that American Religious were initiating "broad developments within religious life" and felt free to determine their own patterns of life, to explore a variety of ministries and to engage in secular occupations. And, the statement concluded that American Religious would listen to Rome, but would make their own decisions about actually following directives from Rome.

The statement did not pass the 1970 assembly of women's superiors because some members complained they had no advance notice that it would be proposed, had no input in its formulation, and did not have time to study and debate its implications. Nevertheless, the officers of the men's and women's conferences of major superiors sent the Statement to members of the Bishops' Liaison Committee with the two conferences, feeling that "the statement could act as a springboard to the meaningful discussion they anticipated having with the Bishops' Liaison Committee."[3] The Statement had shared the agenda at the 1970 assembly with some other controversial matters, including an address by Father Haughey, who encouraged sisters to ignore directives from Rome that were not communicated directly to them and about which they were not consulted.[4]

Consortium Perfectae Caritatis

These events of the 1970 assembly were just too much for some major superiors who had been concerned for some time that the Conference of Major Religious Superiors of Women's Institutes was headed in the wrong direction, that is, away from Rome. According to the recollections of Sister of Notre Dame Mary Elise Krantz,[5] some of these superiors, who had not been acquainted before, shared their concerns with one another during coffee breaks at the 1970 assembly. Among those sisters were: Sister of St. Joseph Alice Anita Murphy of Chestnut Hill, Pennsylvania; Immaculate Heart of Mary Sister Mary Claudia Honsberger of Immaculata, Pennsylvania; Sister of St. Joseph Marie Assumpta McKinley of Watertown, New York; and Franciscan Sister Sixtina Reul of Alton, Illinois. During the days of the assembly, these women discussed forming an organization dedicated to studying the documents of Vatican II regarding religious life. Their determination resulted in the formation of the Consortium Perfectae Caritatis, an organization which would prove to have limited influence during its twenty-plus years of existence, but eventually was a major influence in forming a new conference of major superiors representing thousands of women Religious.

The first formal meeting of the group took place at Sister Mary Elise's motherhouse in Chardon, Ohio, on December 2, 1970. Attending that meeting was Cardinal Egidio Vagnozzi, president of the Prefecture for Economic Affairs of the Holy See and former apostolic delegate to the United States, as well as two bishops, several priests, and about sixty sisters from throughout the United States. About thirty other bishops sent their greetings.[6] One proposed title for the organization was "North American Association of Religious Women," but the name Consortium Perfectae Caritatis was adopted instead, referring to the Vatican II document on religious life, *Perfectae Caritatis*.

At the group's first general assembly February 28 to March 2, 1971, in Washington, D.C., Bishop Fulton J. Sheen spoke, along with apostolic delegate Archbishop Luigi Raimondi. At that assembly, the essentials of religious life — as the sisters interpreted them to be defined in Vatican II documents — were adopted as the guiding principles of the consortium. These essentials included: 1) pursuit of holiness through the vows; 2) a "clear and unequivocal position in support of the Holy See and the right she has to interpret the norms of religious life for the universal Church and the local Churches"; 3) belief in a permanent ecclesial commitment to a corporate and institutional apostolate under the guidance of the hierarchy; 4) willingness to respond to the pope and the Congregation for Religious; 5) "acceptance of life in a Eucharistic Community under legitimately elected superiors"; 6) wearing of a religious habit; 7) life in community with communal and liturgical prayer; 8) concern to foster vocations.

The main activity of the consortium was sponsoring semi-annual assemblies which were designed to be educational in nature. Among speakers at those assemblies were prominent members of the hierarchy, such as John Carberry, Jean Danielou, John Krol, William Baum, James Hickey, and Fulton Sheen. The consortium also published an educational newsletter, which included documentary material from the Congregation for Religious. Funding was obtained by conference fees and donations from sympathetic clergy and hierarchy as well as lay individuals. The Knights of Columbus organization also was a generous donor.

Originally the consortium was made up of major superiors of women Religious who endorsed the essentials of religious life as professed by the consortium. The consortium never was a membership organization, but it invited any Religious who shared the philosophy of the consortium to attend its meetings and subscribe to its mailings. While the consortium was intended to be an educational enterprise to enable sisters to accomplish the renewal mandated by Vatican II, it took on an additional role of trying to help sisters address excesses and abuses which they encountered in their communities. Indeed, consortium records indicate that many Religious found support and comfort in the organization at a time when renewal in their congregations seemed to them to be moving far beyond the guidelines of Vatican II. This excerpt from a 1971 letter to the consortium reflects the contents of similar letters in the consortium records:

> . . . I am a Sister for thirty-five years. . . . I have been happy in my religious life. I have changed to a modified modern habit and have found some of the other changes in community life helpful. However, I am concerned when I see how we continue to see changes occur in our life which are almost a practice by a large number of sisters before one realizes what has happened. I believe in a habit — a sign of our place among the people of God. But a

large number of our Sisters no longer wear either a veil or an emblem. I know that clothes does not make the sister. But I am worried when I see many of my sisters out in slacks, shorts and other non-sisterly attire.

Community prayer and personal prayer appears to be superficial. Sisters are on the go and away from the community many week-ends and the holidays and any kind of work or living arrangements seem to be permitted.

Those of us (I would guess that we are in the minority) who speak out or take a different stand are quickly and easily out numbered and out-voted — at least it has been this way in the past. We are encouraged to join NAWR [the National Assembly of Women Religious] but I do not go along with the thinking of that group.

My concern now is this — what can individual sisters do who are not able to make changes in their own situation but believe they see their own associates moving toward a secularized way of life. If the younger sisters believe that the church is asking this of them then, I believe that those who feel the obligations of their original religious commitment should be able to live out their way of life. At the present time I am living with sixteen other sisters whose ideals are in accord with mine so we are able to establish a better religious house than many other places. If the community continues to promote this type of work and we can live together this will take care of us for a while but if we should meet with change we could well find ourselves in the midst of a secularized house.

I want to know what could be done or at least offered to our Sisters at chapter and I also want to know what I can do to be able to live out my promise to God and to the Church for the rest.

. . . Please do not take this as a criticism of my own order because I do not feel I am in a position to do this. But I present it, rather — as an individual Sister who believes in conscience that she cannot live in a situation which is becoming more and more secularized by the individuals rather than by the leaders in community. It seems to me that we are to a large extent ruled or directed by trends — one thing leading to another — with no pro or con coming from a central executive group. Last year at Chapter, a proposal to consider two different life styles was not considered. This year we have a proposal to select a symbol and uniform color for the habit-sign and to consider the establishment of a secular institute and a religious community separate from one another. Though I wish we would not have to take such drastic steps I expect that it too, will not get far in Chapter. Even now, Sisters on the Council and other vocal members are saying it will be voted down without any trouble. I love our community and I want to persevere in it but not to the extent that I would have to be unfaithful to my vows and original promise to God and the Church.

. . . Any suggestions you can offer or material you can share will be appreciated.[7]

The consortium meetings usually drew between one hundred and two hundred sisters, but the organization was not effective in attracting large numbers of mainstream sisters. One difficulty was that many sisters could not obtain permission from their superiors to attend consortium meetings, either because their superiors did not understand what the consortium was about, or they did not agree with its philosophy. Other sisters have indicated that they did not attend consortium meetings because they felt they should have received a specific invitation from the organization.

The consortium probably also did not attract large numbers because it projected an image of being much more conservative than the record indicates it actually was. Rather than trying to return religious life to a preconciliar mold — as its critics charged — the consortium records indicate that it heavily promoted the teachings of the Second Vatican Council, even publishing a book — *Religious Life: A Mystery in Christ* — which collected pertinent documents on religious life from Vatican II, the popes, and the Congregation for Religious. And consortium records contain letters from men and women Religious and hierarchy who attended consortium assemblies for the first time who were pleasantly surprised that the organization was not the ultra-conservative group that they had perceived it to be.

But the consortium sisters seem to have made several key mistakes that saddled their organization with the conservative image, an image they were never successful in overcoming. The first mistake was the name of the organization. In choosing a Latin title, the sisters set themselves apart from the updating called for by Vatican II. And people unfamiliar with the Council documents (i.e. the Council document on religious life was *Perfectae Caritatis,* translated into English as "perfect charity") perceived a holier-than-thou image when the title of the organization was translated as the Association of Perfect Charity.

The consortium further projected a conservative image quite out of step with the legitimate women's movement by maintaining as its coordinator a male, Father James Viall, a priest of the diocese of Cleveland. Further, a hefty majority of the speakers at the consortium assemblies were men, giving fuel to the argument that the consortium sisters felt that women had nothing significant to say about important issues in the Church and religious life. Some members of the consortium board had addressed the problem of a women's organization having a male leader, and some suggested that a committee should have more input into which speakers would address the consortium assemblies, since speakers usually were chosen by Father Viall. But consortium leaders apparently felt a great loyalty toward Father Viall, who had been supportive of the organization from its inception, and who had numerous contacts in the Church through his position as president of the Confraternity of Catholic Clergy.

The organization of the consortium itself also proved to be a weakness. Since it was a loosely defined group with a purpose of education, there was not much formal structure and no official membership. In the early days of the consortium, there was not even a board of directors. Eventually, an administrative board — usually numbering about fourteen — was formed from interested sisters, and four of those board members functioned as president, vice-president, secretary, and treasurer. Eventually one sister became executive director.

Some sisters attending the consortium assemblies found it distressing that there appeared to be no specific leaders in charge of the group. Others who were more familiar with the structure of the consortium suggested that leaders be changed more frequently, as the consortium board had retained many of the same members throughout the years. Additionally, because the consortium was the only organization of women Religious during the early 1970s that vigorously endorsed official Church positions and supported the hierarchy and Rome, it attracted some sisters who were still very resistant to the changes of Vatican II, thus enforcing the image of conservatism. The same thing happened when a few conservative bishops and priests publicly aligned themselves with the organization.

Because of its outspoken loyalty to the magisterium, the consortium had the backing of many prominent members of the hierarchy, both in this country and in Rome. In 1980, the signatures of fifty United States bishops were obtained by the consortium, endorsing a petition that the pope declare the organization a pontifical forum.[8] (Consortium records indicate that the organization repeatedly asked Rome for recognition, not as a major superiors' conference, as its critics charged, but rather to gain pontifical approval and legitimacy that would help attract more sisters to its meetings and mailing list.) In 1972, the consortium received Vatican approval of sorts in the form of a *Decretum laudis* — a decree of praise — from the Congregation for Religious.[9] In 1973, Bishop James J. Hogan, chairman of the NCCB liaison committee with the Leadership Conference of Women Religious, observed that a growing number of bishops saw the consortium as representing a valid point of view, and those bishops were looking for a means of rapprochement with the consortium.[10]

Still, many United States bishops steered clear of endorsing the consortium because the Leadership Conference of Women Religious clearly viewed the consortium as a threat, and most bishops did not want to come down on one side or the other. Bishop William Connare of Greensburg, Pennsylvania, wrote the consortium in 1976 that many bishops supported the consortium but did not say so openly because they did not want to contribute to the division between the two groups of sisters, a division that worried many bishops.

He observed: "Unfortunately the leadership of the LCWR has lost its bearings. I know many bishops feel that way. Privately we discuss the situation, but seem hesitant to criticize openly. Maybe the time has come for the latter approach."[11] Bishop Floyd Begin of Oakland, California, who had worked on the staff of the Congregation for Religious, observed in 1977 that many bishops were confused and uninformed about the Leadership Conference as well as the consortium. He suggested that bishops had been cautious about endorsing the consortium because they wanted to "preserve the wealth of potential service contained in LCWR."[12] Indeed, bishops agonized privately over what would become of the schools and hospitals in their dioceses if they antagonized the orders affiliated with the Leadership Conference by publicly supporting the consortium.

It was true that the consortium and the LCWR were two dichotomous groups that bumped heads frequently. The Leadership Conference feared that the consortium was trying to cozy up to Rome in an effort to replace the conference as the Vatican-approved organization of United States women superiors. The consortium felt that the conference had lost its loyalty to Rome and was leading American sisters away from the model of religious life prescribed by Church documents and canon law. Ironically, some sisters maintained membership in both groups simultaneously. In the midst of this conflict, the Congregation for Religious advised consortium members who were major superiors to continue their membership in the Leadership Conference, even if they did not approve of the direction the conference was taking. Apparently Rome felt that the consortium sisters would bring a moderating influence to the Leadership Conference. Eventually, however, most of the consortium members left the Leadership Conference, thus delineating the differences between the two groups even more dramatically.

A provincial superior wrote the Congregation for Religious in 1977 over her concern about remaining a member of the Leadership Conference and supporting its activities and publications with dues moneys when she disagreed with the direction the conference was taking. She complained that the same people continued to serve on the conference executive board and that she could find no voice in the organization. She charged that the conference was attempting to direct the activities of religious communities at the national level as well as at local levels. And, she asked, "Must communities like ours continue to be represented by an organization such as this? . . . The only way to gain control in this group is by giving up one's apostolic work and spending all of one's time in this kind of contention." She asked for clear direction from the Congregation for Religious so that she would not default in service to the Church.[13]

Archbishop Augustine Mayer, secretary of the Congregation for Religious, responded that the Congregation for Religious had encouraged major superiors to retain their membership in the Leadership Conference to make it clear that not all superiors agreed with the direction taken by the conference. But he admitted the Congregation for Religious no longer felt justified in maintaining that attitude, and that each major superior should decide for herself whether or not to maintain membership in the Leadership Conference since it was a voluntary organization, and no one was obliged to belong.[14]

Dialogue between the sisters' groups

The Congregation for Religious, and eventually the pope, urged the two groups to get together to try to resolve their differences, and these dialogues eventually did lead to creation of an alternate conference of women's superiors in the United States, but in a manner probably none of them would have anticipated.

The first of these formal dialogues occurred March 15, 1972.[15] The consortium presented four points that it wanted to have covered in the dialogue: "1) right to bear as community one's historic witness; 2) right to have a voice in the picking of speakers and being spared Gregory Baum's reflections on pre-marital sex [The former Father Baum had spoken at the Leadership Conference 1971 assembly]; 3) right to get Hans Küng straight, instead of being filtered through Father McBrien [Father Richard McBrien also had addressed the 1971 assembly]; 4) right to have one's positive positions accepted as such, rather than perpetually being labeled 'negative.' "

It became clear during the discussion that the Leadership Conference representatives favored a continuing dialogue with Rome about regulations on religious life. The consortium representatives suggested that dialogue was fine until Rome spoke definitively on a subject, and then dialogue should cease. However, conference president Sister Thomas Aquinas suggested that since the Vatican curia had not yet caught up to Vatican II, sisters were merely being helpful by questioning certain issues. Conference representatives also pointed out that the official Church had made incorrect statements before, as in the case of Galileo.

Then the consortium grilled Sister Thomas Aquinas on her decision not to pass along to members of the conference a 1971 letter from the Congregation for Religious which commented on the pope's evaluation of renewal. Sister Thomas Aquinas explained that in her capacity as president, she had to decide what actions would do more harm than good, and she had decided that passing that information along to conference members would "do more to diminish the image of the Congregation for Religious among many sisters than it would enhance it. . . . I feel that very very often I am placed in a position of trying to uphold the Congregation for Religious against its own acts. And this is a terrible position to be in."[16]

So went the dialogue; instead of coming to agreement on any issues, the two parties had merely succeeded in elaborating on their differences.

The two groups met again in November of 1974, this time in Rome, in the presence of officials from the Congregation for Religious.[17] Cardinal Arturo Tabera, prefect of the Congregation for Religious, led the meeting, assisted by his undersecretary, Franciscan Father Basil Heiser, an American.

Proceedings of that meeting[18] indicate that Cardinal Tabera was very concerned over the polarization between the two groups of sisters. The conference sisters contended that there were acceptable, diverse ways of renewing religious institutes. The consortium sisters countered that they were obliged to accept the authority of the Church and the official interpretation of documents. And Cardinal Tabera observed that in response to the Vatican II call for renewal, there had been some "immobility" as well as "progressivism which went beyond" what was required by the Church for renewal and adaptation. He cited problems with religious institutes whose renewal was based not on Church doctrine, but on "ideology not proper to the Church, on authors who speak and write as independent and autonomous authority, without the due regard which the magisterium rightfully merits." He stressed that Religious must not lose their identity or betray the fundamental values of religious life by embracing secularization.

The conference representatives admitted that there had been abuses in the renewal process, but they contended that those abuses were largely a matter of the past. Cardinal Tabera stressed that the principal responsibility of a national conference of Religious was "to follow the norms of the documents of the Magisterium for the promotion of religious life." He observed that the Leadership Conference had made mistakes in some of its assembly speakers and some of its publications, but he said those abuses could be remedied. The consortium sisters reported that many of the documents of Vatican II had not been disseminated to grassroots sisters, and they asked the Congregation for Religious to issue a specific document on religious life (which actually happened in 1983, with *Essential Elements*). About the only issue agreed on by the two groups of sisters was that the consortium did not cause the polarization that existed among women Religious, as that polarization was already present when the consortium was founded.

It was the desire of the Congregation for Religious that the dialogue between the Leadership Conference and the consortium continue, so in 1975, Archbishop Mayer, secretary of the congregation, asked Archbishop James J. Byrne of Dubuque to preside at another meeting between the two groups. (Archbishop Byrne was head of the United States Bishops' Liaison Committee with the Leadership Conference.) However, the Leadership Conference executive committee was "disconcerted and saddened" that Archbishop Byrne had been asked to mediate the dialogue, as it was the executive committee's contention that Cardinal Tabera had wanted the sisters to continue their dialogue alone. So, the conference executive committee wrote Cardinal Tabera of "our concern about the necessity of a third party presiding at any sharing between LCWR/CPC."[19]

After Archbishop Mayer convinced the conference sisters that Archbishop Byrne was to act as a representative of the Congregation for Religious,[20] a meeting eventually took place in Chicago on September 3, 1975. The same sisters who had participated in the 1974 meeting in Rome again represented their organizations at the 1975 meeting. The differences between the two groups of sisters continued to be obvious. The conference sisters suggested that since canon law was being revised, it was acceptable to act in anticipation of the new code. The consortium sisters stressed following the official documents of the Church. But again, the only area of agreement that surfaced was the acknowledgment that the two groups held two quite different theologies of religious life.[21]

Even though these dialogues had not resulted in any meeting of the minds, they did serve a useful purpose of at least highlighting the enormous gap between the two groups of sisters: The conference leaders had made it clear they could not accept the premise of the consortium sisters that the conference was leading sisters along a false renewal path; and the consortium sisters were unwilling to consider any renewal ideas that did not follow the pronouncements of Rome to the letter.

During the next few years, the two organizations of sisters treated one another with civility, usually inviting a representative of the other group to their annual meetings, but clearly not arriving at any meeting of the minds.

In 1974, the Leadership Conference of Women Religious published a book titled *Widening the Dialogue,* a collection of essays criticizing the apostolic exhortation *Evangelica Testificatio* and defending the renewal practices undertaken by the more change-oriented religious institutes. The Leadership Conference's book claimed that *Evangelica Testificatio* was not a conclusive document, and the papal document's tone was "not one of finality but of ambivalence." Further, ". . . [*Evangelica Testificatio*] interprets religious life in a traditional frame and in traditional language, both of which point religious life to the past." Hence, the book's authors concluded, it was necessary to dialogue with the papal document.[22]

In early 1976, the consortium published its own booklet entitled *"Widening the Dialogue . . ."?* The consortium booklet was a critique of the Leadership Conference's 1974 book, *Widening the Dialogue.* The consortium's booklet asked, "Does one 'dialogue' with a document?" and it disputed, point by point, the conference's version of Pope Paul VI's exhortation. The consortium booklet claimed that "errors, several of which are basic to the understanding of the Church," were being promulgated to women Religious through the Leadership Conference's book and nationwide seminars based on their book.[23]

New organizations emerge

Clearly, no progress was being made in bridging the gap between the vision of each group of sisters regarding modern religious life. In the meantime, a third party entered the picture. The Institute on Religious Life was founded in Chicago in 1974 by a coalition of hierarchy, clergy, Religious, and laity, including Cardinal John Carberry of St. Louis, Bishop James J. Hogan of Altoona-Johnstown, and Sister Mary Claudia Honsberger, who also was a member of the consortium. According to information published by the Institute, its purpose is to gather bishops, priests, Religious, and laity "to work together to find solutions confronting religious communities," to "promote authentic religious life as taught by Vatican II," and to encourage vocations. The institute sponsors regional and national meetings, as well as various educational programs. It publishes a newsletter, *Religious Life*, and a journal, *Consecrated Life,* which is the English edition of *Informationes-SCRIS*, the journal of the Congregation for Religious. Membership is open to religious communities as well as individual Religious and laity.

The key person in starting the institute was Jesuit Father John Hardon, a theologian. Father Hardon had been a theological advisor to the consortium for a few years, but eventually he and consortium leaders disagreed on tactics. Minutes of the November 20, 1973, meeting of the consortium administrative council reveal that Father Hardon felt he had a mandate from the Congregation for Religious to do more about the crisis in religious life in the United States. He urged the consortium to become more activist, to get better organized, to become a decision-making body, and to provide to Religious the documents coming out of Rome. But the consortium council felt that the Congregation for Religious had made it clear to them in a 1973 letter from Archbishop Mayer[24] that the consortium council should continue doing what it had been doing without any "heavy structure." And the consortium council agreed that it was the responsibility of the Vatican — not the consortium — to disseminate official Vatican documents to Religious.[25] So, the consortium and Father Hardon parted company and Father Hardon went on to see many of his goals realized in the establishment of the Institute on Religious Life.

Initially there was some tension between the institute and the consortium, including some hard feelings when both organizations scheduled their 1977 annual meetings at the same time, thus forcing some sisters who held membership in both organizations to choose between the two. But eventually those tensions diminished, partly because of the efforts of Sister Mary Claudia Honsberger, who as a member of both groups convinced her colleagues that the two groups were organized for two distinct purposes and were complementary rather than competitive.

However, other groups of women Religious did not look so kindly on the Institute on Religious Life. The January 1978 newsletter of the National Coalition of American Nuns carried a long harangue about the Institute's 1977 conference in St. Louis titled "Whatever Happened to Religious Life?" The NCAN newsletter said the title of the conference was insulting to thousands of religious men and women, and "the conference will not diminish the undeniable reality which is twentieth century religious life, not over-the-shoulder nostalgia." The newsletter also observed that the speakers addressing the Institute's meeting looked like "Who's Who in Right Wing America." (Speakers included Phyllis Schlafly; Congressman Henry Hyde; Virgil C. Dechant, supreme knight of the Knights of Columbus; Geraldine Frawley of *Twin Circle*; and Dale Francis of *Our Sunday Visitor*.)[26]

The Leadership Conference of Women Religious wasn't any too happy with the arrival of the Institute on Religious Life, either. Minutes from the 1979 annual assembly of the conference indicate a growing concern by conference leaders over the Institute's activities, especially since the institute had set up an office in Rome to communicate directly with the Congregation for Religious. Additional concern was raised about financial contributions "from conservative lay persons in the church, and the endorsement of some of the Bishops." The minutes indicate that conference leaders had already discussed the institute with the apostolic delegate Archbishop Jean Jadot, with Archbishop John Quinn, and with the United States Bishops' Liaison Committee with Religious.[27]

The Leadership Conference was further dismayed by the Institute on Religious Life in 1983 after the pope had appointed Archbishop John Quinn to lead the study of religious life in the United States. Along with the papal charge to study religious life, the pope authorized the Congregation for Religious to issue the document summarizing the church teaching on religious life, *Essential Elements*. Some conference members had railed against the papal-mandated study at their 1983 assembly, calling it an effort to get American sisters "back in line."[28] Then, just two months after the conference assembly, the November 1983 newsletter of the Institute on Religious Life carried an "Open Letter to U.S. Bishops." The open letter referred to "discordant voices" that had publicly questioned the right of the pope to direct Religious in the United States, an obvious reference to the remarks at the Leadership Conference assembly and to some disparaging remarks made at the annual assembly of the Conference of Major Superiors of Men just days before the women's assembly. The institute letter went on to welcome the study of religious life and thanked the pope for *Essential Elements*. The Institute's open letter contained the signatures of superiors from one hundred twenty-six religious institutes, as well as several lay persons.[29]

The Institute on Religious Life apparently did not suffer from the opposition of any of the sisters' groups that criticized its activities. It has attracted several prominent members of the hierarchy to its board of directors, including Cardinals William Baum, Anthony Bevilacqua, John Carberry, James Hickey, John Krol, and John O'Connor, and its membership rolls in 1995 had one hundred fifty-two affiliated religious communities, twelve Catholic lay Associations, one secular institute and a number of individual laity and Religious. The institute also played a major role in the erection of a second conference of women's superiors in the United States.

At the Institute's national meeting in 1986, a special session was set aside for major superiors to discuss the possibility of forming an association of women's superiors within the Institute. Dominican Sister Assumpta Long, who had served on the consortium board, became chairperson of a committee to study the possibility. One year later, the Forum of Major Superiors was established as a part of the institute at the institute's 1987 national meeting. Sister Assumpta was elected first president of the forum and was succeeded by Little Sister of the Poor Mary Bernard Nettle in 1989. The forum was designed to promote communication and cooperation between the superiors and was open to any women major superiors, even those not affiliated with the Institute on Religious Life.

By 1988, most women superiors who belonged to the Consortium Perfectae Caritatis also held membership in the Institute's Forum of Major Superiors.[30] A few of these sisters also maintained membership in the Leadership Conference of Women Religious, but most of them had severed ties with the conference over ideological differences.

Cardinal Hickey's critique

Meanwhile, Pope John Paul II was becoming increasingly concerned about the state of religious life in the United States, particularly about the polarization between United States sisters, and the bland report of the Quinn Commission had done little to calm those concerns. In early March of 1989, thirty-five United States bishops met with the pope and Vatican officials for four days in a wrap-up meeting for the Quinn Commission study on religious life.

In the March 9 session of the meeting, Cardinal Jean Jerome Hamer, prefect of the Congregation for Religious, addressed the bishops on "The Pastoral Responsibility of the Bishops Relative to Religious Life in the United States." As reported in Chapter Twelve, the Vatican was not entirely satisfied with the results of the Quinn Commission study. Cardinal Hamer told the bishops that they were responsible not only for the apostolates of Religious, but the bishops also were responsible for overseeing the observance by Religious of their vows, their "fraternal life in community; the witness they must bear to God before the people of God; and their fidelity to their distinct charism, which ought to place its stamp on all religious life." Cardinal Hamer said that the mandate given the bishops by the pope in 1983 when he established the Quinn Commission did not carry new powers, but rather highlighted powers the bishops already had to carry out their pastoral office, and which should continue. "This pastoral service of religious life must be not only pursued, but intensified," Cardinal Hamer said.[31]

That same day, Cardinal James Hickey of Washington also spoke at the meeting, and his remarks would turn out to be more significant than most people realized at the time. Cardinal Hickey highlighted the deep divisions among Religious in the United States, even Religious living in the same institute. And he talked about the fact that many women Religious felt they had no formal communication link with Rome since they did not support the views of the Leadership Conference, and therefore did not hold membership in the superiors' conference.

Cardinal Hickey spoke about a "crisis which many religious congregations in the United States are facing" because of an overall membership decline and a rising average age. Cardinal Hickey said that "Within the same religious institute divergent views have arisen on many seminal issues which previously bound members closely together." These issues included living in community, the value of various religious practices, and the authority of the ordinary magisterium. And, he said, "In some cases the very meaning of vowed religious life and its relationship to the church, both local and universal, remain points of disagreement and even division among members of the same institute." Cardinal Hickey also observed that an emphasis on justice issues and social needs had "profoundly affected" the way Religious view themselves and their ministries, with the result that political activism often overshadowed the "transcendent nature of religious life."

Cardinal Hickey identified two basic orientations toward religious life in the United States. The first model describes the change-oriented institutes discussed in this book. Cardinal Hickey said this model stresses mission and ministry and seems to characterize the majority of religious institutes in this country. These Religious embrace "the importance of being in the midst of the world in order to address its needs," he said, and so "the external structures of religious life are de-emphasized." In some cases, these Religious "describe the fundamental purpose of religious life as 'community for mission.' " Cardinal Hickey listed characteristics of some of these religious institutes as: living in small communities or alone, choosing one's own ministry, engaging in works not associated with the Church, turning away from corporate commitments in order to work on social justice issues, and becoming more politically active. "Many religious are convinced they are developing new forms of religious life while at the same time living in a manner consonant with membership in an approved religious institute," he said.

The other approach to religious life identified by Cardinal Hickey fits the description of traditional institutes discussed in this book. Cardinal Hickey said this second model focused on "consecration through the vows as a value in itself and a basis for community apostolate." He said these institutes emphasize "the centrality of common life, common prayer, the religious habit and community-based ministries." Such institutes are sometimes described as "conservative" or "traditional," Cardinal Hickey said, and they "often feel they are a minority whose views are not adequately considered." These institutes, he said, "look to the magisterium and their own traditions to determine future directions."

Cardinal Hickey enumerated five duties of bishops regarding religious life: 1) sharing the teaching of the Church on religious life; 2) spending time with Religious to develop mutual understanding; 3) strengthening communication between Religious and the Holy See; 4) holding up to the young the highest esteem for religious life; and 5) assisting Religious with pressing problems, such as recruitment, adequate wage compensation and retirement funding.

Regarding his third point about communication between Rome and Religious, Cardinal Hickey pointed out that the Conference of Major Superiors of Men and the Leadership Conference of Women Religious were the only official channels between the Holy See and Religious in the United States. But, he said, "A significant number of religious relate to the Consortium Perfectae Caritatis or the Institute on Religious Life. I see a need for us as bishops to foster discussion at the local and the universal level among religious holding divergent points of view. We should also remember that many religious women not represented by the LCWR desire some representation with the Holy See."[32]

The pope acts

Just a little over two weeks after that Vatican meeting, Pope John Paul II addressed a letter on March 29 to United States Bishops in which he asked them to continue their "special pastoral service" to Religious begun in 1983 when he appointed the Quinn Commission. He said that the bishops had done the listening and dialoguing he had asked for, but that the teaching of "a sound theological exposition of religious life" must be ongoing, not temporary. In the letter, the pope expressed his concern about "polarization, particularly among women religious" and stressed that all superiors of women Religious had the right to belong to the Leadership Conference of Women Religious and that all members of the conference had the right to make their concerns heard. "The conference must find realistic and equitable ways to express the concerns of all women religious," he urged, and he directed bishops to find "effective ways to remove the causes of their division." He also exhorted the women to "speak to one another about the issues which divide them." Obviously referring to the consortium and the Institute on Religious Life, the pope acknowledged other organizations had been founded to promote religious life and said that such associations of the faithful were distinct from superiors' conferences, but there was a legitimate place in the church for them.[33]

Then just a month later, in an unprecedented move, Pope John Paul II gave a clear indication that he had heard the pleas of the traditional sisters. The pope appointed Cardinal Hickey to a three-year term as official liaison to the Vatican for sisters who were not affiliated with the Leadership Conference of Women Religious. In a May 2 letter making the appointment, the pope also asked Cardinal Hickey to act as a facilitator of communication between the Leadership Conference of Women Religious and the sisters who were not affiliated with the Leadership Conference.[34] Thus, Cardinal Hickey had a clear mandate from the pope to use his personal influence to attempt to bring the sisters together.

In response to the pope's directive, Cardinal Hickey arranged for a series of dialogue sessions between the Leadership Conference of Women Religious, the Consortium Perfectae Caritatis, and sisters representing both the Forum of Major Superiors from the Institute on Religious Life and the institute itself. The first session took place in October of 1989, followed by sessions in April and September of 1990.

A "Transcribed Text of the Meeting of the consortium and the LCWR Dialogue Teams, September 8, 1990, Silver Spring, Maryland" reveals that in the nearly twenty years the groups had been dialoguing, little had changed in their divergent theologies.[35]

According to the meeting transcript, the first half of the meeting was devoted to discussing the groups' differing theologies and interpretations of revelation, authority, tradition, and Church structure, particularly about how those elements impact religious life. The consortium sisters wanted to discuss "absolute truths that would transcend . . . any age, any period of time, any period of history," as well as "the relationship between the living tradition . . . and the hierarchy, or the teaching office of the Church."[36] However, Sister Doris Gottemoeller of the Leadership Conference responded: "I can't think of anything that's infallibly taught, nor anything in Scripture, about religious life. The Church has given us a great deal of latitude in terms of the way in which we live out the calling that we received, that our founders have received and that we, in concert with them, follow, and the Church sort of blesses it in retrospect, the Church doesn't originate it."[37]

The second part of the meeting concerned plans for future dialogues. The sisters from the consortium, forum, and institute understood that the groups of sisters were meeting because the pope had asked them to do so, through Cardinal Hickey, and they expected to discuss the definition of modern religious life. The Leadership Conference sisters said that they had been trying to get such a dialogue going for up to ten years, and that the pope's directive just coincided with their own efforts to approach the forum to establish communication and to clear up misconceptions and rumors about the various groups of sisters.

Regarding the future, the Leadership Conference president indicated that her organization had little patience for continuing conversations with either the consortium or the Institute on Religious Life. She said that her conference would be willing to continue "official communication" with the Forum of Major Superiors, since it was an entity made up only of superiors of women Religious, and thus was a comparable group to the conference (even though the forum really was an arm of the Institute on Religious Life). But the conference leaders did not see any benefit to a continuing relationship with the consortium or the Institute on Religious Life, since they were "a mixture of grass-roots Sisters, their leadership, membership, including priests, religious and laity." The Leadership Conference suggested that if the consortium and the institute wished to continue dialogue with the Leadership Conference, the conference would send a representative to such a meeting, but that such a dialogue should probably bring in other grass-roots organizations, such as the National Assembly of Religious Women. Finally, Sister Doris suggested that if women superiors wished to continue dialoguing with the Leadership Conference, they should simply join the conference. The meeting ended with the groups agreeing to give further thought to when or if future dialogues would take place.

After the meeting, consortium president Sister Vincent Marie Finnegan, a Carmelite, had her secretary transcribe the audio tapes of the meeting into a ninety-four-page text. These transcripts then were sent out to all parties for approval. However, the Leadership Conference representatives refused to approve the text as the official record of the meeting and instead proposed a six-page summary as the official record. The consortium representatives felt that the conference's six-page summary did not adequately represent the deep theological divisions that had become evident at the meeting, so they eventually signed the conference minutes under protest and with appended comments of their own.[38] Sister Mary Bernard, representing the Forum of Major Superiors, also was unhappy with the conference's version of the meeting and suggested retaining the transcript for the historical record rather than accepting the six-page summary.[39] The complete ninety-four-page transcript of the meeting was given to Cardinal Hickey by the consortium sisters. Cardinal Hickey then shared the transcript at a meeting of the National Conference of Catholic Bishops and eventually took it to Rome. The transcript of the "dialogue" between the sisters' groups apparently thus helped set the stage for approval of a new conference of women's superiors.

A new conference of major superiors

In April 1991, the consortium administrative board met to discuss the previous September's dialogue meeting and to plan future strategy. It was suggested at the meeting that Rome had ordered dialogue between the groups of sisters in order to get in writing the clear differences between the groups. Holy Cross Sister Mary Gerald Hartney observed that the Leadership Conference did make a valid point about the various groups — the consortium, forum, Institute on Religious Life — being so disunited and diverse. The sisters also discussed their concern that the emerging new communities of sisters who were basing their constitutions on Vatican II teachings about religious life had nowhere else to go if they did not feel comfortable with the direction of the Leadership Conference of Women Religious. The consortium was not a leadership group, and the Forum of Major Superiors really was not an independent body, but a part of the Institute on Religious Life. The idea eventually emerged that the best course of action would be to create a new entity, and the consortium board agreed to approach the Forum of Major Superiors about this possibility.[40]

The consortium and forum officers met September 5, 1991, to discuss uniting the two groups. But during discussion of a possible merger, a consensus surfaced that rather than merging the two groups, it would be more helpful to women Religious all over the country to form one distinct new organization composed only of major superiors. And, for this new group to be effective, the sisters felt that it should have the approval of Rome.[41] Consultation with canon lawyers verified that there was nothing in canon law to prevent the approval of more than one conference of superiors in a country, though this had never before happened. The two groups of sisters decided to proceed by having the consortium board meet with the board of the Institute on Religious Life — the parent organization of the forum.

The eventual conclusion reached at a December 14, 1991, meeting of the officers of the consortium, the forum, and the institute was that a new council of major superiors of women Religious should be formed. Cardinal Hickey was present at the meeting as papal liaison for the non-LCWR sisters, and was supportive of the idea after apparently concluding that the dialogue sessions he had orchestrated had made no progress in resolving the differences between all the groups of sisters.

However, once the decision was made to form the new conference of women's superiors and to apply for Vatican approval, the sisters had to work fast because Cardinal Hickey's three-year papal appointment as Vatican liaison to women Religious was due to expire in May of 1992, just five months later. And clearly the sisters realized they needed the assistance of Cardinal Hickey in making the whole unprecedented plan work. A steering committee was formed to draft a mission statement and statutes for the new organization. Serving on that committee were Sisters Vincent Marie Finnegan, chairperson; Mary Bernard Nettle; M. de Chantal St. Julian, a Sister of the Holy Family; and Franciscan Sister Leticia Rodriguez. Assisting the committee were Bishop John J. Myers of Peoria; Bishop John Sheets, a Jesuit and auxiliary bishop of Fort Wayne-South Bend, Indiana; and an unnamed canon lawyer.[42]

In just three days, the steering committee wrote an initial draft for a mission statement, which began: "There is a need for religious not aligned with LCWR to have a permanent organization or structure by which their needs could be represented to the Holy See and through which the Holy See could communicate its concerns, directives and encouragement."[43] The flurry of activity continued over the Christmas holiday season, as the sisters worked overtime to put the final touches on proposed statutes for the organization and tried to gather support for their proposal from religious institutes and ecclesial authorities across the country.

In January of 1992, Cardinal Hickey presented the proposal for the new conference to Pope John Paul II and Cardinal Eduardo Martinez Somalo, prefect of the Congregation for Religious. Cardinal Hickey told the February 15 meeting of the Forum of Major Superiors that the pope and Cardinal Somalo had been in favor of their proposal, but approval was not yet official, so the sisters held their breath. Obviously, there was a good deal of behind-the-scenes maneuvering going on, for the Vatican was moving uncharacteristically fast. On February 19, Archbishop Agostino Cacciavillan, apostolic delegate to the United States, met with representatives of the Leadership Conference of Women Religious and the Conference of Major Superiors of Men and informed them that a Vatican-approved new Council of Major Superiors of Women Religious was coming into existence.

14: The Leadership Conference Splits

After hearing the news, the stunned president of the LCWR requested a meeting with the Congregation for Religious. On April 10, Cardinal Somalo, prefect of the Congregation for Religious, and members of his staff met in Rome with Leadership Conference president, Dominican Sister Donna Markham, and conference executive director Sister of St. Joseph Janet Roesener. Accompanying the sisters for moral support — and indicating the tacit support of their conferences — were Christian Brother Paul Hennessy, president of the Conference of Major Superiors of Men, and Monsignor Robert Lynch, general secretary of the National Conference of Catholic Bishops. Sister Donna reported after the meeting that Cardinal Somalo had assured her that the new council would not be perceived as equal to the Leadership Conference nor would it be considered as a parallel or alternative national conference.[44] According to Brother Paul's recollection of the meeting, the Americans "all expressed concern that the canonical approval of a small group of religious as parallel to a conference could be hurtful and divisive. They listened to us very attentively and with great courtesy, and we were assured that a parallel group would not be established. I informed the gathering that in my years of interaction with LCWR, they had reached out over and over, with little success, to those women who had formed their own unofficial union."[45]

However, at the very moment the American contingent sat in the meeting with the Congregation for Religious, pleading the case of the LCWR, a bombshell was exploding in other parts of the Vatican. A new book, *The Transformation of American Catholic Sisters,* had just been released which told the story of the Leadership Conference from the perspective of two former executive directors of the conference, Sisters Mary Daniel Turner (executive director 1972-78) and Lora Ann Quinonez (executive director 1978-86). The two authors spared no details in characterizing the transformation of the superior's conference from an entity created by and loyal to Rome, into an independent organization of sisters determined to conduct their business the American way. The book also detailed the conference's ongoing conflict with Rome over the nature of religious life and the conference's relations with ecclesiastical authority.[46] Supporters of the new traditional superiors' conference made sure that plenty of copies of the book were made available in Rome. The book could not have been published at a worse time for the LCWR or a better time for the fledgling new council, for it confirmed and detailed what the traditional sisters had been saying about the philosophy of the Leadership Conference.

The new Council of Major Superiors of Women Religious was formally erected by the Congregation for Religious on June 13, 1992, with tentative approval of its statutes for five years. The approval was made known to the United States bishops by Cardinal Hickey in a closed session of their spring meeting on June 19. Sister Donna Markham, president of the Leadership Conference, also was informed of the decision while she was at the bishops' meeting.[47] Announcement to the public came in a June 22 press release from the Archdiocese of Washington, which said that the new Council of Major Superiors of Women Religious had equal canonical standing with the Leadership Conference, and was an alternative to the conference. The press release also stressed that the status of the Leadership Conference of Women Religious remained unchanged, and it noted that, while the two groups of women superiors had equal canonical status, they were not linked organizationally, though the Holy See desired cooperation between them. The June 22 announcement also brought the news that Cardinal Hickey had been re-appointed to serve as papal liaison to sisters not affiliated with the Leadership Conference of Women Religious.

After the new council was formally erected by the Vatican, the Consortium Perfectae Caritatis and the Forum of Major Superiors were dissolved by their own memberships, and the assets of the consortium were transferred to the council. Sister Vincent Marie Finnegan acted as spokesperson for the new organization.

When the council was approved, some eighty-four superiors had applied for membership, representing about ten thousand professed sisters and another nine hundred in formation.[48] These statistics give some indication about the future orientation of religious orders. The new council's members represented only about ten percent of women Religious at that time, but a significantly higher percentage of the women who were then in formation. The statutes of the new council included membership criteria that were based, as Sister Mary Elise had suggested, on the papally-defined essential elements of religious life. Consequently, membership in the new council was open to major superiors and vicars of institutes which live in community, follow the teaching of the magisterium, share common prayer, practice community-based ministries, adhere to the authority of a superior, and wear religious garb. Potential members were required to apply for membership in the organization and then be approved by the council's board.[49]

Needless to say, the Leadership Conference of Women Religious was not happy with approval of the new group, nor was the Conference of Major Superiors of Men. Adding to their discomfort was the fact that there had been some misunderstanding about the canonical standing of the new council. A joint statement issued by the two conferences on June 22 observed that both conferences, as well as the International Union of Superiors General had "directly expressed" to the Congregation for Religious "their opposition to the plans to take this action." And, the statement contended that at the April 10 meeting in Rome, the Congregation for Religious "affirmed LCWR as the official conference for women religious leaders in the United States and assured the representatives that any new group would not be parallel to or a substitute for LCWR." The joint statement declared, "LCWR and CMSM are concerned that the establishment of this separate council will open old wounds within congregations and between congregations. Such an action is contrary to a primary function of leadership — to promote unity and understanding."[50]

Brother Paul Hennessy, president of the Conference of Major Superiors of Men, expressed his dismay in a letter to members of the men's conference, saying that approval of the new conference was "offensive" and "not unifying." The CMSM president also reported that he would write Cardinal Somalo "to express my regret and disappointment that despite my trip to Rome and all our communications, we were not included in a notification about the establishment of the new council. We clearly indicated to him our belief that this is not [a] 'women's issue' but a religious life issue, and we had to learn of the establishment through hearsay and through the press."[51]

Sister Donna Markham, president of the Leadership Conference, wrote Cardinal Somalo, complaining about the language used to describe the new council, being particularly disturbed that the new group was depicted as being an alternative to the Leadership Conference. She told Catholic News Service that Cardinal Somalo had responded in July that each conference had its own distinct purpose, and that superiors could belong to either or both organizations.[52] A further clarification came in August from a spokesman for Cardinal Hickey. Monsignor William Lori said that the new council had the same "juridical nature" as the Leadership Conference, and it was an official established association of major superiors in the United States that had been "erected canonically by the Holy See." Monsignor Lori said the chief differences between the new council and the Leadership Conference were in their specific purposes and their membership.[53]

National Conference of Catholic Bishops' president, Archbishop Daniel Pilarczyk, extended good wishes to the new council, but he indicated that approval of the new council was a big surprise, and he tried to smooth over matters by adding, "I wish to assure the members of the LCWR that their valuable contribution and witness in the life of the church in the United

States continues to be greatly appreciated by the bishops of our conference."[54] Archbishop Quinn, who had headed the papally-mandated study of religious life in the 1980s, seemed similarly surprised and perplexed by the move, saying, "In faith and obedience to the church I accept this decision and pray that the new council will be effective for the church." Archbishop Quinn also hastened to praise the LCWR and its members, saying that the conference still was approved by the Vatican and that "The constitutions of the individual congregations belonging to the Leadership Conference have also been approved by the Holy See, giving authenticity to the way of life lived in accord with those constitutions."[55] (Note: Most, but not all constitutions of communities affiliated with the Leadership Conference had been approved by the Vatican at that time. Moreover, in practice, many women Religious do not live in accord with the approved constitutions of their institutes.)

Message from Rome?

Why did Rome approve the new council?

Some Vatican watchers speculate that the "special pastoral service" the pope had asked United States bishops to render under the Quinn Commission by "proclaiming anew . . . the church's teaching on consecrated life" had not been very effectively rendered among, or accepted by, a good many women Religious. Further, the Leadership Conference had made a habit of "dialoging" about directives from Rome rather than implementing them, and Rome may simply have run out of patience with these debates. Since so few sisters still staffed Catholic institutions in the United States, the prospect had disappeared that religious orders might withdraw large numbers of sisters from service if Rome alienated the Leadership Conference by approving another conference of women's superiors. Another factor certainly must have been the delivery to Rome of the text of the September 1990 sisters' dialogue, which should have made very clear to Vatican officials the deep theological and philosophical differences dividing the groups of sisters.

Additionally, it was becoming clear statistically that the orders which maintain a traditional religious lifestyle — living in community, praying regularly and together, wearing religious garb, working in Catholic Church institutions, espousing fidelity to the pope — are attracting most of the new vocations and have a lower median age than the more diverse communities. Indeed, the largest average group of sisters represented by the new Council of Major Superiors of Women Religious is the thirty-to-thirty-nine-year-old age group.[56] Approval of the new council may reflect Rome's recognition that future growth of religious life in the United States appears to be taking the direction pursued by the new council members.

Also, the communities affiliated with the new Council of Major Superiors of Women Religious clearly are more inclined to make a corporate commitment to staff Catholic institutions within dioceses — something orders with the open placement policy cannot effectively do. A 1995 demographics survey of the new council showed that the 103 member communities (representing about 12,000 sisters) were working in over 500 schools, colleges or day-care centers, and almost 300 homes for the aged, hospitals, or clinics in 143 of the 198 dioceses in the United States.[57]

However, acceptance of and enthusiasm for the new Council of Major Superiors of Women Religious has been mixed. Sister Vincent Marie observed in 1996: "Overall, we have been very well accepted at the NCCB [National Conference of Catholic Bishops] level."[58] But one could easily get the impression that the new council is looked upon much more favorably by Rome than by some of the ecclesial establishment in the United States.

When this author was working on an article for *Our Sunday Visitor* about the 1994 Synod on Consecrated Life, the National Conference of Catholic Bishops' Committee on Religious Life and Ministry was contacted on September 12, 1994, regarding papal appointment of synod observers. Sister of Mercy Sharon Euart, who is one of the three associate general secretaries for the National Conference of Catholic Bishops, and who serves as staff for the Committee on Religious Life and Ministry, gave the names of the bishops appointed, as well as the names of the president of the Conference of Major Superiors of Men, Sulpician Father Gerald Brown, and the president of the Leadership Conference of Women Religious, Sister Doris Gottemoeller. Sister Sharon also said that another sister had been appointed, but she said she could not remember that sister's name. As it turned out, the "other sister" appointed by the pope as a synod observer was the president of the Council of Major Superiors of Women Religious — Sister Vincent Marie Finnegan. In addition, a board member of the new council had been named by the pope as a synod expert, Dominican Sister Christine Born. Yet, the names of these two sisters and their organization — which was two years old by that time — apparently were so obscure to an associate general secretary of the NCCB that she did not even recognize or remember the names.

Other such incidents have occurred when persons holding official positions in the Church have espoused ignorance or misinformation about the council. For example, a June 13, 1995, memo from the chair of the Eastern

Region of the National Conference of Vicars for Religious contained this piece of misinformation: "I did not realize until now that membership in the Council [of Major Superiors of Women Religious] is a personal membership, not by congregation or by leadership. A habit and veil makes a religious eligible for membership. To me, it seems that this organization is structured more like NAWR than the LCWR."

Yet, Rome apparently has been well pleased with the council's performance during its first three years in existence, for in late 1995, the Vatican gave final approval to the statutes of the council, two years before its probationary period was up.

In spite of all the hard feelings and misinformation, the Leadership Conference of Women Religious and the Council of Major Superiors of Women Religious have managed to interact gracefully since the new council was approved. In fact, the Leadership Conference suggested that the new council be invited to join the Tri-Conference Commission on Religious Life and Ministry. The Tri-Conference Commission had evolved out of the former NCCB Liaison Committee to the conferences of men and women superiors, as a means of continuing the rapport established between bishops and Religious during the Quinn Commission listening sessions. The Tri-Conference Commission originally was made up of members of the Bishops' Committee on Religious Life and Ministry and the officers of the men's and women's conferences of superiors, with a purpose of effecting good communications between Religious and the bishops. Since the new council was invited to join, the "Tri-Conference" was dropped from the title, and the new title became simply Commission on Religious Life and Ministry.

15: Turn out the Lights: Finances, Vocations, the Elderly, and Denial

> "How did all this ever happen to us? . . . All this did not just *happen*. We did it to ourselves."[1]
>
> **Sister Elizabeth McDonough, OP**

Two distinct models of religious life for women have evolved in the United States. Between ten and twenty percent of the orders of women fall into the traditional category, and most of these traditional institutes have affiliated with the new Council of Major Superiors of Women Religious. The rest can be described as change-oriented, and most of these orders are affiliated with the Leadership Conference of Women Religious. Both of these models of religious life for women share some common problems as they enter the twenty-first century, but the future for the traditional orders looks much more optimistic than the future of the change-oriented orders.

While most of the traditional institutes are not being overwhelmed with new vocations, many of them are attracting sufficient numbers of new candidates to sustain the institute in future years. A few are even attracting significant numbers of new members and actually have instituted waiting lists so that they are not overwhelmed with too many new members at one time. Also, a number of new religious institutes have been founded since 1970 with the expressed purpose of living religious life as it is understood by the Church. As of late 1996, approximately eighty of these new communities belonged to the Fellowship of Emerging Religious Communities (formerly the Fellowship of New Religious Communities.)[2] Although many of these new institutes are very small, and their future is tenuous, they are indicative of an ongoing interest by contemporary men and women in living religious life according to Church teachings.

The apparently viable institutes of women have these elements in common: specific corporate identity, common apostolate, community living, common prayer, religious garb, traditional practice of the vows, outspoken fidelity to the pope and the magisterium, and religious governance based on the religious superior model. In short, they practice the elements of religious life repeatedly set forth in documents such as Vatican II's *Perfectae Caritatis,* the apostolic exhortation *Evangelica Testificatio,* numerous instructions emanating from the Congregation for Religious, various papal discourses, and again in the 1996 apostolic exhortation on consecrated life, *Vita Consecrata.* (However, a few of the traditional institutes still cling to a pre-Vatican II model of religious life in many areas, and have a great deal of updating to do before they can consider themselves to be operating in compliance with the Vatican II renewal.)

As Father Albert DiIanni contends, young people are attracted to religious institutes that have retained their identity as religious institutes and have specific spiritual practices. Father DiIanni, a theologian and former vicar general of the Marist Fathers, has noted: "Young people are telling us that something has gone wrong with some forms of religious life. They are doing it by staying away in droves. Part of their message, I believe, is that religious groups may have taken the religious heart out of things, that the center has not held. Instead, the young are being attracted by people who invite them to love God because God has loved us, and to assume an unashamedly explicit and classical religious identity. They are being drawn to a strong community life which does not shun ritual and common practices. . . . They desire to belong to a group that tends to its 'being' as well as its 'doing,' its consecration as well as its mission. They want the example and edification of their brothers or sisters. . . . They do not desire to become part of a suffocating tribe, but neither do they want to be a collection of atoms, lovely marbles loosely contiguous in a box."[3]

In contrast to the traditional religious institutes that are attracting some new vocations, most of the institutes of women Religious that carried experimentation and renewal to extremes neither intended nor authorized by the Second Vatican Council, are in decline. Studies have found that these change-oriented institutes lost a greater percentage of their membership than did the traditional institutes, and they have not attracted significant numbers of new members. In many of these institutes, the lifestyle of the sisters has evolved to a point where it is impossible to distinguish sisters from their lay professional counterparts. In some institutes the only connections some sisters have to their community is the umbrella of a tax exemption for their income and occasional formal community mailings.

Since young people are not joining, the median age in some of these "change-oriented" institutes has soared well into the seventies. A myriad of problems have arisen, including retirement funding, building maintenance, and even decisions about continuing the existence of the institute. Still, many leaders of women Religious seem more willing to accept the inevitable demise of their institutes than to admit that many mistakes were made and that their renewal efforts should be re-evaluated by taking into account those mistakes.

The population of sisters most adversely affected by this unraveling of women's religious communities is the elderly. Some of these elderly sisters helped promote the ill-advised, rapid deconstruction of their orders, but most of them had no role in the remaking of religious life, and in fact many of them tried to advocate a more moderate, gradual renewal. And some of them still are working to try to divert their institutes from the destructive path that is leading inevitably to the folding of many religious orders.

Financial crisis

Regardless of what philosophy has motivated them, many orders of women Religious find themselves in dire financial straits, although many of the change-oriented orders seem to be worse off than the more traditional orders, which tend to have a lower median age. According to the 1995 report of the Tri-Conference Retirement Office (a project of the National Conference of Catholic Bishops, the Leadership Conference of Women Religious and the Conference of Major Superiors of Men), nearly forty-seven percent of all women Religious were over the age of seventy in 1995. The retirement office projects that the percentage of sisters over seventy will climb to fifty-four percent in 2000, sixty-one percent in 2005, and sixty-eight percent in 2009. During those fifteen years, the actual number of sisters in the over-seventy category is expected to decline by only eight percent, while the number of sisters in the under-seventy category is expected to decline by a dramatic sixty-two percent.

This means that if present trends continue and this projection is accurate, there will be only one-third as many sisters working in the year 2009 as were working in 1995, but there will be almost as many retired sisters as there were in 1995.[4] Thus, retirement programs for Religious suffer from a similar problem as the Social Security System — a smaller percentage of younger workers to support retirees. And for years, the only retirement program many women's institutes had was the practice of relying on large numbers of young workers to support the elderly population. (Dioceses traditionally provided retirement benefits to diocesan priests, but not to the Religious working in the diocese, as they were considered to be the responsibility of their religious institutes.)

In addition, Religious were not eligible to enter the Social Security system until the law was changed in 1972. So, in 1994, the average retired sister received about $3,300 in Social Security benefits per year, compared to the average retired lay person, who received $7,870. And, according to a 1994 study by the Arthur Anderson accounting firm completed for the NCCB Tri-Conference Retirement Office, it cost about $15,000 a year to support a retired sister in 1994. At the same time, the average salary of a Religious employed by a diocese was less than $15,000, so the financial difficulties become very obvious, especially since many institutes of women Religious already have fewer working sisters than retired sisters. Taking into account the Social Security picture and the retirement funding of both men's and women's institutes, Arthur Anderson estimated an unfunded past service liability of about $6.3 billion in 1994, and that shortfall had increased $1.4 billion between 1992 and 1994.[5] This means that religious orders do not have these billions of dollars that will be necessary to cover the retirement needs of their members.

Some orders have attempted to deal with their financial deficiencies and membership decline by joining two or more orders together into a new entity. This practice is called amalgamation or union, and thus far it has occurred usually with orders that were founded under the same rule. For example, in 1995, three Dominican congregations — the Dominican Sisters of St. Catherine of Siena of Fall River, Massachusetts; the Dominican Sisters of the Most Holy Rosary of Newburgh, New York; and the Dominican Sisters of the Sick Poor of Ossining, New York — merged into the new Dominican Sisters of Hope. At the time of the merger, the Fall River order had 69 members, the Ossing sisters had 53, and the Newburgh community had 248. The median age of the new community was 66.[6] Many other institutes have done the same thing. During the 1980s, for example, the Sisters of St. Joseph of Superior, Wisconsin, merged with the Sisters of St. Joseph of Carondelet of St. Paul Minnesota; and the Franciscan Sisters of Maryville, Missouri, merged with the Franciscan Sisters of St. Mary, of St. Louis, Missouri.[7]

While this may sound like a practical solution to financial and personnel problems, it is not easy for sisters who have lived all their lives in one order to suddenly be faced with accepting an entirely new constitution, an entirely different experience of spirituality, and a whole batch of people they have never met but who are supposed to be their community members, their family. As discussed in the preface to this book, communities that were founded under the same rule often have no more in common than an early founding principle. In practice, sisters whose communities are named after the same tradition can be radically different in philosophy, lifestyle, apostolate, and spirituality.

Canon law requires that the majority of members of an institute must agree to such a merger or union, but there isn't much latitude for any minority dissenting members. They have only three choices, and two of them hardly qualify as choices. One, they can find another religious institute that is willing to accept them as a transfer. Two, they can leave religious life and live on their own. Or, three, they can go along with the whole merger deal, whether they like it or not. In practice, the first two choices are not viable for a sister who is elderly or infirm. Most orders would not accept an elderly or infirm sister who wanted to transfer because of the financial burden of her retirement and health-care needs. And, unless an elderly or infirm sister had a wealthy family willing to support her, she could not afford to strike out on her own in her "golden" years or burdened with an infirmity. In addition, most such sisters take their vows quite seriously, and they do not consider their own personal discomfort with lifestyle or spirituality changes to be adequate grounds to ask for dispensation from their vows.

There is a single precedent for another alternative — formation of new institutes. An instance in 1991 so far appears to be unique.

During the 1980s, several autonomous congregations of Mercy Sisters worked toward forming a single institute. In 1991, seventeen congregations of Mercy Sisters received the permission of the Holy See to form a single institute, the Sisters of Mercy of the Americas.[8] However, twelve Sisters of Mercy of Portland (Maine) did not wish to accept membership in the new institute. Bishop Joseph Gerry of Portland agreed to establish the twelve sisters as a diocesan institute, and a financial settlement was reached between the twelve sisters and the Sisters of Mercy of Portland. The Holy See gave permission, and the Diocesan Sisters of Mercy of Portland were formally established as a separate institute.

The Vatican is very cautious about establishing new institutes, but apparently the new Portland institute was approved because it had several assets: a bishop willing to establish the order as a diocesan institute, a financial agreement with the original congregation, a varied age span among the sisters, and a previously approved and revised constitution (that of the original Mercy Sisters of Portland, which had been finalized a few years earlier).[9] However, this option of establishing a new institute has not been a viable possibility for most sisters who are unhappy with amalgamations.

Sisters in Crisis

Ordinarily, sisters simply have to accept the will of the majority, whether they like it or not.

Many lay people first became aware of the financial problems of sisters when the *Wall Street Journal* published an article on May 19, 1986, about sisters who were selling their property, eating meatless meals, and clipping coupons to make ends meet.[10] On July 1, 1986, the Tri-Conference Retirement Project was founded, and in 1988 the United States bishops instituted an annual appeal, the Retirement Fund for Religious, administered by the Tri-Conference Retirement Office. By 1995, that fund had gathered and distributed about $175 million.[11] A separate campaign sponsored by lay people, Support our Aging Religious (SOAR!), began raising money in 1986, and by 1995 had distributed about $1.5 million to religious orders who were experiencing immediate problems in caring for their elderly. And many local fund-raising efforts on behalf of retired Religious have been undertaken since that 1986 *Wall Street Journal* article. But it is very, very difficult to address an unfunded past service liability in the billions of dollars, even though many religious institutes have adopted new financial management guidelines with the help of the Tri-Conference Retirement Office.

Additionally, fund raising personnel are encountering resistance from a number of lay Catholics who are unhappy with the image projected by some sisters. Many lay people who are struggling to support their own families do not understand why so many sisters live alone or in twos in apartments when a convent with empty rooms is nearby. They wonder if it is necessary for so many sisters to own their own cars and to have wardrobes that rival the best-paid professional lay women. They wonder if it is financially responsible for religious institutes to continue supporting members who spend year after year after year taking university courses or conducting research projects instead of requiring those sisters to hold down jobs and provide income to their institute. Lay people — who cannot afford to take lengthy vacations themselves — wonder if it is financially responsible for religious institutes to allow many of their members to forego gainful employment for the sake of lengthy sabbatical projects or six-month retreats to "discern where the Spirit is leading" them. Lay people wonder if it is necessary for Religious to travel as far and as frequently as some of them do. They wonder if extensive bureaucracies that consume a large portion of the annual budget are necessary in religious institutes. And potential donors have withheld funds because they do not approve of some of the projects sisters are spending their money on, money that instead could have gone toward care of the elderly.

Some elderly sisters resent the fact that, as one sister put it, "the elderly are used as bait" in general fund-raising efforts for their communities. She observed that whenever her institute wanted to launch a fund drive for any reason, the leaders would choose a couple of the elderly sisters who still wear a habit and "parade" them before the media. Predictably, the lay people who remember how much the sisters did for them, respond when they see sisters in habit, she said. However, she noted that this is the only time the leadership of her community sees any benefit to the religious habit.

Similar tactics are being used by other orders, some of which are now offering to put former students in touch with their retired teachers and are asking former students to recount tales of how much the sisters meant to them. One 1996 fund-raising letter received by the author — accompanied by the photo of an elderly sister in habit praying in the chapel — invited donors to send our prayer requests along with our donations so that the retired sisters could include our intentions in their "power-house of prayer." The letter also assured donors that "the Sisters are taking some bold and courageous steps to decrease by half, their expenses in caring for the retired Sisters." It would seem that most donors who wish to support the elderly sisters would prefer that the budgets of religious institutes be cut in other areas, not in the funds going toward care of the elderly sisters. Furthermore, the fund-raising letter and the return envelope offered no indication that the donations being solicited in the name of the elderly would indeed go toward care of the elderly. Many sisters — active as well as retired — recommend that lay persons who wish to contribute toward the care of retired and infirm Religious should restrict those donations to the specific use the donors wish if they do not want their donations diverted to other uses.

Unselfishness or pathological denial?

Several sociologists who have studied the demise of institutes have observed that declining organizations normally stop taking outside risks and direct their attention inward to try to reorganize in order to fend off the pending cataclysm. However, most religious institutes of women that are in decline have taken the unexpected course of downplaying or ignoring their own demise, and instead are concentrating on exterior works, such as finding additional ministries that their few remaining active members are interested in addressing. Some observers have attributed this attitude to the typical unselfishness of women Religious; others consider this attitude to be either sheer stupidity or a total dysfunctional denial that mistakes have been made that led to the institute's decline. In any event, it is an attitude that puts at risk the sisters who depend on the continuation of the institute for their sustenance.

Sociologist Helen Rose Fuchs Ebaugh reported in her 1993 book, *Women in the Vanishing Cloister*, that: "As religious orders have begun to decline in the past fifteen years, they have opted to reduce internal positions and allocate increasing resources to external goals. Most notably, in line with their ideological stance of 'opting for the poor,' many orders have encouraged their members to take jobs working with the poor, jobs that frequently provide very low pay and poor benefits. As a result, the order has to subsidize these members from its general fund, a practice that has contributed to the severe financial crisis in most orders today. . . .

"During the same period that orders have focused upon service to the poor and risk taking, there has been a corresponding de-emphasis upon internal concerns such as membership recruitment and maintaining a unique group identity. . . ."[12]

Likewise, sociologist Sister Patricia Wittberg has observed that "Far from evincing an unwillingness to risk, an inward-looking focus on turf battles and boundary maintenance, and an attempt to alter the environment to one more favorable to their organizational existence, women's religious communities are doing the opposite — celebrating risk-taking, blurring the boundaries of their orders in solidarity with the poor, and committing their resources toward systemic change, not for their own survival, but for the empowerment of the most oppressed."

But Sister Patricia cautioned that ". . . an extroverted focus and a willingness to risk may actually be dysfunctional for organizational survival. During the same period that congregations have been moving toward risk-taking and solidarity with the poor, there has also been . . . a corresponding de-emphasis on internal concerns such as membership recruitment or maintaining a distinct group identity." She added that several studies have shown that a major reason for decline in vocations is that Religious no longer actively try to recruit young people.[13] Sister Patricia also noted that "Rather than squander valuable, and increasingly scarce, human resources in outside positions, the organization could enhance its power, including its power to serve the poor, by utilizing the efforts of all its members to strengthen its own institutions."[14]

An example of this trend to de-emphasize internal concerns in favor of liberating women and the oppressed can be found in the decisions of the 1995 general assembly of the Sisters of Charity of Nazareth, as described by an associate member of the community. She reported that there were 845 sisters in the community in 1995, compared to 1,500 in the 1960s. And, in 1995, only 17 of those 845 were under the age of 30. The largest category in the congregation's ministry profile was retirement. In fact, there were three times as many retired sisters as there were sisters working in the next-largest category, education. Only 37 percent of the community's members were drawing a salary in 1995. And, in 1995, the sisters were forced to give up 164-year-old Presentation Academy in Louisville, Kentucky, because of declining enrollment and financial demands.

Yet, even with this aging population and obvious financial burden, the community's new mission statement was filled with feminist rhetoric. The statement described the Sisters of Charity of Nazareth as: "an international community in a multicultural world, committed to caring for the earth and willing to risk their lives and resources for the sake of justice in solidarity with oppressed peoples, especially the economically poor and women."[15]

It seems not to have occurred to such orders that their own large elderly population may fit the description of oppressed people.

Getting over the numbers game

The debate over why vocations have declined so dramatically ranges wildly from one extreme to another. Some Religious believe that the renewal process begun after Vatican II is still just that — a process. They believe that the Church is in a second, or ongoing, stage of renewal, and Religious must continue to search and experiment until they hit on the right combination, and then everything will just fall into place. The Leadership Conference of Women Religious seems to espouse this philosophy, as one of its five-year goals drawn up in 1994 is "to work for a just world order by using corporate influence to effect systemic change and to foster a transformed religious life."[16] Feminist theologian Sister of St. Joseph Elizabeth Johnson has observed: "In fact, the very effort to keep alive forms of religious life that have for the most part run their historical course may well be counterproductive to the evangelical following of Jesus. Rather, what is needed is vigilant patience, profound prayer and the ability to act boldly toward that future where new forms of evangelical life will develop."[17]

Other Religious seem to feel the problem is with the young people, who are simply too materialistic and selfish to consider a religious vocation. But some observers contend that the very aspects that attracted young people to religious life in the past — self-sacrifice, a sense of belonging to a community, a clear sense of identity, a specific corporate ministry — are the very aspects that most religious institutes deconstructed after Vatican II. In a synthesis of several studies of religious life done under Lilly Endowment grants since 1985, Sister of St. Joseph Sean Peters and Vincentian Father John Grindel observed in 1992 that "confusion dominates the current picture of the nature of religious life. . . . Confusion not only about the nature of religious life in general (as a social institution), but also about the charism, mission, membership, and structures of individual communities and the attempts of individual religious to live out their religious commitments."[18] Most studies on religious life verify this theory, yet few religious institutes seem willing to admit that they have brought on their own demise by the decisions they have made.

Some Religious simply do not bemoan that demise. They believe that religious life is dying a natural death that should not be mourned, so they see no point in inviting new candidates into their institutes. In October of 1995, Sister Sandra Schneiders hinted at this position when she told the ninth National Congress of the Religious Formation Conference that "We must resolutely commit ourselves to risk-taking. . . . Religious must not allow diminished resources to call the shots.

"The Spirit is calling religious to something. Maybe to end religious life. But that's not a foregone conclusion."[19]

Sociologist Helen Ebaugh found some women Religious who believe that "People don't live forever and neither do organizations. There was a time when we were needed in the Church, but perhaps that is not the case any more. Perhaps other types of groups will take over those needs. Our job is to die gracefully and not hold on to something that is no longer needed."[20] In a case study of one order, Ebaugh also found that individualism had taken such a priority that "For many members, survival of the order is no longer a major concern. More important is the sense that one's own meaningful work contributes to the Church and the modern world. As long as membership in the order promotes and sustains this goal, people stay. If however, the order jeopardizes or challenges what individuals value, then some members are prepared either to leave the order or simply to refuse to comply. Presently, the order has virtually no mechanisms of social control over members, other than in the area of budget requests. Because the order depends upon the salaries of these members, the risk of alienating and losing members, especially those drawing high salaries, is too risky. For those reasons, the demise of the order in time seems almost inevitable."[21]

This tension between individual desires and congregational needs was alluded to in 1992 by Sister Margaret Cafferty, executive director of the LCWR. She reported that a conference study of ministry found: "The experience of individual members is currently a stronger factor in ministry decisions than corporate commitments of the congregations. This finding may suggest a need to find a new balance between the common good and reverence for individual rights of community members."[22]

Other women Religious have indicated that to be concerned about the dearth of vocations or the aging of the sisters and the decline of their institutions is to deny the very mission of Religious. Sister Marjorie Tuite, a leader in the National Assembly of Women Religious, observed that "There is no concern for this or that community of sisters to endure, or even for nuns as such to endure, but that there be Christian witness however God chooses to evoke it."[23]

Sister Joan Chittister (president of the LCWR, 1976-77) wrote in 1989 that ". . . we need to get over the numbers game. Numbers are not the essential witness to either the value or the beauty of the life. The numbers game, in fact, is surely the residue of a culture that operates always as if bigger were automatically better in everything."[24] Five years later, when the number of United States sisters had dropped by over 10,000, Sister Joan still insisted: "Viability has been computed in terms of numbers far too long. . . . We have been consumed by concern for median ages, number of candidates and size of our infirmaries far too long. . . .

"History is certain: Religious life is viable only as long as it finds its life in the living dead around it and breathes new life back into those who are dead. When religious life becomes a monument unto itself, it is not viable even if it goes on existing."[25]

Ironically, it is these leaders of the change-oriented orders with rapidly declining populations who seem least concerned about vocations. A newspaper article about the 1994 annual assembly of the Leadership Conference of Women Religious reported:

"Among these women religious, their declining numbers were not a major concern. 'We're more concerned for ministries than numbers,' remarked LCWR staff member Suzanne Delaney of the Sisters of the Immaculate Heart of Mary.

"One sister after another reflected the view that the bulging convents of the past were an anomaly, a product of an era that limited women to a handful of roles in society.

" 'Today, the laity are assuming roles within the church,' said Sr. Regina Murphy, a regional coordinator for the Sisters of Charity. 'We aren't needed in the big numbers we once were. And we're quite content to be small.' "[26]

Such examples of denial are widespread among the leaders of change-oriented institutes. These leaders seem to be unable to step back far enough to see that the "new paradigms of religious life" their institutes have created for themselves, beginning in the 1960s, are exactly what brought them to the tenuous position they are in today. As Father DiIanni said, "the center has not held," for these sisters took "the religious heart out of things" and deconstructed religious life so completely that they even they, themselves, see little difference between the religious vocation and the lay vocation.

On the other hand, religious orders which identify themselves with the essentials of religious life espoused by the Church continue to expend a good deal of energy on recruitment. Some of these traditional institutes have been relatively successful in attracting new members. But it is difficult for religious institutes of women to overcome the public image of sisters that has evolved during the last thirty years, as sisters came to be viewed as the most rebellious group within the United States Catholic Church.[27] As one sister observed, regarding the public image projected by some sisters: "It's no wonder that the people don't love us any more."

The plight of the elderly

In spite of the retirement short-fall identified by the Tri-Conference Retirement Office in 1994, most retired sisters seem to be receiving good physical care from their institutes, although there is legitimate concern about continuing to fund this level of care in the future as the number of working sisters declines every year. Some religious institutes are reluctant to take government subsidies for their members, such as Medicare, but the elderly Religious are eligible for this coverage, and some also are eligible for Medicaid because of their low incomes.

A larger problem affecting the retired sisters in the late 1990s is both spiritual and psychological. Many retired sisters feel that the philosophy of religious life adopted by their institutes makes it difficult for them to sustain their spiritual life and to be faithful to their vows. For example, one sister reported that her congregation built a beautiful new retirement home for the sisters, but did not include a chapel in the facility. She noted that there is a beauty shop in the building, but if a sister wants to attend daily Mass, she must go outside to another building, not an easy task for the elderly or infirm.

In some places, sisters regularly leave their convents to attend Mass at other locations because at the convent Mass, sisters or other non-ordained persons read the Gospel, preach the homily, and perform other functions reserved to a priest or deacon by canon and liturgical law. Other liturgical aberrations in convents have included improper reservation of the Blessed Sacrament and illicit changes in the language of the Sacramentary and the Lectionary. As one sister noted, many women Religious "are repulsed by rituals that center on shells and stones, streams and twigs, windmills and waterfalls and at which so fundamental a Christian symbol as the cross of Jesus Christ is often noticeable only by its absence."[28]

In a 1985 statement to the United States bishops, the national board of the Leadership Conference of Women Religious reflected a more radically feminist attitude about liturgy than most sisters espouse:

The exclusion and/or negation of women in liturgy

and worship is one of the most demoralizing experiences which women sustain. This is particularly true because of the church's longstanding assertion that liturgy (especially the eucharist) is the "center of our lives." If one is *de facto* invisible in something said to be 'the center,' one is, quite literally, displaced or alienated.

Women may not, given the church's prohibition of their ordination, preside; the ritualization, symbols and language of liturgy and worship are more often than not sexist; concelebrated liturgies multiply the presence of males (especially hard to take when the congregation is exclusively or primarily female as is the case in religious communities and organizations of women); qualified women are not permitted to preach (except through subterfuges like giving the homily a different name and dislocating it); God is addressed and referred to in language and images which identify the deity as male, manlike, possessing male traits. Some liturgical roles are barred to women; others they may experience but cannot be formally installed in.[29]

In addition to a feminization of the liturgy in countless congregations, the leadership also has completely renovated the convent chapel or church, removing pews, altars, statutes, and stained glass, erasing nearly every vestige of the sacred that had inspired the elderly sisters for most of their years in religious life.[30] The end result in many of these cases is a "modern liturgy space" that is not designed for long-term Eucharistic adoration, a customary occupation of many elderly and infirm Religious.

Critics of such renovations have argued that the finished product of these renovations is more suitable for holding community meetings than for any liturgical ceremonies that are intended to invoke the transcendent.[31] One sister even said she believed that these renovations of chapels have been orchestrated precisely so that the elderly will not be able to spend so much of their time in prayer and Eucharistic adoration. And, some observers of these "renewed" chapel configurations have suggested that some renovations are orchestrated for the explicit purpose of de-emphasizing the presider role of the priest-celebrant. For example, in some convent chapels, the sanctuary space is not delineated in any way — not even by one raised step; the altar has become a small, moveable table placed in the middle of the congregation; and the presider's chair is placed in the midst of the assembly. The purpose of this configuration seems to be to create the feeling that the priest blends in with the congregation so that the "pain" of women's exclusion from the priesthood is thus lessened.

In any event, regardless of how good the intentions of the "change-oriented" orders might be, the fact is that many of the elderly — and some not-so-elderly — sisters have suffered immeasurably and continue to suffer.

First of all, sisters who entered religious life prior to 1970 entered the convent under an entirely different set of circumstances than those which prevail in a change-oriented institute today. In orders that based their renewal on the Vatican II documents, changes in religious life may have been difficult for some of the elderly and even younger members who were resistant to change. But when Church guidelines were followed, and change was implemented intelligently and slowly, and essentials of religious life were maintained, the sisters could be reassured that they were complying with the mind of the Church simply by reading the documents of Vatican II, papal communications, and decrees from the Congregation for Religious. However, in orders that totally transformed the whole concept of religious life and tried to re-engineer a new definition, many of the elderly feel totally disenfranchised. Some simply were not consulted about sudden and massive changes that affected the very heart of their communities. Others were coerced to give their tacit approval to sweeping changes or to remain silent about actions they could not and would not approve. And many of these sisters disapprove of what they perceive to be their leaderships' open disrespect for the hierarchy, traditions, and teachings of the Catholic Church.

In general, these sisters take very seriously the vows they made, and they are disturbed not only that religious life has been fundamentally restructured in their own communities, but even more alarmed that in the restructured model, it is difficult, if not impossible, for them to live out the vows they made to God. And many of them are very troubled when they see that their leadership either rejects or ignores directives from the Vatican, apparently with impunity, for most bishops seem reluctant to intervene, even in areas where bishops do have authority.

One elderly sister explained that "We are refugees in our own communities." She said that her community's leadership considers the elderly well cared for if their physical needs are met. But, she said, the spiritual and emotional needs of the elderly are not understood. The active members of her community give more of their time and attention to the prisoners in the local jail than they give to their own sisters in the community, she observed. Also, many sisters who do not need nursing-home care find themselves living a solitary existence in apartments because there simply are no other community living facilities left in their orders, which have sold off convent and mother house properties.

Certainly, this treatment of the elderly is contrary to what Pope John Paul II promoted in *Vita Consecrata* when he wrote that care and concern for elderly Religious should be derived from a "clear obligation of charity and gratitude" as well as "an awareness that their witness greatly serves the church and their own institutes." Further, he wrote that the mission of the elderly is "worthwhile and meritorious" even after age or infirmity causes them to retire from their apostolates. "The elderly and sick have a great deal to give in wisdom and experience to the community, if only the community can remain close to them with concern and an ability to listen.

"More than in any activity, the apostolate consists in the witness of one's own complete dedication to the Lord's saving will." The pope also noted that the elderly live out their vocation by persevering in prayer, accepting their condition, and "by their readiness to serve as spiritual directors, confessors or mentors in prayer."[32]

Apparently many elderly sisters in change-oriented institutes also live out their vocations by simply persevering in their day-to-day lives. One sister who has been in religious life for fifty years expressed the point of view of many elderly sisters in the following essay, included here with her permission. This sister embraces the decrees of Vatican II, wears a contemporary habit of a dark suit and a veil, and has been active in civil rights work, including many years of teaching in inner-city schools and working with underprivileged children. She is now retired, but still works part-time tutoring and writing.

> The present turbulent time in the Church is a challenge to everyone, but what is it like to go through it as an older religious? I can tell you, from experience, that it is both a time of martyrdom and a time of Faith. Most religious my age — 50 years in religious life — came from homes in which our Faith was nurtured from the cradle on. We were led to love and respect our Church and its leaders. We had a deep and abiding devotion to the Mass. When we became old enough to go to school, the sisters and the pastors of our parishes took up where the family left off, and our faith continued to grow and deepen in Catholic schools.
>
> When we entered the novitiate, the Faith was again the very reason for our choice. Customs and training — at times a little ridiculous — took place in an atmosphere which always had the transcendent as backdrop. After novitiate, we went out to serve the Church. That's how we understood our role then: to SERVE in the Church. In our order,

that meant going into Catholic classrooms all over the United States to teach about God and the things of God. Don't laugh, but for a while there, we even put God into the math and grammar books. Who of my age group does not recall teaching *Progress in Arithmetic*'s lesson on how many cupcakes were needed for the Little Jesus party? And *Voyages in English*, with all its religious and moral sentences and paragraphs? Maybe we did overdo it a little, but when I look at our world today and our world then, I have to conclude that it was better to err on the side of Faith.

One of history's "turmoil periods" hit us in the 1960s. Turmoil entered the novitiates, too, and strange formation programs (so-called) began to emerge. In many cases, persons as yet unformed themselves, began to be appointed as formation directors, replacing older, experienced, seasoned religious. The rationale was that older religious were unable to give the "young" — if you can call women in their 30s and 40s young — the training needed to "adapt to the times." The results of that mistake are evident in religious congregations today: A generation of religious who haven't the slightest notion of what religious life is about, and who are so "adapted to the times" that they cannot grasp the concept that religious life is supposed to be countercultural rather than adapted to every un-Christian ideology.

In the 30 years that followed 1960, all hell broke loose in some congregations. Questionable elections were held, and carefully controlled processes were used to give the stamp of legality to decisions which were totally unacceptable to the majority of Sisters, most of them older and irrevocably loyal to the magisterium of the Church and the original charism of their congregations.

The reactions to this state of affairs have been varied. Most sisters, accustomed to obedience by long practice of their vow, and untrained in how to deal with the bulldozing methods of controlled (and at times dishonest) processes, suffer martyrdom in silence and in indescribable pain, at seeing their congregations being turned into entities to which they can in no way relate, at witnessing the destruction of the original values, charisms and traditions of their founders and foundresses.

Other sisters, unable to endure being cut off, threatened and persecuted, are giving lip-service to a leadership whose actions they despise, because they don't know what else to do. A third group of sisters, outraged by the injustice and oppression being inflicted upon the majority of sisters by their misguided leaderships are reacting courageously and fearlessly, in spite of threats and persecutions.

One thing is certain; no matter what the reaction, all of these sisters share in the martyrdom being inflicted upon older religious at this time. They are shamed and saddened by the public behavior of their leadership, who brazenly and openly dishonor and ridicule the Holy Father, the magisterium, the Catholic priesthood and the sacred traditions of the Church concerning Faith and morals. The radical feminist leadership of besieged congregations devalue the Eucharist, the Creed, Scripture and all things sacred, putting in their place the worship of goddesses, sacrilegious liturgies, and support of immorality and deviant sexual behavior.

When I said this turmoil period (1960s to 1990s) is a time of martyrdom for older religious, I was not using a metaphor. Physical martyrdom is merciful compared to the assault being made upon the Faith, the values and the sacred traditions of older sisters in congregations whose leadership has been seized by radical feminists. But, besides being a time of martyrdom, this period is also a time of faith for older religious. These sisters who are reacting to this tragedy with silence are not helpless bystanders. As never before, they have intensified their prayer life, spending long hours before the Blessed Sacrament and/or slipping their rosary beads through their fingers, interceding for their congregations, hour after hour, day after day. Those older sisters who, confused, give lip-service to radical feminist leaders do so because they don't know what else to do, and this seems the safest course of action to them. They, too, have deepened their faith life, and their attempt to deal with opposing ideologies and matters of conscience is no small contribution to the welfare of their congregations. Then, there are those older sisters, who, armed with fortitude and prayer, with the strength which comes from the Eucharist and with an overwhelming sense of outrage in the face of injustice, have resolved that their congregations will NOT be secularized and/or destroyed without a struggle on their part.

Realizing that the era of peace before the 1960s did not prepare them for this crisis, they have begun to study the documents of the Church concerning religious. They have unearthed the documents and histories of their congregations in order to be able to get a clearer idea of specific charisms, of the real meaning of their consecration and their role in the Church. They are taking a second look at the vows, community life, personal and communal prayer for the purpose of updating them. They are becoming acquainted with canon law for religious and communicating with persons and organizations in the church whose responsibility it is to give assistance to religious congregations. They are beginning to network among themselves, not only in their own congregations, but with other congregations who may be experiencing the same problems. In this way, sisters who refuse to accept the secularization of their congregations can give one another support and encouragement and share research and insights so that we can act as responsible Christians.

This retired sister reflects the viewpoint of many other sisters. Indeed, these are the sisters who literally built the Catholic parochial school system. These are the sisters who founded or sustained most of our Catholic hospitals and other social service institutions. Yet, in spite of this legacy, their voices are seldom heard in the ongoing debate over religious life. Their voices are not being heard by many of their leaders who are prepared to see their institutes die rather than admit that the decisions they made during the last thirty years should be re-evaluated. The voices of these sisters are rarely heard by many Church officials, who seem to accept as a fact of Church life that religious institutes come and go, and thus they overlook the ongoing human tragedy in the many religious institutes that celebrate more funerals than any other occasion. Instead, the public and the official Church hear the more strident voices of a leadership that does not reflect the attitude of the majority of sisters. And the media regularly carry an image of the sisterhood not based on the works and beliefs of these faithful sisters, but rather based on an image projected by a handful of militant rebels.

16: Where Do the Sisters Go from Here?

"What must be avoided at all costs is the actual breakdown of the consecrated life, a collapse which is not measured by a decrease in numbers but by a failure to cling steadfastly to the Lord and to personal vocation and mission."[1]

Pope John Paul II
Vita Consecrata

This book has attempted to answer the journalists' questions that were posed in the preface about the "who, what, why, when, where, and how" of the crisis now confronting American Catholic sisters. The answers to these questions are complex, and the facts presented here inevitably will be interpreted in different ways, for some sisters, clergy, hierarchy, and laity continue to deny that a crisis exists. Others who may admit there is a crisis will seek to place the blame on anyone except themselves or their organization, and surely there is a lot of blame to go around. But the purpose of this book is not to point fingers or to place blame; it is to report the facts so that the answers to these questions can be used to help address the crisis in women's religious communities.

Who?

Women Religious, who once were revered as models of deep spirituality and Christian virtue, now have a reputation as the most rebellious group within the Church. The names of sisters are prominent in organizations which challenge the Church on issues such as abortion rights, women's ordination, and internal authority structures of the Church. In many orders of women Religious, sisters no longer live together, pray together, or work together. Sisters, who once were the backbone of Catholic institutions, have left those institutions in growing numbers to pursue "ministries" in the secular sphere that have little to do with the Church or the vows they profess as consecrated women.

As a result, numerous Catholic institutions have closed because of lack of personnel even as the Catholic population has grown. Over 100,000 sisters taught in Catholic schools in 1965, compared to fewer than 13,000 in 1996. During that time frame, nearly half of all Catholic grade and high schools closed, and many Catholic health care institutions were secularized or forced to close. Also in the years between 1965 and 1996, the number of sisters declined by half, and many of the communities of women Religious have unraveled to the point that their survival is questionable, for the median age in many orders has soared into the seventies because young women are not attracted to the sisters' new self-styled way of life.

What happened?

Few people would debate the fact that by the 1950s, many religious institutes were bogged down in a lifestyle that was so authoritarian and regimented that Religious often could not even think for themselves, let alone grow spiritually. Some of these institutes were held together only by traditions that modern sisters did not understand, and some orders were so mired in an eighteenth-century mindset that they were not effectively serving the twentieth-century Church or nurturing the spiritual needs of their members. The Second Vatican Council (1962-65) called on religious institutes to renew themselves, to take a fresh look at the charism of their founders, and apply that charism to modern times. This renewal was to involve removing meaningless rules and regulations, taking into account the physical, psychological, and spiritual needs of the members. The renewal also was aimed at fostering a more mature understanding of the call to holiness and a contemporary application of the institutes' apostolates to the needs of the times. While doing this, the religious institutes were to retain their rich heritage, their primary apostolate, and the essentials of religious life such as life in community, authority vested in a superior, religious garb, and common prayer.

As reported in the previous chapters of this book, the documents of Vatican II laid out this charge to Religious to renew themselves, and women Religious went about this task more enthusiastically than any other group in the Church.

However, the renewal intended by the Church was effectively co-opted by activist sisters who had been influenced by the feminist movement, campus radicalism, dissident theologians, and the cultural upheaval of the 1960s. These sisters managed to get into positions of power in many religious institutes as well as in the women superiors' conference. From these positions of influence, and over the objections of most grassroots sisters, these change-oriented leaders used their authority to direct a renewal process that reordered the emphasis of religious life from the sanctification of self and service to the Church, to a secular agenda based on women's liberation and other left-wing ideologies.

Why?

These events occurred for a number of reasons. Prior to Vatican II, sisters were consistently overworked and expected to accept without question the demands of superiors, pastors, bishops, and laity. They were the workforce of the Church, but they were not sufficiently appreciated for what they did or for their considerable talents and intelligence. Sisters were seldom consulted about issues that affected their lives, and were almost never asked their opinion about larger Church issues. As a result, many women Religious resonated with the liberation movement sweeping the United States in the 1960s.

Then, in the middle of those tumultuous 1960s, Religious were asked to rewrite their constitutions and rules, at the very time when society was questioning the role of authority and re-evaluating the place of women in the culture. There could hardly have been a less stable time in recent history for the religious institutes in the United States to re-evaluate their rules and constitutions. In addition, most religious institutes of women were made up of sisters trained to teach, nurse, or perform social work. Most of these orders did not have the skilled personnel for orchestrating a major overhaul of a complex institution that already had many organizational problems.

At the same time that religious orders were being asked to rewrite their constitutions, the Church announced that the *Code of Canon Law*, which had been adopted in 1917, was being revised. Yet, Religious were supposed to proceed with writing their new constitutions while adhering to the old code and interim documents, and then be ready to revise those constitutions again when the new *Code of Canon Law* was issued. It took nearly twenty years to issue the new code, so many Religious simply ignored most existing legislation and conciliar documents and wrote their constitutions "in anticipation" of what they hoped would be in the new canons.

In a few cases, Rome protested these points, but during the 1970s and even into the 1980s, the Vatican bureaucracy was notoriously slow in responding to the new constitutions sent for approval. This delayed response was caused by the monumental task of having to review the constitutions of religious institutes from all over the world, but also because reviewers sometimes spent considerable time on trivial matters such as grammar and phraseology. Furthermore, because so many constitutions had to be read, outside consultants were employed by the Congregation for Religious to review the constitutions. The result of so many different reviewers being involved in the process was that inconsistencies were common — items which may have been rejected in one constitution may have been approved in another, depending on who did the paperwork. Many religious institutes simply proceeded to operate under their proposed new constitutions, assuming Rome's eventual approval some time in the future. If that approval did not eventually come, many institutes simply played the game of prolonged "dialogue" with Rome, hoping to win approval for practices that already had been in effect for years.

Further complicating the picture was the fact that the Vatican seemed to be at a loss in trying to deal with women who had allowed themselves to be walked on for so long, but now were standing up for their legitimate rights. And when the progressive sisters saw Rome's difficulty in coping with some of the most reasonable requests of women Religious, these change-oriented sisters seized the opportunity to push their more radical agenda to make a complete break with past traditions and define religious life in their own terms.

How?

Clearly, one of the key elements that has enabled the unraveling of women's religious communities is denial. Many sisters, many leaders of women's institutes, and some members of the American hierarchy simply haven't wanted to believe that the kind of renewal effected by most women's communities actually led to the disintegration of those communities. They prefer instead to blame the selfishness of young people or the influence of modern culture.

There was strong evidence of such denial in 1983, after the pope requested that United States bishops study religious life in this country to try to determine why vocations had decreased so dramatically. Astoundingly, that study, led by Archbishop John Quinn (detailed in Chapter Twelve of this book), reported back to the pope that religious life was basically in good shape in this country, even as many religious orders were declining at an alarming rate, individual Religious were feeling more and more alienated from their communities, and Catholic institutions were closing their doors because of lack of personnel.

Such denial is still characteristic of many Religious and some members of the hierarchy as we approach the twenty-first century, in spite of strong evidence that the elements of religious life that were discarded by most change-oriented communities of women Religious — a corporate aposto-late, life in community, regular prayer in common, religious garb — are the very elements that attract young people to religious life and sustain the commitment of existing members. These progressive communities which discarded the essentials of religious life include some of the largest and most prestigious congregations of women Religious in the United States, with over half of the professed sisters in this country belonging to such institutes. But many of these progressive institutes haven't received any new members under the age of forty in years, and the average age of their members is rising fast.

Some sobering statistics

Various studies of religious life during the past ten years have con-cluded that the kind of deconstruction of religious life that was pursued by these progressive congregations of women is directly related to defections and declining vocations.

Immaculate Heart of Mary Sister Eleace King, a former research asso-ciate at the Center for Applied Research in the Apostolate (CARA) at Georgetown University, tracked data on religious institutes from the late 1980s and into the 1990s. The *CARA Formation Directory for Men and Women Religious 1994-1995* edited by Sister Eleace reported data that was based on about seventy-five percent of the religious institutes in the United States. Regarding new vocations to the religious life, CARA found that in 1992, fifty-seven percent of the women's communities had no new candi-dates enter their institutes, and seventy-one percent had no one make final vows.[2]

The CARA study attempted to identify the characteristics of community life that tend to attract new candidates. Communities were termed "intrinsic" if they provided their members with renewal and retreat experiences that were specific to the "guiding spirituality" of the institute. Communities were termed "varied" if their spirituality was derived from a variety of traditions. Thirty-four percent of the women's institutes were categorized as intrinsic, and those communities had a higher average of candidates in the novitiate or temporary vows than did the varied groups, with an average of 1.2 new mem-bers taking final vows in the intrinsic group in 1992, compared to 0.5 in the varied group. Likewise, communities that consider living in a religious house "important" received a higher average of new members than did institutes that consider living in a religious house to be "not important." So too did communities who operated their own novitiates, rather than sending candidates to inter-community novitiates. But, two out of three women's institutes send their candidates to inter-community programs.[3]

At the time the statistics were gathered, 1993, about eighty-one percent of the women Religious in the United States belonged to institutes whose superiors were affiliated with the Leadership Conference of Women Religious. About twelve percent belonged to institutes whose superiors were affiliated with the Council of Major Superiors of Women Religious (the new group of superiors of women which was approved by the Vatican in 1992).

The CARA study broke down the statistics according to affiliation in these two groups and found some interesting trends. Of the sisters who have taken final vows, the groups affiliated with the Leadership Conference represented eighty-nine percent, while those affiliated with the new Council of Major Superiors represented ten percent. However, while the new Council's affiliates represented only ten percent of the women in final vows, they had approximately twenty-five percent of all women in initial formation and about thirty-one percent of the women making final vows. "If this pattern continues and attrition rates do not differ, then the proportion of sisters represented by CMSWR [Council of Major Superiors of Women Religious] communities will increase, while that represented by LCWR [Leadership Conference of Women Religious] will decline," according to the CARA study.[4]

The CARA report concluded: "Men and women entering religious life are more apt to select institutes that are strongly grounded in their own spiritual tradition, deem living together in religious houses important, and maintain their own novitiate programs. Earlier CARA research indicates that communities with a clear corporate ministry are more inclined to attract new members than those offering diversified service. When these findings are considered together, the need for religious 'identity' becomes clear. Communities having a distinct lifestyle and ministry rooted in the guiding spiritual tradition of the institute are apt to attract new candidates. Those with diversity in lifestyle, ministry and spirituality are not. . . .

"The future of any religious institute depends on new candidates and the number of religious, both men and women, has declined steadily for the last 27 years. Therefore, it seems urgent that men and women religious be rooted in the guiding spirituality of their institutes and that this spirituality inform and shape the corporate ministry and lifestyle of the community."[5]

16: Where Do the Sisters Go from Here?

Roger Finke, a Protestant sociology professor at Purdue University, used the statistics from CARA in a sociological analysis of membership growth in orders of women Religious, and his study confirmed the CARA conclusions. Finke found that "Rather than 'secure the growth' of religious orders, the new reforms [after Vatican II] have been associated with eliminating growth and securing membership decline." Finke examined why vocations declined when religious orders made membership easier by increasing individual freedoms and reducing communal demands. He found that "The decline in communal living, the loss of distinctive dress, and the increase in individual autonomy all increased nongroup activity." And, as sisters spent less time with their community, they received fewer rewards from the community's social networks, which also made it easier for them to leave religious life.

Finke also found that group solidarity is important for supporting a member's religious commitment, because members of the group offer support and confirmation to one other. But, "As members reduce their investments in community activities and increase their nongroup activities, the group is less capable of supporting the extremely high levels of religious commitment associated with religious orders." This theory explains why traditional religious orders are more successful in attracting recruits, according to Finke. Since membership demands are high for religious life, the order must offer the member "a religious lifestyle that is distinctive from that of the laity." But Finke also observed that a traditional religious order does not mean a pre-Vatican II order, for there are successful orders that have heeded the call of Vatican II to return to the spirituality of their founders in a creative way while still retaining the strict demands of common life.[6]

The "Future of Religious Orders in the United States" project

The most comprehensive study ever done of the opinions, beliefs, attitudes, and practices of men and women Religious also reflected the findings of CARA. Begun in 1989 and completed in 1992, the "Future of Religious Orders in the United States" (FORUS) study involved 10,000 sisters, brothers and priests from 816 religious congregations that had a total of 121,000 members. The study was funded by Lilly Endowment, Inc., and conducted by Father David Nygren, an organizational psychologist, and Sister Miriam Ukeritis, a clinical psychologist. The study consisted of a national survey of the 10,000 Religious, as well as group and individual interviews and regional workshops.

Some of the conclusions of the FORUS study were:

- Dramatic changes are necessary in most religious institutes for religious life to continue to have an impact on the Church or the world.
- Individualism and self-preoccupation have replaced the virtue of generosity in some Religious, and have affected the concept of obedience.
- While most Religious institutes espouse the importance of the preferential option for the poor, "a significant number of religious" do not have a personal commitment to this concept.
- There is a lowered respect on the part of Religious for authority within their congregations, the Church magisterium and the United States hierarchy.
- Many religious institutes have no sense of corporate identity and no specific mission focus, resulting in few new vocations and little inspiration for current members.
- A "significant percentage" of Religious don't understand their role in the Church, with women Religious — over thirty percent — being the most uncertain.
- Women Religious express disagreement and confusion about how their consecrated life differs from that of lay women.
- Many Religious do not seem to realize how laicized they have become and how inaccessible they are to the people who need them the most.
- The orders that are most stable are characterized by traditional practices of common life and prayer and a clear sense of mission.[7]

Sister Miriam and Father Nygren also studied members of visioning groups in religious orders. The people in these groups were nominated by their superiors, and were supposedly people who were able to articulate beliefs, attitudes, and choices about the future. Since superiors chose the group participants, it is not surprising that FORUS concluded that the values of these visioning groups often were shared by the community's leadership, but did not always reflect the opinions of the general membership of the community — another indication of the gulf between superiors and grassroots Religious. Further, the visioning groups anticipated that religious congregations of the future will be ecumenical, possibly interfaith, and made up of persons who are lay or cleric, married or single, vowed or unvowed, of various cultures, races, and sexual orientation. However, Father Nygren, reflecting Finke's conclusions, warned that "The breadth of view among leadership and the visioning groups stands in contrast to another dominant strain in our study; namely, that such inclusiveness leads to boundaryless conditions which can lead to neutralizing the impact of religious orders and to losing their identity as a group."[8]

Regarding those leaders, the FORUS study concluded that "the vast majority" of the leaders in religious institutes in the 1990s are "average performers," and that the concept of leadership is an increasing concern in religious orders. Father Nygren said that "The most striking weakness among current leaders is their inability to formulate a strategy to achieve a purpose or mission." Also, "Average leaders of religious orders, on the other hand, are motivated more by acceptance than achievement and are more inclined to act on behalf of individual members, thus resulting in a greater proclivity towards maintenance of the status quo."[9]

The FORUS study also praised a number of accomplishments in religious life, and, like the Georgetown CARA study, it offered ways to use its conclusions to revitalize religious life in the United States. For example, Sister Miriam Ukeritis also echoed the thesis supported by Roger Finke when she said, "Religious orders with a focused mission typically exact a higher cost among members with respect to belonging and commitment. Religious orders that define clearly the boundaries and expectations of their members and distinguish them from other members of the Church will be revitalized."[10]

Further, the FORUS study found that ninety-two percent of women Religious were willing to work in an institute sponsored by their congregation, and eighty-four percent were willing to live in an institute sponsored by their congregation. This information gives congregational leaders and planners the opportunity to revitalize a community by recapturing the concept of a corporate mission, FORUS concluded.[11]

However, since the FORUS report was issued in 1992, there is no evidence that leaders of change-oriented institutes of women Religious have made any effort to identify a corporate apostolate on which to focus the ministry of their members or to recall their members into community living, even though the majority of women Religious are willing to live in community and pursue a common apostolate with the other members of their order.

As Sister Miriam observed during an October 3, 1992, teleconference on the FORUS report, there is "a resistance on the part of many people to see what a crisis we're in and what a crisis we're facing. . . . In some cases it may be denial."

Denying the obvious

Ironically, the Leadership Conference of Women Religious was heavily involved in the FORUS study and even had representatives on the FORUS advisory board,[12] including Sister Donna Markham, president of the Leadership Conference 1991-92, and Sister Bette Moslander, president in 1981-82, who also had been a consultant to the Quinn Commission. But rather than trying to learn from the conclusions of the FORUS report in order to strengthen religious institutes, the Leadership Conference of Women Religious hastened to dispute the validity of some of the conclusions in the FORUS study.

Shortly after the findings of the FORUS study were released, the Conference even produced its own "ministry study," *Threads for the Loom*, which contradicted some of the FORUS findings that were critical of women Religious. For example, FORUS found that women Religious were the most uncertain group in the Church about their identity, but *Threads for the Loom* argued instead that these women were "actively engaged in the development of new paradigms of religious life." FORUS found that Religious often talk about the importance of serving the poor, but few Religious are actually engaged in work with the poor; while *Threads for the Loom* claimed that "the opportunity to serve the poor [is] a primary criteria in ministry selection."[13]

Dominican Sister Donna Markham, president of the Leadership Conference of Women Religious 1991-92 took exception to some of the FORUS conclusions in a *Washington Post* interview, suggesting that the FORUS conclusion that younger women Religious were more confused about their role in the Church than were other Religious, was due to the fact that young women view the church as "antithetical to women" since women are denied ordination.[14] Sister Doris Gottemoeller, president of the Sisters of Mercy of the Americas who was elected president of the Leadership Conference of Women Religious in 1993, observed that the FORUS report covered "a snapshot in time" rather than significant trends.[15]

The FORUS report also was attacked at the 1993 annual assembly of the Leadership Conference of Women Religious by assembly speaker Sister of Mercy Janet Ruffing, who said: "The current research on religious life employs images of confusion and chaos, of diminishment and decline, of lack of focus, of invisibility. Others have written of walking where there is no path or of seeing in the dark. Yet I remain convinced that whatever religious life will be in the coming millennium, it will rise up again from the dying embers of the present moment."

Sister Janet then identified five areas of disagreement with the FORUS study, lamenting the exclusion of women from the priesthood, invoking feminist jargon, and calling on a liberation theology concept that Christ's death was more of a political statement than a redemptive act. Among Sister Janet's points about the FORUS study: 1) ". . . The old juridical categories assumed by the questions seemed inadequate to express the new experience of apostolic religious life for women"; 2) ". . . Conclusions of this study suggested some tensions between the prophetic and contemplative poles of religious life. . . . But one is only prophetic when protest, denunciation, lament, and vision are rooted in the mystical impulses of the fiery spirit." 3) "Third, apostolic religious women were not questioned about feeling a call to ordained ministry." 4) "Fourth, some of the questions on spirituality seemed poorly conceived." 5) "I found the questions on Jesus unconnected to the content of that Christology — how an experience of Jesus leads to specific forms of mission. . . . In addition, liberation Christologies, including feminist ones, emphasize that Jesus suffered a political death precisely because he refused to accept the injustice embedded in the religious and social institutions of his day. Jesus is not so much one's Lord and Master to whom one gives obedience by accepting the superior's decisions as he is the animating source of compassion, energy, and love. Obedience is listening and responding to this call wherever it takes us."[16]

Another symptom of denial is the way many leaders of women religious continually downplay what they derisively call "the numbers game," even as the number of sisters declines by thousands every year. While arguing that quality is more important than quantity, these leaders continue to push ahead with developing their "new paradigms of religious life," rejecting the concept of religious life that has been contained in numerous Church documents since the Second Vatican Council, preferring instead an egalitarian, "ecofeminist" model based on their own "lived experience." But these leaders seem oblivious to the fact that young people simply are not attracted to these new models of so-called religious life that some sisters — led by the Leadership Conference of Women Religious — have been experimenting with for the past thirty years. As the Shaker community discovered, and sociologists have confirmed,[17] religious experiments that fail to attract young members do not survive. Nor do religious communities that fail to admit that they have made mistakes and fail to try to discover why young people are not eager to join them.

Further, some leaders of religious congregations are in such a state of denial that they seem unable to recognize the fact that they have transformed their communities from religious institutes into "closet" secular institutes. Members of secular institutes take private vows, live "in the world," engage in individual ministries, and wear ordinary lay clothing. Clearly, the lifestyle of many women Religious today is indistinguishable from that of members of a secular institute, except that the secular institute puts more demands on its members than do some religious institutes of women. Ironically, though, Religious enjoy more benefits than do members of a secular institute — lifetime care by their institute, the tax-exempt status of the institute, and the canonical right of the institute to exercise the apostolate in the name of the Church.

Still, the leaders of many progressive communities of women Religious continue to deny that their congregations no longer conform to the Church understanding of a religious institute. Instead, they claim to be founding new forms of religious life, or transforming the old forms, while still feeling entitled to enjoy the prestige and benefits of vowed members of canonically recognized religious institutes. Rather than change themselves to conform to the model of religious life as understood by the Church, these women strive to change the Church to conform to the model of religious life they are creating through their "lived experience."

The ambiguous role of the institutional church

The institutional Church has appeared to be unwilling or unable to address this crisis among American women Religious, perhaps opting for the recommendation of Archbishop Whealon in 1984 to apply the Gamaliel principle and simply do nothing. Indeed, the hierarchy probably has many reasons for being cautious in dealing with institutes of women Religious in the United States, for such experiences have not always been well advised. In the early history of the Church in the United States, there are documented stories about bishops illicitly interfering in the internal business of institutes of women Religious. For example, one bishop ordered contemplative nuns to leave their cloister to teach in a Catholic school; another bishop removed a legitimately-elected superior from her office and replaced her with a sister of his own choice. Other abuses of hierarchical authority have occurred where Church officials have meddled in areas of religious life which are canonically under the authority of the religious institute, not the local bishop. (Indeed, canon law protects religious institutes' rights to determine how that institute will exercise its own spiritual heritage and founding charism, but this must always be within Church guidelines for religious life.) So, most contemporary bishops in the United States have probably overcompensated for these past abuses by giving little or no oversight to women's institutes, even in areas where they do have authority.

Complicating the picture is the fact that many institutes of women Religious in the United States are pontifical institutes (as opposed to diocesan institutes), meaning that they are under the direct authority of the Holy See — not the local bishop — in matters relating to their internal government and discipline. However, a local bishop still has authority over all religious institutes in his diocese regarding "the care of souls, the public exercise of divine worship and other works of the apostolate" (Canon 678). Yet, many bishops simply do not understand exactly what their relationship with religious institutes should be, and so they solve the dilemma with a "hands off" approach.

Another factor discouraging the official Church from confronting the sisters who deviate from Church teaching is that past confrontations with American sisters have not been very successful. For example, when the Vatican backed Cardinal James McIntyre in insisting that the Immaculate Heart of Mary Sisters of Los Angelos restructure their community in accordance with Vatican II guidelines, that community was virtually destroyed, with over three-hundred sisters leaving religious life. And the media successfully portrayed the official Church as the villain in the whole situation.

In 1984 another confrontation between sisters and the hierarchy caused considerable misunderstanding, resulting in a power struggle that produced years of conflict and reams of adverse publicity. In that situation, twenty-six sisters signed the controversial *New York Times* abortion rights statement sponsored by Catholics For A Free Choice. The Congregation for Religious directed the institutes of all the signers to instruct those sisters to publicly retract their support of the statement or face expulsion from their religious institutes. Most institutes and Religious initially refused to follow the directions of the Congregation for Religious, but eventually the claim was made that some sort of agreement was reached between the Vatican and all the Religious involved except for School Sisters of Notre Dame Barbara Ferraro and Patricia Hussey, who eventually left religious life and attracted considerable publicity when they co-authored the book, *No Turning Back: Two Nuns' Battle With The Vatican Over Women's Right To Choose*.

However, several of the other sister-signers later asserted that they never did back down from their position, even though the Congregation for Religious announced that all but two of the sisters had retracted their statement. According to one 1986 news report, the Congregation for Religious "accepted statements by religious superiors, even though some of the signers still do not know the precise content of these statements."[18] And reportedly, some sisters merely acknowledged that the Church teaches that all human life is sacred, but refused to disassociate themselves from the abortion rights statement.

This confrontation caused a great deal of confusion and ill will toward the Church, so the hierarchy may have concluded from this experience that confronting sisters on their divergence from Church teachings is really counterproductive. Since the sisters who seem to be the most vocal dissidents belong to communities of women Religious that are proceeding rapidly down the path of self-destruction, the hierarchy may well have decided that the best way to deal with these sisters is simply to allow them and their institutes to die out quietly rather than to engage in battle with them.

Traditional sisters in progressive communities

The prospect of oblivion is little comfort to the sisters who are members of these progressive institutes, who did not choose the deconstruction of their communities, and who wish to live religious life according to Church directives. For them, the institutional tragedy is a human tragedy. In most cases where the character and mission of a religious institute was radically altered, the renewal was stolen by progressive sisters who felt the reform mandated by the Council did not go far enough. They created their own version of renewal and imposed it on their communities through political maneuvering, psychological manipulation, and dissemination of incorrect information.

Many sisters who did not agree with the new philosophy and lifestyle adopted by these progressives tried to speak up, but they usually were silenced as reactionaries opposed to any change. Some sisters even petitioned their communities to create separate houses or provinces for the sisters who wished to continue their regular community lifestyle and religious observances.[19] But progressive sisters who preach pluralism and inclusivity have little tolerance in actual practice for sisters who disagree with them and do not accept their radical philosophy of religious life. And so, many sisters, most of them elderly, have struggled to live religious life in communities that do not value or recognize the definition of religious life that was embraced by sisters who entered the convent and made their vows before constitutions were rewritten in the 1960s and 1970s. In many cases, these sisters are subjected to abuses of authority far worse than any of the authoritarianism practiced by mother superiors or the hierarchy prior to Vatican II.

In addition to being faithful to their vows and personal vocation, what can these sisters do about the fact that their religious communities have changed the very definition of religious life?

First of all, sisters can inform themselves about the documents and teachings of the Church on consecrated life. As noted earlier, religious superiors are required by canon law to pass along to the members of their institutes all relevant Church documents, but as this book also reported, many superiors do not follow that canon. Sisters can obtain these documents for themselves from other sources: *Origins,* 3211 Fourth Street N.E., Washington, D.C. 20017-1100, (202) 541-3290; or Daughters of St. Paul, St. Paul Books & Media, 50 St. Paul's Ave., Boston, MA 02130, (617) 522-8911.

Sisters also can make a record of what has happened in their institutes and then make that record available to several appropriate people. For example, sisters have reported rigged elections of their officers, denial of any representation at their chapter meetings, and illicit liturgical practices in their convents, such as sisters reading the gospel and preaching the homily. They have reported that the elderly are denied the opportunity to practice religious devotions, or are chided for loyalty to the Church and the hierarchy, or are threatened with eviction from an order's retirement facility. Many sisters have objected to the way their order's funds are dispensed — without the sisters' consent — to outside organizations which actively campaign against Church doctrine and authority or which promote leftist secular ideologies.

A canon law expert suggests that sisters document such events in writing, giving only the important facts, dates, and names, reporting what is specifically wrong, keeping the report as concise as possible. This information should be included in a letter to the immediate responsible superior, with a request for an answer to the letter. A copy of that same letter should be sent to another person at the same time — perhaps another superior, another sister, or a trusted lay friend — so that someone else knows the letter exists. If several sisters are aware of such an event that violates the rights of sisters or contradicts Church teaching or discipline, they should all follow the same procedure.

Then, if the superior does not address the problem satisfactorily in a month or so, the next layer of authority should be contacted by the same method — a simple, precise letter with documentation, asking for a reply, with a copy going to another responsible person. If the sister gets no satisfaction within her congregation, she should move on to outside authority — the diocesan vicar for Religious, then the local bishop, then the papal nuncio, then the Vatican's Congregation for Institutes of Consecrated Life and Societies of Apostolic Life. Diocesan newspapers and concerned lay persons also should be informed when the rights of sisters are being violated by their communities, or the Church is being attacked by the very people who have consecrated themselves in the name of the Church. But the canon law expert also warns that if sisters want to be taken seriously, they should stick to the facts and avoid form letters, long personal commentaries, and frequent complaints about minor issues.

Sisters in Crisis

At the very least, this approach will provide a record that some sisters tried to address what they perceived as a rejection of Church teachings and a violation of their rights, a record that they were faithful to their vows to the end. Such a record will make clear to present and future researchers, historians, and Church authorities that most grassroots sisters did not agree with the brand of renewal implemented in United States religious institutes. At best, the reported situations might be addressed by higher authority or by congregations that want to avoid adverse publicity, for congregational leaders are well aware that most lay Catholics hold sisters in very high esteem and would withhold contributions from a religious institute that does not respect the rights of its members or follow the teachings of the Church.

The future of religious life for women

It is apparent that some institutes of women Religious will not survive very far into the twenty-first century. And some that do survive will do so still unrenewed spiritually. It is a sad irony that sisters were the most responsive group in the Church in answering the Vatican II call to renewal, and yet women Religious have suffered the greatest destabilization of any group in the Church.

The answer is certainly *not* to return to the past, even though a few disillusioned women Religious long for the "good old days" when some sisters moved in lock-step, and felt they displayed their dedication to God simply by completing all their assigned prayers and tasks in dutiful obedience. There is much more to religious life than just doing as one is told, and the reforms mandated by the Second Vatican Council were intended to guide Religious to a more mature practice and understanding of their vocation.

The good news is that some institutes of women Religious have been successful in following the charge of the Council to return to the original inspiration of their order and adapt that inspiration to contemporary times while still preserving each institute's heritage. They have been able to relate the life, prayer, work, and government of their institutes to the needs of their members, while addressing the apostolic needs in contemporary culture and society.[20] These orders are more successful in attracting new candidates than are the more progressive women's institutes which carried renewal well beyond the mandates of the Second Vatican Council. These institutes also have a lower median age than do women's institutes as a whole. The same is true for some new institutes of women Religious that have been founded since the Second Vatican Council, and have based their original constitutions on the Council documents.

16: Where Do the Sisters Go from Here?

The studies of religious life cited above found that the religious institutes that maintain a distinct identity, a specific ministry, community life, regular prayer schedule, and in general place specific demands on their members are the institutes that probably will survive into the next century. Perhaps these institutes may even thrive if they can convince women that they offer an opportunity to live a life of dedication to God that is not available to laywomen on their own. These institutes may be even more successful in increasing their memberships if they can overcome the media stereotype of the naive, mindless nun as portrayed in movies such as "Sister Act," as well as the negative image of nuns shaped by American sisters who attract newspaper headlines by challenging Church authority and doctrine.

But, these moderate institutes that have followed the Council documents on renewal represent far fewer than half of the professed women Religious in this country. Because of social and cultural shifts since World War II, it seems doubtful the United States Church ever again will see the large numbers of women Religious that filled American convents in the 1950s and 1960s.

What will become of religious life for women in the United States?

As sociologist Sister Patricia Wittberg has pointed out, there always will be people who want to live out the universal call to holiness in a more radical manner than the lifestyle pursued by the ordinary lay person.[21] And Pope John Paul II has stressed that "the profession of the evangelical counsels indisputably belongs to the life and holiness of the church" and will always be an essential characteristic of the Church.[22] He has made it clear that the Church will continue to nurture and support the true renewal of religious life, and young people have responded by entering the traditional religious institutes. Some communities of women Religious surely will survive and perhaps even prosper, especially those communities that initiated reforms after Vatican II to update their institutes while still retaining their heritage and the essentials of religious life.

The prospects for "refounding"

What about the other two models of women's communities: a small number of communities that remain in a pre-Vatican II mindset, whose "renewal" has been superficial, and at the opposite extreme, the large number of progressive communities who remade their orders into entities that are more like secular corporations or sororities than religious institutes?

Some of these religious orders undoubtedly will disappear as their aging populations die out. But it also is possible that some of these institutes

327

may experience a "refounding" in the twenty-first century, and like the legendary phoenix, rise from the ashes of their self-immolation.

The refounding of religious orders has a rich history in the Catholic Church, exemplified by women such as Teresa of Ávila, who led the sixteenth-century reform of her Carmelite order after the Carmelites allowed their observance of poverty and communal life to deteriorate; and Mother St. John Fontbonne, who refounded the Sisters of St. Joseph after the order was almost destroyed during the "Reign of Terror" of the French Revolution.

This refounding must be accomplished by the sisters within those institutes themselves, for refounding of religious orders cannot be mandated or directed by hierarchy, clergy, or laity, though legitimate refounding efforts should be supported by these other groups of people. In the refounding process, some members of a religious institute may come to the realization that their concept of consecrated life really does not fit the Church understanding of a religious institute, and so those women may wish to pursue one of the other forms of consecrated life defined by the Church, such as secular institutes, consecrated virgins, or societies of apostolic life. Certainly these other forms of consecrated life allow for holy lives of dedication, and these other forms of consecrated life are also highly esteemed by the Church — but they are distinct from religious life.

Perhaps some other women who identify themselves as sisters will honestly assess their lives and their personal philosophies and realize that they do not effectively practice the vow of poverty in their lifestyle or the vow of obedience in their attitude toward superiors and Church authority, and that a more honest role for them would be that of a lay person. By making clear the various categories of consecrated life, and by making clear the distinction between religious life and the lay life, the women who desire to persist in religious life should be better able to attract new members since their distinct identity as Religious will emerge.

If the Holy Spirit does inspire some women Religious to refound their institutes in the twenty-first century, those women will need the support of the official Church and the laity to empower them to bring order out of the chaos that exists among many institutes of women Religious today. These refounders of the twenty-first century have an advantage that Teresa of Ávila and Mother St. John did not have in previous centuries — the rich collection of Church documents that have been developed since the Second Vatican Council to assist them in relating the original heritage of their institutes to the contemporary Church. They also can benefit from the growing body of information about religious life that has been accumulated by the social sciences in the last thirty years.

16: Where Do the Sisters Go from Here?

In her 1996 book *Pathways to Re-Creating Religious Communities*, Sister Patricia Wittberg uses the analogy of taking a trip to analyze the elements needed for successful refounding of religious orders. She concludes her book with this advice:

"So find a vision which consumes and vitalizes you, one which you are willing to die for — and to live the rest of your life for — and start the journey. Don't wait until fifty, or twenty, or even ten people are ready to go with you. If others do not see religious going anywhere that is clear and distinctive, why on earth would they join them? Start the journey, alone if need be, and then invite others to come along.

"Expect to 'fail.' Expect to fail several times. Expect to lose your way, to forget essential supplies, to suffer breakdowns (and breakups), to journey painstakingly for years only to face dead-ends and washed-out roads. Even if the larger congregation mentors your attempt, if they publicize your experiment and recruit new members for you, if they challenge you when you stray from your ideals and encourage you when you return to them — and this is precisely the role which established congregations should be playing to support their members' various refounding attempts — you will, quite possibly still fail. Learn from your mistakes and try again . . . and again. That is what founders, and refounders do. That is the crucifixion, the 'Passover,' to which they are called. The resurrection, we know by faith, will also occur."[23]

Meanwhile, many institutes of women Religious are faithfully going about the business of mentoring their members in their vocations and serving the Church loyally in countless ways. In addition, numbers of faithful sisters in the congregations which are not supportive of Church teachings on religious life still remain faithful to their vows under difficult circumstances and persist in their determination to imitate Jesus, to be a sign to the world that the ultimate goal of every person is union with God. This is exactly what the Holy Father asked of Religious in his 1996 apostolic exhortation, *Vita Consecrata* when he said:

"Rather, by persevering faithfully in the consecrated life, consecrated persons confess with great effectiveness before the world their unwavering trust in the Lord of history, in whose hands are the history and destiny of individuals, institutions and peoples, and therefore also the realization in time of his gifts. Sad situations of crisis invite consecrated persons courageously to proclaim their faith in Christ's death and resurrection that they may become a visible sign of the passage from death to life."[24]

Surely, the sisters who have persevered in their vocations in spite of the "sad situations of crisis" in their orders perpetrated on them by radicals who want to re-order religious life have fulfilled the Holy Father's expectation. These women indeed have led transfigured lives as they set their sights on "our heavenly homeland and the light which will never grow dim."[25] Even if a successful refounding in their orders does not occur, these faithful sisters have fulfilled their vows and transcended the tragic unraveling of their religious communities.

Notes

For citations of material found in the University of Notre Dame Archives, the archives location code for the material is included. These abbreviations are used: UNDA is the University of Notre Dame Archives; CLCW is the collection of the Leadership Conference of Women Religious; CMAS is the collection of Sister Rose Eileen Masterman, CSC; CCPC is the collection of the Consortium Perfectae Caritatis; CARW is the collection of the National Assembly of Religious Women. The box number in the collection is cited first, then the folder number.

Preface

1. Information on orders found in: Eleace King, IHM, ed. *CARA Formation Directory for Men and Women Religious 1994-1995* (Washington: CARA/ Georgetown University, 1993).

Chapter one

1. *Our Sunday Visitor*, Oct. 25, 1992, p. 3, as quoted from Oct. 3, 1992, teleconference on the "Future of Relgious Orders in the United States."
2. *LCWR Occasional Papers*, Spring 1994, p. 21.

Chapter two

1. *Catholic World*, June 1964, p. 144.
2. Elizabeth Kolmer, ASC, *Religious Women in the United States* (Wilmington, Del.: Michael Glazier, Inc., 1984), p. 35.
3. Abbé Gaston Courtois, ed., *The States of Perfection* (Westminster, Md.: The Newman Press, 1961), p. 154.
4. Ibid., pp. 216, 218.
5. Ibid., p. 349.
6. *Review for Religious*, Nov. 1954, p. 298.
7. *Jubilee*, Apr. 1967, p. 35.
8. *Liguorian*, Feb. 1976, pp. 39-43.

9. Mother Mary Florence, SL, ed., *Religious Life in the Church Today* (Notre Dame, Ind.: University of Notre Dame Press, 1962), p. 222.

10. *Review for Religious*, Nov. 1961, p. 453.

11. Notice from California Fire Marshal's Office, Dec. 12, 1962, Records of the Leadership Conference of Women Religious (hereafter cited as CLCW), box 1, folder 17 (hereafter cited as 1/17), Archives of the University of Notre Dame (hereafter cited as UNDA).

12. *Sister Formation Bulletin*, Autumn 1966, p. 2.

13. Courtois, op. cit., p. 199.

14. Ibid, p. 218, footnote 8.

15. Ibid., p. 291.

16. Telephone interview with author, Nov. 27, 1995.

17. *Catholic Parent*, Jan./Feb. 1995, p. 15.

18. Unless otherwise indicated, all such statistics are from the appropriate year of the *Official Catholic Directory* (New Providence, N.J.: P.J. Kenedy & Sons in association with R.R. Bowker, a Reed Reference Publishing Co.).

19. *America*, Apr. 27, 1957, p. 122.

20. George Stewart, *Marvels of Charity* (Huntington, Ind.: Our Sunday Visitor Publishing Division, Our Sunday Visitor, Inc., 1994).

21. *The Priest*, Feb. 1957, pp. 125-130.

22. See Pope John Paul II, *Vita Consecrata*, in *Origins*, Apr. 4, 1996.

23. *Our Sunday Visitor,* May 7, 1995, p. 5.

24. Christopher J. Kauffman, *Ministry and Meaning: A Religious History of Catholic Health Care in the United States* (New York: The Crossroad Publishing Co., 1995), p. 273.

25. Jules Archer, *The Incredible Sixties: The Stormy Years That Changed America* (San Diego: Harcourt Brace Joanovich, 1986).

26. *Passionist*, Vol. 27 (1994), p. 83.

27. Christina Hoff Sommers, *Who Stole Feminism? How Women Have Betrayed Women* (New York: Simon & Schuster, 1994).

28. Mother M. Alcuin, OSF, National Executive Chairman CMSW, to Regional Chairmen, Sept. 12, 1957, CLCW 158/13, UNDA.

29. Sister Andree Fries, CPPS,"Transformative Leadership—Key to Viability," Aug. 26, 1995, address to joint CMSM/LCWR Assembly, p. 3.

30. Felician A. Foy, OFM, ed., *1966 National Catholic Almanac* (Paterson, N.J.: St. Anthony's Guild, 1966), p. 535.

31. Felician A. Foy, OFM, and Rose M. Avato, eds., *1996 Catholic Almanac* (Huntington, Ind.: Our Sunday Visitor Publishing Division, Our Sunday Visitor, Inc., 1995), p. 536.

32. *Modern Healthcare*, Aug. 8, 1994, pp. 80-81.

33. *Our Sunday Visitor*, Nov. 20, 1994, p. 21.

34. See Pope John Paul II, *Vita Consecrata*, in *Origins*, Apr. 4, 1996.

Chapter three

1. *Homeletic and Pastoral Review*, Dec. 1984, p. 21.
2. *Review for Religious*, Jan./Feb. 1994, p. 142.
3. Ibid.
4. "Remarks of Reverend Bernard E. Ransing, CSC," executive committee meeting, CMSW, Chicago, Ill., Jan. 22-24, 1965, CLCW 2/23, UNDA.
5. *Proceedings for the Institute for Local Superiors 1967* (Notre Dame, Ind.: University of Notre Dame Press, 1968), pp. 23-24.
6. Ibid., pp. 31-32.
7. National Assembly of Women Religious press release, undated, titled "Re: American Religious — Sacred Congregation," Records of the National Assembly of Women Religious/National Assembly of Religious Women (Hereafter cited as CARW) 10/14, UNDA.
8. Sandra M. Schneiders, IHM, "Towards a Theology of Religious Obedience," in Lora Quinonez, CDP, ed., *Starting Points* (Washington, D.C.: Leadership Conference of Women Religious, 1980), p. 73.
9. Archbishop Augustine Mayer, Jan. 11, 1972, Records of the Consortium Perfectae Caritatis (hereafter cited as CCPC), 5/41, UNDA.
10. See *Review for Religious*, July 1970, p. 587 and other "Questions and Answers" sections in the *Review* during the 1960s and 1970s.
11. Kolmer, op. cit., p. 79.
12. Ibid., p. 53.
13. Archbishop Augustine Mayer at Oct. 18, 1973, meeting of provincial superiors, CCPC 5/38, UNDA.
14. Helen Rose Fuchs Ebaugh, *Out of the Cloister* (Austin: University of Texas Press, 1977), p. 37.
15. CMSW *Proceedings of the Annual Assembly*, 1967 (Washington: Conference of Major Religious Superiors of Women's Institutes of the United States of America, 1968) p. 150.
16. Brother Bernard M. Ryan, A Critique of *Experience in Community: Should Religious Life Survive?*, Papers of Sister Rose Eileen Masterman, CSC (hereafter cited as CMAS), 4/1, UNDA.
17. Administrative Board of the Consortium Perfectae Caritatis to the Congregation for Religious regarding topics for the Oct. 23, 1972, plenary assembly in Rome, CMAS 2/11, UNDA.
18. Joseph M. Becker, SJ, *The Re-Formed Jesuits* (San Francisco: Ignatius Press, 1992), p. 72.
19. "Unity in Diversity," Interim Statement of Renewal of Franciscan Sisters of Perpetual Adoration, St. Rose Convent, LaCrosse, Wisc., CLCW 172, UNDA.
20. Report on the Medical Missionary Sisters' Sixth General and Special Chapter, Nov. 15, 1967, CLCW 158/19, UNDA.
21. Proceedings of the General Chapter 1971 Franciscan Sisters of the Poor, Brooklyn, N.Y., CLCW 172, UNDA.

22. *National Catholic Reporter*, July 9, 1969, pp. 1, 8.
23. Results of Detroit Province Government Survey, undated, CMAS 2/8, UNDA.
24. Joan Chittister, OSB, et al., *Climb Along the Cutting Edge* (New York: Paulist Press, 1977), p. 41.
25. *National Catholic Reporter*, Feb. 18, 1972, p. 5.
26. *Sisters Today*, Oct. 1972, pp. 71-77.
27. *Review for Religious*, Jan. 1973, pp. 114-116.
28. Father Paul Boyle to Sister Mary Luke, July 1, 1966, CLCW 158/20, UNDA.
29. Maureen McCormack, "Uprooting and Rerooting," in Ann Patrick Ware, SL, ed., *Midwives of the Future* (Kansas City: Leaven Press, 1985), p. 100.
30. Cardinal Vagnozzi to Sister Mary Luke, Jan. 12, 1967, CLCW 1/9, UNDA.
31. *Proceedings of Annual Assembly, 1967*, pp. 148-149.
32. Msgr. Joseph T.V. Snee to Sister Mary Luke, July 8, 1966, CLCW 158/20, UNDA.
33. John C. Haughey, SJ, "Where Has Our Search Led Us," delivered at CMSW National Assembly, Sept. 9-13, 1970.

Chapter four

1. NAWR press release, undated, titled: "Re: American Religious — Sacred Congregation," CARW 10/14, UNDA.
2. *Review for Religious*, Mar./Apr. 1994, pp. 306-307.
3. *National Catholic Reporter*, July 16, 1971, p. 3-B.
4. Sandra M. Schneiders, IHM, *New Wine-Skins* (New York: Paulist Press, 1986), p. 23.
5. Leadership Conference of Women Religious, *Widening the Dialogue* (Ottawa: Canadian Religious Conference and Washington: Leadership Conference of Women Religious, 1974), pp. 245-246.
6. Archbishop Augustine Mayer to Dear Reverend Mother, July 10, 1972.
7. "Interview with Cardinal Danielou by Vatican Radio, October 23rd, 1972," CLCW 2/25, UNDA.
8. *Origins*, June 17, 1976, pp. 61-64.
9. *Origins*, July 7, 1983, p. 133.
10. Ibid., pp. 133-142.
11. Ware, op. cit. p. 3.
12. Dorothy Vidulich, "Finding a Founder," in *Midwives of the Future*, p. 170.
13. *New Catholic World*, Jan./Feb. 1988, pp. 25-26.
14. *National Catholic Reporter*, Mar. 2, 1984, p. 17.
15. Lora Ann Quinonez, CDP, and Mary Daniel Turner, SNDdeN, *The Transformation of American Catholic Sisters* (Philadelphia: Temple University Press, 1992), p. 62.
16. Ibid., pp. 86-87.
17. Cardinal Eduardo Pironio to Archbishop John Quinn, Jan. 18, 1984, CLCW 85/9, UNDA.
18. Marie Augusta Neal, SNDdeN, *From Nuns to Sisters* (Mystic, Ct.: Twenty-Third Publications, 1990), p. 89.

19. Margot H. King, ed., *A Leaf From the Great Tree of God* (Toronto, Ontario: Peregrina Publishing Co., 1994), p. 39.
20. *The Homiletic & Pastoral Review*, Dec. 1984, pp. 19-27.
21. *Journal for the Scientific Study of Religion*, 1993, 32 (1), pp. 76-82.
22. Fries, op. cit., p. 4.
23. *Origins*, Mar. 24, 1994, pp. 693-712.
24. *Origins*, Dec. 10, 1992, p. 435.
25. Ibid, p. 444.
26. *Origins*, Apr. 1, 1993, pp. 724-726.
27. Ibid., p. 730.
28. *Origins*, July 15, 1993, p. 124.
29. NCAN newsletter, Jan. 1994, p. 2.
30. *National Catholic Reporter*, Nov. 5, 1993, p. 18.
31. *National Catholic Reporter*, Sept. 9, 1994, p. 5.
32. *Review for Religious*, May/June 1995, pp. 462-466.
33. Catholic News Service, Oct. 4, 1994.
34. *Origins*, Oct. 20, 1994, p. 334.
35. Catholic News Service, Oct. 5, 1994.
36. *Origins*, Oct. 20, 1994, p. 333.
37. Ibid., pp. 331-332.
38. Cardinal John O'Connor, written intervention at World Synod of Bishops, Oct. 27, 1994.
39. *Origins*, Apr. 4, 1996.
40. Undated LCWR news release, circa Apr., 1996.

Chapter five

1. Sister Joan de Lourdes to Dear Sister, May 2, 1970, CLCW 34/33, UNDA.
2. Foy and Avato, op. cit., p. 523.
3. *Origins*, Apr. 4, 1996, p. 698.
4. Sister Merle Nolde to Sister Lora Ann Quinonez, July 18, 1980, CARW 38/37, UNDA.
5. *Proceedings of the Annual Assembly*, 1965 (Washington: Conference of Major Religious Superiors of Women's Institutes of the United States of America, 1966) pp. 19-22.
6. Sister Mary Rose Emmanuella Brennan to Sister Mary Luke Tobin, May 17, 1966, CLCW 158/20, UNDA.
7. *National Catholic Reporter*, Sept. 1, 1965, p. 1.
8. Father Bernard Ransing to Sister Emmanuella, Apr. 23, 1967, CLCW 1/12, UNDA.
9. Cardinal Antoniutti to Mother Omer, Feb. 16, 1968, CLCW 34/07, UNDA.
10. *Proceedings of the Annual Assembly*, 1967, pp. 193-194.
11. *National Catholic Reporter,* Feb. 2, 1973, p. 2.
12. *Proceedings of the Annual Assembly*, 1967, p. 158.
13. Ibid., p. 151.

14. Sister Mary Daniel to CMSW executive committee, Apr. 8, 1968, CLCW 34/09, UNDA.

15. Sister Cecilia Abhold to Sister Mary Daniel, Apr. 13, 1968, CLCW 34/09, UNDA.

16. Mary Luke Tobin, "Doors to the World," in *Midwives of the Future*, p. 185.

17. *Proceedings of the Annual Assembly*, 1968 (Washington: Conference of Major Religious Superiors of Women's Institutes of the United States of America, 1969) p. 87, CLCW 10/14, UNDA.

18. CMSW notes on resolutions from 1968 assembly, dated Oct. 21, 1968, CLCW 1/23, UNDA.

19. Vote cited in Sister Emmanuella memo, Mar. 17, 1969, and cost cited in Sister M. Rose McPhee to CMSW members, July 24, 1969, CLCW 1/24, UNDA

20. Sister Mary Rose McPhee to CMSW members, July 24, 1969, CLCW 1/24, UNDA.

21. Mother Omer to members, Aug. 19, 1969, CLCW 1/24, UNDA.

22. *National Catholic Reporter*, Oct. 1, 1969, p. 8.

23. Quinonez and Turner, op. cit., p. 153.

24. Sister Corita Kemble to Mother Paulita, Sept. 23, 1969, CLCW 5/18, UNDA.

25. Sister Mary Claudia to CMSW members, Oct. 13, 1969, CLCW 5/18, UNDA.

26. Mother Mary Omer to Sister Mary Claudia, Oct. 22, 1969, CLCW 5/18, UNDA.

27. *Ave Maria*, Oct. 25, 1969, p. 2.

28. Sister Mary Claudia to Father Reedy, Oct. 24, 1969, CLCW 158/22, UNDA.

29. Father John Reedy to Sister Mary Claudia, Oct. 27, 1969, CLCW 158/22, UNDA.

30. Members of that task force were: Mercy Sister Maurita Sengelaub, Mercy Sister William Joseph Lydon, Sister Claudia Zeller (conference executive director), Sister of Charity Josephine Marie O'Brien, and Sister Mary Daniel Turner, as related in CMSW letter to membership, July 21, 1971, CLCW 11/4, UNDA.

Chapter six

1. *Review for Religious*, Mar.-Apr. 1990, p. 207.

2. Sister Mary Omer to U.S. Bishops, Apr. 20, 1970, CLCW 10/16, UNDA.

3. Minutes of CMSW national board meeting, Sept. 4, 1971, CLCW 11/1, UNDA.

4. "Summary of Survey of Objectives, Programs, Organization, Administration and Financing, Conference of Major Religious Superiors of Women's Institutes in the U.S.A.," Sept. 19, 1969, pp. 27-28, CLCW 10/15, UNDA.

5. Report of Task Force on Organization and Coordination of CMSW, Apr. 2, 1970, CLCW 10/17, UNDA.

6. Report of meeting of CMSW Task Force on Organization and Coordination with chairmen of all interim committees, Apr. 3, 1970, CLCW 10/18, UNDA.

7. *National Catholic Reporter*, Sept. 18, 1970, p. 4.

8. Ibid.

9. John Haughey, ST, quoted in *The Southern Cross*, Sept. 17, 1970, CLCW 82/ 31, UNDA.
10. Haughey, op. cit.
11. *America,* Sept. 26, 1970, p. 208.
12. Sister Ruth Marion McCullough to Sister Mary Claudia Zeller, Oct. 7, 1970, CLCW 158/21, UNDA.
13. Memo to CMSW Membership, undated, circa Sept. 5, 1970.
14. Several of these individuals supporting the Statement were past or future presidents of the Conference of Major Religious Superiors of Women's Institutes, including: Sister Mary Luke Tobin, (1964-66); Sister Angelita Myerscough, (1970); Sister Thomas Aquinas (Elizabeth) Carroll (1971); Sister Margaret Brennan, (1972); Sister Frances Borgia Rothluebber, (1973); Franciscan Sister Francine Zeller (1974); and Sister of Charity Helen Flaherty (1982). Other prominent names were Sister Mary Daniel Turner, a member of the Sisters' Survey committee and Conference executive director 1972-78; Precious Blood Sister Anthonita Hess, chair of the Conference's East Central Region as well as the Conference's Vocation Committee; Loretto Sister Helen Sanders, president of the Loretto Sisters 1970-78; Anita Caspary, former president of the Immaculate Heart of Mary Sisters of Los Angeles, who in early 1970 had led over three-hundred IHM sisters in requesting dispensation from their vows rather than agree to follow the directives of Rome for renewal; Father Paul Boyle, president of the Conference of Major Superiors of Men 1969-74, a past president of the Canon Law Society of America (1964-65) and canonical advisor to many orders of sisters; Father Francis Gokey of the Society of St. Edmund, executive secretary of the Superiors of Men; and Brother Gabriel Moran, president of the Long Island/New England province of the Christian Brothers, whose 1970 book, *The New Community*, called for dissolution of religious orders.
15. CMSW press release, undated, CLCW 16/3, UNDA.
16. Proposed draft of letter from Sister M. Eucharia Malone to Dear Sister, undated.
17. The other two women Religious attending the liaison meeting were Mercy Sister Inviolata Gallagher and Dominican Sister Leo Vincent Short.
18. Minutes of CMSM/CMSW liaison committee meeting, Nov. 14, 1970, CLCW 6/8, UNDA.
19. CMSW/CMSM Liaison Committee to members of Bishops' Liaison Committee with CMSW/CMSM, Nov. 14, 1970, CLCW 6/8, UNDA.
20. *Searching*, No. 3, CLCW 1/25, UNDA.
21. Report from Chairman of the Liaison Committee with Religious Women to NCCB Administrative Board, Jan. 20, 1971, p. 4, CCPC 5/45, UNDA.
22. Sister Angelita Myerscough to Bishop Joseph Breitenbeck, Sept. 20, 1970, CLCW 84/08, UNDA.
23. CMSW to membership, July 21, 1971, CLCW 11/4, UNDA.
24. Report of the executive director to the national board of CMSW, Jan. 25, 1971, CLCW 2/9, UNDA.

25. Sister Mary Claudia Zeller to Sister Angelita Myerscough, Jan. 2, 1970, CLCW 158/22, UNDA.

26. CMSW memo to members, June 17, 1971, p. 7, CLCW 1/27, UNDA.

27. *Searching,* No. 5, Feb. 1971, p. 6, CLCW 1/28, UNDA.

28. Mother Alice Anita Murphy to Sister Angelita, July 2, 1971, CLCW 10/21, UNDA.

29. CMSW memo to members, June 17, 1971, p. 7, CLCW 1/27, UNDA.

30. *Review for Religious*, Mar.-Apr. 1990, p. 206.

31. Sister Regina Kelly, OP, to members of the CMSW, Jan. 26, 1971, p. 1, CLCW 1/26, UNDA.

32. Sister Eucharia Malone to Sister Angelita, Apr. 20, 1971, CLCW 158/22, UNDA.

33. Sister Claudia Honsberger to Sister Angelita, Apr. 5, 1971, CLCW 10/22, UNDA.

34. Mother Mary Dominic to Sister Angelita, Mar. 22, 1971, CLCW 10/22, UNDA.

35. To Sister Angelita, Mar. 19, 1971, CLCW 10/22, UNDA.

36. Sister Ann Virginia Bowling to members of the CMSW Credentials Committee, Feb. 2, 1971, CLCW 5/2, UNDA.

37. Mother Virgina Janson to Sister Ann Virginia Bowling, Feb. 25, 1971, CLCW 5/1, UNDA.

38. *LCWR 1975 Directory*, CLCW 56/02, UNDA.

39. Sister Ann Virginia Bowling to Mother Virgina Janson, Mar. 3, 1971, CLCW 5/1, UNDA.

40. Bishop Raimondi to Sister Angelita, July 21, 1971, CLCW 56/02, UNDA.

41. Minutes of executive committee meeting, July 21, 1971, CLCW 56/02, UNDA.

42. Report to the U.S. bishops by the NCCB liaison committee with the CMSW, circa Nov. 17, 1971, CLCW 6/21, UNDA.

43. Minutes of CMSW national board meeting, Sept. 4, 1971, CLCW 11/1, UNDA.

44. Presidential address in Official Minutes of Business Meeting No. 1, Sept. 6, 1971, CLCW 11/1, UNDA.

45. Credentials Committee report in Official Minutes of Business Meeting No. 3, Sept. 8, 1971, CLCW 38/20, UNDA.

46. Presidential address in Official Minutes of Business Meeting No. 1, Sept. 6, 1971, CLCW 11/1, UNDA.

47. Undated CMSW press release reporting on 1971 national assembly which ended Sept. 11, 1971, CLCW 11/1, UNDA.

48. Official Minutes of Concluding Business meeting, Sept. 11, 1971, CLCW 38/20, UNDA.

49. Sister Mary Elise Krantz to Cardinal Antoniutti, Sept. 19, 1971, CCPC 5/23, UNDA.

50. Official Minutes of Business Meeting No. 5, Sept. 10, 1971, CLCW 11/1, UNDA.

51. Minutes of CMSW executive committee, Aug. 21, 1971, CLCW 2/24, UNDA.

52. Quinonez and Turner, op. cit., p. 77.

53. *Review for Religious*, Mar./Apr. 1990, p. 207.

54. *Review for Religious*, Mar./Apr. 1993, pp. 166-167.
55. Quinonez and Turner, op. cit., p. 28.
56. *Review for Religious*, Mar./Apr. 1990, p. 207.
57. Sister Thomas Aquinas to LCWR members, Apr. 24, 1972, CMAS 2/10, UNDA.
58. Sister Claudia Honsberger to Sister Thomas Aquinas, May 18, 1972, CMAS 2/10, UNDA
59. Sister Alice Anita Murphy to Sister Thomas Aquinas, May 12, 1972, CMAS 2/11, UNDA.
60. Sister Thomas Aquinas to Sister Alice Anita, May 20, 1972, CMAS 2/11, UNDA.
61. "Minutes of evening briefing," Nov. 18, 1971, appended to "Report of [NCCB] CMSW Liaison Committee," circa Nov. 14-18, 1971, CLCW 6/21, UNDA.

Chapter seven

1. All survey questions quoted in this chapter are taken from the CMSW 1967 "Sisters' Survey," CLCW 86/03, UNDA.
2. Patricia Wittberg, SC, *The Rise and Fall of Catholic Religious Orders* (Albany: State University of New York Press, 1994), p. 215.
3. Quinonez and Turner, op. cit., pp. 43-44.
4. Ibid., p. 49.
5. Elizabeth Carroll, "Reaping the Fruits of Redemption," in *Midwives of the Future*, p. 64.
6. Neal, *From Nuns to Sisters*, pp. 55-56.
7. Ibid.
8. *Proceedings of the Annual Assembly*, 1967, p. 194.
9. Minutes of the meeting of the Research and Study Project on Religious Life, Sept. 25, 1965, CLCW 86/05, UNDA.
10. *Review of Religious Research*, Fall 1970, pp. 5-6.
11. Eugene E. Grollmes, SJ, ed., *Vows But No Walls* (St. Louis: B. Herder Book Co., 1967), p. 170.
12. Sister M. Charles Borromeo Muckenhirn, CSC, ed., *The Changing Sister* (Notre Dame, Ind.: Fides Publishers, Inc., 1965), p. 17.
13. Ibid, pp. 79-80.
14. Ibid, p. 169.
15. Ibid, p. 206.
16. Ibid, pp. 226-228.
17. Ibid, p. 260.
18. Ibid, p. 294.
19. Ibid, p. 319.
20. Father Bernard Ransing to Sister Emmanuella, Apr. 23, 1967, CLCW 1/12, UNDA.
21. Sister Marie Augusta to Mothers, May 2, 1967, CLCW 86/02, UNDA.
22. Sister Marie Augusta to Sister Mary Luke, May 2, 1967, CLCW 86/02, UNDA.

23. Sister Mary Luke to Sister Marie Augusta, May 10, 1967, CLCW 86/02, UNDA.
24. Father Bernard Ransing to Sister Emmanuella, June 4, 1967, CLCW 1/12, UNDA.
25. Kolmer, op. cit., p. 42.
26. *Proceedings of the Annual Assembly*, 1967, p. 193.
27. Ibid., p. 23.
28. Ibid., pp. 24-25.
29. Ibid, pp. 23-24.
30. Ibid, pp. 22-23.
31. "Memo for Congregation for Religious on Sisters' Survey, June, 1969," pp. 1-2, CLCW 10/15, UNDA.
32. *Proceedings of the Annual Assembly*, 1967, pp. 22-23.
33. *Review of Religious Research*, Spring 1971, pp. 158-159.
34. "Memo for Congregation for Religious on Sisters' Survey, June, 1969," pp. 2-4, CLCW 10/15, UNDA.
35. *Renewal Through Community and Experimentation* (n.p., Canon Law Society of America: 1968), pp. 151-152.
36. Gene Burns, *The Frontiers of Catholicism* (Berkeley and Los Angeles: University of California Press, 1992), p. 147.
37. According to the report of the Research Committee on Religious Life given by Sister Mary Daniel Turner, *Proceedings of the Annual Assembly, 1967*, pp. 193-194.
38. Sister Mary Claudia to Sister Marie Augusta, Oct. 17, 1969, CLCW 158/19, UNDA.
39. *Sister Formation Bulletin*, Autumn 1968, p. 7.
40. *Review for Religious*, Mar./Apr. 1991, p. 179.
41. *Studia Canonica*, Vol. 26, 1992, pp. 336-337.
42. Marie Augusta Neal, "The Church, Women and Society," lecture delivered Apr. 4, 1990 (Colchester, Vt.: Saint Michael's College, 1990).
43. LCWR 1995 Conference Report, "Transforming Leadership for the New Millennium," pp. 4-5.
44. Telephone interview with author, Mar. 13, 1995.
45. For a detailed description, analysis, and personal experience of enneagram, see Mitch Pacwa, SJ, *Catholics and the New Age* (Ann Arbor, Mich.: Servant Publications, 1992).
46. *National Catholic Reporter*, Jan. 26, 1996, p. 21.
47. Pacwa, op. cit., p. 19.
48. Albert DiIanni, SM, *Religious Life As Adventure* (Staten Island, N.Y.: Alba House, 1994), pp. 72-73.

Chapter eight

1. Quinonez and Turner, op. cit., p. 11.
2. Sister Maria Assunta Werner, CSC, *Madeleva* (Notre Dame, Ind.: Congregation of the Sisters of the Holy Cross, 1993), p. 158.

Notes to Chapters Seven and Eight

3. Sister Mary Immaculate Creek, CSC, *A Panorama: 1844-1977 Saint Mary's College Notre Dame, Indiana* (Notre Dame, Ind.: Saint Mary's College, 1977), pp. 94-100.
4. *Sister Formation Bulletin*, Vol. XVIII, No. 4, Summer 1972, p. 4.
5. Creek, op. cit., p. 94-100.
6. *Sister Formation Bulletin*, Autumn 1958, p. 13.
7. *The Sign*, Mar. 1963, pp. 45-46.
8. *National Catholic Reporter*, Aug. 14, 1968, p. 1.
9. Ibid., p. 8.
10. Philip Gleason, *Contending With Modernity* (New York: Oxford University Press, 1995), p. 234.
11. *Time*, July 17, 1964, p. 43.
12. *Catholic Historical Review*, July 1993, p. 485.
13. *Sister Formation Bulletin*, Autumn 1966, p. 9.
14. Ibid.
15. *Sister Formation Bulletin*, Summer 1967, p. 13.
16. Father James W. Richardson to Sister Joan Bland, Sept. 11, 1967, CLCW 34/25, UNDA.
17. Sister Emmanuella to Sister Mary Audrey, Sept. 18, 1967, CMSW 34/25, UNDA.
18. *Sister Formation Bulletin*, Summer 1964, p. 35.
19. *U.S. Catholic Historian*, Winter 1988, p. 65.
20. Marjorie Noterman Beane, *From Framework to Freedom* (Lanham, Md.: University Press of America, Inc., 1993), p. 84.
21. Ibid., pp. 85-86.
22. Archbishop Augustine Mayer, OSB, to Most Reverend Aloyisius Wycislo, Apr. 9, 1981, CCPC 1/33, UNDA.
23. *Sister Formation Bulletin*, Spring 1964, p. 5, and Winter 1962-63, p. 11.
24. *America*, Jan. 9, 1971, p. 13.
25. *Sister Formation Bulletin*, Spring 1961, p. 12.
26. Margot H. King, op. cit., pp. 30, 34.
27. Statement of Archbishop Paul Phillippe, OP, to national committee of CMSW and officers of the SFC, Aug. 29, 1963, as recorded in "Restructuring of NSFC," a report on Oct. 16-17 meeting, CLCW 34/16, UNDA.
28. "Sister Formation History," p. 3, CLCW 34/28, UNDA.
29. *Sponsa Regis*, Apr. 1964.
30. Minutes of CMSW Research & Study Project on Religious Life, Sept. 25, 1965, CLCW 86/05, UNDA.
31. *Sister Formation Bulletin*, Winter 1966, p. 24.
32. Matthew Bunson, ed., *Our Sunday Visitor's Encyclopedia of Catholic History* (Huntington, Ind.: Our Sunday Visitor Publishing Division, Our Sunday Visitor, Inc., 1995), p. 814.
33. Cardinal Egidia Vagnozzi to Bishop Karl Alter, Sept. 11, 1961, CLCW 1/9, UNDA.

34. *Sister Formation Bulletin,* Autumn 1966, p. 17.

35. Lillanna Audrey Kopp, "Don't Fence Me In," in *Midwives of the Future,* p. 211.

36. *National Catholic Reporter,* Aug. 13, 1969, p. 1.

37. Report of the CMSW Ad Hoc Committee on the Agenda, Dec. 17, 1970, CLCW 34/28, UNDA.

38. SFC statement, Oct. 1974, in Nov. 1974 *In-formation,* CLCW 35/02, UNDA.

39. *In-formation,* Sept. 1975, CLCW 35/02, UNDA.

40. Mimeographed report concerning a "Brainstorming Session on October 2, 1975," from Futureshop, CLCW 35/03, UNDA.

41. *In-formation,* Lent-Easter, 1978, CLCW 34/34, UNDA.

42. *In-formation,* May 1976, CLCW 35/02, UNDA.

43. Ibid.

Chapter nine

1. Joan Chittister, OSB, *The Fire in These Ashes* (Kansas City: Sheed & Ward, 1995), p. 34.

2. Maureen Fiedler, "Riding the City Bus From Pittsburgh," in *Midwives of the Future,* p. 47.

3. Ibid., pp. 42-43.

4. Janet K. Ruffing, RSM, "Leadership a New Way: If Christ Is Growing in Us," in David L. Fleming, SJ, and Elizabeth McDonough, OP, eds., *The Church and Consecrated Life* (St. Louis: Review for Religious, 1996), p. 199.

5. Neal, *From Nuns to Sisters,* p. 47.

6. Helen Sanders, SL, *More Than A Renewal* (Nerinx, Ky.: Sisters of Loretto, 1982), p. 325.

7. Sister Rose Eileen Masterman to Rev. Barnabas Mary Ahern, CP, Mar. 12, 1974, CMAS, 2/23, UNDA.

8. To the Members of the General Chapter, 1977, CCPC 7/32, UNDA.

9. Unsigned letter to Sister Rose Eileen Masterman, Nov. 15, 1980, CMAS 3/33, UNDA.

10. Elizabeth Carroll, in *Midwives of the Future,* p. 63.

11. *Review for Religious,* Nov./Dec. 1994, pp. 923-924.

12. *Review for Religious,* Oct. 1991, pp. 775-780.

13. *Review for Religious,* Jan./Feb. 1994, p. 124.

14. *Review for Religious,* July/Aug. 1987, pp. 620-624.

15. *Review for Religious,* July/Aug. 1991, p. 561.

16. Fries, op. cit.

17. *Origins,* Apr. 4, 1996, p. 797.

18. *Review for Religious,* Mar./Apr. 1985, p. 262.

19. *Origins,* Sept. 24, 1992, p. 261.

20. *Trans-Sister* Newsletter, Nov. 1970, Vol. 4, No. 2, CMAS 2/6, UNDA.

21. Sanders, op. cit., p. 229.

22. Jesus Torres, CMF, to Sister Mary Ann Coyle, SL, Nov. 11, 1995.

23. *Cross and Crown,* Sept. 1970, pp. 298-299.

24. David O'Connor, ST, *Witness and Service* (New York: Paulist Press, 1990), p. 46.

Chapter ten

1. *Sisters Today,* Jan. 1993, p. 46.
2. *Review for Religious,* Sept./Oct. 1987, pp. 669-670.
3. Joan D. Chittister, "No Time for Tying Cats," in *Midwives of the Future,* p. 17.
4. See Patricia Wittberg, SC, "Outward Orientation in Declining Organizations," in *Claiming Our Truth.*
5. *Liguorian,* Sept. 1974, pp. 46-47.
6. *Our Sunday Visitor,* Apr. 20, 1980, pp. 6-7.
7. Margaret Ellen Traxler, "Gread [sic] Tide of Returning," in *Midwives of the Future,* p. 136.
8. *Review for Religious,* May/June 1988, p. 399.
9. *Health Progress,* Dec. 1986, pp. 72-74.
10. *Origins,* Sept. 24, 1992, p. 264.
11. *The Way Supplement,* Summer 1988, p. 64.
12. Dorothy Vidulich, op. cit., p. 166.
13. Quinonez, *Starting Points,* p. 27.
14. *The Jurist,*Vol. L, 1990, p. 40.
15. Chittister, in *Midwives of the Future,* p. 8.
16. *The Way Supplement,* Summer 1988, p. 68.
17. *Origins,* Mar. 24, 1994, pp. 693-712.
18. Mary Collins, OSB, "Is the Eucharist Still a Source of Meaning for Women?" in Paul J. Philibert, OP, ed., *Living in the Meantime* (New York: Paulist Press, 1994), pp. 186, 189.
19. Margot H. King, op. cit., p. 89.
20. Mary Jo Leddy, *Reweaving Religious Life* (Mystic, Conn.: Twenty-Third Publications, 1990), p. 97.
21. *Origins,* Apr. 4, 1996, p. 712.
22. *Origins,* Mar. 24, 1994, p. 699.
23. Ibid., pp. 705-706.
24. Marie Augusta Neal, SNDdeN, *Catholic Sisters in Transition* (Wilmington, Del.: Michael Glazier, 1984), p. 54.
25. "Patterns in Authority and Obedience," Leadership Conference of Women Religious, May 15, 1978, p. 7.
26. Ibid., p. 12.
27. *Origins,* Sept. 24, 1992, p. 271.
28. Ibid.
29. Schneiders, op. cit., p. 190.
30. *Origins,* Sept. 24, 1992, p. 271.
31. Ibid., p. 270.
32. *Sisters Today,* Jan. 1993, p. 43.

33. Burns, op. cit., p. 143.
34. Marcelle Bernstein, *The Nuns* (Philadelphia: Lippincott, 1976), pp. 265-266.
35. *Studia Canonica*, Vol. 26 (1992), p. 325.
36. *National Catholic Reporter,* Feb. 18, 1972, p. 5.
37. Cardinal Antoniutti to Bishop Leo Pursley, Feb. 5, 1972, CCPC 5/47, UNDA.
38. Sister M. Thomas Aquinas to "My dear sisters," Feb. 21, 1972, CCPC 5/41, UNDA.
39. *The Catholic Mind*, Oct. 1972, pp. 34-35.
40. Bishop Leo Pursley to Cardinal John Wright, Feb. 8, 1972, CCPC 5/47, UNDA.
41. *Review for Religious*, Jan. 1979, p. 54.
42. Archbishop Jean Jadot to Most Reverend Joseph L. Bernardin, Feb. 28, 1976, CCPC 5/37, UNDA.
43. Rev. Msgr. William J. Awalt to Sister Rose Eileen Masterman, CSC, Sept. 19, 1979, CMAS 3/30, UNDA.
44. *National Catholic Reporter,* July 29, 1983, pp. 1, 8.
45. Minutes of the Meeting of the Bishops' Liaison Committee and CMSW Committee for liaison with the bishops, Apr. 25, 1971, and copy of the "Points submitted by various bishops for the consideration of the CMSW. Presented to the representatives of the CMSW by the NCCB Liaison Committee, Apr. 25, 1971 in Detroit." CLCW 6/18, UNDA.
46. Sister Angelita Myerscough, ASC, to Most Reverend James J. Hogan, Apr. 28, 1971, CLCW 6/18, UNDA.
47. Sister Angelita Myerscough, ASC, to Members of the National Board and CMSW Committee for Liaison with Bishops, Apr. 28, 1971, CLCW 6/18, UNDA.
48. "Report of [NCCB] CMSW Liaison Committee," circa Nov. 14-18, 1971, CLCW 6/21, UNDA.
49. Bishop James J. Hogan to Sister Mary Daniel Turner, SNDdeN, June 4, 1973, CMAS 2/11, UNDA.

Chapter eleven

1. *Newsweek*, Feb. 16, 1970, p. 34.
2. *Newsweek*, Sept. 8, 1969, p. 80.
3. Ibid.
4. Sarah Bentley Doely, ed., *Women's Liberation and the Church* (New York: Association Press, 1970), p. 71.
5. 1967 Chapter Decrees of Immaculate Heart of Mary Sisters of Los Angeles, CLCW 34/07, UNDA.
6. *National Catholic Reporter*, Mar. 27, 1968, p. 12.
7. *National Catholic Reporter*, June 30, 1995, p. 19.
8. *National Catholic Reporter*, Nov. 15, 1967, p. 1.
9. Ibid.
10. *National Catholic Reporter*, Jan. 31, 1968, p. 10.
11. *National Catholic Reporter*, Mar. 13, 1968, p. 1.

12. *National Catholic Reporter*, Mar. 27, 1968, p. 1.

13. *Commonweal*, Apr. 5, 1968, p. 63.

14. *Newsweek*, Sept. 8, 1969, p. 80.

15. *Ave Maria*, Feb. 3, 1968, p. 4.

16. *Commonweal*, Apr. 5, 1968, pp. 60, 63.

17. *America,* Oct. 25, 1969, pp. 349-350.

18. Mother Thomas Aquinas Carroll to Mother Mary Omer, Feb. 12, 1968, CLCW 34/07, UNDA.

19. Mother Mary Omer to Executive Committee, Feb. 29, 1968, CLCW 34/07, UNDA.

20. Sister Thomas Aquinas to Pope Paul VI, Mar. 19, 1968, CLCW 34/07, UNDA.

21. Sister Rose Emmanuella and Father Boniface Wittenbrink to Bishop Luigi Raimondi, Mar. 19, 1968, CLCW 1/8, UNDA.

22. National Catholic News Service, Feb. 28, 1968, CLCW 34/07, UNDA.

23. *National Catholic Reporter*, Mar. 27, 1968, p. 1.

24. *National Catholic Reporter*, Mar. 20, 1968, p. 1.

25. Bishop Luigi Raimondi, Apr. 4, 1968, as enclosure to CMSW members from Mother Omer, Apr. 15, 1968, CLCW 1/8, UNDA.

26. *National Catholic Reporter*, June 19, 1968, p. 3.

27. *Newsweek*, Sept. 8, 1969, pp. 80-81.

28. Sister Rosalie Murphy to CMSW members, Sept. 26, 1969, CLCW 34/07, UNDA.

29. *National Catholic Reporter*, Apr. 9, 1971, p. 8.

30. *National Catholic Reporter*, June 6, 1995, p. 19.

31. *Proceedings of the Thirty-First AnnualConvention 1969*, Canon Law Society of America, 1970, pp. 125-127.

32. Ibid., pp. 123-126.

33. Address of Father Donald N. Weber to School Sisters of St. Francis General Chapter Session, Aug. 26, 1969, CMAS 2/9, UNDA.

34. To whom it may concern from Mother M. Clemens, Nov. 24, 1970, CCPC 7/41, UNDA.

35. *National Catholic Reporter*, Sept. 25, 1970, p. 3.

36. Ibid.

37. Letter to Task Force of the General Legislative Assembly, and to each member of the Congregation of the School Sisters of Saint Francis from The Representative Group, Oct. 22, 1972, CCPC 7/44, UNDA.

38. *Review for Religious*, Sept./Oct. 1994, p. 789.

Chapter twelve

1. *LCWR 1993 Conference Report*, p. 9.

2. *Origins*, July 7, 1983, pp. 131-132.

3. Ibid., p. 133.

4. *Origins*, Sept. 1, 1983, pp. 200-204.

5. NETWORK press release, May 15, 1983, CARW 4/47, UNDA.

6. Joint NARW and NCAN press release, May 13, 1983, CARW 4/47, UNDA.
7. *Ms.*, Sept. 1983, p. 102.
8. Ibid., p. 56.
9. *Hospital Progress*, Sept. 1983, pp. 20-21.
10. *Origins*, Sept. 8, 1983, p. 220.
11. *Hospital Progress*, Sept. 1983, p. 20.
12. Quinonez and Turner, op. cit., pp. 86-87.
13. Ibid., pp. 62-63.
14. *National Catholic Reporter*, Sept. 26, 1983, p. 6.
15. *National Catholic Register*, Oct. 9, 1983, p. 1.
16. Ware, op. cit., p. vii.
17. *Origins*, Dec. 1, 1983, pp. 430-431.
18. *Review for Religious*, Mar./Apr. 1984, pp. 161-169.
19. "Report of Archbishop John R. Quinn, Pontifical Delegate, on the Meeting of the Bishops of the United States and Related Matters Concerning Religious Life in the United States," Dec. 21, 1983, CLCW 85/9, UNDA.
20. *Newsweek*, Mar. 19, 1984, p. 100.
21. Robert J. Daly, SJ, et al, eds., *Religious Life in the American Church* (New York: Paulist Press, 1984), pp. 152-153.
22. Ibid., pp. 173-174.
23. Ibid., p. 300.
24. The administrative board of Consortium Perfectae Caritatis to Most Reverend John R. Quinn and the National Conference of Catholic Bishops, Sept. 10, 1984, CCPC 2/14, UNDA.
25. Ibid.
26. *New York Times*, Oct. 7, 1984, p. E-7.
27. The women Religious whose names appeared on the Oct. 7, 1984, *New York Times* Catholic statement on pluralism and abortion were: Loretto Sisters Mary Ann Cunningham, Mary Louise Denny, Maureen Fiedler, Pat Kenoyer, Ann Patrick Ware, and Virginia Williams; Sisters of Notre Dame de Namur Barbara Ferraro and Patricia Hussey; School Sisters of Notre Dame Jeannine Gramick and Margaret Ellen Traxler; Dominican Sisters Kathleen Hebbeler, Donna Quinn, Ellen Shanahan, and Marjorie Tuite; Sisters of Charity Roseann Mazzeo, Margaret Nulty, Margaret A. O'Neill, and Marilyn Thie; Sister of St. Joseph Judith Vaughan; Mercy Sister Margaret A. Farley;Ann Carr, a Sister of Charity of the Blessed Virgin Mary; Religious Sister of Charity Mary J. Byles; Maryknoll Sister Rose Dominic Trapasso; and Kathryn Bissell and Caridad Inda, Sisters of the Humility of Mary.
28. See Barbara Ferraro and Patricia Hussey, *No Turning Back* (New York: Ivy Books, 1992).
29. *Origins*, Nov. 29, 1984, p. 392.
30. Ibid., p. 393.
31. Rev. Thomas Dubay, SM, to Most Reverend John R. Quinn, Aug. 18, 1984.
32. As read by Archbishop John Whealon in presentation to Oct. 13, 1984, meet-

ing of the Consortium Perfectae Caritatis, entitled "Religious Life as Unchanging,"CCPC, 2/16, UNDA.

33. John W. Padberg, SJ, "The Contexts of Comings and Goings," in *The Crisis in Religious Vocations*, Laurie Felknor, ed. (New York: Paulist Press, 1989), pp. 26-29.

34. Mary An Donovan, SC, "A More Limited Witness: An Historical Theologian Looks at the Signposts," in *The Crisis in Religious Vocations*, pp. 87-90, 97.

35. Mary Ewens, OP, "The Vocation Decline of Women Religious: Some Historical Perspectives," in *The Crisis in Religious Vocations*, pp. 179-180.

36. Donna J. Markham, OP, "The Decline of Vocations in the United States: Reflections from a Psychological Perspective," in *The Crisis in Religious Vocations*, p. 195.

37. Rose McDermott, SSJ, "A Canonical Perspective on the Departures from Religious Life," in *The Crisis in Religious Vocations*, pp. 225-226.

38. *Origins*, Dec. 4, 1986, pp. 467-470.

39. *LCWR 1993 Conference Report*, p. 9.

40. *Origins*, Mar. 23, 1989, pp. 691-692.

41. *Origins*, Apr. 13, 1989, pp. 745-748.

Chapter thirteen

1. *National Catholic Reporter*, Aug. 13, 1969, p. 2.

2. *Origins*, Apr. 1, 1993, p. 730.

3. Quinonez and Turner, op. cit., pp. 101-102.

4. *National Catholic Reporter*, Sept. 29, 1972, p. 21.

5. Burns, op. cit., Note 130, p. 261.

6. Quinonez and Turner, op. cit., p. 99.

7. Ibid., p. 57.

8. *National Catholic Reporter*, Sept. 13, 1974, p. 1.

9. Quinonez and Turner, p. 100.

10. Ibid., p. 101.

11. Quinonez, *Starting Points*, p. ii.

12. Nadine Foley, OP, ed., *Claiming Our Truth* (Washington: Leadership Conference of Women Religious, 1988), p. 2.

13. Quinonez and Turner, op. cit., p. 60.

14. *Origins*, Nov. 3, 1977, pp. 315-317.

15. Sister Mary Daniel Turner to LCWR members, with enclosed documentation, Nov. 11, 1977, CMAS 2/21, UNDA.

16. *National Catholic Register*, Sept. 25, 1977, p. 4.

17. *National Catholic Reporter*, Oct. 19, 1979, pp. 1, 14.

18. Sister Theresa Kane to LCWR members, Feb. 18, 1980, CLCW 36/24, UNDA.

19. *National Catholic Reporter*, Nov. 9, 1979, p. 12.

20. *Washington Post*, Oct. 12, 1979.

21. LCWR memo to members from Sister Lora Ann Quinonez, executive director,

Dec. 28, 1979: Report of Nov. 5, 1979, meeting with the Congregation for Religious, p. 8, CMAS 3/31, UNDA.

22. *National Catholic Reporter*, Aug. 27, 1982, pp. 1, 19.
23. *LCWR 1986 Conference Report*, p. 10.
24. *National Catholic Reporter*, Sept. 7, 1984, pp. 1, 23.
25. See the work of Wittberg, Ebaugh, Eleace King, Nygren, and Ukeritis.
26. *LCWR 1989 Conference Report*, "Goals and Objectives 1989-94," p. 11.
27. 1995 LCWR Assembly Resolution #1.
28. LCWR *Update*, Oct. 1995, p. 1.
29. LCWR *Update*, Dec. 1995.
30. *Time*, Mar. 20, 1972, p. 64.
31. *National Catholic Reporter*, May 1, 1970, p. 1.
32. Newsletter, task force/NAWR, Mar. 1970, Vol. 1, No. 4, CARW 4/50, UNDA.
33. "The National Assembly of Women Religious (NAWR) 1968-1979" History, CARW 10/05, UNDA.
34. A report on the Cleveland meeting of NAWR, Apr. 17-19, 1970, CARW 4/50, UNDA.
35. NAWR membership report as of 1980, CARW 10/32, UNDA.
36. "The National Assembly of Women Religious (NAWR) 1968-1981 history," CARW 10/06, UNDA.
37. NAWR membership report as of 1980, CARW 10/32, UNDA.
38. *National Catholic Reporter*, Aug. 30, 1974, p. 3.
39. *Probe*, Summer 1995, p. 4.
40. *Commonweal*, Sept. 27, 1974, p. 516.
41. NAWR membership report as of 1980, CARW 10/32, UNDA.
42. Sister Maggie Fisher to John W. McDevitt, Oct. 8, 1974, CARW 4/23, UNDA.
43. *National Catholic Reporter*, Aug. 29, 1975, p. 1.
44. Ibid., p. 3.
45. *National Catholic Reporter*, Aug. 27, 1976, p. 1.
46. *Commonweal*, Sept. 10, 1976, p. 578.
47. *Origins*, Sept. 8, 1977, p. 178.
48. *Origins*, Aug. 11, 1977, pp. 136-137.
49. NAWR affirmation, CARW 10/43, UNDA
50. *Origins*, Sept. 8, 1977, p. 178.
51. Sister Lorraine Biebel to Sister Maggie Fisher, Nov. 19, 1977, CARW 10/43, UNDA.
52. Sister Maureen Connelly to Sister Kathleen Keating, Nov. 16, 1977, CARW 10/43, UNDA.
53. Sister Martha Gleason, OSU, to Sister Kathleen Keating, Sept. 21, 1977, CARW 10/43, UNDA.
54. Sister Kathleen Cooney, OSU, to Sister Kathleen Keating, Jan. 30, 1978, CARW 10/43, UNDA.
55. NAWR membership report as of 1980, CARW 10/32, UNDA.
56. Ibid.

57. *Probe*, Summer 1995, p. 8.
58. Sister Hope Steffens, OP, to Sister Kathleen Keating, Mar. 14, 1978, CARW 10/43, UNDA.
59. Sister Merle Nolde to Sister Virginia Ann Driscoll, Apr. 28, 1980, CARW 4/13, UNDA.
60. Sister Merle Nolde to Sandra Ardoyno, SL, Sept. 29, 1981, CARW 4/13, UNDA.
61. Sister Maggie Fisher, RSCJ, to Sister Elizabeth Dyer, May 11, 1978, CARW 4/13, UNDA.
62. Sister Marguerite Ternus to National Assembly of Women Religious, Feb. 27, 1980, CARW 4/07, UNDA.
63. *National Catholic Reporter*, Aug. 29, 1980, p. 3.
64. *Probe*, Summer 1995, p. 9.
65. Ibid., p. 3.
66. *National Catholic Register*, Aug. 26, 1984, p.1.
67. *New York Times*, Oct. 7, 1984, p. E7.
68. *New York Times,* Mar. 2, 1986, p. 24E.
69. *Probe*, Summer 1995, p. 11.
70. Ibid., p. 12.
71. *New York Times*, May 1, 1993, p. 10.
72. *Commonweal*, June 4, 1993, p. 7.
73. Ibid., p. 6.
74. *Probe*, Winter 1995, p. 3.
75. *Probe*, Summer, 1995, p. 12.
76. *If Anyone Can, NCAN* (Chicago: National Coalition of American Nuns, 1989), p. ii.
77. *National Catholic Reporter*, Aug. 13, 1969.
78. *The Catholic Voice*, Mar. 4, 1970, CLCW 27/9, UNDA.
79. NCAN News, Vol. 6, No. 2, undated, circa 1975, CLCW 27/8, UNDA.
80. NCAN reprint, "A Backward Glance: Twelve Years in Remembering," insert in Dec. 1981 NCAN News, CARW 39/40, UNDA.
81. NCAN Newsletter, Feb. 1, 1976, CLCW 27/8, UNDA.
82. *If Anyone Can, NCAN*, pp. 29-40.
83. *Ms.*, Sept. 1983, p. 105.
84. *Origins*, Jan. 27, 1983, p. 536.
85. NCAN newsletter, May & June 1986, Vol. 16, No. 4 & 5, CARW 39/42, UNDA
86. *Time*, Jan. 7, 1985, p. 83.
87. NCAN News, Fall 1986, Vol. 17, No. 1, CARW 39/42, UNDA.
88. NCAN newsletter, Jan., 1986, Vol. 16, No. 1, CARW 39/42, UNDA.
89. *If Anyone Can, NCAN*, p. 72.
90. NCAN News, Jan. 1994, p. 1.
91. NCAN News, Oct. 1994.
92. NCAN News, Dec. 1994.
93. Ibid.
94. *National Catholic Reporter*, Sept. 29, 1972, p. 13.

95. Carol Coston, "Open Windows, Open Doors," in *Midwives of the Future*, p. 155.

96. *New York Times Magazine*, Nov. 28, 1976, p. 94.

97. *Network*, Nov./Dec., 1995, p. 16.

98. *National Catholic Reporter*, Dec. 19, 1975, p. 16.

99. *National Catholic Reporter*, Sept. 5, 1975, p. 15.

100. Flyer, Public Endorsements, Ordination Conference, "Women in Future Priesthood Now: A Call For Action," Nov. 28-30, 1975, Detroit, Mich., CLCW 28/12, UNDA.

101. Sister Mary Daniel Turner to Sister Mary Luke Tobin, Aug. 31, 1978, CCPC 2/31, UNDA.

102. *National Catholic Reporter*, Dec. 28, 1984, p. 4.

103. *National Catholic Reporter*, Dec. 1, 1995, p. 10.

104. Ibid., p. 9.

105. Ibid.

106. Ibid., p. 10.

107. *New York Times*, Nov. 14, 1995, p. A17.

108. *National Catholic Reporter*, Dec. 1, 1995, pp. 9-11.

109. *National Catholic Reporter*, Dec. 29, 1995/Jan. 5, 1996, p. 5.

110. *Cross Currents*, Spring 1989, p. 98.

111. Ibid.

112. Ibid., p. 99.

113. *Call to Action News*, Dec. 1995-Jan. 1996, p. 7

114. Ibid., p. 1.

115. From biographical material enclosed in LCWR Aug. 18, 1993, press release.

116. *Origins*, Nov. 4, 1976, p. 324.

117. Ibid. pp. 311-319.

118. *Origins*, May 19, 1977, pp. 757-764.

119. *Churchwatch*, Feb.-Mar., 1991, p. 4.

120. Call to Action Internet homepage, July 27, 1996.

121. Call to Action 1996 National Conference promotional tabloid.

122. Ibid.

123. Call to Action Internet home page, July 29, 1996.

124. *Origins*, June 6, 1996, pp. 36-38.

125. *St. Louis Post Dispatch*, May 25, 1996.

126. *National Catholic Reporter*, May 31, 1996, p. 5.

Chapter fourteen

1. Elizabeth A. Johnson, CSJ, "And Their Eyes Were Opened," address presented to CMSM/LCWR Joint Assembly, Aug. 24, 1995.

2. *America*, Apr. 11, 1970, pp. 388-389.

3. John C. Haughey, SJ, CMSW publication, *Searching*, No. 3, Dec. 1970, CLCW 1/25, UNDA.

4. Haughey, op. cit.

5. Personal interview with author, May 13-14, 1995.
6. "Consortium Perfectae Caritatis," informational reprint on history and purpose of the organization, circa 1979, pp. 1-2, CMAS, 3/28, UNDA.
7. To Mother M. Elise, undated, circa 1971, CCPC 1/07, UNDA.
8. Minutes of CPC administrative council meeting, Apr. 13, 1980, CMAS 3/31, UNDA.
9. *Origins*, Oct. 3, 1985, p. 252.
10. Bishop James J. Hogan to Sister Mary Daniel Turner, SNDdeN, June 4, 1973, CMAS 2/11, UNDA.
11. Bishop William Connare to Sister Rose Eileen Masterman, July 12, 1976, CMAS 2/23, UNDA.
12. Bishop Floyd Begin to Sister Patricia Marie Mulpeters, PBVM, Feb. 25, 1977, CMAS 3/15, UNDA.
13. To Archbishop Augustine Mayer, June 1, 1977, CMAS 3/16, UNDA.
14. Archbishop Augustine Mayer, Aug. 3, 1977, CMAS 3/6, UNDA.
15. Representing the Leadership Conference of Women Religious were members of its executive committee: Sisters Thomas Aquinas (Elizabeth) Carroll, Angelita Myerscough, Joan DeLourdes Leonard, Francis Borgia Rothleubber, and Margaret Brennan. Also attending was the conference executive director, Immaculate Heart of Mary Sister Ann Virginia Bowling. Representing the Consortium board were: Sisters Mary Elise Krantz, Alice Anita Murphy, Mary Claudia Honsberger, Dominican Sister Marie William MacGregor, Little Sister of the Poor Gertrude Elizabeth McGovern, and Sister of Notre Dame Mary Nathan Hess.
16. CPC record of meeting between CPC administrative board and LCWR executive committee, Mar. 15, 1972, CMAS 2/29, UNDA.
17. Representing the Leadership Conference were Sister Francine Zeller, conference president; Sister of Charity Barbara Thomas, vice-president; Sister Mary Daniel Turner, executive director; and Sister Margaret Brennan, conference president 1972-73. The consortium representatives were Sisters Mary Elise, Mary Claudia, Marie William, and Holy Cross Sister Rose Eileen Masterman.
18. Proceedings of combined meeting of Congregation for Religious, LCWR and CPC, Nov. 12-14, 1974, CMAS 3/4, UNDA.
19. Sister Francine Zeller to Sister Mary Elise, Mar. 11, 1975, CMAS 3/7, UNDA.
20. Archbishop Augustine Mayer to Sister Mary Daniel Turner, Apr. 4, 1975, CMAS 3/4, UNDA.
21. Unofficial transcript of Sept. 3, 1975, meeting with Archbishop Byrne and representatives of the CPC and LCWR, O'Hare Airport Hotel, CMAS 3/4, UNDA.
22. *Widening the Dialogue*, pp. 245-246.
23. Consortium Perfectae Caritatis, *"Widening The Dialogue . . .?"* (Huntington, Ind.: Our Sunday Visitor, 1974), p. 1.
24. Archbishop Augustine Mayer to members of CPC administrative council, June 16, 1973, CCPC 1/15, UNDA.

25. Minutes of CPC Administrative Council meeting, Nov. 20, 1973, CCPC 1/15, UNDA.

26. NCAN News, Jan. 1978, CLCW 27/8, UNDA.

27. Minutes of LCWR 1979 assembly, Aug. 28, 1979, CMAS 3/31, UNDA.

28. Quinonez and Turner, op. cit., p. 87.

29. *Religious Life*, Nov. 1983, pp. 3, 11-13.

30. Minutes of the Oct. 9, 1988, CPC administrative board meeting, CCPC 2/04, UNDA.

31. *Origins*, Mar. 23, 1989, pp. 691-692.

32. Ibid., pp. 692-693.

33. *Origins*, Apr. 13, 1989, p. 749.

34. *National Catholic Register*, May 28, 1989, p. 1.

35. Speaking for the Leadership Conference were Sister of Providence Kathleen Popko, president; Mercy Sister Helen Marie Burns, past president; Sister Nadine Foley, president 1988-89; St. Joseph Sister Janet Roesener, executive director; Mercy Sister Doris Gottemoeller, elected president in 1993; and Immaculate Heart of Mary Sister Anne Munley, a member of the Conference's national board who became president in 1996. Representing the consortium were Carmelite Sister Vincent Marie Finnegan, consortium chairman of the board; and Sisters Mary Claudia Honsberger, Mary Elise Krantz, and Mary Gerald Hartney, a Holy Cross Sister who was consortium treasurer. The Institute on Religious Life was represented by Sister Mary Assumpta Long. Sister Mary Bernard Nettle represented the Forum of Major Superiors.

36. "Transcribed Text of the Meeting of the Consortium and the LCWR Dialogue Teams September 8, 1990, Silver Spring, Maryland," p. 28.

37. Ibid., p. 30.

38. As reported in minutes of annual meeting of the CPC administrative board, Apr. 24, 1992, CCPC 2/08, UNDA.

39. Sister Mary Bernard, LSP, to Sister Mary Elise, Jan. 11, 1991.

40. Minutes of CPC administrative board meeting, Apr. 5, 1991, CCPC 2/08, UNDA.

41. As recounted in Oct. 13, 1991, minutes of Consortium Perfectae Caritatis administrative board, CCPC 2/08, UNDA.

42. As reported in minutes of annual meeting of the CPC administrative board, Apr. 24, 1992, CCPC 2/08, UNDA.

43. "The Formation of an Association of Major Superiors of Women Religious," Mission Statement, Initial Draft, Dec. 17, 1991, CCPC 6/66, UNDA.

44. Catholic News Service, July 29, 1992.

45. Paul K. Hennessy, CFC, to "Dear Brother Members of CMSM," June 22, 1992.

46. Quinonez and Turner, op. cit., p. 161.

47. Hennessy, op. cit.

48. Press release, Archdiocese of Washington, June 22, 1992.

49. *Origins*, July 23, 1992, p. 161.

50. Ibid., p. 159.
51. Hennessy, op. cit.
52. Catholic News Service, July 29, 1992.
53. Catholic News Service, Aug. 21, 1992.
54. *Origins*, July 23, 1992, p. 159.
55. Ibid.
56. CMSWR Newsletter, Nov. 1995, p. 2.
57. Ibid.
58. Sister Vincent Marie Finnegan to author, Jan. 10, 1996.

Chapter fifteen

1. *Review for Religious*, Mar./Apr. 1991, p. 173.
2. According to Father Martin Farrell, OSD, director, P.O. Box 499, Fort Covington, NY 12937.
3. Albert DiIanni, SM, *Religious Life as Adventure* (New York: Alba House, 1994), pp. 153-154.
4. Report of the Tri-Conference Retirement Office, presented to the NCCB-USCC spring meeting, Chicago, Ill., June 15-17, 1995.
5. *Our Sunday Visitor*, Dec. 4, 1994, p. 16.
6. *Catholic Transcript*, July 7, 1995, p. 5.
7. *National Catholic Reporter*, Mar. 27, 1986, p. 8.
8. The Sisters of Mercy of Albany, Auburn, Belmont, Brooklyn, Buffalo, Burlingame, Burlington, Cedar Rapids, Erie, Hartford, Merion, Pittsburgh, Plainfield-Watchung, Portland, Rochester, Windham, and the Union, which had nine provinces: Baltimore, Chicago, Cincinnati, Detroit, New York, Omaha, Providence, Saint Louis, and Scranton.
9. Catherine C. Darcy, RSM, *The Institute of the Sisters of Mercy of the Americas* (Lanham, Maryland: University Press of American, Inc., 1993), pp. 170-172.
10. *Wall Street Journal*, May 19, 1986, p. 1.
11. Report of the Tri-Conference Retirement Office, presented to the NCCB-USCC spring meeting, Chicago, Ill., June 15-17, 1995.
12. Helen Rose Fuchs Ebaugh, *Women in the Vanishing Cloister* (New Brunswick, New Jersey: Rutgers University Press, 1993), p. 33.
13. Patricia Wittberg, SC, "Outward Orientation in Declining Organizations," in *Claiming Our Truth*, pp. 92-93.
14. Ibid., p. 95.
15. *National Catholic Reporter*, Feb. 16, 1996, pp. 23-24.
16. Leadership Conference of Women Religious, *1995 Conference Report*, p. 35.
17. *Review for Religious*, Jan.-Feb. 1994, p. 24.
18. *Review for Religious*, Mar.-Apr. 1992, p. 269.
19. *St. Louis Review*, Oct. 20, 1995.
20. Ebaugh, *Women in the Vanishing Cloister*, p. 150.
21. Ibid., p. 132.

22. *Origins*, Sept. 10, 1992, p. 222.
23. *St. Anthony Messenger*, May, 1977, p. 26.
24. *National Catholic Reporter*, May 19, 1989, p. 1.
25. *National Catholic Reporter*, Feb. 18, 1994, p. 14.
26. *National Catholic Reporter*, Sept. 9, 1994, p. 5.
27. Burns, op. cit., p. 131.
28. *Review for Religious*, Jan./Feb., 1992, p. 96.
29. *Origins*, Mar. 21, 1985, p. 653.
30. See *Our Sunday Visitor*, Apr. 26, 1992, pp. 3-4, and Aug. 8, 1993, p. 17.
31. See *Our Sunday Visitor*, July 9, 1995, p. 5.
32. *Origins*, Apr. 4, 1996, pp. 695-696.

Chapter sixteen

1. *Origins*, Apr. 4, 1996, p. 702.
2. Eleace King, op. cit., pp. 2-3, 9.
3. Ibid., pp. 7-10.
4. Ibid., pp. 12-13.
5. Ibid., p. 18.
6. Roger Finke, "An Orderly Return to Tradition," paper presented at the Nov. 1995 annual meeting of the Society for the Scientific Study of Religion.
7. *Origins*, Sept. 24, 1992.
8. "Members of Religious Orders Articulate Models for the Future," Sept. 16, 1992, press release, DePaul University Center for Applied Social Research.
9. "Outstanding Leaders Offer Hope for a Viable Future," Sept. 16, 1992, press release, DePaul University Center for Applied Social Research.
10. "Changes Must Occur So Religious Life Can Continue As Vital Force in the Church and the World," Sept. 16, 1992, press release, DePaul University Center for Applied Social Research.
11. *Origins*, Sept. 24, 1992, p. 265.
12. Members of the FORUS national advisory board were:Patricia Fritz, OSF; Adrian Gaudin, SC; Howard Gray, SJ; Fred Hofheinz; James Jones, OSB; (Bishop) Thomas Kelly, OP; Jeanne Knoerle, SP; Donna Markham, OP; Bette Moslander, CSJ; Basil Pennington, OCSO; Loughlan Sofield, ST; and Barbara Valuckas, SSND, according to David J. Nygren and Miriam D. Ukeritis, *The Future of Religious Orders in the United States* (Westport, Ct.: Praeger, 1993) pp. xv-xvi.
13. From the executive director's message, Conference Report of 1993 LCWR National Assembly, p. 10.
14. *Washington Post*, Sept. 26, 1992, p. G11.
15. *Our Sunday Visitor*, Oct. 25, 1992, p. 3.
16. Sister Janet Ruffing, RSM, "Enkindling the Embers: The Challenge of Current Research on Religious Life," lecture delivered at LCWR annual assembly, Aug. 14-18, 1993.

17. See the cited works of Patricia Wittberg, Roger Finke, and Helen Rose Fuchs Ebaugh.

18. *National Catholic Reporter*, Aug. 18, 1986, p. 20.

19. Sister Mary Cecilia Murray, OP, *Other Waters: A History of the Dominican Sisters of Newburgh, N.Y.* (Old Brookville, N.Y.: Brookville Books, 1993), pp. 287-288.

20. *Review for Religious*, Jan.-Feb., 1994, p. 143.

21. *Our Sunday Visitor*, May 7, 1995, p. 5.

22. *Origins*, Apr. 4, 1996, p. 702.

23. Patricia Wittberg, SC, *Pathways To Re-Creating Religious Communities* (New York/Mahwah, N.J.: Paulist Press, 1996), pp. 199-200.

24. *Origins,* Apr. 4, 1996, p. 691.

25. Ibid., p. 717.

Selected Bibliography

Beane, Marjorie Noterman. *From Framework to Freedom: A History of the Sister Formation Conference,* Lanham, Md.: University Press of America, Inc., 1993.

Becker, Joseph M., S.J. *The Re-Formed Jesuits.* San Francisco: Ignatius Press, 1992. (A history of the changes in Jesuit formation, 1965-1975.)

Bernstein, Marcelle. *The Nuns.* Philadelphia: Lippincott, 1976. (A Jewish journalist explores the life and future of women Religious.)

Burns, Gene. *The Frontiers of Catholicism: The Politics of Ideology in a Liberal World.* Berkeley and Los Angeles: University of California Press, 1992. (A cultural analysis of the Catholic Church in the United States.)

Chittister, Joan, OSB, et al. *Climb Along the Cutting Edge: An Analysis of Change in Religious Life.* New York: Paulist Press, 1977. (How renewal was effected by Benedictine sisters.)

Chittister, Joan, OSB. *The Fire in These Ashes: A Spirituality of Contemporary Religious Life.* Kansas City: Sheed & Ward, 1995.

Consortium Perfectae Caritatis, *"Widening The Dialogue . . . ?"* Huntington, Ind.: Our Sunday Visitor, 1974. (A response to the LCWR book *Widening the Dialogue,* which had criticized the 1971 apostolic exhortation on renewal of religious life, *Evangelica Testificatio.*)

Courtois, Abbé Gaston, ed. *The States of Perfection According to the Teaching of the Church: Papal Documents from Leo XIII to Pius XII.* Westminster, Md.: The Newman Press, 1961.

Creek, Mary Immaculate, CSC. *A Panorama: 1844-1977 Saint Mary's College Notre Dame, Indiana.* Notre Dame, Ind.: Saint Mary's College, 1977.

Darcy, Catherine C., RSM. *The Institute of the Sisters of Mercy of the Americas: The Canonical Development of the Proposed Governance Model.* Lanham, Md.: University Press of American, Inc., 1993.

DiIanni, Albert, SM. *Religious Life As Adventure: Renewal, Refounding or Reform?* Staten Island, N.Y.: Alba House, 1994.

Doely, Sarah Bentley, ed. *Women's Liberation and the Church: The New Demand for Freedom In the Life of the Christian Church.* New York: Association Press, 1970.

Ebaugh, Helen Rose Fuchs. *Out of the Cloister: A Study of Organizational Dilemmas.* Austin: University of Texas Press, 1977.

Ebaugh, Helen Rose Fuchs. *Women in the Vanishing Cloister: Organizational Decline in Catholic Religious Orders in the U.S.* New Brunswick, N.J.: Rutgers University Press, 1993.

Felknor, Laurie, ed. *The Crisis in Religious Vocations: An Inside View.* New York: Paulist Press, 1989. (A collection of essays on religious life by some of the experts consulted by the Quinn Commission.)

Fleming, David L., SJ, and McDonough, Elizabeth, OP, eds. *The Church and Consecrated Life.* St. Louis: *Review for Religious,* 1996. (Articles reprinted from *Review for Religious,* discussing the philosophy of religious life and renewal of religious life since Vatican II.)

Florence, Mother Mary, SL, ed. *Religious Life in the Church Today: Prospect and Retrospect.* Notre Dame, Ind.: University of Notre Dame Press, 1962. (Proceedings of the Women's Section of the Second National Congress of Religious in the United States.)

Foley, Nadine, OP, ed. *Claiming Our Truth: Reflections on Identity.* Washington: Leadership Conference of Women Religious, 1988. (The third book published by the LCWR Contemporary Theology Project.)

Gleason, Philip. *Contending With Modernity: Catholic Higher Education in the Twentieth Century.* New York: Oxford University Press, 1995.

Grollmes, Eugene E., SJ, ed. *Vows But No Walls: An Analysis of Religious Life.* St. Louis: B. Herder Book Co., 1967. (Presentations from the Institute on Religious Life in the Modern World, St. Louis University, 1966.)

Kauffman, Christopher J. *Ministry and Meaning: A Religious History of Catholic Health Care in the United States.* New York: The Crossroad Publishing Co., 1995.

King, Margot H., ed. *A Leaf From the Great Tree of God: Essays in Honour of Ritamary Bradley.* Toronto, Ontario: Peregrina Publishing Co., 1994.

Sisters in Crisis

Kolmer, Elizabeth, ASC. *Religious Women in the United States: A Survey of the Influential Literature From 1950 to 1983.* Wilmington, Del.: Michael Glazier, Inc., 1984.

Leadership Conference of Women Religious. *Widening the Dialogue.* Ottawa: Canadian Religious Conference and Washington: Leadership Conference of Women Religious, 1974. (Critical response by the LCWR to the 1971 apostolic exhortation on the renewal of religious life, *Evangelica Testificatio.*)

Leddy, Mary Jo. *Reweaving Religious Life: Beyond the Liberal Modet.* Mystic, Conn.: Twenty-Third Publications, 1990.

Muckenhirn, Sister M. Charles Borromeo, CSC, ed. *The Changing Sister.* Notre Dame, Ind.: Fides Publishers, Inc., 1965. (Essays on religious life written after the 1964 Grailville meeting by sisters who were consultants for the Sisters' Survey.)

Murray, Mary Cecilia, OP. *Other Waters: A History of the Dominican Sisters of Newburgh, N. Y.* Old Brookville, N.Y.: Brookville Books, 1993.

National Coalition of American Nuns. *If Anyone Can, NCAN: Twenty Years of Speaking Out.* Chicago: National Coalition of American Nuns, 1989. (Selected statements and positions of the NCAN, 1969-1989.)

Neal, Marie Augusta, SNDdeN. *Catholic Sisters in Transition: From the 1960s to the 1980s.* Wilmington, Del.: Michael Glazier, 1984.

Neal, Marie Augusta, SNDdeN. *From Nuns to Sisters: An Expanding Vocation.* Mystic, Ct.: Twenty-Third Publications, 1990.

O'Connor, David F., ST. *Witness and Service: Questions About Religious Life Today.* New York: Paulist Press, 1990. (A canon lawyer examines canonical issues related to religious life.)

Pacwa, Mitch, SJ. *Catholics and the New Age: How Good People Are Being Drawn into Jungian Psychology, the Enneagram, and the Age of Aquarius.* Ann Arbor, Mich.: Servant Pulications, 1992.

Philibert, Paul J., OP, ed. *Living in the Meantime: Concerning the Transformation of Religious Life.* New York: Paulist Press, 1994. (Essays on religious life by prominent men and women Religious.)

Quinonez, Lora Ann, CDP, and Turner, Mary Daniel, SNDdeN. *The Transformation of American Catholic Sisters.* Philadelphia: Temple University Press, 1992. (A history of the LCWR by the two sisters who were executive directors of the conference from 1972 to 1986.)

Quinonez, Lora, CDP, ed. *Starting Points: Six Essays Based on the Experience of U.S. Women Religious.* Washington, D.C.: Leadership Conference of Women

Religious, 1980. (The second book produced by the LCWR Contemporary Theology Project.)

Sanders, Helen, SL. *More Than A Renewal: Loretto Before and After Vatican II 1952-1977.* Nerinx, Ken.: Sisters of Loretto, 1982.

Schneiders, Sandra M., IHM. *New Wine-Skins: Re-imagining Religious Life Today.* New York: Paulist Press, 1986.

Sommers, Christina Hoff. *Who Stole Feminism? How Women Have Betrayed Women.* New York: Simon & Schuster, 1994.

Stewart, George. *Marvels of Charity: History of American Sisters and Nuns.* Huntington, Ind.: Our Sunday Visitor Publishing Division, Our Sunday Visitor, Inc., 1994.

Ware, Ann Patrick, SL, ed. *Midwives of the Future: American Sisters Tell Their Story.* Kansas City: Leaven Press, 1985. (Essays on religious life written in response to the 1983 Vatican document *Essential Elements,* which accompanied the papal letter initiating the Quinn Commission study of religious life.)

Werner, Sister Maria Assunta, CSC. *Madeleva: Sister Mary Madeleva Wolff, CSC, A Pictorial Biography.* Notre Dame, Ind.: Congregation of the Sisters of the Holy Cross, 1993.

Wittberg, Patricia, SC. *Pathways To Re-Creating Religious Communities.* New York/Mahwah, N.J.: Paulist Press, 1996. (A sociologist sister discusses issues involved in refounding religious orders.)

Wittberg, Patricia, SC. *The Rise and Fall of Catholic Religious Orders: A Social Movement Perspective.* Albany: State University of New York Press, 1994.

Index

A

abortion 212, 215, 312, 323
Abzug, Bella 253, 255
Adorers of the Blood of Christ 83
Adrian Dominican Sisters 257
alienation of property 169
Alzamora, Archbishop Augusto Vargas 70
amalgamation 296, 297
American Civil Liberties Union 84
Antoniutti, Cardinal Ildebrando 49, 81, 106, 185, 206, 207, 208
Apostolate 139, 228, 315
apostolate 133, 151, 162-183, 185, 186, 187, 193, 195-196, 198, 206, 207, 209, 213, 222, 227, 231, 239, 269, 280, 282, 294, 297, 307, 312, 315, 319, 322, 323
Archer, Jules 30
Ashe, Sister Kaye OP 259
associate members 158-160

B

Baggio, Cardinal Sebastiano 179
Barrett, Deborah 253
Baum, Father Gregory 99, 274
Baum, Cardinal William 269, 279
Beckman, Mary 246
Beesing, Sister Maria OP 130
Beijing women's conference 242
Benedictine Sister(s) 79, 110, 173
Bernardin, Cardinal Joseph 70, 179, 260
Berrigan, Father Daniel SJ 84, 143
Bevilacqua, Cardinal Anthony 279
Bland, Sister Joan SNDdeN 139
Booz, Allen and Hamilton 48, 83-84, 85, 87, 89, 90, 97
Born, Sister Christine OP 291
Bourg, Father Carroll SJ 82
Bowling, Sister Ann Virginia IHM 100, 101, 104
Boyle, Father Paul CP 48, 49, 79, 80, 82, 93, 95
Bradley, Sister Ritamary CHM 140, 142, 143, 144, 252
Breitenbeck, Bishop Joseph 96
Brennan, Sister Margaret IHM 68, 83, 91, 95, 101, 104, 106, 221, 236
Brennan, Sister Rose Emmanuella SNJM 80, 140, 144
bylaws 89, 90, 91, 94, 97, 98-99, 100, 102-103, 104, 105-106

C

Cacciavillan, Archbishop Agostino 286
Cafferty, Sister Margaret PBVM 125, 211, 231, 241, 255, 260, 302
Call to Action 80, 256, 259-264

Callahan, Father William SJ 148, 256
Camara, Archbishop Helder 236
Cancio, Silvia 258
Candon, Sister Elizabeth RSM 246, 247
Canon Law Society of America 48, 79, 122, 192
Capuchin 95
Carberry, Cardinal John 269, 277, 279
Carr, Sister Anne BVM 256
Carroll, Sister Thomas Aquinas (Elizabeth) RSM 83, 85, 91, 95, 101, 102, 104, 105, 106, 111, 142,155, 178, 189, 191, 275
Casey, Father Thomas J. SJ 161
Caspary, Sister Humiliata (Anita) IHM 61, 82, 111, 142, 184, 185, 187, 190, 191, 207, 245, 252
Catholic Coalition for Gay Civil Rights 253
Catholic Organizations for Renewal 263, 264
Catholic Sisters in Transition: From the 1960s to the 1980s 228
Catholic University 136, 145, 170, 173, 236
Catholics and the New Age 131
Catholics for a Free Choice 223, 241, 253, 254, 323
Center for Applied Research in the Apostolate at Georgetown University (CARA) 228, 315
Center of Concern 245, 259
chapter decree(s) 41, 45, 57, 123, 126, 182, 186, 188, 190, 191, 192, 196
chapter meeting(s) 38, 50, 152-164, 192, 193, 201, 202
Chapter of Faults 21, 41
chastity 71, 113, 114, 120, 176, 198, 232
Chavez, Cesar 245
Chittister, Sister Joan OSB 48, 149, 163, 171, 239, 260, 303
Claiming Our Truth 238
Claydon, Sister Margaret SNDDN 110
Clemens, Sister M. (Mother M.) OSF 202
Climb Along the Cutting Edge 48
CMSW *See* Conference of Major Religious Superiors of Women's
CMSM *See* Conference of Major Superiors of Men
co-members 158-160
Code of Canon Law 38, 40, 41, 50, 60, 62, 63, 75, 77, 79, 165, 187, 213, 214, 219, 253, 313
Collins, Sister M. Emmanuel OSF 144
Collins, Sister Mary OSB 173
Commission on Religious Life and Ministry *See* Tri-Conference Commission
Committee on Religious Life and Ministry 291, 292
Commonweal 188, 246
community 21, 24, 26, 30, 36, 37, 40, 41, 43, 44, 45, 46, 47, 55, 57, 60, 63-65, 66, 67, 71, 73, 82, 84, 100, 109, 113, 114, 115, 116, 118, 120, 121, 122, 125, 126, 128, 129, 134, 139, 140, 142, 150, 152, 153, 158, 160, 162-183, 184-210, 213, 221, 222-223, 224, 227, 232, 244,

community continued 246, 252, 253, 269, 270, 274, 280, 281, 282, 288, 290, 294, 295, 296, 299, 300-301, 302, 305, 306, 307, 310, 312, 315-317, 318, 319, 321, 323, 324, 327
community without walls 139
Concannon, Sister Isabel SSJ 111
Conference of Major Religious Superiors of Women's Institutes (CMSW) 32, 39, 42, 51-52, 53, 76-87, 88-107, 108-112, 118, 122-125, 133, 137, 146, 181, 182, 189, 191, 207, 256, 259, 267, 268 *See also* Leadership Conference of Women Religious
   1965 assembly 79
   1966 assembly 80
   1967 assembly 81
   1968 assembly 122
   1969 assembly 84
   1970 special assembly 89
   1971 assembly 99
   bylaws 88
   credentials 89
   early years 77, 102
   membership 143, 183
   membership requirements 100
   statutes 123
Conference of Major Superiors of Men (CMSM)48, 67, 77, 93, 189, 216, 217, 240, 241, 266, 279, 282, 286, 287, 288, 289, 291, 295
Confraternity of Catholic Clergy 272
Congregation for Religious 19, 20, 21, 39, 41, 43, 49, 51-52, 57, 59-62, 64, 74, 80, 81, 82, 84, 85, 86, 88, 91, 94, 96, 98, 101, 104, 105-106, 107, 117, 120, 121, 137, 142, 143, 146, 160, 170, 171, 173, 174, 176, 177, 180, 185, 187, 188-189, 190-191, 192, 201, 202, 206, 207, 208, 211, 213, 215, 216, 220, 224, 231, 232, 237, 240, 250, 253, 256, 267, 269, 271, 273, 274-276, 278, 279, 280, 286, 287, 288, 289, 294, 306, 314, 323
Congregation of the Humility of Mary 97, 140
Connare, Bishop William 273
Consecrated Life 278
Consortium Perfectae Caritatis 97, 104, 222, 268, 280, 282, 283, 288
constitution(s) 31, 37, 38, 39, 40, 41, 42, 46, 47, 48, 77, 78, 79, 80, 123, 125, 126, 137, 141, 148, 151, 153, 178, 180, 181, 186, 190, 209, 227, 229, 253, 285, 290, 313, 314, 324, 326
Contemporary Theology Project 238
convent(s) 18, 19, 20, 21, 23, 25, 29, 30, 32, 33, 37, 44, 46, 53, 64, 76, 77, 81, 83, 108, 109, 139, 166, 168, 170, 171, 175, 187, 190, 192, 194, 199, 205, 303, 304, 325, 327
   permissions 20
   reform 18
   rules 36

Coogan, Father John E. 29
Cooke, Father Bernard SJ 79, 136
Coston, Sister Carol OP 255, 259
Coughlan, Father David SJ 156
Coulson, William 126, 127186
council documents 36, 51, 53, 85, 110, 111, 112, 125, 148, 271, 326, 327
Council of Major Superiors of Women Religious 235, 286-287, 290-292, 293, 316
Council of Women Religious from the Archdiocese of Omaha 247
Counihan, Sister Bernadette OSF 209
Cousins, Archbishop William 80
Coyle, Sister Mary Ann SL 160
credentials 89, 98, 99,100, 101, 102, 103
Curran, Father Charles 136, 143, 145
custom(s) 19-24
   changes proposed 19

D
Daly, Mary 83
Danielou, Cardinal Jean 58, 269
Daughter(s) of Charity 135, 165, 216
Davidson, James D. 109
Day, Dorothy 245
departures (from orders) 121, 209
Diekmann, Father Godfrey OSB 136
DiIanni, Father Albert SM 131, 294, 303
discipleship of equals 258
Dominic, Sister Mary OP 100
Dominican(s) 100, 124, 126, 129, 130, 138, 143, 147, 213, 218, 229, 231, 250, 254, 255, 257, 259, 280, 287, 291, 296, 320
Dominican Sisters of Hope 296
Dominican Sisters of St. Catherine of Siena 296
Dominican Sisters of the Most Holy Rosary 296
Dominican Sisters of the Sick Poor 296
Donnelly, Sister Dorothy CSJ 148, 252
Donovan, Sister Mary Ann SC 229
Dooley, Sister Anne Mary SSJ 229, 254
Downing, Sister Mary Omer SC 84, 86, 87, 91, 189, 190
Dubay, Father Thomas SM 83, 226, 231
Dyer, Sister Elizabeth SL 248

E
Ebaugh, Helen Rose Fuchs 299
Ecclesiae Sanctae 38, 40, 41, 42, 43, 57, 59, 60, 177, 178, 180, 187, 201, 213
Ecclesial Role of Women Committee 237
ecofeminist 321
Egan, Monsignor Jack 244
elderly sisters 153, 155, 295, 298, 299, 304-310
election, electioneering 151-157, 158
encounter groups 126-127
enneagram 128, 129, 130, 131, 147, 165
Equal Rights Amendment 79, 142, 148, 237, 247, 252, 255

Sisters in Crisis

Essential Elements in Church Teaching on Religious Life (*Essential Elements*) 59-63, 213-214, 218, 219, 222, 223, 224, 225, 231, 276, 279
Euart, Sister Sharon RSM 291
Eucharist, eucharist 168, 172, 173, 185, 204, 205, 240, 246, 249, 269, 305, 309, 310
Evangelica Testificatio 56, 57, 59, 92, 101, 102, 177, 180, 213, 220, 237, 277, 294
Everett Curriculum 141
Ewens, Sister Mary OP 229
experiment(s) 38-43, 82, 129, 191, 301, 329
Experimenta Circa 57
experimentation 80, 82, 85, 93, 111, 116, 139, 144, 154, 161, 183, 193, 197, 206, 207, 213, 253, 294

F

Farley, Sister Margaret RSM 241, 256
Fellowship of Emerging Religious Communities 293
Fellowship of New Religious Communities 294
feminism 31, 68, 69, 78, 129, 151, 200, 236, 238
feminist(s) 149, 152, 176, 193, 231, 234, 249, 250, 257, 258, 259, 309
feminist theology 151
Ferder, Sister Fran OSF 260
Ferraro, Sister Barbara SSDN 323
Fichter, Father Joseph SJ 61
Fiedler, Sister Maureen SL 150, 253, 258, 260, 263, 264, 265
finances 293, 295
    financial crisis 295, 300
Finke, Roger 317, 319
Finnegan, Sister Vincent Marie OCD 284, 286, 288, 291
Fiorenza, Elisabeth Schussler 253, 257, 258
First International Conference of Councils and Senates of Women Religious 243
Fischer, Father James CM 95
Fisher, Sister Maggie RSCJ 245, 246, 248
Fitzgerald, Sister Clare SSND 216
Fitzpatrick, Ruth McDonough 216, 257, 258
Flaherty, Sister Helen SC 180, 217, 222
Focus on Women 237
Foley, Sister Nadine OP 237, 238
Fordham University 137, 143
Forum of Major Superiors 280, 283, 284, 285, 286, 288
FORUS 65, 168, 174, 175, 317, 318, 319, 320 *See also* "Future of Religious Orders in the United States"
Fox, Sister Sean OSM 220
Franciscan(s) 85, 110, 130, 138, 143, 144, 198, 202, 208, 216, 221, 260, 268, 275, 286, 296
Franciscan Sisters of Christ the Divine Teacher 208
Franciscan Sisters of Christian Charity 46, 47
Franciscan Sisters of Perpetual Adoration, LaCrosse, Wisconsin 45

Franciscan Sisters of St. Mary, St. Louis, Missouri 296
Franciscan Sisters of the Poor, Brooklyn, New York 45
Fraternal Life in Community 64, 65
"Future of Religious Orders in the United States" 65, 167 *See also* FORUS
FutureChurch 260, 263

G

Gabisch, Sister Rose Dominic SC 139
Gallen, Jesuit Father Joseph SJ 24
Gamaliel principle 227, 231, 322
Gannon, Sister Ann Ida BVM 110
general chapters 38, 49, 57, 177, 178, 222
George, Bishop Francis OMI 70
Georgetown University 228, 258, 315
Georgetown University Center for Applied Research in the Apostolate (CARA) 65, 315, 316, 317, 319
Gottemoeller, Sister Doris RSM 74, 169, 238, 283, 291, 320
government of orders 34, 37, 42, 45, 57, 74, 83, 120, 123, 183, 187, 213, 232, 245, 322, 326
Grailville 110, 129
Gramick, Sister Jeannine SSND 61, 253, 254, 258
Greeley, Father Andrew 82
Grennan, Sister Jacqueline SL 110
Grindel, Father John CM 301
group identity 300

H

habit 20, 21, 22, 25-26, 31, 36, 37, 39, 41, 45, 47, 49, 50, 56, 58, 72, 84, 154, 176-181, 185, 187, 190, 199, 204, 269, 271, 282, 290, 292, 299, 307
    dispute about 176
    hygiene 20
    necessity 177
    style 176
    symbolism 26
    unsafe 25
Hamer, Cardinal Jean Jerome OP 231, 232, 280
Hannan, Archbishop Philip 246
Hardon, Father John SJ 278
Haring, Father Bernard CSSR 79, 80, 136, 138
Harmer, Sister Catherine M. MMM 157
Hartney, Sister Mary Gerald CSC 285
Haughey, Father John SJ 53, 91, 92, 267, 268
Hayes, Diana 258
health (of sisters) 23, 38, 78, 297, 304
Heiser, Father Basil OFM Conv. 275
Hennesey, Father James SJ 221, 287, 289
Hennessy, Brother Paul K. FSC 136
Henning, Clara 236
Heston, Father Edward CSC 39, 40, 84, 85, 86, 189
Hickey, Cardinal James 269, 279, 280, 281, 282, 283, 284, 285, 286, 288, 289
Hill, Father Richard A. SJ 157

Hofstetter, Sister Adrian Marie 91
Hogan, Bishop James 181, 182, 183, 273, 277
Holland, Joseph 245
Holloway, Sister Marcella Marie CSJ 23, 164
Holy Cross 86, 110, 133, 154, 285
Holy Father 39, 62, 72, 179, 183, 201, 202, 214, 222, 223, 240, 261, 329, 330 *See also* John Paul II, Pope; Paul VI, Pope; Pius XII, Pope; and John XXIII, Pope
Honsberger, Sister M. Claudia IHM 36, 63, 100, 106, 268, 277, 278
horariums 19, 26
hospital(s) 30, 31, 33, 34, 165, 166, 170, 188, 203, 231, 273, 291, 310
Huddleston, Sister Mary Anne IHM 162, 175
Humanae Vitae 86, 92, 136, 145, 262
Hussey, Sister Patricia SSDN 323
hygiene 25, 49

I
Illich, Monsignor Ivan D. 142
Immaculate Heart Community 185, 191
Immaculate Heart of Mary Sister(s) (IHM) 40, 68, 100, 104, 110, 144, 162, 168, 175, 255, 260, 268, 303, 315
Immaculate Heart of Mary Sisters of Los Angeles 61, 82, 85-86, 94, 126-127, 184-191, 192, 206, 208, 209, 244, 246, 251, 252, 323, 323
In-formation 147, 148
individualism 64, 66, 70, 123, 147, 167, 171, 174, 175, 186, 215, 237, 302, 318
Institute on Religious Life 277, 278, 279, 280, 282, 283, 284, 285
intensive journal workshops 128
Isasi-Diaz, Ada Maria 249

J
Jadot, Archbishop Jean 179, 279
Janson, Sister Virgina SCC 100, 101
Jesuit(s) 44, 79, 82, 83, 91, 95, 104, 127, 131, 136, 138, 142, 143, 145, 148, 156, 157, 161, 188, 221, 229, 267, 278, 286
John Paul II, Pope 34, 46, 59, 60, 61, 63, 69, 71, 77, 159, 173, 211, 212, 218, 226, 231, 232, 239, 257, 280, 282, 283, 286, 307, 311, 327 *See also* Holy Father
John XXIII, Pope 151
Johnson, Andrea 259
Johnson, Sister Elizabeth CSJ 266

K
Kane, Sister Theresa RSM 215, 216, 239, 249, 256, 257
Kavanaugh, Father Aidan OSB 136
Keating, Sister Kathleen SSJ 245, 247, 248
Kelly, Archbishop Thomas OP 213
Kennedy, Father Eugene MM 79
Kennedy, Sister Ethne SH 244
Kent, Sister M. Corita IHM 110, 114

Kerwin, Father Finian OFM Cap. 95
King, Sister Eleace IHM 315
Kissling, Frances 253
Knights of Columbus 269, 279
Kobler, Father John CP 31
Kopp, Sister Mary Audrey (Lillana) SNJM 139, 140, 146, 191, 251, 252
Krantz, Sister Mary Elise SND 104, 268
Krol, Cardinal John 269, 279
Kuhn, Sister Roberta BVM 103

L
Laghi, Archbishop Pio 215, 240, 241
Larraona, Father Arcadio 20
LCWR *See* Leadership Conference of Women Religious
leaders (in religious institutes) 319
Leadership Conference *See* Leadership Conference of Women Religious
Leadership Conference of Women Religious (LCWR) 32, 33, 48, 56-57, 58, 62, 63, 64, 67, 68, 74, 76-87, 88, 98, 99-107, 108, 124, 125, 130, 137, 142, 146, 147, 155, 159, 163, 173, 174, 178, 180, 192, 211, 216, 217, 218, 221, 222, 225, 229, 231, 235,-243, 244, 249, 255, 256, 257, 260, 265, 266-292, 293, 295, 301, 303, 304, 316, 319, 320, 321
1965 assembly 79-80
1966 assembly 80-81
1967 assembly 81-84, 119
1968 assembly 81-84
1969 assembly 84-87
1970 assembly 90, 91-97, 100, 101, 267-268
1970 special assembly 89-90, 91, 102, 103
1971 assembly 99-107, 142, 182, 275
1972 assembly 236
1973 assembly 236
1977 assembly 239
1977 assembly 239
1982 assembly 240
1983 assembly 62
1984 assembly 240
1985 assembly 241
1989 Leadership Conference joint assembly 241
1996 Leadership Conference annual assembly 242
changing the name 104
Contemporary Theology Project 237
Ecclesial Role of Women Committee 237
goals 242
membership 235
theology committee 56
Leddy, Mary Jo 173
Leibold, Archbishop Paul 107
Leonard, Sister Joan deLourdes CSJ 76
lesbian 250, 259, 263
Lessard, Bishop Raymond 213

liberation theology 150-151, 236, 320
lineamenta 65-71, 235
Linscott, Sister Mary SNDdeN 105
Loes, Brother Augustine FSC 95
Long, Sister Assumpta OP 280
Long, Sister M. Brideen OSF 26
Loretto Sister(s) 79, 110, 129, 150, 160, 165, 173, 190, 248, 258, 264, 265
Loretto Six Percent Committee 248
Lori, Monsignor William 289
loss in membership 224
Loyola University 137
Lozano, Father John CMF 221
Luecke, Sister Jane Marie OSB 110, 116
Lumen Gentium 37, 111, 112, 213
Lynch, Monsignor Robert 287

M
MacDonald, Sister Eileen IHM 190
Maguire, Father Daniel SJ 136
Maida, Cardinal (Dr.) Adam J. 170
Malone, Sister Eucharia RSM 95, 99
Mansour, Sister Agnes Mary RSM 212, 215, 228, 241, 255
Maradiaga, Archbishop Oscar Andres Rodriguez 70
Marillac College 135
Marist 83, 226, 294
Markham, Sister Donna OP 287, 288, 289, 320
Marquette workshops 141
Marshall, Bishop John 246
Marvels of Charity 29
Maryknoll 79
Mary's Pence 259
Maslow, Abraham H. 126
Masterman, Sister Rose Eileen CSC 154
Mayer, Archbishop Augustine OSB 41, 42, 256, 274, 276, 278
McBrien, Father Richard 99, 136, 256, 275
McCormack, Sister Maureen SL 51
McCoy, Father Alan OFM 216
McDermott, Sister Rose SSJ 230
McDevitt, Bishop Gerald V. 80
McDonough, Sister Elizabeth OP 124, 157, 177, 293
McEnroy, Sister Carmel RSM 258
McGrath, Monsignor John J. 170
McGrath thesis 170
McHugh, Monsignor James 238
McIntyre, Cardinal James 82, 85, 142, 184-186, 187, 190, 251, 323
McKinley, Sister Marie Assumpta SSJ 268
Medical Missionary Sisters 45
membership 183, 278, 279, 280, 281, 282, 284, 288, 289, 292, 294, 296, 297, 300, 301-304, 317, 327
  diminishing 125
  recruitment 300
  requirements 77

Mercy Sister(s) 74, 151, 166, 212, 215, 241, 256, 258, 297
merger 285
Meyers, Sister Bertrande DC 135
Midwives of the Future 60-61, 218
Miller, Sister Amata IHM 259
Mooney, Father Christopher SJ 137
Moran, Brother Gabriel FSC 56, 82, 121, 137, 243
Moslander, Sister Bette CSJ 216, 218, 255, 320
Ms. magazine 216, 253
Muckenhirn, Sister Charles Borromeo (Mary Ellen) CSC 110, 113, 144
Murphy, Sister Alice Anita SSJ 98, 106, 268
Murphy, Sister Rosalie SND 95, 97, 101, 104, 191
Mutuae Relationes 220
Myers, Bishop John J. 286
Myerscough, Sister Angelita ASC 83, 85, 91, 95, 96, 99, 101, 104, 111, 191, 256

N
National Assembly of Women Religious (NAWR) 40, 55, 79, 180, 243-251, 252, 255, 256, 270, 303 *See also* National Assembly of Religious Women
National Assembly of Religious Women (NARW) 243, 249-251 *See also* National Assembly of Women Religious
National Catholic Conference for Interracial Justice 146, 251
National Catholic Educational Association (NCEA) 134, 143
National Catholic Reporter 45, 60, 61, 69, 91, 110, 136, 144, 180, 190, 207, 237, 239, 245, 249, 251, 259
National Coalition of American Nuns (NCAN) 63, 69, 91, 101, 140, 142, 146, 148, 166, 191, 215, 218, 243, 251-255, 256, 259, 263, 264, 278
National Conference of Catholic Bishops (NCCB) 95, 96, 102, 105, 107, 177, 179, 181, 182, 218, 238, 241, 250, 253, 260, 261, 265, 285, 287, 289, 291, 295
National Conference of Vicars For Religious 292
National Council of Catholic Women 247
National Organization for Women 237
National Sister Formation Committee 91, 135, 143, 145
NAWR *See* National Assembly of Women Religious
NCAN *See* National Coalition of American Nuns
NCCB *See* National Conference of Catholic Bishops
NCEA *See* National Catholic Education Association
Neal, Sister Marie Augusta SNDdeN 62, 80, 82, 108, 110, 112-113, 117-125, 151, 174, 221, 228, 244, 256
Nettle, Sister Mary Bernard LSP 280, 286
NETWORK 215, 255-256, 259, 260

New Age 129, 131, 138
New Ways Ministry 61
New York Times (The) (ads) 223, 241, 249, 253, 262-263, 323
Nix, Dr. J. T. 23
No Turning Back: Two Nuns' Battle With The Vatican 323
Nobody Owns Me 209
Nolde, Sister Merle OSB 79
Nouwen, Father Henri 99
Nugent, Father Robert SDS 61
Nygren, Father David CM 160, 167, 317, 318, 319

O

obedience 20, 22, 37, 44, 47, 56, 60, 62, 66, 71, 92, 109, 113, 114, 139, 154, 164, 174, 175, 178, 180, 186, 198, 215, 216, 224, 232, 237, 238, 240, 290, 308, 318, 321, 326, 328
occupations 165, 167, 175
O'Connor, Cardinal John 71, 279
O'Connor, Father David F. ST 160, 161
Olley, Sister Michelle OP 254
open placement 33, 34, 42, 164, 168, 192, 291
Ordinatio Sacerdotalis 258
ordination of women 142, 147, 229, 237, 245, 256, 258, 262, 264 *See also* women's ordination
O'Rourke, Father Kevin OP 50
orphanages 30
Orsy, Father Ladislas SJ 83
O'Sullivan, Sister Maureen RSM 250
Our Sunday Visitor 165, 279, 291

P

Pacwa, Father Mitch SJ 131
Padberg,Father John SJ 221, 229
Page, Brother Thomas More CSX 217
paternalism 32
Pathways to Re-Creating Religious Communities 329
Paul VI, Pope 38, 55-57, 58, 59, 61, 277
Penet, Sister Mary Emil IHM 144
Peoria 286
Perfectae Caritatis 37-38, 43, 46, 50, 53, 56, 58, 59, 72, 77, 97, 104, 110, 111, 112, 154, 177, 180, 187, 201, 213, 220, 268, 272, 294
Peters, Sister Sean CSJ 301
Phelps, Sister Jamie OP 250
"Phil Donahue Show" 253
Philippe, Archbishop Paul OP 143
Pieper, Sister Bernadine CHM 97
Pilarczyk, Archbishop Daniel 289
Pilla, Archbishop Anthony 265
Pinkerton, Sister Catherine CSJ 180, 245, 249, 255
Piro, Sister Teresa SC 216
Pironio, Cardinal Eduardo 62
Pius XII, Pope 18, 19, 20, 21, 25, 26
polarization 58, 174, 180, 209, 212, 219, 223, 224, 225, 266, 275, 276, 280, 282

political office 214
poverty 44-46, 58, 66, 70, 71, 72, 113, 114, 121, 163, 164, 169, 175, 176, 178, 182, 198, 221, 223, 232, 328
prayer (community) 19, 22, 25, 36, 37, 42, 44, 45, 46, 47, 55, 56, 58, 60, 64, 66, 83, 84, 113, 131, 132, 147, 150, 162, 168, 172, 173, 185, 187, 190, 192, 195, 204, 207, 213, 222, 224, 245, 246, 250, 269, 270, 282, 288, 294, 299, 301, 305, 307, 309, 310, 312, 315, 318, 326, 327
Prejean, Sister Helen CSJ 242
Priests for Equality 148, 264
Providence Heights College 135
Pursley, Bishop Leo A. 177, 179

Q

Quigley, Sister Carol IHM 255
Quinn, Archbishop John 211-233, 241, 279, 314
Quinn Commission 63, 211-233, 241, 280, 282, 290, 292, 320
Quinn, Sister Donna OP 216, 254
Quinonez, Sister Lora Ann SP 62, 79, 88, 99, 105, 109, 217, 221, 236, 237, 238, 240, 287
Quixote Peace and Justice Center 257

R

Rahner, Father Karl SJ 138
Raimondi, Bishop Luigi 101, 177, 178, 268
Ransing, Father Bernard CSC 39, 52, 80, 82, 89, 117
Redemptorist 79, 138
Reedy, Father John CSC 86
reform 18, 21, 24, 25, 28, 32, 33, 39, 43, 76, 77, 108, 110, 114, 116, 122, 131, 133, 150, 156, 164, 192, 243, 256, 259, 262, 264, 265, 324, 328
reformers 43, 113, 114
refounding 327, 328, 329, 330
Regina Mundi 134
Reilly, Sister Mary RSM 245
Religious Formation Conference 76, 148
religious life, departures from 33
Religious Life in the United States: The Experience of Men's Communities 228
Religious Life: A Mystery in Christ 271
renewal 18-35, 36-54, 55-57, 58-59, 60, 61, 62, 66, 71, 74-75, 76-87, 92, 93, 95, 101, 102, 107, 108-132, 139, 144, 146, 148, 150, 151, 155, 160, 161, 172, 174, 176, 183, 184-195, 202, 206-209, 213, 214, 218, 223, 224, 225-228, 236, 237, 243, 244, 247, 252, 263, 264, 265, 266, 267, 269, 275, 276, 277, 294-295, 301, 306, 312-315, 324-326, 327
Research Committee on Religious Life 111, 118
retirement (of sisters) 29, 153, 166, 171, 252, 282, 295-299, 300, 304, 325
Retirement Fund for Religious 298
Reul, Sister Sixtina OSF 268

Sisters in Crisis

Review for Religious 50, 156, 157, 158, 209
Richardson, Sister Jane Marie SL 110, 114, 190
Rodriguez, Sister Leticia OSF 286
Roesener, Sister Janet CSJ 287
Rogers, Carl R. 126
Rohr, Father Richard OFM 221
role of authority 139, 174, 313
Rothluebber, Sister Francis Borgia OSF 56, 83, 95, 101, 104, 189, 192, 209, 236, 237, 244
Ruether, Rosemary Radford 259
Ruffing, Sister Janet RSM 151
rule books 19, 78, 181
rules 21, 22, 23, 37, 41, 58, 127
Ryan, Brother Bernard M. FSC 43

S

Sacred Heart Sister(s) 245
Sager, Dr. Alan 34
Saint Mary's College 133, 134, 170
scales 119
Scarpino, Sister Georgine M. RMS 166
Schaldenbrand, Sister M. Aloysius SSJ 110, 114, 190
Scharper, Philip 80
Schenk, Sister Christine CSJ 260
Schillebeeckx, Father Edward OP 138
Schneiders, Sister Sandra IHM 40, 56, 168, 171, 175, 238, 260, 302
School Sister(s) of Notre Dame 61, 140, 166, 216, 323
School Sisters of St. Francis 95, 184, 189, 192, 193-210, 241, 244, 251
schools 26-28, 29, 30, 31, 33, 34, 45, 64, 72, 126, 134, 135, 143, 151, 163, 170, 183, 187-188, 205, 208, 231, 273, 291, 307, 312
Schum, Sister Agnes Ann SL 258
Schwarz, Karen 258
Second Vatican Council 19, 23, 30-31, 32, 36, 39, 41, 43, 46, 47, 54, 55, 56, 60, 70, 76, 78, 79, 83, 92, 105, 110, 123, 125, 139, 148, 177, 221, 271, 294, 312, 321, 326, 328 *See also* Vatican II
    abuses (of the teachings) 59, 165, 179, 193, 203, 225, 232, 269, 276, 322, 324
secular institute 40, 42, 62, 227, 170, 183, 271, 280, 321
secularism 66, 199, 206
Senate of Religious Women of the Diocese of Cleveland 247
Seng, Sister Angelica OSF 110, 115
sensitivity training 126, 127, 128
Sheahan, Father Gerald SJ 95
Sheen, Bishop Fulton J. 268
Sheets, Bishop John SJ 286
Sister Formation Bulletin (*SF Bulletin, Bulletin*) 123, 138, 139, 140, 143, 145, 146, 147,252
Sister Formation College 135, 137

Sister Formation Committee 91, 110, 111, 123
Sister Formation Conference 76, 123, 133, 134, 143, 145, 146, 147, 148, 252, 256
Sister Formation Movement 133-148
Sister Formation program 135, 137, 138, 140, 142
Sister(s) of Charity 84, 135, 139, 180, 217, 218, 229
Sister(s) of Charity of the Blessed Virgin Mary 45, 110, 165, 256
Sister of Christian Charity 100
Sister(s) of Loretto 34, 51, 110, 144, 160, 165, 218, 257
Sister(s) of Mercy 95, 150, 155, 158, 169, 178, 180, 189, 214, 215, 245, 246, 250, 291, 320
Sister(s) of Notre Dame 82, 104, 268
Sister(s) of Notre Dame de Namur (SNDdeN) 62, 88, 105, 110, 139
Sister(s) of St. Joseph 97, 98, 110, 111, 142, 147, 152, 153, 164, 167, 172, 190, 216, 230, 242, 245, 254, 260, 268, 287, 301
Sister(s) of the Holy Names of Jesus and Mary 80, 139
Sisters' Conference of the Diocese of Peoria 246
Sisters Council of the Diocese of Grand Island, Nebraska 248
Sisters For Christian Community 252, 253
Sisters Forum 144
Sisters of Charity of Nazareth 58, 130, 300, 301
Sisters of Mercy of Portland (Maine) 297
Sisters of Mercy of the Americas 297, 320
Sisters of St. Francis of the Martyr St. George 239
Sisters of St. Joseph 296, 328
Sisters of St. Joseph of Carondelet 64, 180, 296
Sisters of St. Joseph of Cleveland 257
Sisters of St. Joseph the Worker 58
Sisters, Servants of the Immaculate Heart of Mary 63
Sisters' Survey 81, 82-83, 108-126, 132, 144, 151, 155, 163
    scales 118
Sisters Today 49, 144
Snee, Monsignor Joseph T.V. 53
Social Security System 295, 296
Society of Helpers 244
Somalo, Cardinal Eduardo Martinez 286-287, 289
Sommers, Professor Christina Hoff 31
Sponsa Christi 19
St. Julian, Sister M. de Chantal SSF 286
St. Mary's Seminary and University 137
Starting Points: Six Essays Based on the Experience of U.S. Women Religious 238
statutes 77, 78, 81, 83, 85, 89, 90
Steps in the Journey 237
Stewart, George 29
Stratman, Sister Judanne OSF 46

Index

Stuhlmueller, Father Carroll CP 256
Suelzer, Sister Alexa OP 216
Suenens, Cardinal Leon Joseph 18, 197, 199
superior(s), role of 19, 20, 21, 22, 23, 24, 26, 28,
    32, 37, 39, 40-41, 42, 43, 45, 47, 49, 57, 58,
    60, 62-63, 65, 66, 72, 74, 75, 77-79, 83, 88-
    107, 108-109, 122-123, 136, 137-138, 141, 144,
    145, 147, 150, 152, 153, 154-155, 158, 159,
    162, 164, 171, 174, 175, 177, 180, 187, 189,
    191, 192, 203, 214, 217, 232, 253, 288, 294,
    312, 325
Support our Aging Religious 298
Sylvester, Sister Nancy IHM 260
Szoka, Archbishop Edmund 214

T

Tabera, Cardinal Arturo 275-276
tax status 167
teaching sister(s) 26, 27, 33, 182, 188
Teilhard de Chardin, Father Pierre SJ 110, 145
The Changing Sister 110-116
The Church and the Second Sex 83
"The Education of Sister Lucy," 134
The Incredible Sixties 30
"The Statement on American Religious Life in the
    Seventies" 93-97
    "American manifesto on religious life" 93
The Transformation of American Catholic Sisters
    287
Third way 44
Thompson, Margaret Susan 63, 254, 259
Threads for the Loom 320
Timlin, Bishop James 70
Tobin, Sister Mary Luke SL 51, 53, 79, 82, 110,
    111, 117, 255, 256, 257, 259
*Transformative Elements for Religious Life in the
    Future* 241
Traxler, Sister (Mary Peter) Margaret Ellen SSND
    140, 146, 148, 166, 191, 218, 234, 243, 251,
    253, 254, 259
Tri-Conference Commission on Religious Life and
    Ministry (Commission on Religious Life and
    Ministry) 292
Tri-Conference Retirement Office 295, 296, 298,
    304
Tuite, Sister Marjorie OP 218, 249, 255, 256, 302
Turner, Sister Mary Daniel SNDdeN 62, 81, 88,
    99, 104, 109, 110, 111, 116, 118, 183, 217, 236,
    237, 238, 240, 256, 287
twenty-year plan 26

U

Ukeritis, Sister Miriam CSJ 317, 319
unemployment 166
University of Notre Dame 136, 229, 253
Update 130

V

Vagnozzi, Cardinal Egidio 51, 117, 145, 268
Valeri, Cardinal Valerio 32
Vatican Congregation for Religious 21, 39, 142,
    143
Vatican directives 45
Vatican documents 49, 51, 53, 65, 82, 104, 109,
    112, 187, 188, 206, 213, 235, 268, 278, 306
Vidulich, Sister Dorothy CSJP 60, 69, 187, 216
Villot, Cardinal Jean 58
Vita Consecrata 34, 46, 71, 77, 159, 173, 294,
    307, 311, 329
vocation(s) 20, 21, 29, 30, 33, 46, 55, 59, 65, 67,
    70, 71, 72, 74, 76, 78, 143, 167, 175, 181, 209,
    211, 213, 217, 222, 226, 228-230, 248, 261,
    269, 278, 290, 293, 294, 300-304, 307, 314-
    318, 329
vows 19, 37, 39, 44, 46, 57, 60, 70, 71, 92, 108,
    113, 114, 134, 139, 142, 160, 164, 165, 168,
    174, 175, 191, 198, 205, 209, 213, 214, 215,
    234, 269, 271, 280, 282, 294, 297, 304, 306,
    310, 312, 315, 316, 321, 324, 326, 329, 330

W

Walter, Sister Annette CSJ 142, 143, 144, 252
Ware, Sister Ann Patrick SL 60, 173, 253
Waters, Bishop Vincent 178
We Are Church 254, 263, 264, 265
Weakland, Archbishop Rembert OSB 220
Weber, Father Donald N. 193
Weems, Reverend Renita J. 243
Western Behavioral Sciences Institute 126
Whealon, Archbishop John 221, 226, 227, 228, 231,
    322
Who Stole Feminism? 31
Widening the Dialogue 56, 237, 277
Williams, Sister Virginia SL 265
Wittberg, Sister Patricia SC 109, 300, 327, 329
Wolff, Sister Madeleva CSC 133, 134
Wolff, Sister Mary Florence SL 144
Women in the Vanishing Cloister 299
Women-Church Convergence 250
Women's Liberation 91, 179
women's liberation 139, 313
women's ordination 147, 148, 239, 252, 257, 259,
    262, 263, 312 *See also* ordination of women
Women's Ordination Conference (WOC) 148, 216,
    237, 252, 256,-259, 260, 263, 264
World Synod of Bishops 65, 254
    October 1994 65, 69
Wright, Cardinal John 179

Z

Zeller, Sister Mary Claudia OSF 85, 86, 92, 97,
    123, 237, 256
Zeller, Sister Mary Francine OSF 144

Our Sunday Visitor...
Your Source for Discovering the Riches of the Catholic Faith

Our Sunday Visitor has an extensive line of materials for young children, teens, and adults. Our books, Bibles, booklets, CD-ROMs, audios, and videos are available in bookstores worldwide.

To receive a FREE full-line catalog or for more information, call **Our Sunday Visitor** at **1-800-348-2440**. Or write, **Our Sunday Visitor / 200 Noll Plaza / Huntington, IN 46750.**

Please send me: __ A catalog
Please send me materials on:
    __ Apologetics and catechetics   __ Reference works
    __ Prayer books   __ Heritage and the saints
    __ The family   __ The parish

Name_____

Address_____Apt._____

City_____State ____Zip_____

Telephone (   ) _____

A73BBABP

Please send a friend: __ A catalog
Please send a friend materials on:
    __ Apologetics and catechetics   __ Reference works
    __ Prayer books   __ Heritage and the saints
    __ The family   __ The parish

Name_____

Address_____Apt._____

City_____State ____Zip_____

Telephone (   ) _____

A73BBABP

Our Sunday Visitor
200 Noll Plaza
Huntington, IN 46750
1-800-348-2440
OSVSALES@AOL.COM

Your Source for Discovering the Riches of the Catholic Faith